HUMAN DEVELOPMENT

The Neglected Dimension

Human Development

The Neglected Dimension

Edited by

**Khadija Haq
Uner Kirdar**

Papers prepared for the Istanbul Roundtable on Development:
The Human Dimension, September 2-4, 1985

North South Roundtable   **Islamabad, Pakistan**

Published in 1986 by the North South Roundtable
P.O. Box 2006, Islamabad, Pakistan
© 1986 by the North South Roundtable. All rights reserved

United Nations Sales Number: E. 86. IIIMB. 2
International Standard Book Number: ISBN. 92-1-126003-5

Printed in Pakistan

TO BRADFORD MORSE

This book is dedicated to Bradford Morse, Administrator of the United Nations Development Programme (1976-86), on the occasion of his retirement. During his ten years as UNDP Administrator, Bradford Morse has never missed an opportunity to bring to the attention of the international community the vital role of the human element in the development process. Indeed, his name has become synonymous worldwide with the human dimension in development. He has long warned the international community that neglect of this element will significantly retard long-term, self-sustained development. His commitment to these ideals is not limited to his international career, but finds its roots in his personality and the deep convictions which have guided him throughout his life and work.

ACKNOWLEDGMENT

Funds for North South Roundtable activities are provided by the Canadian International Development Agency, the International Development Research Centre of Canada, the Netherlands Government, the OPEC Fund, the Swedish International Development Authority, the United Nations University and the World Bank. The funding organizations are, however, not responsible for views presented in North South Roundtable documents.

CONTENTS

Chapter

PART I
THE HUMAN FACTOR

PART II
COMPARATIVE DEVELOPMENT EXPERIENCE

PART V
IMPACT OF SCIENCE AND TECHNOLOGY

PART VI
CONTRIBUTION OF THE PRIVATE SECTOR, NGO'S AND INSTITUTIONS

APPENDICES

TABLES AND FIGURES

Chapter 31

Chapter 31

PREFACE

"Recent economic pressures, national and international, have led to serious neglect of the human dimension in development. Unless remedied, this neglect will distort and handicap the future development of at least a generation to come."

This dramatic message emanated from the Roundtable on Development: The Human Dimension, jointly convened by the North South Roundtable and the UNDP Development Study Programme on September 2-4, 1985, in Istanbul, Turkey. It brought together a group of more than fifty leading national and international personalities, academicians, development experts and business leaders from developed, developing and socialist countries to take a fresh look at the human dimension in the economic and social development process in order to identify the major issues and to mobilize international support for required policy changes.

The history of the development process over the last thirty years shows that the transfer of financial resources for physical investments has not in itself created an adequate foundation for self-sustaining development. The experience acquired during this period clearly demonstrates that one of the major obstacles to economic progress in developing countries is the insufficient attention given to the development of human resources. Also, in the midst of an ongoing world financial and debt crisis, the adjustment measures in most developing countries have been secured at unfortunately high human costs — high in terms of lost output, depressed employment and rising poverty levels. Austerity programs at their implementation level have resulted in a serious curtailment of investment in human resources. The attention of national and international policymakers has shifted from long-term goals to short-term financial and adjustment concerns. The international community is more interested in ensuring the timely payment of debts and interest rates than in seeking to eradicate poverty and in strengthening the human dimension of development. Thus, anti-poverty and human development programs have been pushed aside. Poverty can wait, the banks cannot!

This was the economic environment which set the stage for the first meeting of the Roundtable on the Human Dimension of Development in Istanbul on September 2-4, 1985. The ongoing crisis brought into focus the larger illumination of thirty-five years of development experience and thinking: that human development is both an input and an objective of development. Yet the statistics tell the story of our failure to recognize it as an objective. The conventional wisdom of each decade has tended to offer single-factor recipes for economic development — investment in physical infrastructure, industrialization, export promotion, import substitution, basic needs, etc. The latest thinking acknowledges that while all these elements are necessary conditions for growth, they are not sufficient without inputs into human capital formation, since it is on human beings and their capacity to utilize their skills and experience that self-sustaining development ultimately depends.

The new Roundtable met with the primary objective of reasserting the central importance of human well-being as the objective of all development. It started from several assumptions: that the neglect of this basic fact leads to misguided policies and deprivation of the poorest; that the human factor is the most vital ingredient for promoting development in the long term and for enabling countries to weather external shocks in the short term; and that in a rapidly changing technological environment, developing countries will have to pay special attention to skill formation and training.

The Istanbul Roundtable made a strong joint appeal for a general redirection of policy and planning toward the human dimension in development. It called for intensified action in four specific areas: education and training, nutrition and health, the role of women, and new technologies. It emphasized the need for initiatives to help break the impasse many developing countries face in the areas of finance and adjustment, as well as action to increase global awareness, including a World Conference on the State of the Human Condition.

The papers collected in the present volume reflect the proceedings and findings of the Istanbul Roundtable. The authors give their personal views, which should not be attributed to the organizations with which they are affiliated.

The Istanbul Statement, which summarizes the major highlights of discussions and conclusions, appears at the beginning of this volume. The Statement was presented, discussed and broadly approved at the final session. It was published after the Istanbul Roundtable and was widely circulated by the North South Roundtable and the UNDP Development Study Programme.

Part I contains papers that address the issues of the theory and definition of the human dimension in development. Fundamental questions are raised as to whether a definition of the human element is needed at all, and whether current indicators of economic development can realistically measure human development and human welfare in a society.

The chapters of Part II look at the comparative development experience of a few countries in respect of human development. East Asian countries that have done well in this regard are the focal point of this part.

Part III contains chapters on individual country experience in developing human resources. The experiences of countries such as Benin, Turkey and Japan are analyzed. The candid reports of the authors are imbued with the enthusiasm of development plans that have worked or are working. At the same time, there are valuable insights into the problems that can arise.

Part IV begins with an examination of the role of women in development, and of the fact that to give the human dimension a proper focus requires that women's status be improved. Contributions of various social sectors such as education, health and employment in building human capital are analyzed in this part.

The important issue of the contribution of science and technology to human development is discussed in Part V. From a general consideration of the impact such issues can have on the people living in developing countries, the chapters move on to more detailed suggestions on exactly what kinds of technology are useful for the Third World.

In looking at the ways in which the human dimension is a vital force in the private sector, nongovernmental organizations and institutions, the chapters of Part VI draw heavily on the individual experience of the authors. Successful business enterprises in both the developed and developing countries are shown to be greatly dependent on skilled and trained personnel. The final chapter provides a critical examination of the institutional aspects of the human dimension.

The Istanbul Roundtable was merely the beginning of a process of creative thinking and dialogue on the question of the human dimension of development that we intend to continue by organizing a series of further meetings. We hope that these discussions will make a valuable contribution to reemphasizing that the objective of development is *people,* and that people must be the center of all concerns. We believe that in the final analysis, all efforts in the development process, all policy options, all adjustment measures and institutional alternatives should be judged by the same yardstick — the impact they have on promoting human welfare. It is in this spirit that this volume has been put together.

We offer our grateful thanks to the host country, Turkey, for the very gracious hospitality provided to the Roundtable. We thank all the participants in the Istanbul Roundtable for the valuable contributions they made toward the success of the meeting and to this volume. We are greatly indebted to His Royal Highness Hassan Bin Talal, Crown Prince of Jordan, for chairing the Istanbul Roundtable and for providing such eminent leadership. Finally, we are grateful to the Chairman of the North South Roundtable, Mr. Maurice F. Strong, for his continuing leadership and guidance.

We cannot conclude this preface without thanking those who helped us in the preparation of this volume: Dr. James Lee and Ms. Karen Pasha for helping with the editing and Ms. Teresita Caballero for her able and valuable administrative and secretarial assistance. Final responsibility for the selection and editing of papers rests, of course, with the editors.

KHADIJA HAQ   UNER KIRDAR
April 1986

xviii

AN OVERVIEW

[The main themes discussed in the Istanbul Roundtable were summarized by Richard Jolly and Frances Stewart in the form of a Statement which was presented to the final session. This Statement represents an overview of the significant conclusions reached during the Roundtable deliberations.]

The objective of development is people. The process of development may be measured in economic aggregates or technological and physical achievements. But the human dimension of development is the only dimension of intrinsic worth.

It is important to begin with this truism, because it has been increasingly neglected. The economic difficulties of recent years have led to increased poverty and unemployment, worldwide cutbacks in expenditure on health and education, and a deterioration in nutritional standards, especially among vulnerable groups.

Spending on health and education has dropped substantially in all classes of developing countries over the last decade — in low-income countries from 21 per cent of central government expenditure in 1972 to 9 per cent in 1982! Meanwhile, military expenditures worldwide and in the developing countries themselves have continued to increase.

The human effects are especially severe in Africa (greatly reinforcing the effects of drought) and Latin America, but they are also emerging elsewhere, including in some industrial countries. Today's setbacks for the poor and underinvestment in human resources will have long-lasting effects. The damage done by increased malnutrition among pregnant women and small children, for example, is lifelong.

Paradoxically, at the very time when more attention to this human situation is required, less attention is being given. The overwhelming preoccupation with the pressing economic problems of debt, balance of payments and economic survival has shifted the attention of national and international policymakers from long-term goals to short-term adjustment, and from broader concerns to narrower financial matters. This shift has been encouraged by current economic philosophies which, in stressing a market view of economic efficiency, have often neglected the social sectors and small-scale production, in spite of the evidence that investment in these sectors can produce high economic returns.

The situation is serious, but there is no need for despair. The Roundtable identified several examples, both recent and historical, showing the positive results which could follow when resources available — large, small — are consciously directed toward more human ends.

The history of today's most successful economies shows the vital importance of a country's providing adequate resources and attending to the health, education and broader preparation of all its population, but especially of the younger generation. Review of the diverse experience of a number of countries also shows that the varying capacities of human beings largely explain differences in economic performance. These variations in human capacity are partly a consequence of formal investment in education — especially in primary education — and health facilities. But the Roundtable noted that training, and especially learning at work, forms an equally vital element: a challenging and rewarding work environment, when linked to corresponding motivation and incentives, leads to full development of human capacities. Policies to develop human capacities, therefore, need to include those affecting the economic environment, work experience, motivation and incentives, as well as policies to promote formal education and training.

The accelerating influence of new technologies, also reviewed in the Roundtable meeting, makes the current neglect of the human dimension even more dangerous for the future. The computer revolution in particular makes urgent the need in all countries to develop a new and creative approach to primary education.

To respond to a spectrum of need — from rising poverty and malnutrition to the future challenges of technology — a serious shift of attention toward the human dimension of development is urgently needed. To this end, the Roundtable identified four areas of action:

a) A general redirection of policy and planning toward the human dimension.

b) Intensified action in education, nutrition and health, the status of women and new technologies.

c) International action to break the debt impasse.

d) Steps to increase global awareness of the current crisis.

Redirecting Policy and Planning Toward the Human Dimension

It is essential that the human dimension be much more clearly recognized as the essential objective of economic development, as well as a critical input to all economic activity. This requires that assessment of economic performance include the human dimension as a major element. While GNP remains important as a vital source of achieving human fulfillment, it is necessary to adopt new indicators which explicitly and centrally incorporate the human dimension to measure country performance in this area.

Indicators of the human dimension include those measuring the physical health and well-being of people — such as life expectancy, infant mortality rates, rates of morbidity, levels of nutrition and literacy rates — as well as nonphysical indicators to measure achievement in employment (in quantity and quality), social cohesion and stability, and political liberty.

There is an urgent need to develop an internationally accepted set of indicators of the full life which will permit assessment and monitoring.

The indicators that do exist are often grossly deficient, leading to delayed and sometimes misleading conclusions which sometimes threaten the lives of many people.

International and national efforts are needed to improve measuring techniques ensuring up-to-date and reliable data, to be collected on a regular basis.

Statistical indicators of the various elements of the human condition are at least as important as conventional statistics such as GNP, yet they are normally given relatively scant attention.

The redirection of policy and priorities to give greater weight to human needs is also essential. This should focus on :

a) More effective use of resources.

b) Allocation of resources.

c) Increasing the total resources available in all areas where human investment is involved.

Intensified Action in Four Specific Areas

A Broader View of Education

The Roundtable unanimously agreed on the importance of universal primary education from every perspective.

All studies show that primary education, especially of girls, is the single most important factor determining family health. Countries with universal primary education invariably have low rates of infant mortality and high levels of life expectancy, while countries with low levels of primary education have very substantially lower life expectancy — in some cases, twenty years or more less than those countries with universal primary education.

Primary education is also an essential prerequisite to successful economic performance. Primary education reduces the manifold disadvantages suffered by very poor people, enabling them to make the most of a poor environment both in their lifestyle and in their work.

The new information revolution further accentuates the need to support primary schooling at the same time that it extends the definition of basic education. Some level of computer literacy has to be added to the basics of reading, writing and arithmetic.

Primary education is relatively cheap. While international support is desirable, every country can afford universal primary education for its children. Indeed, from a longer-run perspective, no country can afford not to educate its people at a basic level. Special efforts should be made so that all girls go to school. The health and education of future generations depends on female education.

The Roundtable proposed that universal primary education be accepted as a target for all countries of the world, and that appropriate international and national action be taken to support the acceptance of the target and its rapid achievement.

The workplace is also an important site for learning skills (which identifies an important contribution often made by the private sector). Specific job-oriented skills can be learned best in the workplace, which complements the more basic education that can be offered through formal schooling.

The workplace, when well managed, is also a setting for the development of motivation and initiative. The Roundtable noted how successful corporations show respect for their human resources, treating employees as an investment and not simply a cost. Many successful work environments have been restructured so that they also function as informal learning environments. The features of motivation and hard work encouraged in these enterprises are, the Roundtable believes, also possible in publicly owned industries, with intelligent management.

Primary education can never be divorced from the totality of a country's educational system, and adequate provision must be made for secondary schooling and beyond.

The Roundtable agreed on the importance of training in basic sciences in developing countries and stressed that technology cannot flourish without a base of fundamental science in these countries. Science must be broad-based if it is to support a broad spectrum of technological applications.

Nutrition and Health

The serious deterioration in nutritional standards, especially of young children, underlines a special need for urgent action. Since improving nutrition requires action in several sectors — agriculture, health, education and the mass media, as well as in general economic policy — multisectoral support is needed both nationally and internationally. Governments must obviously take the lead, but NGOs and the key international agencies need to provide critical support. The Roundtable identified several specifics for action:

a) The need for increasing agricultural production, especially of basic foodstuffs.

b) The need for well-focused nutritional schemes directed to the nutritional needs of vulnerable groups, especially children under five years of age and pregnant mothers.

c) The need for accelerated action in such priority areas as immunization, diarrhea disease control and basic health education as part of more general action to build up better structures of primary health care.

d) The need for greater emphasis in agricultural policy and action on the need for expanding income and household food production of poor families.

e) The mass media have a vital and often underused role in spreading information and helping to mobilize nationwide action.

Support for an Enhanced Position for Women

Putting the human dimension as the central element in development means an explicit recognition of the role of women.

In most societies, women have substantially less access to education, to jobs, to income and to membership in the ruling elite than men. Women's levels of health and nutrition are often inferior to men's, and girls' welfare is almost invariably less than boys' in these respects. Women, therefore, generally account for he largest proportion of deprived people. Giving the human dimension a central role requires that women's status be improved.

Moreover, women are the main source of childcare and of family health and nutrition. Therefore, the welfare of the whole population depends largely on how women perform their role. From every point of view, it is essential to give explicit recognition to the critical role of women and to enhance their position in society. This requires:

a) Access to primary school for all girls.
b) Improved access to education at all other levels for girls.
c) Increased access to employment and improved conditions at work.
d) Extension and training schemes directed toward women.
e) Improvements in social organization and promotion of women's participation in decision making at all levels to reinforce their active integration and motivation.

New Technologies

The Roundtable recognizes that the world is in the midst of scientific and technological revolutions that are taking place in four different areas: informatics, biotechnology, materials and energy. These developments can open important new perspectives for developing countries, providing the technologies are oriented toward solving the human problems of development.

The Roundtable also stressed the importance of sustaining traditional technologies which are used mainly in crafts and small-scale enterprises and blending those technologies with modern ones. Traditional technologies are so well fitted to local skills and available resources that they are literally the social pivots of many populations in developing countries. The blending of modern with traditional technologies can help to maintain and enhance the living standards of the mass of the population.

Special attention in the Roundtable was focused on computers. The new information technology offers great potential for developing countries but threatens to widen the gap between rich and poor nations, and between social groups within nations, unless special efforts are made to harness the technology appropriately. This requires more resources to be devoted to the development of suitable software for use in developing countries, especially in areas directly affecting the most deprived. Applications which enhance the productivity of agriculture and rural and small industries, and which contribute to basic health care and education, could aid in the alleviation of poverty. The Roundtable recommended that:

a) Efforts be made to develop appropriate uses of the new technology which will contribute to the human dimension of development. These efforts should be both national and international.

b) International support be provided to national, regional and international centers in the developed and developing countries to create software suited to the needs of developing countries.

c) International support be provided for the acquisition and adaptation of existing software and hardware where these meet the needs of developing countries.

International Action

The international organizations too need to reaffirm the central importance of the human dimension in all their activities and take steps to ensure that their programs and practices are redirected to offset the dangerous tendencies which have been occurring.

Both the World Bank and the IMF have had a special role in this because of their dominant international roles in adjustment and development policy. Their policy and approaches need to recognize more clearly the importance of protecting nutrition and basic human needs in the adjustment process, and of ensuring the sustained expansion of employment and incomes in the longer run. In collaboration with others, they need to ensure adequate attention and financing for human investment in the development process.

The United Nations organizations and the specialized agencies, including the regional development banks, also need to focus their efforts and resources more clearly on these priority areas and to identify and support more human-focused actions. A shift toward the human dimension in development in the developing countries would be greatly assisted if the analytical capacities, technical services and financial resources of the various U.N. agencies were devoted centrally to this need.

The bilateral aid agencies also have an obvious role, partly by increasing financial support for human investment. But equally, if not more, important is for them to ensure a stronger focus on the human dimension in the projects they support. Here, collaboration with, or more support for, NGO programs and projects can be especially cost-effective. NGO programs are often more closely related to grassroots action and more in touch with people and communities. Thus, they help to strengthen the approaches and local organization on which sustained development depends.

Breaking the Impasse

There is an impasse for many countries in the area of finance and adjustment. Despite obvious need, many countries, especially in Africa, are not receiving finance from the IMF or from structural adjustment loans of the World Bank because of their failure to agree on an adjustment program, or to fulfill its requirements once agreed.

Many finance/conditionality packages are unrealistically short-term and give inadequate attention to the human dimension. Other Roundtables have discussed problems of international debt and finance in more detail. They have stressed the need for more and longer-term official finance for adjustment. Another aspect of the problem has been sequencing; the limited objectives of the IMF have so far tended to dominate the adjustment process, partly because the World Bank and other development agencies have generally waited until an IMF program is agreed before proceeding with additional finance.

New international initiatives, as well as continuing efforts in the developing countries, will be needed to break the current impasse. Adjustment is an inescapable necessity, but more growth-oriented and human-focused approaches need to be actively explored. Various possibilities were discussed. One suggestion is closer cooperation between the IMF and the World Bank, perhaps with encouragement from the Development Committee. Another suggestion is a stronger role for consultative groups from all sources in exploring a broader approach to adjustment on the basis of the financing available. U.N. agencies other than the Bank and the Fund should give more attention to problems and policies of adjustment. Finally, future sessions of the North South Roundtable could focus on the adjustment experience of particular countries and explore lessons for more general applications.

Previous Roundtables have proposed that governments might invite independent working teams (including country representatives, independent experts, and representatives of the financial community) to help them in developing programs of adjustment and finance that would include prominent attention to the human dimension.

Initiatives in South - South Cooperation

Cooperation within the South also has an important role to play in many of the areas identified :
a) In exchanging information and experience on adjustment programs incorporating the human dimension.
b) In monitoring technological developments in the North, especially new technologies, and their implications for production, trade and development, including skill formation and utilization.
c) In adapting computer technology and identifying uses of such technology in education and elsewhere, and in exchange of information on these issues.
d) In improving indicators of the human dimension and in evolving schemes for skill cooperation among developing countries.

Africa

The human situation in Africa is so serious that it requires special mention. Important actions are underway by governments in many African countries to respond to the urgent needs of famine and to prevent its recurrence. Once world public opinion was aroused, the international community provided increased support. But as the rains return, an equally desperate drought of foreign exchange remains which is holding back development in almost all countries of Africa. Unless substantial increases in net inflows of foreign exchange become available, the human situation in most countries of Africa will remain desperately constrained to a degree which no amount of national or regional effort can overcome.

Steps to Global Awareness

Finally, there is a need to increase national and international awareness of these human dimensions of the current crisis in development, of the costs and risks of neglect, and of the opportunities for action.

Thus, the Roundtable welcomed the proposal by the ILO to convene in 1986 an international tripartite conference, with the participation of principal development financing agencies and the IMF, to consider the effects of the structural adjustment process on employment and other aspects of social development.

The organizations of the U.N. system might together collaborate:

a) On research focused on specific aspects of the changing human condition, in the context of both past trends and future prospects and challenges.

b) In the production of a periodic report on "The State of the Human Condition" covering the changing human situation in all parts of the world.

The Roundtable calls on all governments to support vigorously the initiative of the UNDP Administrator to convene a World Conference on the State of the Human Condition, to which the various organizations of the U.N. system would contribute.

PART I

THE HUMAN FACTOR

CHAPTER 1

The Human Factor in Development

Louis Emmerij

Today, in the middle of the 1980s, practically all efforts seem to be concentrated on getting back to a high and sustained rate of economic growth. This is true in both the industrialized and the developing countries. The warnings of ten years ago about the quality of economic growth — environmental factors, income distribution, employment and patterns of work — seem to be forgotton. Also forgotten is the human resources revolution of twenty-five years ago. The education and health sectors are among the first to be cut in the face of the new orthodoxy in the realm of financial and economic policies. In general, it looks as if physical investments are again given prime of place relative to investments in human capital.

At the same time, one tends to be too pessimistic about what has been achieved to date in terms of economic and social development, particularly in developing countries. Practically no one in the late 1940s and early 1950s could have anticipated the economic and social achievments that have since been realized in the Third World, particularly in Asia and Latin America. It is probably also true that one tends to be too pessimistic about the future because there is always the tendency to extrapolate the present situation. Since the present situation is bleak, its inherent negative characteristics are projected into the future.

We are thus in a state of contradiction. On the one hand is the urge to get back to economic growth, forgetting the lessons of the past or the lessons of other countries and continents. On the other hand is the nasty feeling that in the future, things in the economic, financial and social fields will never be what they were in the past. We are once more at a crossroads, and we may have partly to retrace our steps in order to proceed in the correct direction.

Development Theory and Practice: A Review

Fads and fashion are useful in restoring balance to an unbalanced situation. At the end of the 1950s, for example, we witnessed a "human resources revolution." More modestly, it could be called a renaissance of the economics of education and health. The classical economists, including Marshall, did not ignore the importance of such things as literacy, education and training for increasing the quality of the labor force. However, in the aftermath of World War I, with its galloping inflation followed by the great crisis of the 1930s, as well as during the aftermath of World War II, economic policy was fully concentrated on reconstruction and a return to sustained economic growth at the expense of most other factors, including human capital.

The turning point came at the end of the 1950s, when economists such as Theodore W. Schultz showed that important components of education and health should be considered an investment, i.e., a prerequisite for economic development, rather than a consumption good, to be afforded only after more essential needs have been taken care of. Throughout the 1960s, the study and practice of human resource development were restricted mainly to such aspects as literacy, education, training and health. However, those were also the days of the search for, and quantification of, the so-called residual factor. For example, Denison showed convincingly that economic growth could not be explained by the inputs of capital and labor alone. A host of other factors, such as education and training, research, innovation and management, also accounted for this residual factor. In retrospect, it can be said that the heyday of the economics of education and human resource development occurred in the 1960s.

There was yet another turning point somewhere in the early 1970s. This time, the pendulum swung in the opposite direction. Because of the economic difficulties leading to the depression of the 1970s and 1980s, attention was turned once again to the question of how to get out of the crisis and to return to economic growth. Education, health, etc., are once again considered commodities, luxuries to be afforded in good times but not in bad.

Most of the theoretical and empirical work on human resource development was done in the countries of the North and in Japan, a country that has experienced and recognized the importance of education and training since the end of the nineteenth century. Japan has always put tremendous emphasis on the quality of its population, in particular of its labor force. The developing countries more or less followed in the wake of events as they occurred in the North. During the 1960s, both UNESCO and the ILO became very active in the fields of education and manpower planning respectively, an emphasis that faded away during the 1970s.

At the end of the 1960s, social factors such as employment and income distribution came to the fore. This resulted during the 1970s in the search for employment-oriented development strategies and later in that decade, in the elaboration of growth and redistribution models, which will be discussed a little later.

All this was pushed to the background again, however, during the depression of the 1980s.

The orthodoxy in development theory has always been the modernization theory, although it has been adapted and attacked over the years. The modernization paradigm has undergone changes and adaptations of greater or lesser significance, some examples of which have been given above. During the 1950s and 1960s, maximization of the economic growth rate was considered the driving force which would almost automatically lead to advances in the social sphere, including employment creation and fair income distribution. Almost, because in the writings of those days, including those by W. Arthur Lewis, more subtle reasoning could be found. On the whole, however, it was assumed that a high and sustained rate of economic growth would carry in its wake most of the other objectives of government policy. During the 1970s, the "economic growth alone" concept was abandoned in favor of a much more explicit growth and redistribution development approach. The story of how this new emphasis on redistribution and basic needs came about is well known. In the face of the rapidly increasing populations of the developing countries, growth in the modern sector alone could not create enough productive employment opportunities within an acceptable period of time. A much heavier emphasis on the informal and traditional sectors, on the redistribution of income and wealth, was therefore a natural consequence. Toward the end of the decade, one could have thought that the ruling orthodoxy of development theory had been changed and adapted to such an extent as to become acceptable to a wide variety of countries, regimes and ideologies, and to be able to face the extremely complex situation of the development of nations and peoples.

It is true that at the end of the 1960s and in the early 1970s, a challenge to the modernization paradigm arose when the dependency theory originated in Latin America. The modernization theory puts heavy emphasis on the responsibility of *national* policies. The dependency theory, on the other hand, starts with the assumption that crucial factors are beyond the control of national governments of developing countries, and that national policies are therefore helpless in the face of the current international order.

An important point is that the debate between the modernization and dependency theories did not result in an acceptable compromise between national and international responsibilities in the development strategies of national governments in the South, nor in any clear position on the role and weight of trade and aid in the framework of development.

Turning now to the practice of development, although most countries are in more or less serious economic trouble today, this does not change the fact that throughout the 1970s, Latin America enjoyed an annual rate of economic growth of six per cent, while that of Southeast Asia was even higher than eight per cent. In fact, from the beginning of the 1950s until the end of the 1970s, the average rate of economic growth of developing countries as a whole has been around five per cent per annum, an unprecedented achievement in economic history. Africa has, unfortunately, been the exception, to such an extent that this continent has now largely deteriorated into a real problem area.

Within this general picture, certain developing countries have done much better economically than others, but this cannot always be explained according to the evolving theory set out above. The growth record of the 1970s shows that certain countries, such as the newly industrializing ones, seem at first sight to have done much better than others that were often the "darlings" of the development lobby. Why have certain Southeast Asian countries, and also some Latin American countries, done so much better than, say, Jamaica, most African countries, and Sri Lanka? There may be many reasons for the poor economic performance of certain countries and for a more reasonable performance by others. For the time being, we are only able to ask questions without being able to provide definite answers.

The first of these questions is about the role of the state versus the role of the market, or the emphasis that is put on central planning, as compared to giving private initiative sufficient scope to flourish. Clearly, the right balance must be struck between leaving the prevailing market forces completely free on the one hand, and repairing the damage that this may cause with the aid of state intervention in the form of economic planning on the other. This delicate balance between the free interplay of market forces and safeguarding the interests of the community at large through planning is of vital importance. It may well be that in some countries, the pendulum has swung too far toward one extreme or the other.

The difference in development performance observed during the 1970s could also be due to the fact that the dethronement of economic growth as top-priority objective has caused the pendulum to swing too far in the direction of redistributive policies, thereby putting obstacles in the way of an economic growth-path that still has to be followed. The emphasis given in that decade to growth and redistribution strategies, basic needs strategies, etc., was due to the realization that the balance has swung too far toward the extreme of economic growth. The rebalancing that then took place was severely attacked by those who still believed that a highly skewed income distribution is an essential precondition of economic growth, and by those who contended that the proposed development strategies had nothing to do with economic growth, but were mainly concerned with the "redistribution of poverty." It is thus somewhat ironic that a similar counterattack is now being made to get the pendulum back to where it was some ten to fifteen years ago. Nevertheless, it seems justified to study whether the right balance was struck.

A third question that must be asked is whether countries have found the right balance between decentralized decision making on the one hand and a more participatory decision-making process on the other, a question that is related to the implementation process. Those who maintain that this process is the principal culprit also say that the above reasons are too general, that *many* policies could probably be successful, and that therefore what was wrong was not so much the overall objective, or development strategy, but the specifics of the day-to-day implementation process. These people also posit that there is no clear correlation between economic growth rates on the one hand and income distribution performance on the other. In other words, countries with high economic growth rates may have either a fairly uneven or a fairly even income distribution.

Countries with low economic growth rates may also show the same spurious results in income distribution. All this tends to prove the point that income distribution in itself either stimulates or hinders economic growth. The important factor is the way in which redistributive measures of income and wealth are implemented.

The price that has been paid by those countries that played the game of the existing international order, as compared to those that chose more self-reliant paths, also has to be considered. In looking at that particular balance, one must avoid the facile trap of continually blaming "the international order." International aspects are important, of course, and also the international order, while international trade is crucial. It is not true, however, that this line of reasoning generally leads to the conclusion that the national will to change can have no effect!

These are some of the questions that have been raised by critical evaluators of the development record over the past ten to fifteen years. Differences in human resource development and endowment, or more generally, differences in the human factor, have not been advanced so frequently as explanatory factors of varying economic and social development performances over the past decade. If at all, they have been put forward timidly, and in the most general terms. Someone may mention the differences in education and skills. Another may go much further and discuss the differences in innate ability. Comparative advantages are sometimes also mentioned, but these are very complex and sensitive issues. Are the Chinese populations the reason why Southeast Asia is doing so well? Can this be the entire story, because Thailand and the Philippines have also started to do well? Why do Jamaicans at Harvard perform so much better than American blacks at the same university? What is the secret of Japan?

These questions may well lead us to the heart of the development problem, but they bring us in the first instance to the question of definition.

Defining the Human Factor

There is evidence that the pendulum has swung too far toward neglecting human resource development. In the North, economic, financial and social policies emphasize inflation, government deficits, balance-of-payments equilibrium, economic restructuring and new technologies. If anything, human capital is being destroyed through such schemes as early retirement, introduced in an effort to do something about the mounting unemployment problem. The education and health sectors are under attack: their structure and their past growth have caused consumption aspects to gain the upper hand in comparison to investment aspects.

In the South, many countries are forced to undergo severe adjustment programs, as a result of which education and health budgets are sacrificed, because they are considered less vital to the economy. An extremely dangerous mechanism has thus been put into motion. The formation of skills is jeopardized on behalf of the short-term objective of adjusting the economy and reducing financial deficits. However, as soon as these countries start to grow again in the medium term, the need for human resources will increase. In other words, medium- and long-term losses will be incurred to obtain a short-term gain.

Three definitions of human resources are discussed below, starting from the definition which emerged twenty-five years ago and ending with a much more complex and broad definition of the human factor in development.

The Traditional Definition

As indicated earlier, the traditional definition of human resource development as it emerged some twenty-five years ago focused heavily on matters of education and secondarily on health. Skill formation was seen as an investment in human capital that had to be undertaken parallel with investments in physical capital. Within this definition, such instruments as manpower forecasts and rate of return analyses were used to determine how the future educational systems should evolve. For example, should relatively more emphasis be put on expanding primary and lower secondary education than on upper secondary and university education? Within the latter, which disciplines should be stressed that would be more in line with the country's economic and technological requirements over the coming period? Important debates about the structure of education have been the result of such forecasts and calculations.

During the 1970s, however, an entirely new school of the economics of education came to the fore; one could almost speak about a "second generation of the economics of education." Emphasis was shifted towards the socialization function of schooling, examining the screening hypothesis and studying labor market segmentation. The trend now is to see effective educational planning as based on a realistic assessment of the operations of labor markets. These are in a continuous state of flux, particularly in terms of employment patterns rather than relative wage differentials; with the best will in the world, it is difficult to avoid a situation in which every educational reform is addressed to curing the ills of yesterday rather than of today. Economic growth and technical progress are just as capable of de-skilling existing jobs as of generating new jobs and new skills. Consider, for example, the way in which the development of hand-held calculators and word processors has reduced the importance of functional numeracy and literacy in the work force and increased that of favorable attitudes to computer aids. The expansion of new industries and contraction of the old ones, changes in employment legislation and changes in trade union regulations are able rapidly to alter existing patterns of recruitment. No method of educational planning can keep pace. In this sense, there is real economic merit in general academic education as a hedge against technical dynamism.

The old demand for vocational and job-specific education, which at first might seem to be a rallying call for economists, is actually the opposite of what is implied by the "new" economics of education. A major conclusion is that instead of trying to forecast the impossible, the educational system should be turned into a much more flexible body, able to react swiftly and effectively to changes in the economy and in society in general. Policymakers need to realize that transformation includes the introduction of recurrent education and greater emphasis on the training and retraining of adults.

A Broader Definition of Human Resource Development

A distinction should be made between (i) the creation of human resources, (ii) their deployment and (iii) the setting up of an incentive structure with which to realize such a desirable deployment.

The first of these would broadly follow the lines of the traditional definition. In other words, the creation of human resources would still focus principally on education and training.

The second component, however, would explicitly draw the matter of deployment and utilization of human resources into the definition. The emphasis would then be on entrepreneurial and managerial abilities, research and technology, general skill formation of the masses, participation in the decision-making process, etc. In other words, not only investment in human capital, but also the possibility to deploy it over a wide range of social, economic and cultural activities, must be assured. Thus, not only certain types of education and training, but also employable skills, including those of management, should be provided. Moreover, what purpose does a widely educated population serve if it may not participate in the decision-making process? Highly qualified scientific and technical personnel should be deployed in research and development activities. The *World Bank Report, 1980* defines human development along such lines by including education and training, better health, nutrition, fertility reduction, entrepreneurial and administrative abilities, and research and technology. The report states, "Human development increases productivity, reduces fertility, and thus promotes long-term growth in average incomes." In terms of educational policies, greater emphasis should be put on basic education, with the possibility of alternating work with education and training. These alternate periods would concentrate on the specifics, including middle-level management and training. Research and development should be pursued in a few carefully selected centers of excellence, and developing countries should concentrate on such things as research on solar energy. Management training should be on-the-job, with the possibility of selected high-level training aspects being undertaken abroad. All this would mean a quite different policy package in the field of human resource development than has so far been pursued.

If human resources are to be deployed in the right direction, a number of actions must be undertaken — actions that will affect the incentives which cause people to undertake certain things rather than others. This is the third component of the definition. If the deployment of human resources is to move in the direction indicated here, at least three types of action will be required.

a) The income structure — both monetary and non-monetary incomes — will have to be adapted in such a way that people will find it more remunerative to choose occupations, types and levels of education that are in line with the future development of society.

This is not only a matter of wages or salaries, but also of so-called fringe benefits. i.e., nonmonetary incentives that go with certain jobs. For example, if the need for middle- and high-level managers is more urgent than that for clerical workers, this must be reflected, first of all, in significant wage differentials between the two kinds of occupations, but probably also in differences in a whole range of facilities that cannot immediately be translated into financial terms.

b) Changes must be introduced into the decision-making structure at the national government, local government and enterprise levels. If human resources are to be deployed so that people can take a more active part in decisions that affect them, this will have to be reflected in a decision-making structure that is horizontal rather than hierarchical. That this is a delicate matter has been shown in the European context during the late 1960s and early 1970s. However, this experimental process has taught us many lessons, resulting in a decision-making structure that combines a maximum amount of participation with speed and efficiency.

c) If the reasoning of the previous section is correct, changes must also be introduced into education and research policies. These should be directed towards the following:

- Primary education and lower secondary education should be given priority in the allocation of funds.
- Additional funds should go to selected research institutes.
- More emphasis should be given to middle-level management.

In addition to the adaptations in the income structure set out above, parallel changes must be introduced in educational and research structures and facilities in order that human resources may be deployed along the lines set out in this paper.

The Human Factor in Development

The question of human resources can obviously be interpreted much more broadly than has been done in the framework of the two previous definitions. This leads us to the question of the human factor in development, touching upon such questions as innate ability, motivation and achievement, and even more importantly, upon the question of whether systematic differences in these factors occur across races and cultures. This is clearly an extremely delicate matter; if it is not done carefully, such an analysis will bring back reminders of old (and fortunately, almost forgotten) racist theories.

It seems somewhat paradoxical to undertake such a search in times when both cultures and the objectives that different societies set for themselves tend to become more homogeneous across continents. It should be borne in mind, however, that this trend towards homogeneity has caused reactions. In more and more cases, national culture and religion are being reemphasized.

Nevertheless, it is in such directions that one must search in looking for the answers to questions like: Why are the countries of East and Southeast Asia doing so much better economically than almost any other country, including those of Europe? Why will Singapore soon be the richest spot in the world? Why is Africa doing so poorly that it is gradually becoming a disaster area? Can all this be explained only by economic factors, resource endowments, organizational skills, etc.?

It is clear that psychological factors also come into play. Anyone who visits Southeast Asia today will gain the impression that the people there feel they have a world to conquer. No one who returns from that part of the globe to Europe can escape this impression. This is part of the answer to the question of why Europe is now doing so poorly.

On the other hand, one might be tempted to say that Asia and Latin America, despite certain drawbacks due to the world economic crisis, are well on their way towards sustained economic and social development. The times of Gunnar Myrdal's *Asian Drama* seem long past. Today, one should write about the "African Drama." On the whole, however, things have been moving far better than observers in the late 1940s and early 1950s thought possible.

The most fascinating questions, however, remain: Why did it happen in certain areas and not in others? Why did it happen at certain points in time and not at others? In the eighteenth century, western countries were no richer than the rest of the world. It has been shown that a combination of managerial ability and a high marginal propensity to save is a sufficient condition to start economic progress even in a very low-income country. A few years ago, it had become a platitude to state that the poor countries were too poor to accumulate enough capital, and therefore they must remain poor. But if western countries, which were also poor to start with, were able in the past to increase their rates of investment considerably, it is worthwhile to find out how they did it. Why did capable people suddenly appear in England, and later in Japan, and still later in Singapore? Why did *they* see favorable conditions and possibilities? Possibilities never exist; they are created by people.

The creation of new possibilities means change. As a point of departure in the analysis of economic development, one might introduce the thesis that traditional man does not like change and in fact resists it. In a traditional society, the desire of the younger generation to be different from the older is on the whole very weak. The societal attitude is rather: Things are good, because they have already been good for a long time.

It is thus clear why many societies have not been able to adapt themselves to fundamentally new conditions. The history of man is a graveyard of cultures that came to catastrophic ends because of the lack of planned, rational and voluntary reaction to change. Cultures have disappeared because climatological conditions changed, trade routes changed, etc.

Some rulers have realized these facts and have tried to make their people "change-minded." Czar Peter the Great, who personally cut off the beards of his *bojars,* and Kemal Ataturk, who banished the *fez,* are famous examples. One will never understand economic development if one continues to think only in quantitative terms of five, ten or fifteen per cent investment without understanding the enormous resistance that nonconformists – the independent thinkers who wanted to analyze problems themselves – had to overcome before a traditional society could be changed into a dynamic one. No theory of economic development is possible unless man is seen as the creator of his own environment.

At the beginning of the seventeenth century, a wood shortage jeopardized the English economy. This led to a strong tendency to substitute coal for wood. This in turn necessitated fundamental technological changes and a complete change in the system of transportation. It took more than 150 years before these problems were solved, but at the end of this period, man *had* changed his environment. Man had come to understand that as soon as his actual living conditions were no longer considered inevitable, rational action could improve his situation. From that time onwards, an important part of western culture concentrated on this improvement.

The Japanese were able to copy western techniques, but they understood immediately that such techniques could not be introduced into the existing feudal society. Instead, they managed to adapt themselves to western science and part of the western outlook without neglecting their own traditions and their historically developed pattern of life. Theirs was the gift of assimilation and adaptation, not merely of imitation. Furthermore, they showed both courage and a talent for compromise. Courage, because they had to eliminate feudal society, partly sacrificing the interests and properties of the very classes to which most leaders of the restoration belonged. They destroyed feudalism, but some of the old feudal leaders became the leaders of modern society. Those who say that the Japanese "only" imitated western technology fail to see that economic development means not only the introduction of new machinery, but the creation of a society in which these machines can function. By doing this, the Japanese leaders were less concerned about the price that had to be paid by certain groups of the population — for example, the peasants. Their aim was the glory of Japan, and individual sacrifices counted little in the face of that objective.

All traditional societies are agrarian economies, and a settlement with agrarian interests must first be achieved. The stories of England, Japan and the Soviet Union are different, but the pattern of events is the same: productivity in agriculture increased and agrarian employment decreased, first relatively, and later also absolutely. Everywhere this has been a harsh process, because rural interests have persisted to the bitter end.

To sum up, the most difficult situation that a government may have to face is to break through a Malthusian low per capita income equilibrium. This is not only an economic problem. A fundamental overall social change is necessary to set in motion a process of economic development. When in the early 1950s economists realized the urgent need for a solution to the problems of low-income countries, they immediately devised a number of theories for the guidance of policymakers. The Harrod-Domar model was used to demonstrate that poor countries remained poor because they were not able to invest enough. Rosenstein-Rodan's "big push" theory showed that a huge increase in investments was needed to break through the low per capita income equilibrium, whereas Rostow's "take-off" theory demonstrated that foreign aid might not be needed for longer than twenty years, because such a period would be sufficient to change a stagnant economy into a progressing one.

Subsequently, it has been realized that lack of organizational ability and lack of skilled labor in general prevent the realization of development plans even more than the lack of capital.

Here we are back at the fashions which, despite obvious inter-relationships, assert that some one factor is more important than all the others. W. Arthur Lewis in his *Theory of Economic Growth,* published exactly thirty years ago and still one of the best books on the subject, recalls these one-sided underlinings over the decades. For example, to Adam Smith and a long line of liberal economists, what was needed to promote economic growth was primarily the right institutional framework. Given this framework, there was not much need to bother about willingness to make an effort, or about the accumulation of knowledge, or capital accumulation, since all these were instinctive human reactions inhibited only by faulty institutions.

Malthus, on the other hand, maintained that one of the major obstacles in underdeveloped countries was lack of demand, which we would translate in our days as "a low evaluation of income in relation to leisure." Another school fastens upon low technological skills as the bottleneck. President Truman's program for underdeveloped countries, for example, claimed that technical assistance was what the underdeveloped countries chiefly needed from the developed ones. Or, there is the school which points to capital as the bottleneck, claiming that if only enough capital were available, new technologies could be made available too, and that in the process of economic growth, all institutions hostile to economic growth would be adapted or swept away. Finally, there is the school which puts all emphasis on national resources, claiming in fact that every country gets the capital and institutions which its natural resources warrant.

Of course, it is true that one obstacle to growth may stand out above all others in some particular place at some particular time, either in the sense that the deficiency is greatest at this point, or else in the sense that it is easier to make a start there than at any other point. All this, however, is only a temporary tactic, in the sense that if one succeeds in breaking one bottleneck, the result is usually that another one comes into prominence. Hence, though the reformer may start out by working upon one factor only, he has to bear in mind that if he is to have complete success, a great deal of other change is involved beyond the factor with which he is immediately concerned.

Conclusion

Human resources no longer play the role they used to play in development theory and practice. This is a mistake. Several definitions of human resources are possible, moving from the traditional to the more complex. Questions that must be discussed are the following:

a) Are we entering a period where the human factor is becoming the limiting factor in economic and social development?

b) If so, which of the three definitions presented is the most appropriate one?

c) If it is the more complex, i.e., the third definition, how can we turn this into an operational concept?

CHAPTER 2

The Human Dimension in Development: Objective and Resource

Frances Stewart

Human welfare is the fundamental objective of economic activity. There may be disagreement about how to define and measure this objective, but there is no quarrel — in the *secular* world — about the primacy of the objective. Moreover, human beings are also the ultimate productive resource. Human labor is essential to design and make the machines we use (or, increasingly, to design and make the machines which design and make machines), while without people and machines, natural resources would be useless as well as valueless. Human beings confer value on things and also make their production possible. Hence the topic under discussion — the human element as an objective and resource — in fact covers the *whole* of economic activity.

Despite the fact that human beings and human welfare underlie all our notions of value and resources, they are disguised in the normal discussions of GNP and economic activity. Indeed, the disguise goes so far that it merges into neglect, with harmful effects on human welfare and economic efficiency. Let us then consider economic activity explicitly from the point of view of people ("economics as if people matter," as Schumacher put it).

"Human welfare" is a vague concept. We will consider problems of definition; planning approaches which explicitly incorporate the human element; how such approaches bear on those of conventional economics — that is, how far our thinking as *economists* has to be revised if the human element is incorporated centrally; and how the incorporation of the human dimension can lead to a radical revision of country ranking, as compared with a more conventional approach.

Human Welfare as an Objective: Definitional Issues

What constitutes (defines and measures) "human welfare"? Gross National Product (GNP) per head is the conventional measure, and, despite the many well-rehearsed objections to it, it continues to be the main way of ranking countries' economic performance. (For example, the World Bank's *World Development Report* lists countries in order of income per head). A closer look at the question suggests that GNP per head bears little relationship to human well-being as we commonly understand the term. Human welfare is about whether children live or die; whether people eat well, are malnourished or starve; whether women lead healthy and tolerable lives or are burdened with annual childbearing, the high risk of maternal mortality, and the certainty of lifelong drudgery; whether humans control their lives at work or are "details" of the machinery, spending most of their lives in tough, unpleasant activity, at the dictation of management and machinery; whether people have access to work at all; whether people control their political lives or are subject to arbitrary decisions taken by others, with the possible removal of their liberty and even their lives for political reasons; whether their education is sufficient to permit men, women and children to partic- ipate in the world around them as full members of society with some control over their destinies, rather than as victims in a world where to be uneducated is akin to being blind, and where schooling is a universal passport. One could go on; the important point is that none of these aspects of human fulfillment — all of which must be obvious to anyone who thinks about these questions — are intrinsic to the usual measure of human welfare, GNP per capita. We need a definition which does incorporate these objectives.

We have called the human objective "the full life"[1] to provide a name for such an objective — i.e., one which does incorporate the many dimensions which together constitute human welfare. The full- life objective (FL) incorporates physical well-being, which requires various goods and services necessary for people to lead healthy and educated lives (e.g., food, water, shelter, schooling, etc.). In addition, it should also include nonphysical aspects such as those mentioned above (e.g., employment, conditions of work, political liberty, etc.). With this view, GNP per capita should not be regarded as the objective of economic activity, but rather as a means (quite possibly a rather ineffective means) of achieving the full-life objective. Much more needs to be said on the FL objective before it can be used operation- ally. While there is no space here for a full discussion, certain impor- tant points should be noted.

a) It is multidimensional. The precise dimensions to be included may be a matter of dispute, and the weighting to be given to each one is bound to be arbitrary (e.g., how much weight should be given to the health objective as against political liberty?). These problems are essentially insoluble from a technical perspective, because there is no uniquely correct definition or weighting. It is the task of the political process to provide some political solution. This type of issue has led to criticism of efforts to provide an index of human welfare.[2] While the criticisms are valid, they are not a justification for throwing the whole approach aside and returning to GNP. Rather, they point to the need to measure the various aspects separately (e.g., life expectancy, literacy, arbitrary imprisonment), without attempting to provide one composite index.

b) The FL requires certain physical goods and services such as those listed above, but the provision of these goods is not the objective, which is ultimately a quality of life for which the consumption of certain goods is essential. Consumption is a means to, not the end of, human welfare. Different goods and services may be appropriate, or even essential, depending on the particular situation (e.g., heating in cold climates, transport in remote regions). Moreover, goods and services may substitute for each other or complement each other. A very important empirical relationship is that between physical goods and services, about which planning decisions are made, and the FL objective. We describe this relationship as the *metaproduction function*:

$$FL = f(a,b,c,d....)$$

where FL is the objective and a,b,c,d, are the relevant goods and services. Clearly, the function will depend on which dimensions of the FL are being considered. Knowledge about the relationship is essential for formulating policies and plans. In general, there is very great ignorance in this area. The way it has been presented above, the metaproduction function may sound rather abstract, pedantic and obscure. It is not: it is about important and familiar issues — for example, whether child health would be better promoted by the provision of clean water, or by maternal education, or whether both are necessary; how nutritional standards can be best raised, and so on. While these questions can be avoided when the objective is maximizing GNP, answers to them are essential for planning with human welfare as its prime concern.

c) There is a definite *distributional* aspect to the FL objective — i.e., the aim is to give priority to those most deprived of essential aspects, over and above further enriching those whose minimum needs are already met. But the precise interpretation of this distributional aspect, like all issues of distribution, is a difficult question, subject to the usual problems (e.g., of whether to give zero weight to people with need fulfillment above some minimum, how to define the minimum, how to deal with people well below the minimum, as compared with those just below).[3]

d) There is also a critical question of *timing:* is the concern only with today's achievements, with next year's too, with ten years hence, with the next century and beyond? To what extent the people of today should be sacrificed for those of tomorrow is a difficult political question. Most would agree that the aim is to achieve a *sustainable* position, which means that to make gains now at the expense of the environment, whose destruction will threaten future generations, is definitely undesirable. Beyond that, the FL approach would not normally justify sacrificing minimum FL achievements of people today for the sake of luxury consumption now or in the future (though for political reasons, this normally does happen). In contrast, the GNP objective may justify just such a sacrifice.

e) The objective is related to individuals — i.e., to women, men and children as individuals. The family, of course, normally provides the essential context in which individual fulfillment occurs, but in order to assess achievements, it is necessary to go beyond the household (where analysis often stops — e.g., in looking at household income distribution) to distribution *within* the household.

Plans and Policies

In devising plans and policies with the human dimension as the essential objective, it is helpful to consider three types of planning framework — concerned with production, with organization and with incomes. The three frameworks are summarized in figures 1, 2 and 3. These frameworks, as presented here, focus on the physical aspects of FL achievements, which are the natural concern of economic planning. However, incorporating other aspects would also have some implications for economic planning. This would arise, for example, if employment were taken as a vital objective. The first (production) diagram shows the steps necessary to ensure the production of the appropriate bundle of goods through resource allocation between different activities. The FL is the ultimate objective; it is also a vital productive resource. This is indicated in the diagram showing the feedback between the FL objective and the increase in resources in subsequent periods. Despite acknowledgment of the importance of human resources to economic productivity, the precise relationship remains very much a black box about which additional research is urgently needed.

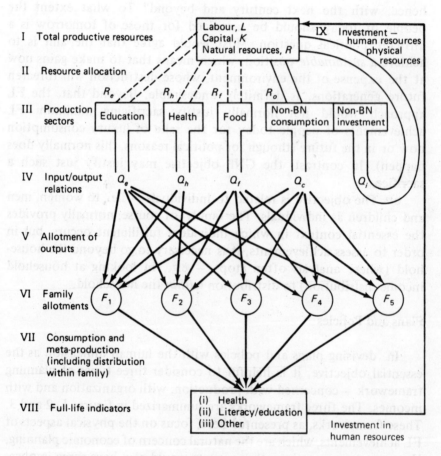

Figure 1 Production Framework

Most of the items most closely related to meeting minimum human needs in poor societies are produced outside the conventional private capitalist system; much is done within the household, or in the public sector. Consequently, the appropriateness and efficiency of *organization* is a critical issue. This is described in figure 2. To ensure that people are able to consume the goods and services, they

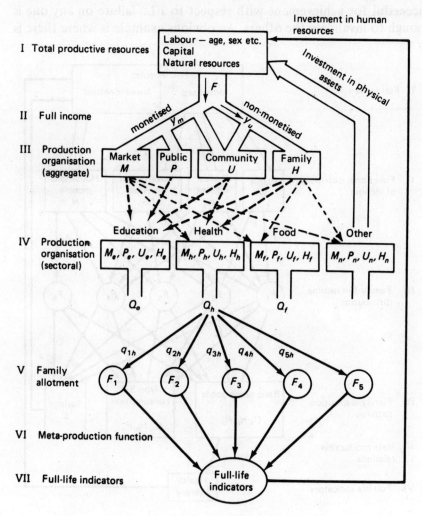

Figure 2 Full income and organisational choices

must have sufficient real incomes, in cash or kind, through economic activity or *subventions* from the state or elsewhere: i.e., they must have sufficient *entitlements,* to use Sen's terminology.[4] Figure 3 traces the way in which incomes derived from the productive system generate patterns of household income, which in turn lead to expenditure and consumption of the basic goods and services relevant to the FL objective.

It should be noted that all three types of planning must be successful for achievement with respect to FL: failure on any one is enough to invalidate the others. An obvious example is where there is

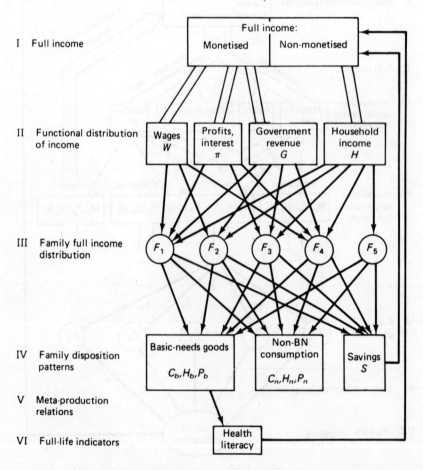

Figure 3 Income distribution and basic needs

plenty of food, but people have inadequate money to buy enough. The metaproduction function is an essential link in each of the frameworks, relating the consumption of goods to the FL achievements. Within this framework, intrahousehold distribution of consumption is of critical significance in determining how household consumption affects individuals' achievements. This is indicated in figure 4.

The same level of household income may lead to very different FL achievements according to (i) how it is spent on different categories of goods (e.g., cigarettes or food); (ii) how each category is distributed among different household members; (iii) how efficiently each good is used (e.g., how many nutrients are retained from any given food as a result of storing/cooking, etc.).

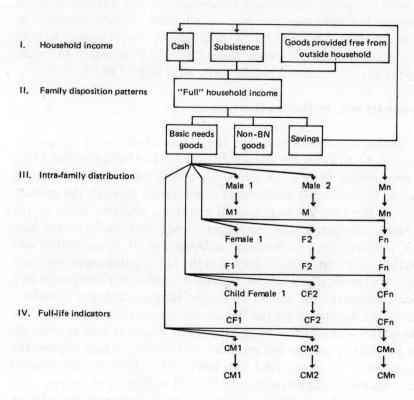

Figure 4 Intrahousehold income distribution and basic needs

The GNP per capita story thus stops before the important aspects of human fulfillment:

a) It ignores how incomes are distributed among households.
b) It ignores how expenditure is allocated between goods.
c) It ignores intrahousehold distribution.
d) It ignores the efficiency of consumption.

Approaches to development strategies which incorporate distributional objectives explicit — e.g., the redistribution with growth approach[5] — allow for the first of these problems but do not deal with the remainder.

From a policy perspective, these lacunae are enormously important. While the GNP maximization strategy was criticized for assuming, without justification, the "trickle down" of incomes to the poor, the human dimension approach suggests even more tenuous links with GNP, since is it necessary to assume not only a trickle down of incomes, but also the presence of all other aspects involved, as discussed above. Direct focus on these aspects — with respect to both economic planning and policy formulation — is necessary to ensure that the system functions satisfactorily with respect to FL.

Economics and the Human Dimension

Neither the neoclassical nor the Marxist framework adequately describes or analyzes the human dimension. The basic building block of neoclassical theory, on which all normative economics rests, is reliance on consumer preferences as expressed through the marketplace as the ultimate indicator of economic welfare. Some of the problems associated with consumer choice and welfare have long been acknowledged — notably, externalities of consumption and questions of income distribution. But the human dimension approach more fundamentally weakens reliance on consumer preference as a guide to welfare. The human dimension approach requires consideration of the welfare of all the family and not just the "consumer"; it necessitates examination of the supply of goods as well as demand; and in focusing on the metaproduction function, it goes beyond the consumption of *goods* (and also beyond the Lancasterian view of consumption of *characteristics)* to the real well-being of people.

Arguably, this is a step that Marx took in distinguishing between the *use-value* of goods as against their *exchange-value*. But the analysis has not been carried significantly beyond using this as a critique of capitalism.

Sen's entitlement approach[6] is of obvious relevance. As initially formulated, it was a measure of real income in terms of one item (food) and one need (hunger). This, however, omits the step incorporated in the metaproduction function which relates the consumption of the relevant goods (food, in this case) to the actual achievement in terms of real human welfare (i.e., nutrition). In more recent writing, Sen has used the concept of *capability*, which comes closer to doing this.[7] But the capability approach is concerned with *potential* for meeting a specified need, not actual achievement. For human welfare, we are not interested so much in potential as in actual achievements. This can involve important differences. For example, it is possible to calculate how much money a family needs, potentially, to fulfill the nutritional needs of its children. But suppose family expenditure is actually determined by someone who will spend a large proportion of additional income on drink? Then the capability-determined income will have little bearing on actual achievements with respect to child nutrition. Extra income or other policies would be needed to ensure the FL achievement. Moreover, extra expenditure on food may not be the best way of achieving improved nutrition − maternal education, for example, or reduced incidence of certain diseases, might be more effective. The metaproduction function focuses directly on exploring such multifactoral relationships.

Country Performance on Human Welfare

Country performance on improving human welfare will, of course, depend on the particular dimension of the FL being considered. Among developing countries, infant mortality rates, life expectancy and adult literacy are three obvious indicators of achievement on the physical side. Indices of political prisoners, freedom of the press, voting rights, etc., could be used to measure political rights. Other indicators would be needed to measure other aspects, such as access to, and quality of, work. On the whole, these nonphysical dimensions are usually treated qualitatively rather than quantitatively. While this may be justified because of the difficulties of devising nonsubjective indicators, it tends to mean that such aspects are given smaller weight than those that are measured quantitatively. An important agenda for research is thus to identify human welfare objectives and devise systematic measures.

This paper focuses primarily on just one simple measure of the physical dimension — life expectancy at birth. This statistic has the advantages of incorporating infant and child mortality and of being highly correlated with measures of literacy. It is also available (admittedly somewhat inaccurately) for every country for which income figures are available. Table 1 ranks all developing countries by life expectancy and by rates of infant mortality, showing how these rankings differ from ranking by per capita income. Although there are some differences in ranking between life expectancy and infant mortality, they are not very sharp, while there are some huge differences between both these indicators and per capita income ranking. For example, China has the same rate of infant mortality as Venezuela, although Venezuela's per capita income, at $3,840, is over 12 times as great as that of China at $300. Costa Rica has the same income per head as Peru, but its rate of infant mortality is one-fifth that of Peru. Algeria, with an income per head of over $2,000, has a rate of infant mortality equal to or higher than countries with incomes of about one-tenth of this, such as Lesotho and Tanzania. These big differences in ranking show that incorporating the human dimension into objectives and strategies may make a radical difference in drawing conclusions, as compared with an approach focusing solely on growth in incomes.

TABLE 1
Country Ranking: Life Expectancy, Infant Mortality, Income Per Capita
1983

Country	Life Expectancy		Infant Mortality		Income Per Capita	
	Rank	Years	Rank	Per 1,000	Rank	$
Afghanistan	1	36	1	200*	29	n.a.
Guinea	2	37	6	158	19	300
Sierra Leone	3	38	2	198	24	330
Bhutan	4	43	4	162	30	n.a.
Chad	4	43	13	142	31	n.a.
Ethiopia	4	43	16	140*	1	120
Angola	4	43	8	148	68	n.a.
Burkina Faso	8	44	8	148	6	180
Malawi	8	44	3	164	8	210

* For 1982

– Cont'd

TABLE 1 – Continued

Country	Life Expectancy Rank	Years	Infant Mortality Rank	Per 1,000	Income Per Capita Rank	$
Lao PDR	8	44	5	159	33	n.a.
Yemen AR	12	45	7	152	42	550
Mali	12	45	8	148	3	160
Niger	12	45	18	139	10	240
Somalia	12	45	13	142	13	250
Nepal	15	46	12	143	3	160
Mozambique	15	46	33	109	34	n.a.
Senegal	15	46	17	140	36	440
Mauritania	15	46	20	136	38	480
Yemen PDR	15	46	19	137	41	520
Burundi	20	47	23	123	10	240
Rwanda	20	47	22	125	15	270
Central African R	22	48	13	142	16	280
Benin	22	48	8	148	18	290
Sudan	22	48	28	117	28	400
Uganda	25	49	35	108	9	220
Togo	25	49	31	112	16	280
Madagascar	25	49	65	66	22	310
Liberia	25	49	32	111	38	480
Nigeria	25	49	30	113	53	770
Bangladesh	30	50	21	132	2	130
Pakistan	30	50	27	119	27	390
Zaire	32	51	38	106	5	170
Tanzania	32	51	46	97	10	240
Bolivia	32	51	23	123	40	510
Zambia	32	51	42	100	44	580
Ivory Coast	36	52	25	121	47	710
Morocco	36	52	44	98	50	760
Lesotho	38	53	33	109	37	460
Oman	38	53	25	121	95	6,250
Haiti	40	54	36	107	19	300
Indonesia	40	54	40	101	43	560
Papua NG	40	54	46	97	50	760
Cameroon	40	54	29	116	54	820
Burma	44	55	49	93	6	180
India	44	55	49	93	14	260
Zimbabwe	46	56	63	69	49	740
Saudi Arabia	46	56	40	101	97	12,230
Kenya	48	57	57	81	26	340
Algeria	48	57	36	107	83	2,320
Egypt	50	58	39	102	46	700
Nicaragua	50	58	53	84	56	880
Peru	50	58	44	98	58	1,040
Libya	50	58	51	91	96	8,480
Ghana	54	59	46	97	22	310
Iraq	54	59	60	71	94	n.a.

Cont'd

TABLE 1 – *Continued*

Country	Life Expectancy		Infant Mortality		Income Per Capita	
	Rank	Years	Rank	Per 1,000	Rank	$
Honduras	56	60	57	81	45	670
Guatamala	56	60	64	67	59	1,120
Iran	56	60	42	100	93	n.a.
Tunisia	59	62	54	83	62	1,290
Congo	60	63	55	82	60	1,230
Turkey	60	63	55	82	61	1,240
Dominican R	60	63	66	63	64	1,370
Ecuador	60	63	59	76	66	1,420
Thailand	65	64	72	50	55	820
Vietnam	65	64	69	53	35	n.a.
El Salvador	65	64	62	70	47	710
Colombia	65	64	69	53	67	1,430
Jordan	65	64	67	62	73	1,640
Brazil	65	64	61	70	77	1,880
S. Africa	65	64	51	91	84	2,490
Paraguay	71	65	76	45	65	1,410
Korean DR	71	65	84	32	70	n.a.
Lebanon	71	65	75	48	71	n.a.
Mongolia	71	65	73	49	72	n.a.
Mexico	75	66	71	52	82	2,240
China	76	67	79	38	19	300
Syrian AR	76	67	68	56	74	1,760
Malaysia	76	67	86	29	75	1,860
Korea R	76	67	86	29	78	2,010
Venezuela	80	68	79	38	87	3,840
Trinidad and Tobago	80	68	89	28	92	6,850
Sri Lanka	82	69	82	37	24	330
Yugoslavia	82	69	84	32	86	2,570
Jamaica	84	70	89	28	63	1,300
Chile	84	70	78	40	76	1,870
Argentina	84	70	83	36	79	2,070
Panama	87	71	91	26	80	2,120
Portugal	87	71	92	25	81	2,230
Kuwait	87	71	86	29	98	17,880
UAE	87	71	77	44	99	22,870
Uruguay	91	73	79	38	85	2,490
Singapore	92	74	97	11	91	6,620
Costa Rica	92	74	94	20	57	1,020
Israel	92	74	96	14	89	5,370
Cuba	95	75	93	20	69	n.a.
Greece	95	75	95	15	88	3,920
Hong Kong	97	76	98	10	90	6,000

SOURCE: World Bank, *World Development Report, 1985*; UNICEF, *State of the World's Children, 1985.*

Table 2 lists countries whose ranking for 1983 was very different according to different indicators. Countries are included where there is a difference in ranking of 20 or more between the life expectancy indicator and the income per head indicator.

TABLE 2
Country Performance: Life Expectancy
Compared With Income Per Head

"Good" Countries*		"Weak" Countries†	
Sri Lanka	+57	Angola	−60
China	+57	Oman	−57
Burma	+37	Saudi Arabia	−51
Costa Rica	+36	Libya	−46
Ghana	+32	Iraq	−40
Vietnam	+30	Yemen AR	−34
Bangladesh	+28	Iran	−34
Zaire	+27	Nigeria	−29
Cuba	+26	Afghanistan	−28
Jamaica	+21	Chad	−27
Tanzania	+20	Bhutan	−26
		Yemen PDR	−26
		Mauritania	−24
		Sierra Leone	−21
		Senegal	−21

SOURCE: World Bank. *World Development Report 1985.*

* Countries whose ranking according to life expectancy is 20 or more better than their ranking by per capita income.

† Countries whose ranking by life expectancy is 20 or more worse than by per capita income.

As can be seen, this assessment of performance throws up rather different "success stories" than the normal ranking in terms of growth in GNP or incomes per head. Tables 3 and 4 contain lists of "successes" and "failures," using the human dimension as a criterion but adopting a more complex methodology to identify "success" and "failure." Table 3 indicates special sucess/failure on life expectancy in relation to per capita income in 1979, using regression techniques to identify "success" and "failure". Table 4 uses adult literacy as the criterion with data for 1976. There is very substantial overlap in the lists of countries in tables 2, 3 and 4.

TABLE 3
Exceptional Performers in Basic Needs (Life Expectancy)
1979

	"Good" Av. % deviation on 3 methods † 7.5% or more above predicted		"Poor" Av. % deviation on 3 methods † 7.5% or more below predicted level
1. Sri Lanka*	+ 37.2	1. Ivory Coast*	− 22.0
2. China*	+ 30.9	2. Angola*	− 20.3
3. Albania*	+ 20.3	3. Yemen AR*	− 19.8
4. Burma*	+ 18.2	4. Senegal*	− 18.0
5. [Bangladesh*	+ 16.4]	5. Yemen PDR*	− 15.8
6. Jamaica*	+ 14.2	6. Mauritania*	− 14.7
7. Cuba*	+ 13.7	7. Cameroon*	− 14.0
8. Thailand*	+ 12.5	8. Algeria*	− 13.2
9. Philippines*	+ 12.3	9. Niger*	− 12.6
10. El Salvador*	+ 12.1	10. Congo*	−111.4
11. India*	+ 11.1	11. Central*	− 11.4
12. Panama*	+ 10.7	12. Afghanistan*	− 11.1
13. Mongolia*	+ 9.5	13. Guinea*	− 11.0
14. Syrian AR††	+ 8.1	14. Ethiopia††	− 10.0
15. Malaysia††	+ 8.0	15. Burundi*	− 9.7
16. Kenya†††	+ 6.7	16. Nigeria*	− 9.5
17. [Bhutan††	+ 6.5]	17. Papua NG††	− 8.9
18. Hong Kong†††	+ 6.4	18. Zambia††	− 8.8
19. Costa Rica†††	+ 6.2	19. Sudan††	− 8.6
20. Uruguay††	+ 5.4	20. Bolivia††	− 8.3
		21. Togo††	− 7.9
		22. Upper Volta††	− 7.5
		23. S. Africa†††	− 6.6
		24. Chad†††	− 5.4
		25. Venezuela†††	− 5.2
Taiwan ⊕	12.8	Iran ⊕⊕	
Vietnam ⊕	35.6	Saudi Arabia ⊕⊕	
		Iraq ⊕⊕	
		Libya ⊕⊕	

SOURCE: Stewart (1985).

† The three methods involve comparing actual achievements on life expectancy with those predicted by three different "best fit" relationships relating life expectancy to income per capita.

* Achieve 7.5% or more above/below predicted on each of 3 methods.

†† Achieve 7.5% or more above/below on 2 of 3 methods.

††† Achieve 7.5% or more above/below on 1 of 3 methods.

[ ] Countries with lowest incomes per capita in sample.

⊕ Using estimates for 1979 income per capita.

⊕⊕ Oil exporters, not included in regressions.

TABLE 4
Exceptional Performers on Basic Needs (Literacy)
1976

"Good" % deviation from predicted level † more than 20% above			"Poor" % deviation more than 20% below	
1.	Burma*	+ 113.3	1. Senegal*	− 80.4
2.	Sri Lanka*	+ 112.6	2. Yemen Arab Rep*	− 70.2
3.	Somalia	+ 100.1	3. Niger*	− 69.7
4.	Tanzania	+ 72.7	4. Ivory Coast	− 65.9
5.	Philippines*	+ 69.3	5. Mauritania*	− 65.1
6.	Thailand*	+ 65.7	6. Mali	− 64.8
7.	S. Korea	+ 54.5	7. Togo*	− 63.9
8.	Cuba*	+ 49.2	8. Sudan*	− 56.7
9.	Nicaragua	+ 45.0	9. Zaire	− 55.8
10.	Indonesia	+ 44.2	10. Chad*	− 52.2
11.	Paraguay	+ 41.4	11. Morocco	− 50.5
12.	Lesotho	+ 39.6	12. Algeria*	− 47.5
13.	Romania	+ 34.1	13. Ethiopia*	− 47.2
14.	Costa Rica*	+ 33.3	14. Liberia	− 44.0
15.	Uruguay*	+ 29.9	15. Guinea*	− 43.1
16.	Ecuador	+ 29.6	16. Yemen PDR*	− 40.8
17.	Peru	+ 26.7	17. Nepal	− 39.5
18.	Argentina	+ 25.4	18. Afghanistan*	− 39.3
19.	Madagascar	+ 25.1	19. Kuwait	− 37.9
20.	Bolivia	+ 23.7	20. Iran*	− 35.8
21.	Mexico	+ 20.0	21. Pakistan	− 35.7
			22. Libya*	− 28.3
			23. Zambia*	− 26.5
			24. Malawi	− 26.5
			25. Burundi*	− 20.5

SOURCE: Stewart (1985).
† Semi-log relationship, covering all countries (81) for which data is available.
* Also appear as "good," "poor" performers on life expectancy on table 3.

Incomes are, of course, an important mechanism for assessing achievement on the physical side of the human dimension, as suggested by the planning frameworks described above, where national income provides the resources from which allocations to provide for basic needs are made. Correlation analysis suggests that between 50 and 70 per cent of variation in country achievement on the human dimension are to be "explained" by variations in incomes per head.[7] The lists of successful countries, therefore, tend to underemphasize the achievement of countries where income growth has been strong (e.g., South Korea), whose life expectancy would be good for a lower-income country. It also may show countries as successes which have experienced very stagnant incomes (e.g., Zaire).

Taking tables 2, 3 and 4 together, it is possible to identify three types of strategy as being particularly successful:

a) High-growth capitalist countries which have experienced labor-absorbing industrialization (e.g., Taiwan, Hong Kong, Singapore).

b) Socialist countries which have given high priority to planning for basic minimum needs, both from a production and an entitlement perspective (e.g., Cuba, Vietnam, China).

c) Mixed economics where state intervention in support of social services and low-price foods has been significant (e.g., Sri Lanka, Costa Rica, Tanzania).

While the third type of strategy would appear to be the most feasible — politically and economically — for most countries, it seems to be more vulnerable than the other two. During economic difficulties, and subject to pressure from the international community (notably the IMF), a strategy which relies heavily on welfare-state interventions may be reversed, as has happened in Sri Lanka and will probably happen in Costa Rica and Tanzania. Domestically, such a strategy needs to be bolstered by an underlying pattern of economic performance which supports it (i.e., by land reform, successful agricultural performance and labor-absorbing industrialization). Internationally, performance on the human dimension needs to be acknowledged as a vital element in country achievement and not a luxury to be sacrificed when there are difficulties.[8]

The list of failures includes many whose *organizational* structures are especially weak, and also countries where mineral resources (oil, natural gas) have raised incomes without spreading the benefits widely.

Conclusion

While human welfare supposedly provides the underpinning of economic objectives and economic methodology, in reality, the human dimension has been seriously neglected in economic policy-making and planning. Explicit consideration of the human dimension would radically transform plans, policies and assessments. It necessitates a new look at economic theory, as well as providing an agenda for research.

Notes

1. See Fei, Ranis and Stewart in Frances Stewart, *Planning to Meet Basic Needs* (Macmillan, 1985).
2. See the discussion of PQLI in N. Hicks, and P. Streeten, "Indicators of Development: The Search for a Basic Needs Yardstick," *World Development* 7 (1979).
3. Many of these issues – to which there are no simple answers – are discussed by A.K. Sen in *Poverty and Famines: An Essay on Entitlement and Deprivation* (Clarendon Press, 1981).
4. Ibid.
5. H. Chenery et al., *Redistribution with Growth: An Approach to Policy* (Oxford University Press, 1974).
6. Sen, *Poverty and Famines*, 1981.
7. A.K. Sen, *Resources, Values and Development* (Blackwell, 1985), Chapter 24.
8. Richard Jolly, "Adjustment with a Human Face," (Barbara Ward Lecture to Society for International Development, Rome, July 1985). [See chapter 32 of this volume. – Ed.]

CHAPTER 3

Human Resource Building in the Development Process: Beyond the Paradigm

Jean-Guy St-Martin

In recent years, the issue of building an indigenous human resource capacity in Third World countries has been subject to major shifts with respect to ideological orientation, political concerns and objectives of international cooperation. It is now at the center of a broader issue — the human dimension of the development process. A consensus has in fact existed, at least in theory, since the end of the 1950s on the necessity of stimulating an acquisition of knowledge that could respond to the imperatives of accelerated economic growth and social development in the Third World. What has developed over the last thirty years is a series of paradigms focusing essentially on the definition of "human resource development" and on the means to achieve it.

When strategies of cooperation were being developed, that is, at the time many colonies were achieving independence, the importance of developing human capital was already established as a priority. Although defined to various degrees, depending on the specific conditions existing in individual countries and the resources available, this priority was translated during the 1960s into a number of major activities greatly influenced by the economic theories that had inspired the Marshall Plan. First, a massive transfer of both capital and technology was to improve de facto living conditions for the people of developing countries, and in the process, encourage them to seek higher education and to adapt quickly to the changing conditions generated by the transfer. Second, the traditional models of education and professional training used at that time in the industrialized countries were to be adopted in the Third World, regardless of national priorities and the labor-related absorptive capacity of a given country. International cooperation in the field of education was therefore isolated from the transfer of capital and technology and was, moreover, characterized by the implementation of educational infrastructure and systems often having very little in common with the current and future needs of the newly independent states. Technical assistance was considered to be the major instrument for the development of human capital, with the assumption that it was to be a unilateral transfer from those possessing the knowledge — the industrialized countries — to those needing the knowledge — the developing countries. In that context, there was no differentiation among the learners in terms of their specific needs and/or specific interest to learn; knowledge was considered to be a universal and homogeneous requirement, and the standards for assessing the stage of human resource development were the ones applied by the industrialized countries at a time when they were entering into a major postwar technological revolution.

The massive literacy campaigns were probably one of the few exceptions to this "imported" approach to the development of human resources. If the fight against illiteracy has achieved remarkable results in the first twenty years of development cooperation, many of the efforts to develop a Third World institutional capacity and an appropriate resource base have caused a number of distortions, including: the development of a national expertise not related to the needs of the labor market; a brain drain phenomenon; the emergence of a new elite of bureaucrats often far removed from the real needs of the masses and, more specifically, from the rural population; a progressive loss of interest and hope on the part of large segments of the poorest people in controlling their own development; and the use of technical assistance far beyond the time limit originally planned — a result of the lack of appropriate trained resources to take over, and the unrealistic hopes of the planners of that period.

In all fairness to the donors and the leaders of developing countries of the time, no one can really assess the relevance of the decisions made during the 1960s without considering a number of significant factors. Most of the leaders in the developing countries had been educated in Europe and North America; their comprehension of human resource development was therefore essentially based on the models they experienced in industrialized countries. Furthermore, North-South cooperation had no precedent to compare with, if one takes into account the extremely scarce resources and the urgency of tackling underdevelopment on all fronts. In that context, defining national priorities was at the least an uncertain process. With no common experience to fall back on, industrialized and developing countries also had to establish their respective positions vis-a-vis international cooperation, and to evaluate the potential evolution of the related power balance.

The mistakes, together with a better knowledge of players involved and a greater experience of the needs of Third World countries with respect to human resource development, contributed during the 1970s to some readjustments based on the principles of a true partnership. Some donors, including Canada, started to integrate training activities and technical assistance into the transfer of capital and technology in development projects and programs. The objective was to establish a better equation between the knowledge transferred and the specific development problems of a given country, as well as to build an indigenous resource base with the capacity to take over the outputs of official development assistance. But the most significant change of that period was undoubtedly the predominant influence of the Schumacher school. Rejecting the western models, the government leadership associated with them, and the priority given to institution building, many of the development specialists redefined human resource development in terms of the *individual* involved in a learning process. *Grassroots* cooperation was to be the cornerstone of an indigenous takeover to deal with short-term needs. The well-documented successes of literacy campaigns, together with the long experience of nongovernmental organizations (NGOs) working with people at the grassroots level, reinforced the belief that only this approach could have an effective impact on the development of human resources.

The Canadian government has just terminated an evaluation of nongovernmental development activities covering some 2,000 projects completed between 1979 and 1982. The results indicate that to various degrees, NGOs have also had their problems in attempting to transfer knowledge and promote a true, indigenous self-reliance. For example, less than one-third of the projects achieved the objective of self-reliance; the others required an extension or further external financial support. Only 23 per cent of the local organizations affected by the projects were significantly improved as a result of the interventions. Only 35 per cent of the projects analyzed have had a significant impact on the degree of participation of the populations at different stages of the project. There is in these preliminary results some serious food for though. Obviously, a lot remains to be done if we want to pursue effective cooperation in the development of human resources; it is certainly true with respect to the importance of integrating that dimension in the planning process.

Toward a More Integrated Approach

The decade we are going through has seen the establishment of an equilibrium which takes into account the need for a learning process centered more on the individual in his or her social, economic, cultural and political environment. There is now an attempt to approach human resource development in a more global way. It means not only the integration of all traditional activities, but also the creation of favorable conditions for the transfer of knowledge, the adaptation to change and self-reliance.

With that in mind, it is especially important to focus our attention on a number of considerations which could be decisive in pursuing the human resource development objective.

a) All individuals engaged in a learning process will, at a more or less sophisticated level, proceed with a cost/benefit analysis of what they should retain or reject. To accept change, these individuals must find some short-term benefits, aside from the long-term advantages being offered.

b) Individual choices made on the basis of this cost/benefit analysis are by nature biased. They derive from a rationale made by each individual and closely linked to his or her cultural, social, economic and political experience. Factors such as a negative experience of change, religious or moral considerations, values related to the notion of better well-being, social and political conditioning, a change in power balance, could accelerate the development, or stop it if the relative importance of each of these factors is not considered when the transfer of knowledge takes place. The difficulties related to population control provide a good example of this.

c) We should avoid restricting the definition of human resource development to sectors contributing to the short-term satisfaction of basic needs. If health, nutrition and basic education are important in the perspective of a minimum level of self-sustained development, other sectors, such as agriculture, energy and transportation — even telecommunications — could constitute the turning point in adapting to change.

d) It is now possible to plan and design large projects in which the development of human resources goes together with capital investment, as long as the target groups are clearly identified and an exhaustive analysis is made of their needs and interests at the planning stage. It is indeed vital that in the context of such projects as the implementation of a national railway transportation system, the very groups affected by the project be identified. It means essentially that we must know: (i) the groups for whom the project is designed in terms of specific impact objectives – that is, those that we have identified as "target groups" and who should receive the benefits of the project; (ii) the groups that will eventually take over the project and operate it; (iii) the groups receiving indirect benefits; and finally, (iv) the groups that could be directly or indirectly negatively affected through a loss of benefits or privileges. In all cases, the information pertaining to the balance of power between the groups, their organization patterns, the cultural factors likely to generate a resistance to change, and the previous experience of these groups in adapting to a new environment would facilitate the integration of a human resource development dimension and therefore contribute to the success of the project and the subsequent takeover by the country concerned. This information could also have an important influence on the design of the project, as much at the level of the content that is transferred as at the level of the transfer process itself.

e) The increasing use of associate financing and, more specifically, of mixed credits could in some cases compromise a human resource development objective. In the specific context of "turnkey projects" in the poorest countries, the objectives related to the project's efficiency may be pursued at the expense of an objective associated with the transfer of knowledge. To offset this risk, greater attention could be given to the possibility of financing parallel and complementary human resource development projects – which is not always the case at the present time.

f) Despite the difficulties they have encountered, NGOs remain the most credible partners in dealing directly with the populations, mainly because of their extensive experience in grassroots projects. We could therefore benefit from a greater association with NGOs in large projects requiring the integration of a human resource development component.

g) A *realistic* definition of the human resource development priority must take into consideration situations where a recipient country has very little latitude when having to introduce some drastic changes and force the populations to adapt. For example, the necessity of reducing the external debt service and the balance-of-payments deficit could force some countries to take decisions, at least in the short term, which sacrifice certain aspects of human resource development.

No one can deny the political impact of a global approach to human resource development. People that are better trained, more sensitized, better informed, better prepared to be critical of the decisions taken by their leaders, and in a position to take over their own process of adapting to change could be perceived as a threat by the established power. But that threat is nothing compared to the one of starving and desperate people. Where there is intelligence, initiative and hope, there is always room to negotiate. Nothing can be done when despair is ready to explode.

The Learning Vehicles

We will now look briefly at the learning vehicles which constitute the basis of international cooperation in the area of human resource development. They are essentially formal education, technical and professional training on the job, awareness and participative techniques, and information flows.

Traditionally, the first two vehicles have always been favored by the leaders of developing countries and their partners in the industrialized world. They are likely to continue to be extensively used because of the need for coherent policies in education and employment and the tremendous need to follow up on the results of literacy campaigns. Some changes can, however, be noticed in the use of these vehicles by several developing countries as a result of the lessons drawn from past experience. Among the major trends, the following are worth mentioning:

a) Greater priority is being given to higher education in the home country or in a country of the region, the choice of an industrialized country as a place of study often being made only if there is no national or regional teaching expertise.

b) Greater priority is being given to middle management and technical training in order to overcome the difficulties experienced by several developing countries in dealing with, at one extreme, a growing mass of literate people receiving no further education or training, and at the other, with a pool of highly specialized experts too qualified for the needs of the country. In the middle is a dramatic gap in well-trained resources.

c) A more concise definition of labor force priorities is being sought in order to further refine national priorities in the education sector.

With respect to awareness and participative techniques and information flows, they have been used, until very recently, mainly by nongovernmental organizations involved at the grassroots level. These vehicles are, however, the very ones that could offer the greatest possibilities in terms of a complementary or support activity to the large projects in order to optimize their long-term developmental impact. A closer cooperation between NGOs having a long experience of direct involvement with target groups and a deep knowledge of their specific characteristics when adapting to change and the planners and executing agents of large projects could provide some acceptable solutions to the collective indifference of certain populations vis-a-vis long-term development efforts.

In the specific case of increasing and improving information flows, there is already a clear tendency on the part of some countries to decentralize some elements of the decision-making process to facilitate the use of this vehicle as a tool in human resource development.

The Canadian Experience

Canada's cooperation with Third World countries has always allowed for the development of human resources. However, the understanding of this priority, and the means to implement it in the official development assistance program, have evolved over the years.

From 1968 to 1975, Canada, in large part, followed the traditional models with respect to the implementation of the institutional infrastructure of formal education, the scholarship program and technical assistance. Apart from the fact that this approach was in line with the major trends of that period, there were very few questions raised about its effectiveness. The needs were indeed so great, especially in Africa, that benefits were considered inevitable no matter what the approach taken.

While continuing the institutional infrastructure projects, Canada, starting in 1975, gave progressively more importance to the integration of technical assistance and scholarships within development projects and programs. There was therefore a subsequent reduction of the general scholarship program, which was often not suited to the real and urgent needs of the countries. The major change of that period was, however, the introduction of a new concept — institutional partnership — which called for a totally different type of activity in the area of human resource development. This partnership had a double objective: to develop a self-sustained institutional capacity in a recipient country, and to develop as well a Canadian expertise capable of meeting the needs of that country. It was a recognition of a mutual transfer of knowledge in which each of the partners progresses equally to the benefit of all, and most certainly to the benefit of international cooperation. It was also a recognition of the importance of a long-term institutional link going beyond the ad hoc traditional involvement of technical assistance. Many Canadian institutions then took the initiative of linking themselves with counterparts in Third World countries to develop and implement projects together, with each one identifying its own priorities and interests, its own strengths and weaknesses, in the transfer process. The most recent example is a program initiated two years ago between Chinese and Canadian institutions with the financial support of CIDA.

At the beginning of the 1980s, Canada was definitely influenced by the trend towards an approach more centered on the individual and his or her basic needs, as well as by the idea that indigenous development must start in the cultural and social system specific to each individual society. This concern was already a characteristic of NGO activities financed by Canadians and their government; but it was not reflected in the overall aid program. Canada was in fact cooperating with Third World countries in many areas implicity considered to be human resource development areas and using all the delivery channels available without, however, there necessarily being a complementarity and convergence of the different activities within a country program with a view to achieving a stated priority objective of developing the human resources. One of the first important readjustments was the decision to start making optimal use of the delivery channels according to their specific capacities and strengths. As an example, CIDA started to use nongovernmental organizations more and more often, first as executing agents of multicomponent projects, where the participation of the target groups is an essential prerequisite for an optimal impact, and second as *maitres-d'oeuvre* of grassroots projects that could increase the expected impact of a large project in a given area.

It was in 1982 that CIDA established the development of human resources as a priority for the years to come. Its definition is formulated in the *Annual Aid Review 1982*, submitted to the Development Assistance Committee of OECD, and in the Agency Programming Framework covering the period between 1982-83 and 1986-87. It reads: "Human resource development emp¹ ᴀᴄ'ᴢes people as both the means and the end of development... Ir the short term, it means education and training to meet the immediaᴛᴄ need for skilled technical, managerial, and administrative personnel, and measures directed towards specific target groups to facilitate their participation in the main socio-economic system of the country. These target groups can include women, landless rural/urban poor, young people, isolated communities, etc."

In 1983, CIDA commissioned an evaluation assessment of our interventions in human resource development since 1978. The ultimate objective was to draw some lessons from past experience, with the idea of eventually developing a policy and strategy of cooperation with Third World countries in this area. Following this study, the decision was made to develop a theoretical framework for data collection and analysis in order to ensure a better impact assessment of our activities, insititutional support and technical assistance. Concrete results are expected within a year and will be communicated to all donors interested in sharing their experience with Canada.

In the meantime, important decisions have been taken to start targeting the groups within the context of the human resource development priority and broadening the concept to include all activities capable of creating the necessary conditions for learning and self-reliance. The most concrete example has been the development of a policy and operational strategy to integrate women into the national development process. Approved in November 1984, the policy framework stipulates that the first objective of the new orientation is to "ensure that Third World women are included as both *agents* and *beneficiaries* of CIDA's development program. Within the framework of a five-year action plan covering the period 1986-90, the specific objectives will be defined in view of (i) supporting the efforts of Third World women to participate in their national development, and their initiatives to improve their situation; (ii) understanding better the existing roles of these women in their society, and the potential one they can play; (iii) collaborating with recipient countries in taking positive measures to close economic gaps between women and men."

Much remains to be done, especially with respect to the dialogue with recipient countries to integrate training and labor priorities in the national planning and to identify target groups and conditions of impact. There is, however, no place for illusions. In the context of scarce resources, concrete results deriving from giving priority to human resource development will greatly depend on the capacity of all partners in international cooperation to better coordinate their efforts. There are already encouraging signs regarding the plan to better coordinate technical assistance in the sub-Saharan region. At their last meeting, DAC members were especially sensitive to the necessity of this coordination, and there are hopes that it will materialize in the near future. It is also hoped that the UNDP will play a major role in this effort.

CHAPTER 4

The Human Element as Means and End of Development

Oscar Nudler

To speak about the human element in development is indeed quite legitimate, since we may distinguish in development processes, along with the human element *strictu sensu* many other elements or factors, such as the economic, the tech ıolo, ical, the political, the cultural, and so on. However, such talk abc ʾt tʾ.e human element can also be misleading — in some cases, just a new bottle for the same old wine. As long as we are led to take the human element in development as something which is comparable on an equal footing with nonhuman elements, we might fall, in spite of using a human-laden discourse, into a nonhumanist way of thinking. Fortunately, the heading under which this discussion is being carried out — The Human Element as Means and Objective of Development — suggests a questioning of a purely instrumental view of the role of human beings in development. The human element is certainly a means or resource of development and to this extent is comparable to other means, such as natural resources, equipment, technology, and so forth — no question about that. But the human element is the only element which is at the same time the final end or objective of development. As such, it is not comparable to other elements which are just means.

These two sides of the so-called human element are indeed logically distinguishable. However, the crucial claim of the human-centered approach has always been that for all theoretical and practical purposes involving human beings, the end side should be granted priority. In other words, an exclusive means logic is inherently defective. This stance explains, for example, the humanist resistance to accepting development policies which are based on considering the human element in the early phases of development — the so-called takeoff stage — just as a means, allowing end concerns only at a later stage. The argument here is that once the split between means and ends is accepted, however provisionally, it determines a tendency which is very difficult to reverse afterwards.

Defining Human - Centered Development

Now, let us call any development process which takes the human element not only as a means, but also as an end, "human-centered development" or, for short, "human development." The question is, how can we define such a human development concept? Instead of attempting a direct answer, it is more useful to see first what are the formal features of our concept which any adequate definition or theory of human development should take into account. In this connection, there are at least two seemingly opposing features. On the one hand, the human development concept shows a certain *analytical complexity,* that is, a complexity which can be meaningfully broken into parts which are less complex. On the other hand, however, this atomistic type of analysis turns out to be insufficient to come to grips with our total meaning field, so that we are led to admit, together with its analyticity, its nonreducible, *holistic nature.*

Let us start with the analytical, step-by-step procedure. We may divide, for example, development processes into economic, political, social and many other subprocesses and try then to characterize each of them separately from a human-centered perspective. If we take, for instance, economic development, it is clear that important consequences follow from the adoption of such a perspective. There is implied a sharp change of focus with respect to conventional, particularly neoclassical, economics. As a result, humanist economists consider human economy as being a wider, more inclusive domain, with market or formal economy as a part of it. Their starting point is usually a critical assessment of some traditional assumptions such as invisible hand, perfect market and *homo oeconomicus* and its current versions. The main point they stress is the need to internalize the so-called externalities, that is, the need to consider ecological, social, cultural and psychological preconditions and consequences of economic activity. Issues such as the quality of work, to be measured not only in terms of its tangible output, but also in terms of its impact on workers' well-being and creativity, the scale of production processes, the decentralization of economic wealth and power, the various limits to growth, and so on, are some of the typical concerns which are linked to the human-centered approach to economic processes. Now, one of the serious challenges still to be faced by such an approach is to make it truly operative. Sometimes the complexity of the linkages in the real world is not duly taken into account by some human-oriented proposals which, however well intended, look thus a bit naive. But there are, of course, other developments. To cite just a couple of examples, there is Vanek's work on self-management, and the work inspired in Gandhi's view of economic progress in conditions of mass poverty, which are serious attempts to articulate a human-centered economic vision and at the same time get it down to earth.

If we turn to the political aspects of development processes and the human-centered approach to them, one of the main problems which this approach has confronted is the need to link global or "macro" views to local or "micro" perspectives. While the former emphasize the economic and political constraints on human development deriving from the structure of the world system, the latter stress conciousness-raising, participation, direct democracy and community building at a micro level. My personal experience, particularly as a participant of the Goals, Processes and Indicators of Development Project of the United Nations University, where both perspectives were represented, taught me that the dialogue between them is very difficult, though necessary, to face the sociopolitical aspects of development processes in all their complexity. Let me quote from a GPID report on the difficulties and possibilities of bridging the two levels :

> Perhaps the most intractable problem faced by the GPID project has been the effort to conceptualize links between the micro and macro in ways that would be consistent with human development and that might even open up new potential for human development... As we pursued our efforts to bridge the micro and macro, we had many GPID resources to draw upon. The important challenge, now perceived more clearly in retrospect than earlier, was to synthesize relevant elements from a number of studies through sustained dialogue over a period of time among small groups of people with contrasting views. Four themes contributed to our beginning efforts: First, knowledge and images of potential for individual human development... Second, at the other extreme of the micro-macro continuum, analyses of global systems as they reveal the domination of powerful global forces and their implications for people everywhere... Third, reactive to problems of domination of local people by powerful global forces is work explicating how local people can, through new kinds of local education and organization, confront these forces in their local communities.[1]

The introduction of a human-centered perspective has thus, among other consequences, the effect of requiring of the partial approaches, whether economic or political, an increased openness and sensitiveness to the complexities of the real world, and a refusal to get stuck into narrowly defined boundaries. A similar enlargement of our vision appears when we consider other aspects of development processes. So, for instance, the human-centered approach does not equate social development with the satisfaction of basic needs. In the early 1960s, the basic needs approach was indeed a step forward as compared with the GNP approach; but its fragmentary nature, its disregard of the system of human needs as a whole, was probably a factor allowing its later misutilization. From a human development perspective, the satisfaction of basic needs is also seen as a fundamental objective of social development, but the satisfaction of needs beyond the basic ones is not postponed or left to chance. Their satisfaction is in fact envisaged through the satisfaction of the basic needs in themselves. Thus, for example, if the housing need is considered, room should be left for the active participation of the people concerned in the design and building of their houses and their habitat. But in fact the human-centered approach leads us beyond the human needs satisfaction discourse, at least when this latter implies a view of the human being as just a product or reflection of the social structures in which he is immersed. Although the influence of these structures is surely not denied, the human being is also conceived by the human-centered approach as having the potential for being *an autonomous center of experience and freedom.* In this regard, the notion of human development implies, among other things, a notion of personal growth through an enrichment and expansion of the realm of inner experience. This is not to be interpreted in an individualist sense, but as a requirement posed to development planning to avoid rigid, homogenizing formulas. The aim is to increase the space for expressing and applying individual and group creative potential in the context of their culture. Self-development and codevelopment are thus seen as mutually reinforcing processes.

Earlier on, it was argued that a purely instrumental attitude towards the human resource is hardly compatible with a human-centered approach to development. In addition, an atomistic approach to the various development dimensions like the one just hinted at is also, however humanistically inspired, far from satisfying human development requirements. *Although no dimension can be reduced to some other, none is really independent.* On the contrary, there is a complex interrelatedness of the different dimensions, aspects and levels of development processes, an interrelatedness which any adequate theory of human development should take into account. This poses the need, seldom recognized in technocratic or simply naive social theory, planning and action, of somehow approaching the total web of relations into which any particular development aspect or problem is inserted. The cultural context or framework of people's actions is no doubt the most powerful source of concrete, living, holistic qualities permeating and providing meaning to all activities taking place in a given social setting. The inadequacy of merely abstract, universal, acultural models of development, like the model according to which all countries should follow essentially the same path, is now widely recognized. But in spite of the growing number of studies focusing on the relationships between development processes and indigenous culture, we still lack, to my knowledge, a really satisfactory conceptual framework or map which might guide us in this crucial domain.

Organic and Nonorganic Development

An example of a first approximation in the right direction is a short working paper on the subject written for UNESCO by Ivan Vitanyi, Director of the Budapest Institute for Culture. In his paper, Vitanyi reminds us of the center/periphery distinction as introduced by Alexander Gershenkorn. In the central countries, industrialization

> came into being as a result of internal, autochthonous processes: society itself produces, "exudes" the new order. Internal forces (built into the culture, we may add) are responsible for "primitive accumulation," and this is how conditions for the evolution of a social structure more complex and more variegated than the previous one came to ripen. At variance with this the countries of the periphery were compelled to take another road.[2]

In short, in peripheral countries, the style of development is imposed from outside, using the services of a ruling elite anxious to imitate foreign models and benefit from them. As a way of conceptualizing this difference between internally and externally induced forms of development, Vitanyi adopts the organic/inorganic distinction introduced by Hayek, although without endorsing Hayek's liberal interpretation of it. He concludes:

> In the case of organic development, economic, social and cultural evolution went hand in hand in close connection with one another, whereas in inorganic development this connection was rather loose.[3]

This organic/inorganic distinction is a nice example of the systemic, holistic qualities of development processes. However, the appropriateness of equating this distinction with the developed/underdeveloped distinction may be questioned. Although it is true that development in the West has been internally promoted, and to this extent it has been organic, one can still argue that the model of development which has been followed has proven to be nonorganic, at least to a significant extent, as shown by the major disequilibria it has generated. Let me quote in this connection from the introduction to a book on human development in the present world context which was an output of a GPID Human Development Study Group:

> As is self-evident, industrial revolution(s) and the impact of modern science, technology and the type of rationality associated with them in everyday life have brought impressive advancements but, at the same time, have contributed to create a world characterized by extreme tensions in almost every area of human life. If we look at the society-nature relationship, the destructive action of industrialism over the environment has been so convincingly shown that it hardly requires further comment. Concerning the international order, it suffices to mention that the very existence of such "order" rests on mutual total extermination threats, that is, on nuclear arms balance between the superpowers. This shows in a particularly intense light the inherent violent nature of the international order brought about by the modern system, but there are, of course, many other indicators, like, for instance, the debt crisis, which point in exactly the same direction. As to social relations, let us only recall that although, on the one hand, modernization processes have led to the end of feudal, closed structures, particularly through the building of national states and their progressive transformation into more open social spaces, on the other hand the weakening of community links and in general, of all forms of direct participation or influence of people in social decisions affecting their lives, have created a dangerous, increasing power gap batween macro institutions like transnational corporations, government agencies or political parties and what some call the "civil society," that is, the network of mainly spontaneous, non-imposed forms of social organization.[4]

We may thus conclude that there are two nonorganic forms of development in the world today. The first, which is currently called "underdevelopment," is generated mainly, though not only, from outside by the pressure of the ever-expanding modern system and its associated forms of penetration. Such penetration has usually produced a termendous impact on nonmodern societies. As a result of this cultural shock, a variety of disruptive effects — ranging from technology and production systems up to education and everyday ways of life — have taken place. It is in this way that traditional societies have become underdeveloped, nonorganic structures whose traditional equilibrium has been destroyed without having been replaced by a new one.

The second form of nonorganic development, which we might label, in contrast to the previous one, with the symmetrical, though not so happy term "overdevelopment," is mainly generated from inside through the unfolding of forces built into the development model leading to violence over nature, conviviality and inner balance. The contention here is that the simultaneous presence and combinations of the two forms of nonorganic development — or maldevelopment — lie at the foundations of the present world crisis and its multiple manifestations.

Thus, from a human-centered perspective, development should take into account the *complex interrelatedness* of different aspects and levels of social life; and it should be internally motivated, that is, it should be rooted in *people's culture, values and collective will.* The term "organic," as opposed to mechanical, is used here as a convenient shorthand for expressing all this. It is not used in the functionalist sense of conflict-avoiding models. Now, it may be objected that such an organic vision of development is no more than sheer myth or Utopia. Vis-a-vis present world realities, this claim is obviously well founded. However, this does not imply that the organic growth vision is just a fantasy, with no possible anchor in the real world. After all, the dominant mechanical, technocratic view was also in its beginnings no more — and no less — than utopia. What is more important, this view is showing serious signs of being deeply affected by an overall crisis, and is thus open to change. Besides some well-known criticism of the modern system mentioned earlier, there is another question which is of paramount importance, namely, the question of its epistemological or cosmological foundation. Remember John Michell's almost poetic way of putting it:

The forces and institutions that seem so unchallengeably dominant today have one point of vulnerability. They are the creatures of our collective view of the world, and their continued existence depends on that view of the world being maintained. Any cosmology is successful only to the extent that it reflects the world we know and experience. And the cosmology still dominant has revealed an obvious flaw which must in time prove fatal... The universe is not an affair of particles forming themselves into dense, permanent clusters, ever more organized, but of ever fluctuating relationships, defined and limited by the laws of number of proportion. Thus the old Chinese landscape, with the nodes of its energy structure marked by masts and pagodas to create a placid magnetic field, is a truer representation of the real world than is the megalomaniac headquarters of an expanding business corporation. When we think of future societies we must, if we are correctly to reflect the order of the universe, think in terms of dynamic geometry, that is, of types of harmony within societies and between them and their surroundings.[5]

The possibility of implementing a new human-centered development vision is not just a piece of fiction, but a concrete, practical response to the present world crisis. Such questions have been articulated in different, though essentially equivalent, ways by various human-oriented development thinkers. Thus, in one of the final reports of the UNU/GPID project we can read:

How to raise people's consciousness with respect to global processes (e.g. employment, inflation, cultural penetration, as affected by TNC, militarism, etc.) as an element in local communities, and how to energize people to become full participants in actions that shape these processes? How can this local empowerment be applied beyond the local community in regional, national, international and global contexts?[6]

And to quote John Michell again:

How can would be social reformers take practical steps towards reversing the culture drain? How can one act to restore culture and independence to local communities within a system that is programmed not to tolerate such rivalry?[7]

Questions like these imply reasonably clear answers as far as what should *not* be done is concerned. Thus, for instance, the so-called transfer of technology is not conducive, according to the vision which looms behind these questions, to true development, but rather to external dependency and, hence, nonorganic growth. The answers are far less clear, far more controversial, when the definition of positive ways and means is required. One of the positive answers which is most appealing to human-oriented development scholars and workers is no doubt the one suggested by the term *self-reliance*. In the introduction to a book on self-reliance, the late Roy Preiswerk said:

> We suggest that true development is self-reliant development. Whether it be in food and energy production, health, technology or education, self-reliance is a way of bringing about a better life for those left aside or merely exploited by present development strategies.[8]

Generally speaking, self-reliance is a crucial component of human-centered development. However, as soon as we turn to the concrete ways in which the general idea of self-reliance is to be understood and applied, reservations and discrepancies are likely to appear. Just to give an example of this difficulty, let me quote from a paper by Rosiska and Miguel Darcy de Oliveira:

> A project for self-reliant development can be drawn up only if the principal emphasis is placed on mobilizing and making the maximum use of resources available at the level of the unit whose self-reliance is to be achieved, whether this be a small community, a region or a country.[9]

It is certainly not difficult to agree with such a statement, but then the authors proceed to draw concrete conclusions regarding technology and education which are more questionable than their general claim:

> Such an approach is fundamentally inconsistent with the utilization of advanced technology, which is the product of knowledge held by an elite of over-qualified experts. Reliance on such technology for the promotion of development cannot do otherwise than increase dependency still further. So far as education is concerned, this fundamental recognition must lead to a radical re-thinking of the problem of long and costly training for a professional minority.[10]

It is true, as has been mentioned, that advanced technology transfer is usually a means of increasing external dependency, but should we conclude from this that developing countries should abandon any attempt at reaching high technological levels? And should they exclude or deemphasize, by the same token, the professional training of the experts required by modern technology? A positive answer to these questions may be counterproductive, so that backwardness and increasing dependency finally result from such an allegedly radical self-reliance strategy.

The issue is surely not simple, and no straightforward answer is available. However, historical experience seems to indicate that a flexible mix between openness and closedness is often the best option. Actually, the key to a sound development policy, at least at the nation-state level, rests not so much on self-sufficiency as on the possibility of achieving national control over the development process. A necessary condition for such purpose is no doubt the *full mobilization* of human and nonhuman internal resources and *full reliance* upon them. If, as a result of this, a reasonably integrated economic and social system begins to take shape, selective incorporation of foreign advanced technology may reinforce rather than weaken national autonomy. China is obviously a major current illustration of this course, but this is a subject which does not lend itself to easy generalizations. Most countries simply cannot, whether because of physical or social limitations, achieve a degree of internal integration enabling them to avoid external dependency. Even if they do, the risk of falling back into dependency is always there, vis-a-vis the ever-expanding power of the world system center. *Collective self-reliance* seems to be, at least from a Latin American vantage point, a strategy more likely than national self-reliance to succeed in present world conditions. Incidentally, some initial, still timid steps are being taken now in this direction in Latin America, mainly because of the unbearable pressure of the external debt. Whether they will evolve into a systematic policy remains to be seen.

Aims of Human - Centered Development

The preceding brief discussion has centered around two crucial queries, namely, how should a human-centered approach to development be set forth, and what are the difficulties in implementing it in the real world? Now, let me close these brief reflections by coming back to utopia and providing you with a list a of the requirements which a human-centered society should, in my view, satisfy:

1. *Social equity.* Human development should be equally possible for all members of society.

2. *Interregional and international equity.* The society should permit and promote the human development of its members with respect for the integrity of other societies (i.e., no economic exploitation, political domination and or cultural oppression which prevents the members of those other societies from achieving *their* human development).

3. *Living presence of the future.* The human development of present generations is not to be pursued at the cost of endangering the human development of future generations, not only in terms of preserving the natural environment, but also of respecting (not submitting to) historical achievements and values which help to define people's cultural identity.

4. *Sensitiveness to the present.* The development of future generations should not take place at the cost of the imposed deprivation of the present genration. Construction of a human future is a condition for a human-centered social development process, but the oppression of people in the name of a distant future cannot be justified from a human development point of view.

5. *Participation and meaning.* Beyond the preceding principles, concerning mainly different aspects of equity, a human-centered society provides a meaning frame for human existence so that its members share common feelings and goals and have the opportunity of contributing to their realization without losing personal freedom.[1]

Notes

1. "Human Development in Micro to Macro Perspective" (Report to the United Nations University, GPID Project, Integration Group A, June 1983).

2. I. Vitanyi, "Cultural Dimension of Socioeconomic Development" (UNESCO, December 1983).

3. Ibid.

4. C.A. Mallmann and O. Nudler, eds., *Human Development in its Psychosocial Context* (London, Hodder & Stoughton, forthcoming).

5. J. Michell, "The Ideal World-View," in S. Kumer, ed., *The Schumacher Lectures* (London: Abacus, 1982).

6. "Human Development" (UNU/GPID).

7. J. Michell.

8. R. Preiswerk, Introduction to J. Galtung, P.O Brien and R. Preiswerk, eds., *Self-Reliance: A Strategy for Development* (London: Bogle-L'Ouverture Publications, 1980).

9. Rosiska and M. Darcy de Oliveira, "'Learning by Living and Doing: Reflections on Education and Self-Reliance," in Galtung et al., *Self-Reliance.*

10. Ibid.

11. O. Nudler, "On the Human Development Concept and Contemporary Ideological Systems," in Mallmann and Nudler, *Human Development.*

PART II

COMPARATIVE DEVELOPMENT EXPERIENCE

CHAPTER 5
The Human Element in Comparative Development Experience

Goh Keng Swee

Forty years ago, World War II ended with the total defeat of Germany and Japan. Both countries were throughly devastated by Allied bombing, their major cities virtually levelled. Infrastructure such as power stations and communication facilities — ports, railway yards — were largely destroyed, being regarded as legitimate military targets. Industrial plants were also regarded as legitimate targets, as they produced the sinews of war — tanks, guns, aircraft, explosives and ammunition. So they were also destroyed.

In terms of per capita GNP and per capita stock of physical capital, the Germans and the Japanese were worse off than the people of most of the less developed countries (LDCs) of the Third World today. There is ample anecdotal evidence from biographies of successful Japanese and Germans that the major preoccupation of the population was to scrounge around for food to keep alive. Yet within a generation, they performed their economic miracle. And it was done with apparent ease — there was no "Aid Japan Club," no consortium of banks to extend syndicated loans to Germany, no advice or technical assistance from well-meaning donor countries or international organizations. Within another generation, Germany and Japan had reached the front rank of industrial nations, so much so that hardly anybody recollects their impoverished beginnings in 1945.

The experience of these two countries demonstrates, more convincingly than any amount of statistical data can, the importance of the human element in development. This is especially so in the case of Japan, bereft as it is of natural resources. Allied bombers could destroy physical structures and kill large numbers of people, as did the war itself. Most of the population survived and carried in

The author wishes to acknowledge the assistance of Dr. Phua Swee Liang, Education Specialist, Asian Development Bank, in the researching and preparation of this paper.

their minds valuable knowledge and skills, as well as the habit of group cooperation — the software that enabled these countries, within a short time, to rebuild their economies with such outstanding success.

If the lesson of postwar Germany and Japan can be taken to mean that software determines the outcome and that, given the right kind of software, the hardware will eventually appear, the implications for LDCs are many and complex. Instead of striving to build physical structures as the top priority, perhaps more attention should be paid to software — the knowledge in people's heads, their attitude toward work, the political system and leadership which mobilizes their effort (or fails to do so), and similar matters. The issues raised here are wide-ranging and cover several disciplines of study. Economics is involved; so are other branches of the social sciences — politics, sociology, psychology and education, among others.

Perhaps the most important element in the German or Japanese success story is also the most difficult for LDCs to emulate. Germans and Japanese are among the most homogeneous peoples in the world, possessing a strong sense of national identity. In the early, difficult years, their instinct was to rally round a leader. In the early postwar years, both enjoyed long periods of strong leadership, under Conrad Adenauer and Shigeru Yoshida. The early years forged a national consensus, created the institutions and provided the sense of purpose and direction which propelled them rapidly forward.

By contrast, many LDCs contain plural societies with differences of language, religion and even culture. The political process is thereby made more complicated; but social plurality in itself connot be regarded as a wholly negative element. We have in the USA a plural society where a diversity of people has not prevented the country from developing the world's richest and most dynamic economy.

There are too many imponderables here. The relevant discipline of study is known as political development, and the literature does not shed much light on the contemporary scene. For our purposes, we assume that an effective government apparatus exists which can evaluate policy choices available in a given situation, which can relate these options in the most realistic manner to the means available (in terms of money, manpower, stock of physical assets) and in some rational manner seek the best outcome.

Education and Economic Development

Under this assumption, the postwar experience of Germany and Japan sends a message of hope to the LDCs. Much of the software they need consists of knowledge which already exists and can be learned through formal education or training. So far as attitudes to work are concerned, these can be determined to a substantial degree by economic policy and institutions, as will be discussed later. We know intuitively that knowledge and skills can increase the productivity of people who have acquired them. The cost of imparting these skills and knowledge can be regarded as investment in human capital, a form of human resource development whose returns in increased output can be measured against the cost of investment. There is a considerable amount of literature on the subject, and much of it focuses on the relation between education and economic development in LDCs.

Part of the literature consists of empirical studies in various countries of how earnings are related to educational levels, another part discusses what the results mean, and the rest considers the implications for government policy. In all countries studied, it was observed that the average incomes of people who received primary education were higher than those of people never went to school. Incomes of secondary school-leavers were higher than those of primary school-leavers, and graduates of tertiary institutions earned more than secondary school-leavers. The cost per person at each level of education could be estimated, and a comparison of the two sets of figures — cost and returns — gave an estimate of what is commonly called "return to investment in human capital." The World Bank has developed refined techniques of making such estimates.[1] In general, the position is that returns on investments in human capital in LDCs are higher than those on investments in physical capital, such as power stations, ports and railways. Returns on primary education are higher than those on secondary education, which in turn gives a better yield than university education. Returns on education in LDCs at each grade are generally higher than in developed countries.

So far, so good. But what do the results mean? Let us leave aside the fragility of the data in some LDCs. The policy implications of these results clearly favor large expenditures by LDC governments on education, especially primary education, where illiteracy rates are high and on secondary education where most or all children attend primary schools. However, some scholars challenge the "human capital" model on several grounds. Some claim that education confers higher incomes, not because of knowledge or skills acquired, but by the possession of certificates which are a prerequisite in job applications. Another school states that education merely acts as a sieve or filter, separating the less able from the more able, the latter spending more years in school. The differences in earnings merely reflect differences in abilities. Yet another view claims that while jobs can be done equally well by less educated persons, employers will recruit better educated applicants so that less educated persons suffer. I have oversimplified the arguments of these scholars, which are advanced with much learning and subtlety.

It seems that the different strands of opposition to the human capital model rest on one common ground: they do not see a clear, functional link between what is learned in schools and universities and the specific skills needed in occupations in which school-leavers and graduates are employed. Hence, they contest the claim that higher incomes can be attributed wholly or mainly to education. These arguments appear forceful, but they are inadequate. First, it is not necessary to demonstrate a functional link between school education and work skills. All that is required is to show that a person who can read and write simple statements, e.g., a bill for a customer, can become a salesgirl, a meter-reader or a waiter, while his illiterate peer cannot, and that these occupations are better paid than those open to illiterates.

The same line of reasoning can be applied to different earnings for different levels of education. It is true that some occupations can be performed equally well by primary school-leavers and secondary school-leavers. In such cases, the work force is likely to include both. However, there are occupations which require a certain level of literacy or numeracy, or an ability to communicate — skills at which secondary school-leavers have an advantage over primary school-leavers. Again, such occupations are likely to be better paid than the first group, and this raises average earnings for the better educated.

LDC Experience

When the human capital model is applied to LDCs, some scholars observe that a modern industrial state makes great demands on the whole population in order to produce the wide range of manual and intellectual skills needed to operate complex technology in large-scale enterprises. They do not see much relevance in what is taught in LDC primary and secondary schools to the task of building a scientific, technological society. This argument exaggerates the extent to which the mastery of science and technology is diffused in a modern state. We shall later argue that it concerns only a small section of the community.

As for specific skills, occupations in advanced industrial countries, for the most part, make no great demand on the intellect or on manual dexterity. These account for most jobs of a modern state. Compare a bus driver in, say, the United States with his opposite number in an LDC. The latter drives a rickety vehicle on dilapidated roads, and it can be argued that this may well demand more skill and ingenuity than his American colleague needs to have.

For most of the occupations of modern industry, the skills needed can be easily acquired in customized, short training courses provided by enterprises themselves, provided the workers have had academic education in primary and lower secondary schools. The human mind is a wonderful instrument of learning, and its workings are not fully understood by experts. Hence, the unending controversy over so many propositions in education. Even in LDC agriculture, primary school education increases productivity markedly with the advent of the Green Revolution. This has transformed traditional farming methods in two ways — first, by the introduction of better strains of plant; second, by the application of fertilizers. Field studies in Third World countries show that the new techniques demand the ability to keep records, to calculate quantities and to make simple estimates.

Let us consider how some economically successful countries equip their citizens with the knowledge and skills needed in a modern state. Japan is a good starting point. Japanese industry is regarded with great respect by competing industrial nations, and with good reason. In almost every field in which Japanese manufacturers have chosen to specialize, they have beaten the competition in price, quality and reliability. Japanese industries have long since ceased to imitate. Their capacity to innovate, both in consumer goods and capital equipment, has astonished the world in recent years.

Japanese industrial success has been widely ascribed to the skill and diligence of Japanese workers. Yet their educational system pays virtually no attention to instruction in industrial skills. Such vocational training as has appeared in schools seems ad hoc and half-hearted. Japanese schools remain staunchly academic. Skill training takes place in industrial enterprises. Since lifelong employment is the custom in large Japanese enterprises, firms are willing to invest heavily in training their employees, confident that the long-term benefits of such skill formation will accrue to them. In most countries, workers are free to move from employer to employer, and this reduces the incentive of employers to train workers to the limit of their potential, as the Japanese do.

South Korea's experience in education has been closely studied by scholars. The country's commitment to education has remained strong since the foundation of the republic. Despite the great upheavals Korea has experienced, such as the invasion by North Korea in 1950 and the political troubles of the Syngman Rhee era, great efforts were made in expanding the school system. By 1965, while South Korean per capita GNP was US$ 107, the educational system, in terms of pupil enrollment and money spent, reached the level of middle-income LDCs, with a per capita GNP of US$ 380.[2]

In recent years, South Korea has been making increasing provision for technical education in the formal school system. After nine years of education in primary and middle school, education at the upper secondary level branches into an academic or a technical stream. In 1983, enrollment in these two branches was in the ratio of 56 to 44. The technical schools were mostly established after the Korean economy took off on its spectacular ascent and could not be considered the cause of this ascent.

The content of general education revealed no link to the skills regarded by scholars as necessary to achieve Korea's economic miracle. Further, by western standards, the content of education, then and later, left much to be desired. Classroom size was too large, and rote learning and memorizing of facts was the standard learning process. Particularly objectionable to the liberal school of educators were practices such as bowing to the teacher, mass calisthenics and reading in unison. Instead of encouraging education through free and creative thinking, "Korean education places a heavy stress on moral education and discipline. It is hard to fit this characteristic into the human resource development explanation of education."[1] We shall later see that this interpretation of the Korean experience is not the only one possible.

Whereas literacy and numeracy of moderate standards can equip most people for a large number of jobs in a modern economy, certain occupations demand higher levels of knowledge and skill. They include skilled manual occupations, supervisory grades, middle - and upper-level management and professional positions. What distinguishes these occupations from the hewers of wood and drawers of water is the need to process complex information, exercise judgment and make decisions. Work in skilled manual occupations in modern industry is no longer entirely a matter of keen eyesight and manual dexterity. For instance, those who operate computerized machine tools must be able to read blueprints, understand the meaning of digital readouts and know how to make the needed adjustments.

As we progress upwards from foreman to top management, or from laboratory assistant to research professor, the cerebral content of the job increases with the level of responsibility. It is this segment of the spectrum of skills that is most crucial to the development process, and it is here that we see the greatest difference between the societies of the North and South. The difference is observed in both the quantity of manpower in these grades and the quality. The difference in quantity can easily be demonstrated. Risky though international comparisons of educational statistics are, the figures show that developed countries have a much larger proportion of the population with secondary and tertiary education than developing nations.

In the industrial North, universal primary education was achieved long ago, and most countries have at least another three years of compulsory secondary education. Many LDCs have achieved primary education for all, or nearly all, children of primary school age, and most of the others have reached enrollments of 60 per cent or more. As regards secondary education, the situation varies considerably. In some countries in Latin America and the Far East, enrollment reaches between half and two-thirds of the age group. Other LDCs show much lower figures, from negligible, among the poorest, to about a third for the others.

As regards university and college education, the U.S. leads, with tertiary institutions enrolling about half the high school-leavers. Japan and countries of Western Europe are next, with between a fifth and a third, most countries being in the 25-30 per cent range. Tertiary education is a luxury for poorer LDCs, many of whom show negligible rates of attendance, say, 1 per cent. Some of the middle-income LDCs enroll 5 to 12 per cent of age-group youths in tertiary institutions. There are a few who have reached West European levels. These form a mixed bag — Korea at 24 per cent, the Philippines at 27 per cent, Argentina at 26 per cent. Ecuador leads with 35 per cent.

The experience of countries such as South Korea and Taiwan shows that rapid development has two effects on the demand for university graduates. First, in terms of numbers, they are easily absorbed, so that universities and polytechnics expand rapidly to supply recruits to professional and management positions. Second, as industries move up the ladder of technology, the need for high-quality talent becomes critical. Unless it is met, the development process fueled by industrial expansion may grind to a halt. In both South Korea and Taiwan, the supply of high-quality talent was provided, in part, by a reverse brain drain. Scientists and engineers trained abroad, mainly in the U.S., returned home either permanently or on short-term assignments. This situation stands in stark contrast to LDCs, which suffer from both unemployment of young graduates and the brain drain. How did these things happen? We must now examine how the growth process took place in these two different situations.

It is an axiom of classical economics that a competitive market serves the best interests of consumers and producers. By a kind of Darwinian process, the most efficient producers survive to provide consumers with the goods and services they need at the lowest price. The hidden hand of Adam Smith moves to allocate the country's resources of land, labor and capital to the best use in response to consumer demand, far more effectively than any central planning bureau can hope to achieve. That is the theory. What is the reality?

Inward Versus Outward Orientation

The reality is that perfectly competitive markets exist nowhere in the world, except perhaps in Hong Kong today, and possibly in Lebanon before its recent troubles. Rich nations protect their domestic markets through import duties when politically influential producers feel threatened. When duties are ineffective, import quotas are imposed. When quotas look indelicate, voluntary export restraints make their appearance. LDCs are no less culpable in this respect.

The standard technique of establishing manufacturing industries is by import substitution. Producing goods which were formerly imported is a natural starting point for manufacturing industries in LDCs. Imports are kept out by import duties so that the domestic market can be reserved for plants sited in the country. The selection of goods usually starts with simple manufactures, such as shoes, clothes and bottled drinks, which employ simple labor-intensive processes. Low labor and high transport costs give local manufacturers a further advantage.

This phase of industrialization, the easy phase, soon comes to an end, and LDCs are faced with the problem of where to go from there. Bela Balassa indicated that LDCs progressed in two separate directions, which he termed "inward-oriented industrial development" and "outward-oriented industrial development."[4] Inward orientation means progressing from the easy phase of producing simple consumer goods to producing consumer durables such as refrigerators and automobiles and from there, on to making the intermediate goods — steel and steel products, nonferrous metal products — needed by the second-phase factories, as well as components used in the manufacture of these goods. Eventually, the production of capital equipment, machinery of various kinds, is undertaken. All these enterprises require protection from foreign imports of competing goods.

Outward orientation means producing manufactured goods for export. The major export markets are in the industrial North, and this strategy involves the great risk of taking the competition into the adversary's home ground. It is not a course of action that can be contemplated except by governments and peoples who find themselves in desperate straits. Fortune favors the brave, and Balassa's studies showed that those who took this bold course flourished, while the LDCs who took the apparently more prudent strategy found themselves in trouble.

What are the reasons for this strange outcome? Bela Balassa gave the economic explanation. Briefly, certain characteristics of modern industry combine to pose severe problems for the inward orientation strategy in its second phase. Manufacturing processes in the production of consumer durables, intermediate goods, components and machinery require heavy capital investment in plants. This means that ouput must be large to keep the factory going at full capacity. This has two consequences in LDCs. First, large capital funds have to be generated, either by domestic savings or by foreign borrowing. We see here important elements of the origin of the international debt crisis, since domestic savings in LDCs are usually small. Second, the demand for foreign exchange is heavy, as the machinery that has to be imported is expensive. When LDCs proceed to make components and intermediate goods required by their factories, there is a further complication. In the industrial North, these are produced by a myraid of specialized producers competing for orders or contracts. Specialization on such a scale is seldom possible in LDCs because of limited markets, and this leads to high cost or low quality, or both.

This outcome is the result of what economists call "economies of scale" combined with a limited domestic market. Although LDC populations are large, their purchasing power is low, and hence, market size is relatively small. Another unfavorable outcome of limited market size is the emergence of monopolies or quasi monopolies, since one or a few enterprises can supply the market. Where manufacturers are compelled to use locally produced components – under the policy of increasing domestic content – component producers, if they are few in number, as is usually the case, enjoy a seller's market. The purchasers have to take what is available. The outcome of the arrangement is high-cost goods of a quality not up to international standards. Hence, they cannot be exported, except with government subsidies, and perhaps not even then.

The outward-oriented policies are associated with some countries commonly known as the "Newly Industrializing Countries," or NICs. In the Far East, there are four NICs – Korea, Taiwan, Hong Kong and Singapore. There are many differences between them in respect of population size, political systems, products exported, history, etc. But there are common features, which we shall now describe. They embarked on their journey not as a result of a wise choice of policy options examined in penetrating economic analysis. In each case, the NICs found themselves, in the 1950s and 1960s, in dire trouble, without any clear way of avoiding disaster. Endowed with poor or no natural resources and small populations, neither import substitution industrialization nor the export of primary commodities offered a solution. The only resources they had were people willing to learn and to work hard for low wages. In the 1960s, countries of the industrial North were enjoying good rates of growth and full employment. Accordingly, international trade flowed more freely than it does now. The NICs thus had a comparative advantage in low labor costs, which they turned to good account in establishing industries for export.

Another common feature among the NICs was their dependence on free enterprise to promote export industries. Korea, Taiwan and Hong Kong depended mainly on domestic entrepreneurs, while Singapore expanded industries by hosting multinational corporations, most of them producing components for their home or world market. While wages were low at the start in all four NICs, they rose rapidly when industrial growth mopped up the easily available labor. In Korea and Taiwan, urban labor had to be increased by the transfer of labor from agriculture, or by the location of plants in semirural areas. Hong Kong and Singapore supplemented their work force through migration from neighboring countries, but this soon reached a limit through sheer scarcity of land.

As regards government support for industries, this was least pronounced in Hong Kong and most developed in Korea, followed by Taiwan and Singapore. Support usually took the form of tax holidays of various kinds, preferential access to loans and foreign exchange, provision of infrastructure of good quality, technical assistance in various forms of industrial research, and extensive training programs to upgrade skills. NICs looked warily at each other's wage levels and productivity, the cutting edge of their competitive strength. This had to be so, since about half of their output of manufactured goods were exported.

The Human Element in NICs

Let us look at the human element in NIC development. We have discussed Korea's educational system. The experience of other NICs is not broadly dissimilar — the stress on academic education in the first nine years, the attempt to introduce technical or vocational education with varying degrees of success, and special attention paid to tertiary education. What all four NICs experienced was a shortage of manpower in management and professional occupations which attracted high rates of pay. In Hong Kong and Singapore, the problem became acute; since the language of business is English, the ablest managers and professionals command an international price, and local enterprises have to pay them at this rate or lose them.

Enterprises which produced manufactured goods for export to the industrial North attained, by the nature of their business, high levels of economic efficiency. As wage levels increased, they could no longer depend solely on the advantage of low wages, though this still remained substantial compared with the North. However, other LDCs with still lower wage levels presented a permanent threat unless they acquired other advantages and moved upwards on the technology ladder. The unique advantage the four NICs came to acquire consisted solely of their better use of human resources. This was brought about in a number of ways.

First, in the individual export enterprises, management had to be geared to a high level of competence, one result of the fiercely competitive environment. This involved not merely competence in production, such as acquiring up-to-date machinery, ensuring good plant layout, effective materials control, and possessing the ability to innovate and improve in line with fast-changing export market demands; it also involved competence in marketing, financing, personnel management and other aspects of the management of a business enterprise. As in the developed countries, enterprises in NICs had to search for talent to fill senior positions.

The beneficial effects of gearing the economy to the world grid, which is what outward orientation means, were not limited to the export enterprises. After all, the percentage of NIC GNP generated in that sector falls between 12 and 18 per cent. If the export sector were isolated from the rest, the NICs would not be able to sustain good rates of growth. In reality, to function effectively, export industries depended on other sectors. Transport and communications — roads, railways, ports, shipping and air transportation — must perform well, and where these were inadequate, the government had to provide funds to improve them. Telecommunications, power and water supplies were another obvious need. Less obvious, but just as necessary, were commercial services and banks, and financial services that must support the export effort.

As all those in management positions in industry, commerce, finance, and key public sector agencies needed to be provided with accurate and timely information about the world economy, a competent media service was an additional requirement. Finally, all enterprises working in this wide range of activities required people of ability in the higher and middle levels of management and professional staff. Thus, there developed a persistent demand on the educational system to produce them. Since people who rose to high management positions in both the private and public sector got there by virtue of their insistence on high standards of performance, their influence on the educational system was beneficial. The entrepreneur himself might not be, and often was not, an educated man. Mr. Honda of Honda Motors never graduated from high school. But he understood that once corporate business passed a certain size, needing specialist departments within it, the staffing of these departments at middle and senior positions generated a demand for graduates in many disciplines.

The advances made were not regular over the whole front. NICs started as everybody else did, in poverty. In the early phase, the emphasis was placed on what was perceived as essential, mainly infrastructure in transportation and communications, as well as energy supplies. Once NICs began to move from purely low-cost, labor-intensive processes, the development of skills over a wide range had to be undertaken and the educational system overhauled. It should be noted that growth provided both the demand for skill development and the supply of resources to mount the effort. Rapidly increasing GNP boosted government revenues and enabled finance ministries to release more funds for education. Thus, there developed a symbiotic relationship between economic development and human resource development.

Two points should be noted in the NICs' development process. First, the technology used in nearly all instances was transferred from the North. Technology transfers took much the same forms as in countries pursuing inward-oriented industrial policies. There is the purchase of complete plants under a turnkey contract, or of pieces of new machinery to supplement existing stock. Technology might be transferred by licensing agreements, purchase of patent rights and similar arrangements. Direct investment by foreign enterprises provided another means of technology transfer. What was unique in the NIC experience was that such transfers of technology had to be validated by successful export performance. It is this requirement that provided the pressure on NIC enterprises to strive for maximum returns, compelling them to adopt modern systems of management and the institutions of a modern state. In the process, they came to acquire some of the software of the North. However, the route by which they did so did not follow the same path as the northerners took.

Now we return to Korea, whose system of academic education was assessed as deficient in producing both the skills needed in industry and the attitudes of mind associated with modernization. That was the view of scholars of liberal persuasion, and we noted that another interpretation was possible. Strange though it may seem to the western scholar, the heavy emphasis on ethical principles — and Confucian ethics at that — as well as application to work and discipline can provide a rational explanation for Korea's success. Indeed, one can go further and say that if Korea were to adopt the political system and ideas of a pluralistic democracy, her economic takeoff might have been aborted in confusion as political parties battled one another for public support with extravagant promises they were incapable of fulfilling. Meanwhile, the job of providing improved living standards through fast economic growth would have been neglected. This outcome is not unknown in LDCs.

Soon after the foundation of their republic, the people of South Korea suffered misfortunes only slightly less calamitous than the Germans or Japanese. The country was invaded by the communist North. When this invasion was repelled by U.S. armed forces, subsequent operations brought the Chinese armies to the border, with fierce fighting along the border continuing for several years before a truce was signed. The cessation of hostilities provided no respite for Koreans. As a result of prolonged government mismanagement, Korea was regarded for a long time as another LDC disaster.

The misfortunes of the Korean people brought out two points of interest. Fisrt, their postwar experiement with civilian constitutional government failed to solve the problems of development. Second, in respect of cultural homogeneity and strength of national identity, Korea, in her troubled condition made good use of these assets in the way postwar Japan and Germany did. Intangible though these assets were, they were real and could be turned to advantage by a strong leadership to mobilize a national economic effort. These intangible assets — respect for learning, application to work and feelings of group solidarity based on shared common values — were reinforced by the system of education deplored by liberal scholars. However much scholars may regret that strong leadership came to be provided by a general and was not the outcome of a democratic political process, the end result was beneficial to the country.

The other two sovereign NICs, Taiwan and Singapore, also had their share of political and social trauma. In the case of Taiwan, it was defeat on the Chinese mainland by the People's Liberation Army which compelled those loyal to the Kuomintang leadership to migrate to the island to start a new chapter. As for my own country, Singapore, we had our full measure of troubles for more than a decade in the form of chronic unemployment, student radicalism, general strikes, large-scale civil riots and even communal massacres. Our expulsion from Malaysia in 1965 produced a sobering effect, and Singaporeans at last got down to the problem of earning a living.

Hong Kong was unique, in that the political mobilization which was necessary in the independent NICs did not make sense in a colony. The government could not be removed by popular vote or military coup, and political mobilization was contrary to its interest, even if colonial officials knew how to set about it. Instead, the government sensibly aimed at providing a stable administration. Such an environment gave scope to the entrepreneurs who had fled from Shanghai in 1949 and workers who escaped from Guangdong province to exercise their talent. A free enterprise regime made possible Hong Kong's economic miracle.

The NIC Example

Has the experience of the Asian NICs any relevance to other LDCs? It has to some of them, especially those which have made major advances along the path of development through inward-oriented policies and are now compelled by the logic of circumstances to look outwards. This is already happening to LDCs which have acquired a significant manufacturing capability. To mention but two countries, Brazil and India in recent years have made notable strides in exporting manufactured goods, though the proportion of the total output sold in competitive markets remains small. The fact that inward-oriented economies of LDCs are subject to a wide range of government controls through such instruments as exchange control, import licensing, credit allocation and licensing procedures of various kinds does not in itself preclude a policy adjustment toward larger and faster outward orientation. The Korean government exercised wide-ranging controls over the economy and in regard to the manu-facturing industries, intervened actively to establish skill and capital-intensive industries — steel, petrochemicals, shipbuilding and auto-mobiles — geared toward the export market. It is unlikely that free-market forces would have brought about this result.

Transfers of technology from the North are a necessary condition for rapid industrial growth, but they are not sufficient, for reasons described by Bela Balassa, to sustain such growth for long. From the human element viewpoint, the quasi-monopolistic privileges generated in protected domestic markets result in economic inefficiency, not merely through low capacity usage and a low degree of specialization, but also through low management efficiency. In the absence of competition, enterprises do not feel the pressure to get the maximum out of their plant, equipment and technology. Less capable personnel can be appointed to management and professional positions at lower rates of pay. The need to innovate is diminished in a seller's market. In sum, the demand for high-caliber personnel remains weak. Under such circumstances, nepotism and favoritism in senior appointments and overmanning in the general work force make their appearance, especially when political influence is brought to bear, as often happens in quasi-monopolistic situations. Most harmful of all is the absence of stimulus to high performance in the provision of infrastructure, commercial and financial services, eventually extending to the schools and universities. Where the LDC produces people of outstanding quality, a likely outcome is the migration of some of these to the North — the celebrated brain drain.

In the depressed condition of world trade today, when the industrial North comes under heavy and continuing protectionist pressure, a recommendation to increase exports to developed countries may look out of place. It could well be that the experience of the four NICs in the 1960s and early 1970s will turn out to be a unique historical event, and that in the future, they will be hard put to maintain their position, let alone improve on their export performance. Such an outcome would be damaging for everyone. LDC and NIC exports, even of manufactures, may directly (and visibly) affect competing industries in the North and cause unemployment. However with the proceeds of these exports, they import capital goods — machinery, trucks, aircraft, telecommunications equipment — thereby generating income and employment in the North.

Unfortunately, the impact of this is not visible, and no constituencies can be built on it. Protectionist lobbies in the North gain strength from the visible loss of jobs, but if they succeed in persuading governments to further restrict imports, they merely block the restructuring of their economies, to the disadvantage of their technology-intensive industries. However, when more than 30 million workers are unemployed in OECD countries, arguments of this kind carry little political weight.

It is therefore likely that the impediments to world trade will continue for some time. Nevertheless, unless the world gets segmented into self-contained trading blocs — an unlikely development — opportunities will continue to exist for those with a keen nose for money. This means the encouragement of free enterprise and a policy of nurturing of domestic entrepreneurs who are prepared to take risks in the export market. Enterprises in inward-oriented economies are so circumscribed by government controls and, in some countries, so heavily taxed that a relaxation of these controls, together with tax incentives for export performance, might release an an unexpected upsurge of energy. It is worth a try in the case of countries whose manufacturing capabilities have reached fairly advanced levels and whose weakness lies in suboptimal economic performance. A deliberate and sustained change of policy could yield long-term gains which are absent in producing for a protected home market.

Perhaps the most important benefit is to confirm that resource allocation is about right, as wrong allocations are punished by the bankruptcy of enterprises. A competitive market provides a test that is difficult, perhaps impossible, to reproduce in protected markets, in which resource allocation is subject to a wide variety of government controls, resulting in distortions of the prices of goods, services and factor inputs. Next, the bind of foreign exchange shortage widely experienced in LDCs can be eased. Third, we have seen in the four NICs the spread of efficiency throughout the system by the operation of what economists call "externalities." Finally, a symbiotic relationship can be established between economic growth and human resource development.

Notes

1. George Psacharopoulos, "Returns to Education: An Updated International Comparison," World Bank Reprint Series, no. 210.

2. Noel F. McGinn et al., *Education and Development in Korea* (Harvard University Press, 1980).

3. Ibid., p. 228.

4. Bela Balassa, "The Process of Industrial Development and Alternative Development Strategies," Princeton University Essays in International Finance, no. 191 (December 1980).

CHAPTER 6

The Human Dimension in Comparative Development Experience

Gustav Ranis

Sustained maintenance of acceptable levels of welfare of the human race represents the ultimate objective of all development efforts. What is a bit more controversial is that such minimal standards of acceptable welfare have different meanings at different levels of average income, and perhaps even in different sociocultural settings — certainly if one goes beyond the minimal requirements of health, caloric intake, potable water, etc. Not controversial, but difficult to trace theoretically, or to estimate empirically, are the feedbacks from the satisfaction of human needs to the quality of human resources, e.g., the impact on labor productivity from reductions in morbidity, as well as the impact on human intelligence and ingenuity arising from better nutritional standards.

I propose to leave both these issues concerning the ultimate end of development and the interaction between ends and means to one side, not because they are not highly important subjects, but because they have been covered elsewhere. The basic focus of this preliminary look at the human dimension in comparative development experience will be on the relatively neglected role of the human element in achieving the societal objective which we will assert to be some combination of growth with equity.

The Human Element: A Historical Review

The human dimension is usually either neglected or simply equated with the augmentation of human capital via educational inputs. Depending on the level of sophistication, the past literature has consequently focused on problems of education of various kinds: for example, primary versus secondary, formal versus informal, sometimes based on rate-of-return calculations. In the early going, when planning models were still in vogue, manpower projections represented their human resource counterpart. But, as is now generally recognized, such manpower targets assumed far too many rigidities — between output and employment, between employment and occupations, and between occupations and education — to be very useful. This is quite aside from the general recognition today that planning models themselves have seen their best days.

A much more sophisticated area of inquiry focused on the calculation of rates of return, average and marginal, to various types of educational expenditure. There is no denying that when we observe large differences in the rates of return for different types of educational expenditure within one country, e.g., with much higher rates of return to primary than to college education, this is potentially an important beginning of wisdom. Especially when we compare such rates of return with the rates of return on physical capital formation, or when we see large differences in rates of return across countries — for example, rates of return in India, which for every type of education are three times as high as those in the Philippines — this is very useful information.

While I do not wish to denigrate such approaches and calculations, they may be only tangentially related to the basic question being asked here. It is our view, advanced in this paper, that the most neglected area within this overall neglected field should extend beyond educational expenditures as such and encompass the relevance of the accumulation of noncognitive along with cognitive types of human capital, i.e., something which measures the response capacity of individual economic actors to changing economic conditions. To my mind, it is this response capacity which is the critical element in development at each and every stage, and one which is related to, but not captured by, the traditional literature in this area. In other words, it may be much more useful to think of the human dimension as "the" residual in country or, preferably, sectoral production functions, rather than the black box of technological change, which we all know contains such a large measure of the profession's ignorance concerning what differentiates success from failure in development. Technology, in our view, is not manna which falls from heaven; it has to be leavened and baked by human hands. Accordingly, it is how people organize themselves, and how they achieve the ability to adjust to changing environments and solve problems, which constitute the essential part of that "residual" which we need to disentangle and grasp better.

To advance this cause, it is suggested that we utilize more fully the laboratory of postwar development experience, which now stretches over almost forty years. Until quite recently, the profession, understandably, was forced to concentrate on cross-sectional analysis, as well as on the history of the now advanced societies. By now, however, sufficient data has accumulated to permit a look at our problem in a historical context, i.e., to try and isolate meaningful subphases of development, as well as to differentiate among different types of developing countries. It is, moreover, suggested that much more subtle micro studies are required to supplement any new type of macro or sectoral growth accounting.

It is probably fair to say that, historically, during the 1950s and much of the 1960s, most developing countries were deeply immersed in the so-called import substitution, or inner-oriented, subphase of their transitional growth effort. This was basically associated with the big push for industrialization and an emphasis on building up a new industrial entrepreneurial class, the entire process fuelled mainly by natural resource exports, supplemented by foreign capital inflows. What counted most here was the brute act of saving − both domestic and foreign − getting things done, and much more concern with the size than the sophistication or finesse of the effort. In this era, strangely enough, the human dimension was interpreted largely in terms of the extension of five-year plans to manpower requirements and the educational requirements which followed from them in a somewhat mechnical and inflexible fashion.

In the late 1960s and 1970s most developing countries began to shift towards an export-oriented development strategy. This meant that while natural resources remained a major component of the developmental fuel, countries were beginning to recognize that some increased participation in the world economy was required by both the condition of a limited domestic market and, in some cases, the inability of their natural resource base to continue to carry the entire burden of development. When we differentiate countries by typology, as we must, it is the smaller East Asian countries which at this point shifted toward the competitive exportation of labor-intensive goods, while Latin American and other Asian countries generally shifted toward continued import-substituting production and the export of more capital-intensive (i.e., durable consumer and capital) goods, with the continued support of natural resources and/or foreign capital inflows to finance the process.

It is in this context, i.e., a comparison between import substitution and export orientation, and the differential meaning of export orientation in different types of developing countries, that the quintessential role of the human dimension must be analyzed and defined. Penetrating international markets requires the kind of growth in flexibility, in human response capacity, not necessarily evidenced during the earlier, domestically oriented, protected sub-phase of development. The relative success or failure of this effort must be directly linked to the quality of the human dimension "residual" in countries' production functions if we accept this terminology.

Differences Among LDCs

More specifically, as we moved into the 1970s, the Latin American type of developing country, while its objectives may have shifted somewhat from growth to income distribution, poverty alleviation and the provision of basic needs, still inadequately enlisted the human dimension in achieving these objectives. With most countries remaining very heavily tied to their natural resources fuel by virtue of their favorable initial endowment, as well as the generous inflow of foreign capital not unrelated to that endowment — especially as it shifted from public and concessional to private and non-concessional — their new outward orientation was more of the subsidized export promotion type, implanted on top of a basically unchanged import substitution structure. As a consequence, what we were able to witness here is the worst manifestation of the so-called Dutch Disease, i.e., not just the inability to export labor-intensive industrial goods due to a strong exchange rate, but the continued neglect of the human dimension as we have defined it, i.e., the participation of actors at all levels in the development process, in the course of which the capacity for problem solving, thinking, learning and responding is developed. As long as the central policy setting permits a large wedge to be maintained between what goes on in the rest of the world and the country itself, there results a substantial diminution of the experience of enlisting and enhancing the participation of the human resources in this particular fashion. In contrast, the smaller, natural resource-poor East Asian countries were forced to pay increasing attention to their human resources.

They were increasingly unable to expect the rest of the world — as they could their own citizens — to accept goods produced beyond the reach of either the price or nonprice competition usually exerted by international markets.

This typological difference across LDCs over time — for example, between Latin America and East Asia — can be captured by looking at the traditional residual or total factor productivity in the production functions of these two types of developing countries. For example, in the case of Taiwan, in the three decades from 1950-80, it is estimated that 54 per cent of growth was due to "technology," while the same figure for Latin America is closer to 15-20 per cent. Table 1, based on Angus Maddison's work for an earlier period, makes the same point on a specific country-by-country basis. Notice that, as we would expect, the Philippines behaves more like a Latin American country, while Thailand is closer to the East Asian cases.

TABLE 1
Percentage of Contribution to Annual Average Growth Rate of GDP (1950-1965)

	Labor	Non-Residential Capital	GDP Growth Rate	"Residual"
Argentina	1.05	2.80	3.20	−0.65
Brazil	2.35	3.05	5.20	−0.20
Chile	1.05	2.45	4.00	0.50
Colombia	1.80	2.90	4.60	−0.10
Mexico	2.45	3.20	6.10	0.45
Philippines	2.40	2.55	5.00	0.05
South Korea	2.90	2.20	6.20	1.10
Taiwan	1.70	3.50	8.50	3.30
Thailand	2.70	3.40	6.30	0.20

SOURCE: Angus Maddison, *Economic Progress and Policy in Developing Countries* (Norton, 1970).

It is our position that the famous residual is really due to differences in indigenous technological capacities, i.e., it is related to the problem-solving capacity of the human actors, both managerial and blue collar. It should be noted that Latin America accepted much more technology straight off the international shelf without major adaptations and without much domestic, indigenous, innovative activity, while East Asia substantially modified both the processes and products which had been carefully selected from that shelf

Since we know that nothing can really be transferred efficiently without adaptation and be expected to work well, and since we also accept the fact that the existence of the "rest of the world" and its past technological achievements exerts an overwhelmingly powerful influence, no matter how "closed" or self-reliant an economy is, the marked contrast in these residuals warrants more careful investigation. We believe, but need to prove, that such differences are due to subtle variations in the human capacity to carry out more or less intelligent searches, in the willingness to reject, the ability to solve problems and to make technological adaptations of both the blue collar and white collar variety. What we are talking about here is a tinkering capacity among workers, managers and engineers based on some combination of cognitive literacy and noncognitive capacity. There is little doubt that the "human dimension" and "technological change" are really of one piece and need to be analyzed together much more carefully and precisely.

Components of the Human Dimension

One way of trying to disentangle this would be to differentiate between the organizational and educational components of the quality of the human dimension, i.e., differentiating between how people organize themselves for various economic tasks, and what combination of cognitive and noncognitive processes is ideal for carrying out such tasks at different stages of the transitional growth effort. We have a good deal of evidence, for example, that general functional literacy counts for a good deal in the adoption of agricultural techniques and the ability to adapt them to different environments. In nonagricultural sectors, simple numeracy may be equally important. The work of three noted Nobel laureates – Kuznets, Schultz and Simon – though different in focus and method, points in this same general direction, i.e., an emphasis on primary education as a necessary, but not sufficient, condition. The experience of Japan at an earlier, but equivalent, stage of development also supports the importance of literacy for the spread of improved agricultural techniques (Anthony Tang, among others) and of the importance of "nonconventional inputs," including primary education, for the adoption of "appropriate" labor-using technology in the cotton spinning industries (Gary Saxonhouse, among others).

But it is the noncognitive aspects which, in combination with literacy and numeracy, determine how well populations "deal with disequilibria," as Schultz put it, or "respond to problems," as I would. Saxonhouse finds a large effect from "workers' experience" in his econometric analysis. And all of us can cite episodal micro evidence for the crucial importance of organizational adjustments in response to changes in the environment. The combination undoubtedly matures in the crucible of tinkering and learning by doing, and it exhibits itself in the notion that self-improvement is possible, plus a growing confidence that changing environments are inescapable, that problems can be solved and adversity overcome. It is this which gives people in East Asia both the will and the capacity first to penetrate foreign markets and then to overcome rising trade barriers, international recession, oil shocks and the like, while similar adjustment capacity in the face of substantially less provocation, e.g., with respect to oil, was not demonstrated in the Latin American and other Asian countries.

It is also interesting to note (see table 2) that during the 1970s, when countries were forced to adjust to the deterioration of the international environment, it was the East Asians who maintained, and even increased, very high levels of government budget expenditure on education, while it was the Latin Americans (with the exception of Mexico) who further reduced already lower levels under the impact of the forced adjustment regime.

TABLE 2
Public Expenditure on Education

	As Per Cent of Total Expenditure		As Per Cent of GNP	
	1972	1981	1972	1981
Argentina	8.8	7.3	1.5	1.7
Brazil	6.8	3.8	1.1	0.7
Chile	14.3	14.4	6.0	4.5
Malaysia	23.4	15.9	6.5	6.5
Mexico	16.6	18.2	2.0	3.8
Philippines	16.3	14.2	2.2	1.8
South Korea	15.9	17.9	3.0	3.4
Taiwan	17.3	17.5	3.8	4.8
Thailand	19.9	19.3	3.4	3.6

SOURCES: *World Development Report, 1984; Taiwan Statistical Data Book, 1984.*

What is clearly needed is a Dennison-type disaggregation analysis of the residuals, but from the point of view of participation, learning by doing and cognitive educational attributes of various types of human resources within a developing society as it moves through its transitional growth process. This is by no means easy, and we may run the risk of substituting one black box for another. But I would suggest focusing separately on organizational differences, e.g., farmers' associations and the type of patent system – differentiating between the simple, less demanding utility model and a full patent, which process may serve to encourage the medium- and small-scale sectors and would-be inventor or tinkerer. The nature of the distribution and storage systems in agriculture and of the industrial organization structure in industry affect the strength of the workably competitive pressures which are maintained. Nor should one neglect the importance of public organizational mechanisms which facilitate research and diffusion mechanisms, as, for example, in agricultural research and extension.

But individual access, entrepreneurial and managerial, are clearly important, as are the chances for mobility and self-improvement at all levels. A better understanding of the interactions among education, access, experience and investment will not come cheaply, but it is undoubtedly the way to bring the human-dimension Hamlet back to center stage where be belongs.

CHAPTER 7

Third World Poverty: A Reevaluation

Shahid J. Burki and David Beckmann

The proportion of the world's people who are in abject poverty has gone up over the last few years for the first time in decades. During these same few years. the proportion of development policymakers' attention focused on poverty and human development has almost certainly gone down.

Policymakers in developing countries and in the international development institutions have been giving priority attention to the urgent tasks of recovering financial stability and economic growth — with some justice, because economic recovery is a *necessary* condition for progress against poverty. But economic recovery is not a *sufficient* condition for renewed progress against poverty. Even if the global economy as a whole continues to expand, the prospects for poor people in many of the developing countries are grim.

So as we enter the second half of the 1980s, we simply must focus more attention on poverty again. It is not only a matter of giving more funding to the kinds of poverty-focused projects which we developed in the 1970s, however. The world which is emerging from economic crisis is different from the world we knew before, so we need to rethink our strategies for the reduction of poverty.

To begin, we should, for most purposes, give up our generalized image of "Third World poverty." The circumstances which give rise to poverty in, say, Mali are dramatically different from those which give rise to poverty in Brazil, and the global economic crisis has made the differences among various groups of developing countries more striking than ever.

This paper begins with an overview of the three regions of the world where absolute poverty is concentrated. The core of the paper is an analysis of the different characteristics of poverty in each of these regions. The paper then concludes with a discussion of policy priorities for the reduction of poverty in each of these different situations.

The Three Poverty Regions

Table 1 ventures rough estimates of the extent and distribution of absolute poverty. They are based mainly on unpublished World Bank staff estimates of the numbers of people whose intake of calories is below 90 per cent of the FAO/WHO requirement. Also included in the table is China's own estimate of the number of Chinese below the poverty line (equivalent to US$ 70 in rural areas). The term "mainland Asia" includes China and South Asia together.

TABLE 1
Poverty Regions

	Population in Poverty	Total Population
	(Millions)	
Mainland Asia	580	1,940
South Asia	470	940
China	110	1,000
Sub-Saharan Africa	150	340
Latin America	50	385
Other	60	485
Total	840	3,150

These order-of-magnitude estimates indicate that poverty is now concentrated in three regions: mainland Asia, which includes about two-thirds of the poorest people in the world; sub-Saharan Africa, where the proportion of people in poverty is highest; and Latin America. The other groups of developing countries – along the Pacific rim of Asia and around the Mediterranean Sea (southern Europe, northern Africa and the Middle East) – have made substantial progress against poverty over the last generation, so that, with some exceptions (notably Indochina), they are no longer characterized by massive, miserable poverty.

The circumstances of poverty are different in each of the three main poverty regions. As shown on the next page, even the most aggregate economic statistics suggest that different dynamics underlie the persistence of poverty in each of these three parts of the world.

TABLE 2
GDP and Population Growth in Three Poverty Regions

	Mainland Asia	Sub-Saharan Africa	Latin America
GDP growth			
(% per year)			
1965-1973	5.8	5.8	7.1
1973-1983	5.6	1.5	2.2
Population growth			
(% per year)			
1965-1973	2.8	2.6	2.5
1973-1983	2.0	2.9	2.4
GDP per capita growth			
(% per year)			
1965-1973	3.0	3.2	4.6
1973-1983	3.6	−1.4	−0.2

The last two lines of this table — just six numbers — eloquently tell the story of encouraging economic progress in Asia, alarming economic decay in Africa (a 15 per cent drop in per capita income over the ten-year period), and sudden economic reversal in Latin America. Given that population growth tends to be more rapid among the poor, per capita income among the poor has probably gone down at least as much as average per capita income, and declines in income are clearly most painful among families who are struggling at the margin of subsistence.

Looking to the future, the more optimistic scenario for the global economy in the *World Development Report* would allow the larger countries of Latin America to reestablish minimally adequate rates of growth and improve their creditworthiness by the end of the 1980s. But even under the assumptions of the optimistic scenario, some indebted countries are not expected to recover growth and creditworthiness. And for sub-Saharan Africa, even the optimistic scenario projects declining average per capita income in Africa for the foreseeable future.

Moreover, the assumptions which underlie the *World Development Report*'s optimistic scenario are open to challenge. One assumption is that between now and 1990, the industrial countries will maintain a rate of economic growth which is nearly 50 per cent above their average rate of growth since the end of the World War II.

The *World Development Report*'s optimistic scenario also assumes that the commercial banks will increase their exposure by 5-6 per cent annually through the rest of the decade. At least for now, commercial banks have been unwilling to increase their exposure. In the case of Mexico, for example, the banks agreed to a multi-year rescheduling, but the quid pro quo was no new money.

The Varieties of Poverty

To look more specifically at what is happening to poor people in different parts of the developing world, it may be helpful to use the following labor utilization identity:

$$\frac{Income}{Persons} = \frac{Work\ force}{Persons} \times \frac{Employment}{Work\ force} \times \frac{Income}{Employment}$$

This identity is adapted from Paul Streeten and Michael Lipton, and this paper draws repeatedly from Lipton's recent review of empirical studies on labor and poverty.

Households in absolute poverty depend for their well-being mainly on being able to transform time and strength—their own work—into income. Thus, income per person among the poor depends mainly on the three interrelated factors on the right side of the identity:

a) First, *participation* in the labor force. If a family of six has three members in the work force, for example, income per person will be higher than if only two family members are in the work force.

b) Second, *employment.* Income per person in the family will clearly drop if one of its workers is unable to find work, or unable to find as much work as he is ready to do.

c) Third, *productivity.* Income per person in the family also depends very much on how much income its family members derive from their work.

Work Force Participation

The most urgent aspect of the situation of the poor in Africa is the first factor, work force participation.

Work force participation depends heavily on demography. In general, poor people live in large families, with relatively few people of working age. This dependency effect is exaggerated in Africa, where population growth is nearly 3 per cent and rising.

Because of rapid population growth, only 51 per cent of the population of sub-Saharan Africa is of working age (15-64 years), and that percentage is falling. In China and India, by contrast, 60 per cent of the population is of working age, and the percentage is rising. Put simply, for every ten people, China and India have one more potential worker than Africa does.

The first factor in the labor utilization identity also varies according to the proportion of working-age people who actually participate in the work force. Participation rates are generally higher among low-income people; need virtually compels them to work if they can. But at *very* low incomes participation rates decline, mainly because very poor people are more prone to illness; they are more often simply unable to work.

The few empirical studies we have of labor markets in Africa indicate that a higher percentage of work days are lost to illness and disability in Africa than in the low-income countries of Asia.

This is consistent with the generally poor state of health and health care in Africa. Average life expectancy at birth in sub-Saharan Africa is 49 years, compared to 59 years for all low-income countries. There is one physician for every 21,000 people in Africa; even in the poorest South Asian nation, Bangladesh, there is one physician for every 8,000 people.

Indeed, the two greatest achievements of mainland Asia over the last generation were (i) increasing food production fast enough to keep up with population growth and (ii) achieving significant — in China, dramatic — reductions in birth rates. The first achievement averted mass famine. The second set the stage for more significant increases in per capita income among the poor in the years to come.

There is still much work to be done in the area of family planning, especially in Pakistan and Bangladesh. Further improvements in health, in addition to the immediate benefits, would result in higher per capita incomes among the poor. Indian surveys suggest that poor workers may still be losing 6-7 per cent of their potential work time to illness and disability. Work force participation in South Asia could also be substantially increased by relaxing social constraints.

Caste restrictions on the kinds of work different people expect to do keep some people out of the labor force, and *purdah* restrictions keep all but about 10 per cent of the women in Pakistan from working outside their homes.

Latin America is intermediate between Africa and Asia in terms of population growth and dependency. In Latin America, too, rapid and relentless population growth makes any economic malfunction urgent and potentially explosive. But many countries in Latin America have dramatically reduced birth rates. Moreover, health care and other services have been extended to many of the poorest people in Latin America over the last generation, so that absenteeism due to illness probably contributes less to the persistence of poverty there than in Asia and Africa.

Employment

It is the second factor in the work identity, employment, which is most urgent in the current situation of Latin America's poor. The debt crisis forced Latin America to slash imports, inducing a severe and continent-wide depression.

The year 1984 was the fourth straight year in which average per capita income for Latin America as a whole declined or remained stagnant. Average per capita income has dropped back to about the level of 1976. Production lost because of the crisis is equivalent to more than one-third of GDP. What data exist, compiled by the Economic Commission for Latin America, suggest that employed people have done relatively well in maintaining their wage levels. But the crisis has given rise to widespread unemployment throughout the region.

Latin American development has long been characterized by profound social cleavages — between whites and Indians, and between urban and rural areas. The rapid economic progress in recent decades was concentrated in the cities. Public education and, to a lesser extent, health care facilities were extended to the rural areas in the 1950s and 1960s, but the main engine for the reduction of poverty was migration from the countryside to urban jobs. The share of the labor force in agriculture fell from one-half in 1960 to about one-third in 1980. Two-thirds of Latin America's population is now urban.

Today's unemployment has most directly affected the cities, including some of the urban poor. But it also jams the traditional engine for poverty reduction in Latin America, in effect trapping many potential migrants in relatively backward rural areas.

Some Latin American countries – Bolivia, for example, or Peru – are simply floundering economically. They have not taken credible steps to come to grips with their economic problems. These economies will almost certainly remain depressed. Other Latin American countries are undertaking dramatic adjustments which may, if external circumstances are favorable, lead back to economic growth and creditworthiness. Specifically, countries are trying to shift capital and labor from the production of nontradeable goods to the production of tradeables, thus generating export surpluses to reduce the burden of debt. Countries are also trying to reduce economic inefficiencies – cutting back subsidies to inefficient parastatal firms, for example. Such adjustments are essential, but they also throw thousands of people out of work, and some people, for reasons of age or training or geography, will never find their way into the expanding sectors of the economy. Thus, unemployment is likely to be a prominent factor in the persistence of Latin American poverty for some time to come.

The huge nations of mainland Asia are less dependent on the global economy, so the effect of the global recession on employment was relatively mild. And the employment effects of the recession in Africa, although significant, are minor in comparison with the morass of Africa's other economic problems.

Yet unemployment is a more significant factor in South Asian and African poverty than many economists have thought. Poor people are seldom unemployed for extended periods of time, but they are, nonetheless, often unable to find work. One important factor is that agricultural labor is seasonal, and people who have no land or other assets of their own with which to work are the most likely to suffer seasonal unemployment.

One survey of rural India found that the poorest 1 per cent of the population suffered 22 per cent unemployment – that is, people were, on the average, unable to find work on 22 per cent of the half-days on which they sought work. Among the next poorest 10 per cent of the population, unemployment averaged 14 per cent.

Unemployment is two and a half times higher in six of India's states — Andhra, Bihar, Kerala, Maharashtra, Tamil Nadu and West Bengal — than in the other eleven.

The working-age population is expanding by 2.3 per cent a year in India. According to past patterns, income will have to rise at twice that rate, or 4.6 per cent per year, to create jobs for the new workers at past levels of productivity. Moreover, population pressure on the land is important everywhere in mainland Asia. In India, for example, average farm size declined by 17 per cent during the 1970s. Thus, it will be more difficult than in the past to absorb growth in the work force without declines in employment or productivity.

The employment challenge of a growing population is even more formidable in sub-Saharan Africa. Pressure on the land is less severe in some countries than others, but the growth of Africa's working-age population has risen from 1.6 per cent per year in 1960-70 to 2.0 per cent per year in 1970-82 and 2.9 per cent per year for the remainder of the century!

Productivity

Our discussion of labor participation highlighted the ominous implications of rapid population growth and poor health among poor people in Africa. The second term of the labor identity, employment, features most prominently among the circumstances of poverty in Latin America. But if we now look at the third factor in the labor identity, income per unit of work, we come to the most difficult challenge for mainland Asia.

The *average* per capita income for mainland Asia is a little more than half the average per capita income for sub-Saharan Africa. Per capita income for Pakistan, the highest in mainland Asia, is a little more than half the per capita income for Nigeria.

In South Asia as a whole, nearly one-third of the population is caught in absolute poverty, and much of the rest of the population also subsists at very low levels of income. The distribution of income in India, for example, is roughly average for the developing countries. So general increases in productivity and output must be basic to any strategy to reduce poverty.

The present government of China is convinced that for China, too, further progress against poverty will depend on improvements in economic efficiency and a sustained period of rapid economic growth.

Remarkably, the nations of mainland Asia — in many respects, among the poorest of the poor — have in recent years been achieving among the highest rates of economic growth in the world. India has been averaging economic growth of about 4 per cent for over a decade. Except for Nepal, all the other economies of mainland Asia, including China, have been explanding even more rapidly.

The saving and investment rates of this region are among the highest in the world. Many of the region's economic managers are exceptionally competent. The labor force is increasingly healthy and well educated, and much of this region no longer has the burden of population growth rates such as those which prevail in Africa and Latin America.

What counts for the poor, of course, is not return on factors of production generally, but return on their own work. China has been most successful in raising the real incomes of the poor, partly through its initial revolution in the distribution of assets. China also eliminated some of the worst aspects of poverty by securing minimal levels of food and social services for virtually everyone. But incomes are still very low in China generally, and some rural areas, especially remote areas, remain exceptionally poor.

In South Asia, the main gains in real income among the poor have been improved government services (notably, schools, health care, and security against famine). Many of the poor have also benefited from the expansion of agricultural production; food prices would have been higher otherwise, and real wage rates, even for unskilled labor, are higher than average in the irrigated parts of India.

But for India as a whole, wage rates for unskilled labor have generally remained constant. In some places in South Asia wage rates have fallen, and poverty has clearly become worse. In Bangladesh, for example, the average real wage of agricultural workers in 1984 was only two-thirds the level of 1964.

Thus, improvements for the poor in mainland Asia have so far been relatively meager. But past gains in family planning, health and education help to position many of this region's poor for more significant income gains in the future.

By contrast, sub-Saharan Africa is in the throes of general economic decay. Average investment is only 16 per cent of GDP, compared to 26 per cent for mainland Asia, and for some African countries, investment rates have declined sharply. In Ghana, gross domestic investment decreased from 18 per cent in 1965 to 8 per cent in 1983, in Uganda from 11 per cent to 8 per cent, and in the Central African Republic from 21 per cent to 11 per cent. In several cases, the rate of investment is now too low even for maintenance — aggregate capital disinvestment.

The average return on investment is also low — and declining. Trained manpower is scarce. Even healthy manpower is limited.

David Davies' study on African poverty included data on wage rates for unskilled rural labor in six African countries. In all cases, wage rates for unskilled labor have been falling since the early 1970s.

Latin America has long enjoyed a relatively high level of productivity and income. Industrialization and urbanization raised real wages, even for unskilled labor. But average productivity was declining long before the debt crisis, and countries which are unable to come to grips with the current financial crisis are likely to suffer declines in productivity and income over the long term.

In summary, then, we have some reason for optimism about gains against poverty in mainland Asia, where the great bulk of the world's poorest people still live; indeed, we can hope for progress against poverty on an unprecedented scale in the years ahead. But at the same time, we must expect increasing misery in most of Africa and parts of Latin America — misery on a scale which the world has not witnessed for decades.

Policy Priorities

Given the varieties of poverty, policy priorities must also differ. On the Asian mainland, the rates of domestic savings and investment are high. The resource gap, therefore, is manageable — on the order of 2 per cent of GDP — and can be financed from a combination of concessional and commercial capital flows. GDP growth rates of over 5 per cent per year should be attainable for the duration of the century. Low and falling rates of population growth should result in significant increases in per capita income.

Among the Asian poor, nothing is more important than continued increases in agricultural productivity. They usually spend four-fifths of their income on food, and roughly four-fifths of their income, as a class, comes from agriculture. A World Bank study suggests that a 1 per cent increase in agricultural production in India will generate a 2 per cent increase in real incomes for the poorest quintile. In China, the liberalization of agriculture and the resulting increases in production have raised the incomes for most of China's poorest people by at least 50 per cent in five years.

Given the pressure of a growing work force and limited land, employment is also a priority issue. Rural industry is one important solution, and another, perhaps less obvious, is migration. In China, where many of the poorest people are trapped in areas with meager natural resources, labor mobility is a major issue of poverty policy. The concentration of employment in certain states of India suggests that there, too, measures to encourage migration would help the poor. In Pakistan, remittances from international migration have given an important boost to rural incomes.

Finally, social change is also a poverty priority in Asia — to increase the prevalence of schooling and labor participation among women in Pakistan, for example, or to remove discrimination against underprivileged groups such as the scheduled castes in India.

In sub-Saharan Africa, the most urgent priority is a very basic one: the maintenance of the economic system. Top priority should be assigned to funding and other measures to keep the existing stock of public capital — roads, schools, factories, and so forth — from deteriorating, and to make fuller use of it.

As in Asia, agriculture remains basic to both economic growth and poverty reduction — more realistic prices to farmers, progress in rain-fed farming technology, and much more serious efforts than in the past to adapt new technologies to local physical and cultural realities.

Few African countries have yet committed themselves to reducing population growth. A couple of African countries have explicitly pro-birth policies! Until Africa's rate of population growth is reduced, there can be no hope of general increases in incomes for poor people.

Savings rates have fallen sharply — from 13 per cent to 7 per cent in low-income sub-Saharan Africa between 1965 and 1983 — with the result that the resource gap has widened from 2 to 8 per cent of GDP. Yet disbursements of official development assistance are projected to fall over the next several years. Part of the problem is limited project implementation capacity in Africa, but another part is the slowness of donors to shift to fast-disbursing aid in support of systems maintenance and policy reform.

In Latin America, the challenge is twofold — recovery from the debt crisis and redistribution of income.

Latin America may not be able to cope with the debt overhang without some as yet unanticipated expansion of official finance. But in any case, broad reforms in domestic economic policies are vital for the economic stability and eventual recovery of the debtor nations.

Fortunately, some of the reforms which are necessary for economic and financial recovery will also help to redress long-standing inequities. More realistic exchange rates will favor rural people involved in the production of export crops and encourage more labor-intensive investment. Inefficiencies in parastatal and protected industries have benefited a few relatively privileged workers at the expense of the population at large, and government subsidies have been concentrated in the urban areas; so cutbacks, although painful, will, on balance, probably improve the distribution of income.

Adjustment programs should be designed to minimize the costs to the most vulnerable groups and, more generally, to distribute the costs and benefits of adjustment equitably. Latin America's return to democracy will probably encourage equity in adjustment, although perhaps not for some of the very poorest, least articulate groups.

In formulating poverty strategies for the late 1980s, we must squarely face the need — in Asia, Africa, and Latin America — for broad improvements in economic policy and performance. It would make no sense in Peru, for example, to ignore macroeconomic policy and concentrate on rural health projects. Nor is there any feasible way for India or China to substantially reduce poverty without continued economic growth.

For mainland Asia, then, I have suggested agriculture, employment and social reforms as priorities; for Africa, maintenance, agriculture and population; for Latin America, recovery from the debt crisis and redistribution of income. To avert widespread misery in Africa and Latin America, increased official finance seems necessary.

These policy priorities are focused, not on basic needs in isolation, but on accelerating economic growth in a way which is biased toward the poor.

CHAPTER 8

Capital Investment and the Human Element

Henry Ergas

This paper is concerned with the relationship between capital investment and the human element in development. It begins with a warning against focusing on any one factor, such as capital — or, for that matter, the human element — in a discussion of economic development. It issues a warning against the two major pitfalls in such discussions: *oversimplification,* and mechanical *extrapolation* from partially relevant experience. The need is for an integrated, in-depth approach, which becomes all the more necessary in the present crisis, where maximum and most efficient use has to be made of increasingly exiguous resources. The paper concludes by advocating more pragmatic attitudes to capital investment at the level of both donors and recipients, as well as a recognition of the problems and possibilities of combining technical and financial assistance, and of the cooperation of the public and private sectors in the process, within a framework in which the human element plays its rightful role.

Imbalance in Emphasis on Capital and Resources

In the golden age of planning in the late 1950s and early 1960s, at a time when the newly independent countries embarked on the process of accelerated development, and when European reconstruction made amazingly speedy progress with the inflow of capital from the Marshall Plan, it was fashionable for economic planners to produce models which focused on the supply of capital as the major determinant of economic growth and welfare. Development was programmed in an overall framework, set in national account terms, and the supply of foreign and domestic savings was related to output through the magic formula of a capital/output ratio, itself based on scanty statistical evidence, modified on the basis of overall studies. The framework was of limited operational validity, partly because the statistical evidence on which it was based was weak, but mainly because it subsumed a vast array of questions, including the choice of appropriate technologies, the likelihood of achieving a rate of investment of the magnitude and composition required, and the need for a favorable external and domestic environment. Where it failed most was in its assumptions on the effectiveness of domestic institutions and policies, including the realistic possibility of these being changed within a brief planning period. Programs depended initially on the existence of an adequate service and administrative infrastructure (as had been the case with European reconstruction) and, above all, on the responsiveness of the human element.

These framework models were of some use. They helped summarize an overall situation, particularly at the general policy level, and determined the broad magnitude of an "aid gap." It was, of course, understood that overall negotiations on the domestic and international levels as to sector requirements needed highly detailed elaboration and identification. Eventually, because of the weaknesses of the approach, the reconciliation of budgetary allocations and appropriations with framework figures turned out to be artificial and contrived. Thus, the gap between nonoperational global planning and financial and executive decisions led to a series of discrepancies. Instead of adherence to an overall strategy determining policies, many governments resorted to short-term management, with a desperate search for finance for short-term and long-term requirements. It often happened, therefore, that the selection of both investment projects and of the technologies used was determined by financial availability rather than by a combination of criteria.

The major distoration that arose from assigning the determining role to capital investment occurred in the rural sector, the basic sector of the economy in the developing countries. Investment in heavy infrastructure or in lumpy projects lent itself to the hope that it would "unlock" latent productive forces. Also, such projects were relatively more amenable to rapid execution and control than in-depth rural development projects involving a multitude of beneficiaries. Faith in the productivity of capital was further enhanced by two typical examples of misleading extrapolation: the assumption that the TVA experience lent itself to satisfactory duplication (and, hence, could also help solve acute political problems, especially where river basins transcended major boundaries); and the assumption that similar ecological zones warranted faith in similar types of development. Large amounts of scarce scientific and material resources were spent on designing ecological analogues, which on their own were assumed to indicate the pattern for the future. For instance, much was written in purely technical terms on the transition of the Mediterranean countries to the level of California (a process assumed to be relatively simple), or the transformation to American Midwest conditions of vast areas of Latin America.

The balance sheet is mixed. Many of the transport infrastructure projects have indeed played a major role in allowing and stimulating widespread development. A most telling exemple is the impact of the roads program in Turkey in the 1950s. In parts of Asia, the population explosion would have led to a state of total misery had it not been for the impact of major irrigation projects. There has been some successful adaptation of modern technology in Latin America and North Africa. But against this, there has also been a series of distortions, of investments yielding a fraction of what they were expected to yield. These distortions could have been avoided if an integrated view of development had been taken.

The tragedy is that the ecological analogue syndrome persists to this day. Thus, in the midst of the African hunger crisis — a crisis due only partly to natural causes, and due to a larger extent to a failure to tackle basic institutional, policy, management and training problems relating to the agricultural sector — we have been recently reminded that the African continent is three times as large as the United States, that Zaire alone possesses 13 per cent of the world's hydroelectric potential, and that Africa has not lost the capacity for a flourishing agricultural market that could both satisfy local appetites and provide a cornucopia to the world. This may be true in terms of capacity; in fact, every effort should be made, not only to draw attention to the vast potential which lies unused in developing countries, but also to show how a collective effort must be made to take advantage of this potential.

This means, in the first instance, taking stock of the vast array of knowledge which already exists. But it also means both taking cognizance of the enormous level of investment which a fuller exploitation would involve and, at the same time, of realizing how a well-integrated program of modest dimensions could already make a considerable difference. Full exploitation of the potential would, of course, involve some major change in international and national policies, a change in the world trading pattern, and institutional changes of major dimensions, including the establishment of an effective public administration system, such as that of Singapore, to which Mr. Goh has referred.[1] Although Mr. Goh refers especially to the Japanese experience, his own country provides a striking example of what can be done not only with a remarkable labor force and a highly efficient establishment, but also with intelligent use of a factor which is not available to all: location. There may be disagreement over Mr. Goh's drastic downgrading of the importance of problems of trade and aid as they face the developing countries, but there can be no disagreement over the central role of public administration in its broadest sense, and of the need for preconditions for the effective absorptive capacity of capital. This is only too clear from the experience of the oil-rich capital-exporting countries, where although average incomes are higher than in most areas of the world, the bulk of the population is far from being integrated into the modern sector. These countries export capital which, had adequate conditions existed, would have been absorbed to a large extent at home. Although the share of developing countries in these capital exports has been on the increase lately, recent studies show that a major fraction is still destined for mature economies.

Elements of Human Welfare in Both an Input and Output Sense

The need is for an in-depth and integrated approach which recognizes the "human element" as a key factor in development in both an "input" sense, insofar as success depends on the efficiency, productivity and management of the working population at large, and also in an "output" sense, that is, in measuring the outcome of the development effort, not only in conventional global income terms, but also in terms of the various elements which make what Frances Stewart calls the "full-life" objective.[2] Breaking down the global output element into its component parts in the formulation and selection of projects basically means selecting benchmark outputs which are ends in themselves, which are immediate, and whose impact as "inputs" is often difficult to define and evaluate in the long term.

The objective of establishing a *precise* relationship between the full-life objective and the increase in productive resources in subsequent periods may be overambitious. It is possible, however, to associate at least some partial elements of the full-life objective with increases in resources: good nutrition increases efficiency; increases in production and output are associated with increases in the level of education and training, particularly with adequate manpower planning; resettlement and increases in agricultural output are associated with the liberation of vast areas from debilitating diseases (there are some current specific examples in Africa in this context, and the Mediterranean areas also provides dramatic examples of increases in output with the elimination of malaria). If these full-life outputs (higher standards of nutrition, education and better health, which are immediate ends in themselves) are to fulfil their role as inputs, they need to be associated with a series of other policy, current and capital resource inputs, each of which will have its own opportunity cost.

The increase in productive activity due to a higher level of employment results in a "full-life output" over and above the increase in production to which it gives rise, since it eliminates the misery and social conflict caused by a high level of unemployment. It is also to be noted that in the crucial sector of food production in the developing countries, the increase in productive activity is likely to be synonymous with the attainment of one of the major objectives of the full life — a higher level of nutrition — particularly in the poorer countries, where food imports and food aid have to be carefully integrated with overall agricultural policy, including long-term food security.

The references above are, of course, to the physical dimension. When it comes to the nonphysical factors, the problems of defining output responses become even more complex. Such elements of the full-life objective as political freedom, or high standards of morality in the public administration, almost by definition cannot have identifiable outputs. Recent history, however, includes examples where it may be possible to associate *turning points* in the evolution of key sectors of the economy with, for instance, the introduction of a set of administrative reforms, or a return to freedom, political security and stability, all of which may spark off progress. The basic point, however, is the one made earlier — the impossibility of arriving at meaningful relationships in determining an array of different outputs by focusing on one factor only. As the wise old philosopher put it: When you clap your hands, what is the noise made by the left hand?

International Investment in Components of the Full Life

It was partially because of the difficulty of channelling public or private capital resources for the human welfare element that the proposal for Sunfed was made in the early 1960s. Sunfed was designed to be a social investment organization which would take care of "non-self-liquidating investments" and, hence, of rural welfare in its wider sense: of water supply, housing and health, all of which were difficult to judge in terms of commercial viability. Even though Sunfed was never to see the light of day, some of its objectives have been achieved, partly through the establishment of the United Nations Special Fund, which was to finance preinvestment. The establishment of the UNSF coincided with the initiation of the operations of the International Development Association, whose chief concern was to be lower-income countries which could meet World Bank lending terms only partially, or not at all. It also coincided with the enlargement of the scope of operations of the World Bank and its implicit acceptance of a "social cost and benefit analysis" distinguishing between economic and financial returns. Again, in the same context of a broadening designed to give due reeognition to the human element, the Bank established its cooperation with UNESCO. In both cases, an attempt was made to have quantitative indicators of benefits, with emphasis on the economic returns. In these efforts, the Special Fund enabled the agencies to undertake basic studies with the hope that they would be so planned as to take into account a realistic possibility of their implementation. In fact, as the record shows, lending to agriculture and education by the World Bank (with other international financial agencies following its example) rose constantly until recent times and had a significant impact on the economic progress of the LDCs, especially those in the middle range, where institutional factors were more favorable.

Efforts to introduce the human element as the key determinant of the type and allocation of capital investment in developing countries must be considered against the present situation of exiguous resources; of a generally unfavorable climate for aid; of the culmination of an endemic crisis, threatening starvation in vast areas; of drastic, easy, but mostly unjustified cuts in such basic investments as education and rural infrastructure; and of an increase in unemployment. Accordingly, the process of introduction must be viewed under three different aspects:

a) The adequacy of capital investment criteria.
b) The adoption of policies designed to maximize the efficiency of resources.
c) The closely related adoption of innovative policies and attitudes at the national and international levels, designed to increase the absolute volume of resources devoted to development.

Adjusting Investment Criteria to Favor the Human Element

The outcome of a more explicit recognition of the crucial importance of the human element in determining the allocation of investments among different sectors is likely to be different according to the sectors of the economy. Social investment in health and education are longer-term investments as far as their input/output relationship is concerned. Hence, an increase in the allocation to these sectors, based on conventional criteria, is likely to retard growth, though it may be justified in terms of broader policy objectives.

On the other hand, if the criteria for the choice of investments in the productive sectors (agriculture and industry) include social considerations — employment impact, adequacy of the institutional framework, integration into the economy (instead of producing a purely enclave effect), the results on economic growth cannot be defined a priori, and they need not necessarily be adverse. Decisions often have to be made in agriculture involving a choice between mechanization and nonmechanization, between major irrigation and minor irrigation, between extensive and intensive cultivation. All these decisions have inevitable repercussions on employment and on the use of inputs complementary to the initial investments. They also depend on a set of policy measures which are more easily implemented with one type of technology than with another. In the final analysis, these decisions depend on a careful evaluation of the various factors involved. Thus, it is often the case that a certain allocation for minor irrigation projects would be more economically justified than an equivalent sum spent on major irrigation, or that a low level of mechanization may be preferable to a higher level. *The converse may also be true in other cases.* Similarly, in the industrial sector, the use of more labor-intensive technologies than those commonly in use may be economically justified, even if one considers current money costs rather than social costs adjusted for factor supply differences. The point is, by taking explicitly into account social as well as economic criteria, and by applying a social cost-benefit analysis, the range of choice increases, the search for adequate technology becomes meaningful, and social objectives can find their place even in conditions of major shortages of resources and limited time horizons.

The Social and Human Dimension as a Function of Progress

Social objectives vary according to the level of income, or, better, with the degree of advancement of society. In the poorer societies with which we are particularly concerned, indicators of "the basic entitlements" can be fairly easily expressed in terms of calories, and hence, nutritional strength; of prevention against epidemics; of elementary child care; and of a level of involvement synonymous with employment in the productive process. It is possible to assign numerical values to these entitlements. As societies become more advanced, the range and differentiation of these entitlements increases. To take but an example, relief from traffic congestion through mass transit systems may be of a lesser economic priority than other investments in most developing countries. This also seems to be the view of the World Bank, which has rigorously abstained from financing such projects so far. Neverthless, investments in such transit systems may have, in addition to their economic benefits, considerable social benefits in such metropolises as Bangkok or Cairo, where without an improvement in traffic flow, both the economy and the social fabric could be in danger.

Efficiency in Social Investments

Introducing "social criteria" in the allocation of investments need not necessarily imply major increases in the volume of investments allocated to the social sectors. It is the case in many countries, that the composition of investments in the social sector is at times distorted and unproductive: the massive training of undergraduates in humanities and in law, contrasted with the absence of adequate technical training; the absence of a balanced policy in health care, against the undue weight given from time to time to "showpiece infrastructure" such as magnificent hospital buildings with brilliantly designed equipment lying idle; university campuses which have little to envy in California or Australia, but which turn out alienated graduates. Massive primary education and literacy, the building of cooperation with an effective program of agriculture, cheap health or education programs, total vaccination against measles or smallpox, a dramatic cure of endemic syphilis — all these would, of course, yield their maximum if accompanied by other investments, but even taken in isolation, they justify their minor cost a millionfold.

Similarly, not all modern technology need be expensive. Even if expensive, the right technology can be justified by its output, in terms of both primary and secondary effects. A rational allocation among different types of social investment, therefore, far from impinging on scarce resources needed for directly productive purposes, has the effect of increasing and reinforcing these resources.

Increasing the Total Level of Resources for Human Welfare

Whatever improvements are made in the allocation of resources, the volume devoted to investments must increase if both social and economic criteria are to be considered, particularly if minimum full-life objectives are to be met for vast masses of the population of developing countries. In any case, the margin for economy in opting for less of the showpiece investment referred to above is small. A basic question arising is what changes in aid policy are required to ensure that social objectives are not the first to bear the brunt of retrenchment, and to establish what can be done in more propitious times to promote them further. It is taken for granted that the more resources that are channelled in a broader aid effort in coordination with multilateral agencies, the easier the process is likely to be.

The first task will be to focus international aid on taking the human dimension into account. In the present situation of international economic stringency and uncertainty, the possibilities of major increases in multilateral aid, or a considerably higher proportion of multilateral aid in international aid, are likely to be extremely small. Legislators are likely to be increasingly concerned with controlling the uses of their funds and bilateral aid, though the extent of influence over the latter is likely to increase rather than decrease. Moreover, in such circumstances, foreign aid is also likely to be increasingly an adjunct of foreign international and commercial policy. These tendencies give the whole aid process more of a donor outlook than it professes to have, but it needs a coordinated effort by both recipients and donors to combine their respective areas of interest.

In this context, the international agencies have a set of actions to take into consideration. Their first and foremost need is to reinforce the process of evaluation of their activities already initiated. They should thus associate a substantive audit with their "management audit." While it is true that the efficiency of these organizations is primarily a reflection of the views and receptivity of the member governments, there are also a series of endogeneous improvements which they can adopt at all stages of project and program implementation to increase efficiency. Indeed, much has already been done in this direction. An essential part of this evaluation needs to concentrate on the extent to which the human dimension is taken into account in the various projects and activities involved. The more the efficiency of the agencies increases, the more they will be in a position to play a positive role in the multilateralism in which they have become increasingly engaged.

Such improvements in the aid process will be of little avail if the overall conditions for the grant of vital financial assistance are impossible to achieve within a realistic framework. In this context, much of the debate centers on the general conditions imposed by the international financial agencies, primarily the International Monetary Fund and the World Bank. Their assistance has a determining role, especially in the poorer developing countries now struggling with acute balance-of-payments difficulties — difficulties which are due to a minor extent to their own mismanagement, and essentially to factors outside their control. The debate on conditionality as imposed by the IMF/World Bank often results in a generalized attack on both institutions. Misleadingly ignored are their major contributions — in preventing more dramatic crises than those we have experienced in the case of the IMF, or in providing capital for basic development in the case of the World Bank.

The fact is that every grant of aid is bound to be subject to explicit or implicit conditions. As has frequently been noted, however, the conditions imposed by the IMF on various countries are similar in their general features, though some differentiation does take place in practice. The reason is, of course, that although the objectives of the IMF were initially elaborated in extremely broad terms and did in fact reflect the concern of the founding fathers for employment and equity, in practice, given the limits on its resources, the terms of reference the IMF has set for itself are essentially concerned with short-term adjustment. The target becomes a viable payments position within a limited period; consequently, the range of solutions or options is bound to be narrow, and the time required for adopting measures is in most cases too short for the drastic reversal of policies required. The imposition of this severe time limit on a process which needs major changes in structure, and the dependence of World Bank aid on Fund agreement, causes short-term considerations to predominate, with adverse effects on long-term development, particularly in cases where adverse balance-of-payments conditions reflect basic rigidities due to structural weaknesses in the system.

The criticism directed at IMF/IBRD conditionality involves two sets of considerations. First and foremost — and this applies more particularly to the Fund — is the constraint on budgetary expenditures, designed to bring about an improvement in the balance of payments which would allow recipients to fulfill their external obligations. Second is the imposition of shifts in economic and financial policies, designed to give greater weight to individual enterprise and the market mechanism.

The extent of constraint is obviously dictated by the short-term time horizon. Its impossibility becomes obvious when as much as one-half of foreign exchange earnings must be devoted to servicing foreign debt. It should be remembered in this context that the conditionality of the fund is itself a function of the extent of the disequilibrium existing at the time when Fund negotiations are entered into. Be that as it may, the constraint is bound to translate itself into a reduction of expenditures, which inevitably has a major impact on the poorer sections of the community. Whatever efforts are made to correct waste in social programs, strict austerity measures are likely to affect the lower-income groups dramatically before structural changes are effected.

Of these structural changes, the elimination of subsidies is perhaps the most important. The wider economic implications in some cases more than compensate for an adverse social impact. For instance, even if severe hardship is caused, there is justification in conditions of stringency for the elimination — or at least a major reduction — of subsidies on prices of energy in great scarcity, and for the imposition of high tariffs on telecommunications. In other cases, however, unless a set of complementary measures, themselves part of a well-coordinated policy, are taken, the elimination of subsidies may cause extreme hardship, and its economic advantages may be extremely limited. This is particularly so in the case of food subsidies, the policy toward which has to be devised in the context of overall agricultural policy. The latter needs to take into account the effectiveness of price incentives on agricultural production, the requirements in terms of agricultural inputs and, in the context of foreign assistance, the form and distribution of food aid. The food subsidy problem is a particular instance of why Fund/Bank policies and advice need to be effectively coordinated with the work and experience of specialized agencies.

As regards conditions designed to invigorate the market mechanism and the role of private enterprise, here again, there is need for a case-by-case approach, and for realism on both sides. Standardized solutions cannot apply, particularly given the diversity of situations. There is no doubt, however, that on the one hand, the "social role" of state enterprises is often used as a cloak for privilege and inefficiency, and on the other, that "privatization" is more difficult to achieve than is made out by the vigorous advocates of the free-market mechanism.

Consultative Groups and Periodic Reassessment

There is already in existence the institutional machinery for a more effective coordination of aid, for the harmonization of long-term and short-term measures, and for the blending of technical and financial assistance. The World Bank consultative groups could form the nucleus of more wide-ranging discussions which would gain considerably in effectiveness if they also included the specialized agencies. They could thus give the human dimension the attention it deserves. The Secretary-General of the United Nations and the Administrator of the United Nations Development Programme could assist in the wider coordination of efforts and in periodic assessments. It is encouraging that this is already the case for Africa.

Mobilizing Private Capital

The need for a more effective and coherent structure of aid, where short-term and long-term considerations dovetail, becomes particularly apparent if advantage is also to be taken of private capital in the process of development.

In recent years, the role of private capital in this process has been under considerable attack. Anyone familiar with international capital markets has seen credits sold to countries already declared over-exposed by the World Bank or the International Monetary Fund — and this for purposes which were of relatively low priority. There has also been vigorous promotion, favored partly by generous export credits and often granted in conjunction with foreign aid, pressed for by export lobbies and trade unions in developed countries other-wise threatened by unemployment. Similarly, where legislation did not act as an effective barrier, currency fluctuations have been ex-acerbated by capital movements from multinationals. It is true that private capital has to live by its own rule of profitability, and that it behooves individual recipient governments to form and impose their own priorities. It is also true, however, that if the responsibility for bad credit or bad projects were laid equally where it belonged, the world would be in a worse crisis than that in which it finds itself today. Enterprise and capital in many of the developed coun-tries would also be severely hit if it were not for dramatic rescue operations carried out under government and international auspices.

It is, of course, inevitable that after the major crisis of the 1980s, private capital will become not simply cautious, but more timorous in its lending to developing countries. In a situation in whch inter-national financial agencies will have increasing difficulty in obtaining new funds, and considering the need for more purposeful lending, which would also be a key safeguard for private capital, we welcome the new trend towards more *flexible cofinancing systems* adopted by the World Bank in particular as an advance on the parallel financing arrangements of the past. Cofinancing arrangements involving public and private banks would in effect also allow a greater allocation of funds for infrastructure purposes and give considerable comfort to the commercial community.

Similarly, some improvement in the attitude of both multi-nationals and the host governments can be expected with the elab-oration of a new code of conduct for transnational corporations. Some of the adverse effects of the behavior of transnationals in the recent crisis have been noted above. On the other hand, they can play an important part as suppliers of capital and equity and also, as experience has shown, of valuable training and technology, provided they can integrate themselves into the national context in which they operate.

Coordination, the tie-up between international, bilateral and private aid, and the more effective use of transnational enterprise will all depend on the extent to which the world economy resumes its "international" course and departs from the present tendency toward increased fragmentation. The absence of an effective dialogue between donors and recipients has already manifested itself in the tragic paradox of aid being programmed but only partially allocated in Africa, the continent where it is most needed. A resumption, indeed an acceleration, of economic growth is the only lasting solution. It would have a series of collateral economic consequences – an improvement in the terms of trade, an easing of credit conditions, greater investment capcity on the part of multinationals – all of which would make for more tolerable conditions and greater mutual comprehension.

The immediate problem is the protection of minimum standards of human welfare, weakened by the outflow of resources to pay for past capital inflows which have done little to secure long-term growth and economic stability. In the long run, the settlement of the debt problem must depend on adjustments, not only at the level of recipients, but also at that of donors, who need to take a wide range of measures at the national and international levels if basic values over wide areas of the world are to be preserved.

Notes

1.   Goh Keng Swee, "Public Administration and Economic Development in LDCs" (4th Harry G. Johnson Memorial Lecture delivered to the Royal Society, London, 28 July 1983).

2.   [See chapter 3 of this volume. – Ed.]

PART III

INDIVIDUAL COUNTRY EXPERIENCE

CHAPTER 9

Education and Human Development:
The Turkish Case

Ihsan Dogramaci

Human resource development — the creation of adequate and qualified manpower in the professions and trades — is a prime challenge for all countries. But it is more than a technical challenge, since in its full reach it encompasses the prospects of freedom, dignity, and welfare — all the elements of social well-being, and all the ingredients of democracy.

Because man is the building block of society and is both the means and the end in the building of a nation's culture and economy, the sum of his knowledge and skills is of overarching importance. Health is, of course, central also, as are public governance and equity before the law. But no country can have acceptable standards of health, or provide its citizens with justice and good government, in the absence of education — education in the broadest sense.

As a country moves forward in the development of its human resources, it must steadily reshape the values and attitudes of its citizens. From this reshaping, it must build new institutions and replace or reinvigorate any traditional structures which might retard progress.

It is a traditional, and mistaken, belief in industrializing countries that one may adopt part of the mechanical and material aspects of western civilization without at the same time making any change in the old social institutions of the country. This notion is a misguided starting point on the road to healthy economic and social development. As Toynbee points out, economic development inevitably requires changes in other social institutions, replacing the old with the new. Adam Smith, the great representative of classical economics, also emphasizes the importance of the close correlation between education and economy. In his view, education and culture are not only the foundation of an efficient state system, but also the elements upon which the state is based in economic matters and development. In this respect, it may be said that for developing countries, the role of education in development and modernization is much greater than in the industrialized countries.

There is a close connection between the development of a country and the personal and social development of its people. Crucially important in speeding up economic development are the new value judgments brought about through education and the will to develop.

According to G.U. Papy, professor at the University of Rome, the following points regarding the vital modernizing roles of education and human development are of particular importance.

    a) People adjust themselves more easily to modern discoveries and innovations.

    b) More areas of work and employment opportunities are created.

    c) Production techniques are better integrated and more efficiently used.

    d) Innovations and inventions are put to use without delay.

    e) The efficiency and the enterprising ability of the domestic work force are enhanced, benefits which are transmitted to international transactions as well.

    f) The possibility of policymakers taking dangerous and wrong technical, economic and political decisions is reduced.

Theodore Schultz, a leading figure in educational economics, states that money invested in education results in huge increases in production, which in turn contribute to human development. In other words, every dollar spent on the education of individuals causes a greater increase in national income than a dollar spent on such economic investments as railways, dams or heavy industry.

Demographic Considerations

Turkey's rapidly increasing population doubles every 33 years. A high birth rate (2.1 per cent) is the main reason. Another reason is the successful prevention of infectious diseases and nutritional disorders, and the resultant fall in infant mortality.

The Turkish population is fairly young, the 0-25 age group constituting 58.7 per cent. This youthful population may be considered an asset, for it is possible to train such a large group, which has not yet hardened into shape under various influences and which is still intellectually and morally flexible, to serve the higher interests of the country.

Ataturk and Education

In July 1921, during the Sakarya battles, when the nation was still struggling for survival, Mustafa Kemal, the commander-in-chief, summoned and participated in person in a congress of education. This gesture was deeply significant of the importance he attached to the issue education in the midst of the multi-faceted fight of the nation for its survival. In his opening speech to the education congress made on July 15, 1921, Ataturk said that despite war and the necessity of using all material resources to drive out the enemy, the foundations of a national education must be laid soon, and a program of all the work to be done in this respect must be prepared. He spoke about the damage done by the methods of education employed up to that date. In the days when the war was not yet officially over, Ataturk was touring Anatolia and saying to the people in the provinces:

> Friends!... From now on we shall attain very important victories. However, they will not be the victories of the bayonet, but those of learning and culture. The victories so far gained by our army cannot be regarded as having brought real freedom to our country. They have only prepared a valuable ground for our future victory. Let us not be proud of our military victories, but get ready for new scientific and economic victories.

Ataturk's concern for education was reinforced after the War of Independence. Soon after the war, in answer to a question asking what he would have liked to be if he had not been head of state, he said promptly, "minister of education". He set out the fundamentals of the educational policy to be followed by the new state and supervised reforms made in keeping with these principles. He had laws prepared based on these principles, and he followed their implementation closely. Ataturk often emphasized the point that the economic development of a country was as important as its cultural and social development, and they were closely interdependent. In the opening speech to the Turkish Economic Congress, which he convened in Izmir on February 17, 1923, he said:

> All the principles and programs of our new state, our new government, must be derived from the economic program... We must train and educate our children ... we must furnish them with such learning and knowledge that they may be active in the world of commerce and agriculture. Our educational program must be arranged in a way to ensure this.

Secularization in Education

Until the time of the republic, education was largely carried out in *medreses* and in local schools, where it was based entirely on a religious structure. During the reform years of the Ottoman Empire, no one dared to make any change in the *medreses* and religious elementary schools. The fact that schools based on religious structures continued to be established along with the new schools which were set up from the time of the 1839 reforms created a duality in educational life. As a result of this difference in education, two separate, and often conflicating, generations were brought up. This duality in the educational system inevitably continued in the minds of the people as well. In 1924 a law ensured uniformity in education, thus putting an end to this duality.

One of the outcomes of secularization was the equality of man and woman in education. In this connection Ataturk said the following in Kastamonu on August 30, 1925:

> A community, a nation, is made up of two sexes of humans: man and woman. Is it by any means possible to make a whole develop by having only one part of it develop and leaving the other part behind? Could we have half of a body of people tied by chains to the earth, and make the other rise to the sky? There is no doubt progress must be taken, as I have said, in unison and companionship by both sexes and the obstacles in the way of progress and reformations must be overcome together. It is only then that reforms can succeed.

Literacy Campaign

In the late 1920s, the rate of literacy was not more than 6 per cent. Ataturk had realized the significant relationship between literacy and development. One of his radical reforms was to replace the old Turkish script based on the Arabic alphabet with the Latin alphabet as a first step in his literacy campaign. Formerly, it had been difficult for a student to learn reading and writing even after studying Arabic in the local school and *medrese* for years. Turkish being a member of the Altaic language family, which also includes Finnish and Hungarian, is not structurally related to Arabic, although it borrows many words and phrases from the latter. Indeed, there are more than ten vowels in the Turkish language, whereas there are practically none in Arabic.

Today, we know better than ever before that in those countries where the literacy rate is high, the annual national income is also high. Furthermore, in a country where the literacy rate is low and where population increases rapidly, high infant mortality rates are typical. While life expectancy in countries where the literacy rate is low ranges between 50 and 60 years, life expectancy exceeds 70 years in countries with high literacy rates.

In Turkey, while the literacy rate was extremely low in the 1920s, as mentioned earlier, this rate reached 67.2 per cent in 1980. However, due to the rapid increase in population, a new literacy campaign had to be launched in 1981, and it was decided to keep it up through permanent measures. The results have been gratifying, leading to literacy rates of 72.2 per cent in 1982 and slightly over 83 per cent in 1985.

Among other aims of the literacy campaign is the goal of turning literacy into a useful tool in everyday life and in business and to eliminate ignorance for the purpose of achieving the national development objectives, including industrialization and modernization in agriculture, in order to ensure the conscious participation of the people in the process of democracy. Emphasis falls on the importance of better qualified manpower in national development. Undoubtedly, a new dimension has been added through the literacy campaign to the continuing efforts toward the development of the qualifications of the human element in this country.

Reforms in Higher Education

Ataturk patiently waited ten years for the university to renew itself. In November 1922, when he was awarded the title of honorary professor by the Faculty of Letters of Istanbul University, he sent a cable to the university saying, "I am sure it will be your faculty which will help complete the process of our national independence in future."

It was obvious that the university needed substantial reform. However, many of the professors were against this idea and resisted all attempts toward a reform movement. Those anxious to keep their places were particularly against any radical measures. On the other hand, another group of professors was aware of the shortcomings and defects of the existing state of the university. It was this group which anticipated a reform and which was ready to join the efforts for the realization of it.

Finally, in 1933, ten years after the establishment of the republic, Ataturk was ready to bring about radical higher education reform by establishing a new institute for advanced studies in agriculture in Ankara and reorganizing the university in Istanbul. He utilized the services of Albert Malche, a Swiss professor, in upgrading the university education and administration systems to contemporary European standards.

Manpower Planning and Education

An important issue in the interaction between education and the economy is the prevention of unemployment and wastage through manpower planning.

While developing the manpower resources of a country, particular care must be exercised in the planning of the number and qualifications of the people to be trained in various professions, for both must be in keeping with the development requirements of the country. In countries like Turkey, it is crucial not only that the requirements be met, but also that no educated youth remain unemployed. Success in such planning, however, depends on a variety of conditions and seems often doomed to be limited. But if the trends of future manpower demands in the public and private sectors can be calculated accurately, and if a flexible system can be established to allow for a reasonable mobility between branches of the education and training programs, the right balance can be struck.

Child labor, which is the product of poverty and uneven development in many parts of the world, is another concern that merits serious attention in the discussion of manpower planning. Every effort should be made to provide the young of our species with the time to grow, to play and to learn during that period which we call childhood — to provide them from the beginning with the potential for being productive and happy adults.

One of the important events of the early 1960s in Turkey was the establishment of the State Planning Organization. Since 1963, when the plan period was first started in Turkey, it has been continuously emphasized that the most important means for the increase of qualified manpower is education. It is through education that an individual can be given sound information about what citizenship means and what the rights and duties of a citizen are so that he may safeguard and promote the national values and contribute to national unity.

During the four five-year plan periods up to 1985, it has been stressed repeatedly that education is a public service, for which a considerable part of the country's resources should be allocated. It is, therefore, essential to give priority to social and economic requirements in the designation of resources to be allotted to education. For this reason, educational planning is an important part of development planning. The following brief summary of the Fifth Five-Year Plan (1985-89) will shed some light on the current Turkish policy on education.

a) The general principle is to raise the quality at all educational levels. Priority has been given to training medium-level technical manpower. Steps have been taken for training skilled workers through extended training and in-service training, and a decision has been made to open no new higher educational institutions for subjects in which there is no shortage of supply. Importance shall also be given to training highly qualified managers and administrators through in-school and extended training.

b) Regarding higher education, measures shall be taken to enable universities to preserve their character of being the unrelenting seekers of truth, the protectors of cultural heritage and the guarantors of national unity, breeding and fostering future leaders for society. Universities shall be encouraged to cooperate with the private sector in their research activities. Community leaders shall be oriented, trained and educated to use the results of research relevant to their activities.

c) The Higher Education Council established by law no. 2547 has set out its targets and principles in accordance with the plan. At present, the target of 365,000 students which was planned for the year 1984-85 has been surpassed, and the number has already reached 398,000. It is estimated that in 1989, too, the target number of 526,000 will be reached. Steps shall be taken to keep the quality of education from falling, and even to raise it, while raising the quantity of students.

d) The highest proportion of the national budget shall continue to be set for education, with the possible exception of defense. Of the sum allotted to education, over a quarter shall be designated to higher education.

1981 Reform in Higher Education

It is hardly necessary to recall the events which shook Turkey during the 1970s, when the country was engulfed in turmoil that carried it to the very brink of civil war. The universities not only lagged behind the planned targets in contributing to national development, but also became very much involved in that turmoil, and the flaws inherent in the university system as it existed at that time became particularly apparent during that period of tension. Universities became highly politicized microcosms of the unrest in the country as a whole. University students and even teaching staff members sided with the various factions. Campuses became armed camps and, in some cases, training grounds for guerrilla fighters. Actual battles occurred on more than one occasion in the period between 1968 and 1971, with the police powerless to intervene because of "university autonomy."

University administrations themselves were be no means immune to this antagonistic and highly charged atmosphere. According to the interpretation of autonomy at that time, the university rector and the faculty deans were elected for set terms by the teaching staff. There was no government appointee such as the Kuratel in certain Swiss universities, or the Kanzler as in some other European countries, nor was there any outside governing body such as a court or council or university grants committee as in the British system, nor a board of governors, trustees or regents as in the American universities.

Elections on many occasions became politicized and could take weeks of continuous balloting. In one case, at Ege University in Izmir, balloting took six months, day in and day out, before a candidate for the office of rector could obtain a majority. Not infrequently, deans and rectors were elected by rival groups, so there was little possibility of cooperation between them. Anything even remotely resembling the educational process had come to a complete halt.

The situation of the 1970s was, fortunately, exceptional. But even in the absence of such dire circumstances, the system as it then stood was not serving the needs of the country, as we shall see.

Prior to 1981, the university's responsiveness to the community depended on the vision of far-sighted administrators rather than on any established mechanism. Moreover, the absence of coordination among institution of higher learning made it virtually impossible for national priorities to be addressed in any coherent fashion. Thus, while population pressures made expanded admissions policies imperative, the number of students admitted actually declined. From 1975 to 1980, the number of applicants to the universities rose from roughly 50,000 to 190,000, while admissions dropped from roughly 50,000 to 42,000, even though the number of universities had increased from 8 to 18 during the years 1967 to 1975. In a similar vein, whereas the Turkish State Planning Organization and the Ministry of Health and Social Affairs had estimated that an average of 5,000 physicians should graduate annually in order to meet the needs of the population, and despite the fact that the number of medical schools had doubled from 7 to 14 over the preceding decade, the level of admissions did not significantly increase, but remained in the neighborhood of 2,400.

It is true that a shortage of teaching staff made an expanded admissions policy difficult, but this dearth was in turn the result of the system as it existed. Indeed, university regulations at that time made it extremely difficult for the younger generation to embark upon academic careers. Regardless of a candidate's qualifications and abilities, it was necessary to wait a minimum of four years following the doctorate to be eligible to enter a series of examinations, taking a minimum of nine months, leading to the "docentship certificate." Only then did the candidate have the right even to apply for a position. Compounding the barriers presented by these regulations, the universities were often closed shops, with the teaching staff being promoted from within and little opportunity for outside applicants. Once admitted, however, teaching staff members were often promoted on the basis of seniority in what amounted to a system of near-automatic tenure. Indeed, anyone who failed to be promoted to full professorship after five or six years considered his career to be in jeopardy. This could, and often did, lead to top-heavy situations, particularly in the older schools, where it was not unusual for senior professors to outnumber by far the docents, a teaching category comparable to senior lecturers or associate professors.

The arduous procedures required for university appointment and promotion policies of the various universities exacerbated the geographic imbalance in the universities, one of the most serious consequences of the system. As far back as 1937, Ataturk had stressed the need to establish institutions of higher learning throughout the country, including central and eastern Anatolia. In line with this, new universities began to be established, and by 1975 their number had grown to 18, including 11 in small towns around the country. But while these were encouraged to play an active role in the development of their respective regions, their effectiveness was severely limited by the lack of teachers. In the absence of a higher coordinating body such as a board of governors or trustees, there was no mechanism or incentive to encourage young academics to apply for positions in the provincial universities. Consequently, they suffered from intolerable shortages of staff, while there was a surplus of professors in the more established universities, to the point that there were not enough courses to go around, and some professors actually had no teaching load at all. To give some idea of the problem, in November 1981, just before the passage of the higher education reform law, the senior teaching staff in they universities in Ankara, Istanbul and Izmir numbered 3,156, compared to a mere 85 in the nine least-staffed universities in other cities of Anatolia. Similarly, the teaching staff in 5 medical faculties in these larger cities numbered 1,028, compared to only 36 in the 5 least-staffed medical schools in outlying regions. Teaching in the latter institutions was carried out by so-called "traveling instructors" who delivered their lectures and returned immediately to their own cities, making them totally inaccessible to students in need of explanations outside the classroom.

Clearly, something had to be done to make the universities more responsive to the needs of the people and to make the various parts of the system work in harmony with the whole so as to fulfill their mission more efficiently. The nonaccountability of the universities to any higher body was all the more remarkable when one considers that they were, without exception, wholly financed by the state. It should be added that failure to take into account national goals is particularly serious in a country like Turkey, which, for all the characteristics it shares with the West, is still a developing country with limited resources that must be allocated with great care.

As is known, after 1933, Istanbul University lived a golden age for twelve years, because the new reform had brought a new system and new facilities and resources. From 1946 onwards, after the changes made in the university law, the rectors' administrative and supervisory authority was reduced, and decisions began to be made by committees or boards made up of university teaching members.

The deans and rectors were elected by different bodies, and the rector had no authority over the election of deans and directors of schools.

The years of unrest, starting in the late 1960s and reaching their peak in the 1970s, affected the universities a great deal, disrupting education and training and paralyzing some universities. The military intervention of September 12, 1980 brought the country back from the brink of a precipice and reestablished security. Priority was given in this period to radical reform in higher education, and it was realized without delay.

The objectives and innovations of the higher education reform law of November 1981 have been parallel to, and a continuation of, the reform of 1933 made by Ataturk. Higher educational institutions are spread all over the country; an academic hierarchy has been established; academic staff shortages have largely been eliminated; the number and quality of research projects have gone up; and the rate of success in education has remarkably increased.

The 1981 reform essentially created two national bodies to oversee the system: the Inter-University Board and the Council of Higher Education, generally known as YOK. The Inter-University Board, composed of all university rectors and one professor from each university elected by the respective senates, is charged mainly with setting academic standards and degree requirements.

By Articles 130 and 131 of the Constitution of Turkey, the Council of Higher Education is set up as an integral part of the higher education system, with two-thirds of its membership drawn from academics. As an autonomous body, it does not come under any ministry or any other governmental or nongovernmental agency. Provisions of the Constitution guarantee freedom of teaching and research and forbid dismissal, even temporarily, in any form, of any member of a teaching staff by any outside body or authority. The Council is thus an autonomous national board of trustees with the prerogative of drafting budgetary allocations to universities within the context of a national plan of higher education. In this, it has something in common with the university grants committees in some countries.

One of the principal aims of the new law is to set minimum levels of teaching standards and of credit and degree requirements, none of which had existed previously. It also seeks, through the directives of the council, to resolve certain gross disparities between the universities and to establish "centers of excellence." In the past, the length of the academic year could vary from as few as twenty weeks in some universities to more than forty weeks in others. Such disparities have been eliminated. The new law makes student attendance compulsory and limits the number of times that students can repeat a course or re-sit examinations so as to put an end to the situation whereby chronic students occupied coveted, but limited, places at the universities.

Thanks to this expansion of facilities and teaching staff, Turkey has finally been able to respond to the pressures for increasing university enrollments resulting from its growing population. The number of young people of university age in Turkey has risen by over one million in the past decade to reach a total of over 4.5 million. Since the passage of the reform law, admissions to the universities — which had remained virtually static in previous years due to the lack of facilities — have more than doubled, from 42,000 to 90,000 full-time students. In order to accommodate young people who are employed and unable to devote their full time to their education, an Open University Department was established at Anadolu University in Eskisehir three years ago. Lectures are televised, and reading materials and references are mailed to the registered students, who meet with instructors and take periodic examinations at centers set up in the regions serviced by the university. Over 100,000 students are now registered in the program.

One of the most extraordinary results of the new law is the remarkable improvement of the situation in the provincial universities, the correction of the geographic imbalance in the numbers of teaching staff being the result of a variety of incentives enacted to encourage those seeking advancement within the system to take teaching assignments in outlying areas. For instance, docents cannot be promoted to full professorship in their own universities. Holders of doctorates may receive immediate appointment as teaching staff members in another university, while such an appointment in the same university requires a three-year waiting period. In the older, overstaffed universities, teachers who had achieved tenure prior to the reform have been allowed to retain their positions until retirement, provided they serve a maximum total of four semesters in another university requiring staff in their respective fields. This obligation was not welcomed by a number of professors, who resigned on the pretext that "university autonomy has come to an end." On the other hand, the large majority complied with the new regulations and helped the developing departments.

Another provision of the new law is the establishment of post-graduate institutes with formalized admission procedures, regular courses and set degree requirements. Enrollments now total about 20,000, of which about one-quarter have already started work on their doctorates and the remainder are studying for their master's degrees.

We can also take pride in the strengthening ties between the university and the community since the enactment of the new law. The university can now make its equipment, infrastructure and human resources available to the community — an arrangement beneficial to both parties, since the community receives services at a lower cost than it would find elsewhere, and the university earns revenues for its "revolving fund." Certain work off-campus in public and private enterprises by full-time academic staff may be considered time spent at the university. At the same time, academics have become more aware of community problems.

In the three and a half years since the law went into effect, the number of universities in Turkey had increased from 18 to 19 in 1978 and to 27 by 1982: 4 in Ankara, 6 in Istanbul, 2 in Izmir and the remaining 15 distributed in various towns throughout the country. In addition, this year the first private university has been chartered, which will admit students beginning in the academic year 1986-1987. Teaching facilities have expanded enormously, largely due to the removal of many of the previously mentioned obstacles to entering the academic profession. Holders of doctorates may now apply for teaching positions without the four-year waiting period, and research assistantships are now available to qualified doctoral candidates. This easing of regulations has not resulted in any drop of quality in the faculty; the number of publications during the last academic year is more than double what it was three years ago. As to the actual figures, in the 9 universities where understaffing had previously been the most severe, the total number of teaching staff members has increased eightfold in three years, from 85 to 697. The teaching staff for the most understaffed medical schools also increased eightfold over the same period, from 36 to 280.

Vocational Training

In Turkey, vocational and technical education has a comparatively long record and had begun to be institutionalized in the latter half of the nineteenth century with the advent of industrial training schools. During the republic era, vocational and technical education was reformed with a new outlook, and the educational institutions in this field, mainly under the Ministry of Education or attached to other relevant ministries, have undergone an evolutionary change.

Turkey, at the present stage of its economic, social and cultural development, in view of its skilled manpower needs in every field, feels it necessary to attach a greater importance to the development of vocational and technical education than ever before. Postsecondary technical vocational schools have now been reorganized in a comprehensive system under the umbrella of the universities. The aims characteristic of these new vocational schools include the training of skilled manpower to meet the needs of industrial life and also securing a new pattern in technical and vocational education so that they keep pace with the innovations of technology and are better matched with economic and social requirements.

Generally speaking, vocational schools giving two years of short-cycle higher education are intended to cover a gigantic need felt in industry for intermediate-level manpower that represents a need as great as that for university graduates and for those with postgraduate degrees. As some students have to start earning their living as soon as possible for economic reasons, short-cycle, two-year higher education provides them with an educational opportunity suited to their modest means. Short-cycle higher education graduates capable and wishing to continue their studies are not denied access and transfer to the four-year university education. Their right to vertical mobility is recognized under certain conditions of merit and achievement.

Actually, in a country with such a rapidly increasing population as Turkey, every year an increasing number of students apply for enrollment, and the high number of university clientele can cause the quality of education to deteriorate. The short-cycle, two-year educational institutions relieve the pressure of numbers on four-year universities, alleviating the heavy burden on academic education and eventually improving university standards while opening up new horizons for those who have failed to complete their four-year higher education. At present, the total number of Turkish higher vocational schools has reached 56. Thanks to a loan and technical assistance from the World Bank, the Council of Higher Education is currently reorganizing the program of these schools.

Conclusion

The development of human resources in Turkey in the course of the last four decades has taken on greater and more diversified dimensions than was orginally contemplated. The growth of the population, together with the furthering of industrialization, urban development and foreign trade, have all created a suitable climate for a growing desire on the part of the people for higher standards of living. Public and private efforts to extend and enhance educational instituitions and facilities have taken on greater importance. With the demand for education in general, the demand for scientific, technical, professional and vocational education has also risen, and the growth of institutional development commensurate with these needs has followed. Expansion and development of institutions of higher learning have spread throughout the country. From a single university in Istanbul in 1933, there are now some 27 state universities and one private university, with at least one university in most of the major provinces.

This quantitative growth has paved the way for a policy to improve the standards and quality of higher education, with special emphasis on the planning, coordination, coherence and evaluation of universities at a national level. Yet no attempt has been made to achieve uniformity. On the contrary, diversity is welcomed, and each school enjoys a large measure of autonomy. The 1981 education reform law is a cogent response to this urgent need for planning, coordination and coherence.

Within the framework of the same law, the development of scientific research, with particular reference to applied research, takes pride of place. Financial and budgetary requirements for the implementation of a very extensive program have been provided. This will be a significant feature of the current reform, leading to a closer cooperation between universities and private enterprise conducive to industrial and technological progress. Such a cooperative relationship between the business community and the institutions of higher education is most beneficial to the technological progress of industry, as well as to technological teaching, since it will now draw on the accumulated experience of industry.

It is a commonplace that the rapid development of Turkey, and especially its competitiveness in world markets for the production of durable goods, hinges heavily upon the reorganization of our industrial facilities in line with the most up-to-date technology, and its speedy transfer and efficient use in all fields of the production of goods and services. That this deficiency cannot be remedied unless manpower, adequate in number and quality, is trained in all fields of the industrial and service sectors is openly admitted.

This new trend is the harbinger of a new era. With their new laws and regulations, institutions of higher education, including post-secondary vocational schools, have now blended their diversified extension and enrichment with the necessary components of planning and coherence that are vital for their overriding aims and purposes of maximizing their potential contributions to the democratic and free development and welfare of the Turkish nation as a whole.

References

1. R.M. Avakov et al., *The Third World and Scientific and Technical Progress* (Moscow: Nauka Publishing House, 1976).

2. Kemal Aytac, ed., *Ataturk's Speeches on Educational Policy* [in Turkish] (Ankara University Press, 1984).

3. Ihsan Dogramaci, *Ataturk and Education* (Ankara: Council of Turkish History, May 1985).

4. Ihsan Dogramaci, *Child Labor: A Threat to Health and Development* (Geneva: Defence for Children, 1981).

5. Ihsan Dogramaci, *Health of Mankind* (London: Churchill, 1967).

6. Ihsan Dogramaci, *The Higher Education Reform in Turkey: Results After Three Years* (Ankara, 1985).

7. Ihsan Dogramaci, *Urgent Need for Reform in Higher Education in Turkey* (Istanbul: Bosphorus University, June 1980).

8. Ari Inan, *Ataturk and his Ideas* [in Turkish] (Ankara: Council of Turkish History, 1983).

9. Y.K. Kaya, *Human Development in Turkey: Politics, Education, Development* [in Turkish] (Ankara: Hacettepe University, 1981).

10. G.U. Papy, *General Problems of the Economics of Education* (London: Macmillan, 1966).

11. T.W. Schultz, "Investment in Human Capital," *American Economic Review*, (March 1981).

12. Adam Smith, *The Wealth of Nations* (New York: Modern Library Inc., 1937).

13. Eugene Staley, *The Future of Underdeveloped Countries* (New York: F.A. Praeger, 1961).

14. Turkish Ministry of Education, *Literacy Campaign Activities* [in Turkish] (Ankara, 1983).

15. Turkish State Planning Organization, *Fifth Five-Year Development Plan: 1985-89* (Ankara, 1985).

16. Turkish State Planning Organization, *Report on Education Sector* (Ankara, 1982).

17. A.J. Toynbee, *A Study of History* (New York: Oxford University Press, 1961).

18. C.E.A. Winslow, *The Cost of Sickness and the Price of Health* (Geneva: World Health Organization Monograph Series No. 7, 1951).

CHAPTER 10

Reinterpreting the Historical Development of Basic Education in Korea

Choo Hakchung

Rapid economic transformation and socioeconomic development in Korea since the early 1960s are primarily attributable to the human element. The most often-cited characteristics of Korea's people are their relatively high levels of education, motivation, trainability and ability to work together.[1] Of these characteristics, the relatively high educational level of people has been the most important. It is chiefly through the educational process, particularly basic education as a first step,[2] that the other characteristics and properties are able to be attained and cultivated.

A prerequisite to the development of such desirable human resources, so vital to socioeconomic development and modernization, is an educational system emphasizing basic education. For Korea, it is safe to say that the foundations of this basic educational system were in place even before the early years of this century, when one considers the lead time that would otherwise have been necessary to produce the working population of the generations of the 1960s and thereafter.

The prevailing view holds that the development of basic education in Korea began with its annexation to Japan. This view stems from two interrelated assumptions. First, a larger number of academicians, both native and foreign, expound the belief that educational development in the modern sense, patterned after Japan's, was instituted by the ruling colonial government of Korea. Second, the same group overlooks the importance and role of the traditional, indigenous educational institutions know as *Seodangs* in that development.

The purpose of this paper is to reexamine the conventional views on the growth of basic education under colonial rule. It will argue that the historically deep-rooted, traditional and indigenous *Seodang* played a vital role in the development of basic education in the early years of this century. Two hypotheses will be presented: the process of sui generis, and the use of a basic needs approach.

The testing of a hypothesis emerging out of historical experience often encounters a number of serious constraints, due especially to a lack of adequate data and records on such an informal institution as the *Seodang* under colonial rule. An effort will be made in this presentation to interpret fragmented evidence carefully in support of the hypotheses presented.

Development of Basic Education and the Role of Seodang

Explosion of Elementary Education: Facts from Figures

In this century, Korea has witnessed two quantitative explosions in education. The first was in primary education following the annexation of Korea to Japan in 1910; the second was in higher education after the liberation in 1945. The first quantitative explosion of 1910 has been erroneously credited to some benevolent features of Japanese colonial rule. This was widely publicized by the colonial government of Japan. From 1910 to 1935, the number of students enrolled in primary (normal) schools increased thirty-seven-fold, far surpassing the increases in any other socioeconomic indicators during that period, including population, production and trade volume.

If such a quantitative increase is taken at face value, it is indeed a remarkable achievement by any colonial government. However, before one draws general conclusions from these oversimplified figures, one must question their magnitude in the initial year, and the changes in educational systems and policies affecting enrollment in subsequent years.

In the early years of colonial rule, tens of thousands of traditional *Seodangs* were allowed to exist without being integrated into the new system and without much regulatory action by the Japanese government. They provided basic education to a majority of school-age children. However, in quantitatively documenting the development of primary education, formal educational figures of the initial year excluded students enrolled in *Seodangs,* except for a handful of new primary schools established by the Yi Dynasty on an experimental basis during the turn of the century.

The exclusion of *Seodang* enrollment figures from the official records might be overlooked if they were an insignificant number, representing an informal educational sector. But this is clearly not the case. Careful study reveals that the foreign ruling government concealed the educational realites existing in Korea through a calculated and deliberate effort. Table 1 shows that about 141,000 students were enrolled in *Seodangs* in 1912 (the earliest year for which official published statistics are available). This was more than three times the number of primary (normal) school enrollments for that year. Enrollment in *Seodangs* continued to increase. Until 1922 they enrolled more students than the formal sector in elementary education, despite regulatory measures imposed on them in 1918.

TABLE 1
Reported Numbers and Enrollments in *Seodangs*, 1912-42

Year	Reported *Seodangs*			Number of Normal School Enrollments
	Number	Teachers	Students	
1912	16,540	16,771	141,604	44,639
1915	21,358	21,570	204,161	63,854
1920	24,030	24,185	275,920	107,201
1925	18,510	19,101	231,754	407,292
1930	11,469	11,908	162,247	489,934
1935	6,843	7,408	153,634	714,209
1940	4,686	5,245	164,507	1,331,785
1942	3,504	4,097	150,184	1,694,820

SOURCE: Office of the Chosun Govenor-General's *Statistical Yearbook* for the respective years.

In deducing facts from figures, two things must be kept in mind. First, the figures on *Seodangs* contain unknown degrees of downward bias. In resistance to Japanese rule, the founders and teachers of *Seodangs* often did not report their *Seodangs* until 1918, when reporting was made compulsory. Consequently, there were omissions and underreportings in the statistics on Seodangs, while the figures for normal school enrollment, being administratively recorded, were more reliable.

Second, the compared enrollment figures are cumulative. Although there is no evidence of a standard curricular program followed by *Seodangs*, on the average, *Seodang* programs were shorter in years than those of normal schools. Accordingly, enrollment figures for *Seodangs* need to take into consideration omissions and underreportings in the statistics and allow for the differences in school terms for an accurate comparison.

Changes in Colonial Policies on Seodangs

The growth and decline of *Seodangs* as an informal educational institution under colonial rule cannot be completely understood without considering colonial policy changes on education during this period. Therefore, it is necessary to examine briefly the educational policies of the colonial government over a period of thirty-six years.[3]

Educational policies from 1910 to 1922 may be characterized as regulatory, enforcing the decree on education enacted with the annexation of Korea. Being alarmed by some 2,000 authorizations to establish private schools given by the short-lived Imperial Government of Korea in 1910, the colonial government restricted the establishment of Korean private schools by placing priority on the creation of a new public system modeled after the Japanese system. However, it was not until 1918, when the colonial government drew up an eight-year plan to establish one public normal school per three *myuns* and one normal high school per province, that regulatory measures extended to *Seodangs* became more extensive. Curricular contents were supervised; there was a Japanese language requirement; the right to close them down was reserved. Such measures were not enforced in earlier years. Vocational education and training were also emphasized by promoting vocational extension schools to fully exploit the Korean potential.

After the Korean independence movement in 1919, colonial policies shifted from a strict reactionary mood to a moderate expansionism from 1922 to 1938. However, the indigenous *Seodangs* were placed under tighter surveillance and control, especially by reserving the right of the provincial governor in 1929 to shut them down.

In the late 1920s, gaining entry into primary school became a social crisis for Koreans, since the enrollment rate was only about 20 per cent. The colonial government promoted one-teacher, one-classroom, two-year rural extension schools in 1931 and expanded them rapidly after 1936. Another eight-year plan to establish one public normal school per *myun* was also launched in 1927, but completion was delayed until 1936 because of a lack of resource allocation.

In the remaining years of colonial rule, from 1938 to 1945, educational policies, like everything else, turned to a wartime "Japanization." It was during this period that many private schools at all levels were closed down, even those which survived the drastic reform beginning in 1932 to "convert" private elementary educational schools, including *Seodangs*, into public schools.[4]

In the light of major educational policy changes, it is understandable that a rapid decline in student enrollment in *Seodangs* began in the mid-1920s. However, it is worth noting that the average enrollment in *Seodangs* increased significantly by the late 1930s, despite suppression. *Seodangs* continued to function in significant numbers, particularly in remote rural areas, where 3,000 *Seodangs* enrolled over 150,000 students even as late as 1942.

The Seodang as a Basic Educational Institution

From the preceding, it is evident that the *Seodangs*, although classified as an informal sector, constituted a major half of the dual structure of basic and elementary education under colonial rule. However, there still remains a question of whether or not *Seodangs* were appropriate as basic educational institutions in teaching such fundamental skills as writing, reading and mathematics. In order to evaluate this, we will briefly examine how *Seodangs* were established and financed, what curricular programs were followed, what textbooks were used and how *Seodangs* were evaluated by educational experts.

Historically, a *Seodang* was established in one of four ways. In one process, a learned person initiated the establishment of a *Seodang* in a village in pursuit of his own interests. Tuition was often paid in kind as well as in cash. In another process, a well-to-do person, agreeing to bear the costs, would invite a teacher to educate his children and those of his relatives and friends. The founder often set aside endowed properties for a *Seodang*, which defrayed the costs of education. In a third process, a group of concerned villagers formed a *hak-gye*[5] and invited a teacher to educate their children and others. In a fourth process, a village took collective action to establish a *Seodang* by sharing the costs of education among the residents. It is important to note, from the ways in which a *Seodang* was established, that such institutions were created by private initiative and popular participation, without relying on the government and its support.

What is more relevant in light of the purpose of this paper is whether or not the curriculum of a *Seodang* was adequate in providing basic education to its students. Traditionally, a student was expected to learn *Sohak* at the age of seven and to enter *Daehak* at the age of fourteen.[6] Prerequisites for *Sohak* included the mastery of *Chunjamun* (1,000 characters), *Dongmong-seonsub* and *Tonggam.* These prerequisites alone were sufficient to allay any fears about student literacy. Furthermore, under the 1918 regulations on *Seodangs,* arithmetic and Japanese were added as required courses in the curriculum.

In evaluating the *Seodang* as an educational institution, two diverging views must be considered. First, there are negative views advanced by a majority of Japanese scholars, who characterize the *Seodang* as an extremely outdated and tradition-bound institution, narrowly confined to the teachings of Confucianism and lacking relevance to daily life.[7] In addition, they point out the heavy dependence on the ability of one teacher, and the consequent lack of continuity as an institution.

The positive views, on the other hand, take the given conditions at the time into consideration and acknowledge the *Seodang's* evident contribution.[8] Dr. Helen Kim, a pioneer in Korea's higher education for women, points out that, given the socioeconomic and cultural conditions existing then, *Seodangs* had their value in education, especially at the elementary level.[9] In fact, it was the only elementary educational institution economically and geographically accessible to the poor, particularly the rural poor, during the period when the colonial government planned to establish one elementary school per three *myuns* or per *myun.*[10]

In support of these positive views on the *Seodang*, three important aspects must be further explained. First, the majority of the Korean population was politically suppressed and economically very poor, able to afford only the relatively inexpensive and accessible *Seodang* education, as shown in table 2. Second, the *Seodang* was an institution for maintaining the identity of Korea as a race and culture, particularly among patriotic teachers who resisted colonial rule.

TABLE 2
Selected Indicators of Elementary Education In Korea, 1927

	Primary School*	Normal School†	Other School†	Seodang†
No. of teachers per 100 students	2.8	1.9	3.8	8.4
No. of students per class	45.2	54.2	32.6	12.2
Current expenditures per student	52 yen	23 yen	33 yen	8 yen

Notes: * For Japanese
       † For Korean

Finally, it is conceivable, although statistically not verifiable, that *Seodangs* served as the entry point and bridge to higher education in formal schools for many of their graduates, who would otherwise have been deprived of their educational opportunities.

Two Hypotheses on the Development of Basic Education

As already explained, the development of basic education and the educational level of Korea prior to and in the early years of Korea's annexation to Japan were already high. Historically, all primary education was provided solely through the private institutions known as *Seodangs*, while secondary and higher education were offered through limited numbers of public schools until 1910.

Basic education in the Kingdom of Chosun was so widespread that a pioneering missionary and founder of a Christian college in Korea found that nearly every Korean village, regardlesss of its size, had a school comparable in educational opportunity to those of any European country at that time. (This statement was made by the Korean ambassador to the U.S. in 1874.)[11] A leading Japanese historian notes that at the turn of this century, Korea had more of these educational institutions per unit of population than Japan before the Meiji Restoration.[12] To what, then, can one attribute such a high level of basic education and educational development? Two hypotheses, sui generis and a basic needs approach, are proposed here in an attempt to answer this question.

Value of and Motivation Toward Education: Sui Generis

The historical question as to when Koreans began to place a high value on education and learning can be best answered through the findings of further research by historians and linguists. Historically, there is evidence in the language that education and learning were highly regarded. A number of common Korean words and sayings indicate this strong inclination of the people. For example, *Seobang*, the Korean expression referring generally to a man, literally means a study room. *Seobang-nim*, a respectful term of address by a woman to her husband, means a dear person in a study. Both terms imply that men need to be learned. Another example is the Korean saying, "He cannot recognize the first letter of the Korean alphabet even while sitting in front of a sickle" (which looks exactly like it). If there had been many illiterates, this would not have become such a popular saying.

The Korean classics are full of references to learning and educational institutions. One of the legendary statesmen of the Yi Dynasty wrote in the early seventeenth century in his guidelines for ruling a country that a newly appointed local governor must pay his tributes to the local school on the very next day.[13] An anonymous author in the eighteenth century emphasized in his guidelines of government that each country should have a library in the mountains.[14] In later years, a forerunner of the Korean school of pragmatism asserts in his famous writings on how to promote the well-being of people that every four or five villages ought to have at least one study.[15]

This strong undercurrent of support for learning was obviously reinforced as the nation was colonized. Learning and education became an important part of the independence movement. Educational development became synonymous with survival in the early years of this century in Korea. The zeal for learning and education often went beyond sentiment and was backed by action. The kingdom proclaimed an act to establish private schools in 1908; 2,250 applications were given approval in 1910, which impelled the colonial government to pursue regulatory policies on education.

In fact, potential students far exceeded formal educational opportunities provided by the colonial government. As early as 1930, gaining entry into primary school presented a social crisis because of overcrowded classrooms. The unmet needs in basic education in these years resulted in the further expansion of *Seodangs* and other informal institutions, such as evening and training schools.

What is evident from the preceding is the fact that a high social value has historically been placed on education by the people of Korea. Although the colonial government introduced the first public primary schools, basic education in Korea had long been available through the widespread and indigenous *Seodang*.

Meeting Educational Needs: A Basic Needs Approach

No matter how high the potential demand for education may be, it needs to be socially met with appropriate educational opportunities. It was beyond the financial capabilities of the Kingdom of Chosun to meet the extensively felt educational needs of its people. In fact, as is evident from earlier discussions, all basic education was provided by the *Seodang*, a private institution, prior to Korea's annexation to Japan. Without relying on public sector support, how did the historical Korea meet basic educational needs? The answer to this question may be found in those of its features that resemble those of the basic needs approach.

First of all, the *Seodang* was an indigenous institution unique to Korea. It continued to impart basic education even after the colonial government began to introduce its own form of primary education. Consequently, even before the colonial government had provided adequate educational opportunities, a minimum need for basic education, if not more, was sufficiently and effectively met by the *Seodang*.

Furthermore, this indigenous institution had spread so widely because of popular participation and a bottom-up approach in its establishment and operation. As can be seen from table 2, this institution was not only geographically accessible, since it was located in a village, but also economically affordable by the majority of the population at a time when both poverty and low income prevailed in the country.

Except for the Chinese experience with barefoot doctors, there has been no nationwide experiment to support the feasibility of the basic needs approach as a development strategy. The historical experience of Korea in basic education through *Seodangs* certainly provides an interesting case in support of the feasibility of this approach.

Concluding Remarks

The prime mover of national development is undoubtedly the population, when they possess the desirable characteristics conducive to development and when they realize their full potential. In order to develop human resources, the provision of basic education may be the most important requirement, for other desirable factors can be acquired and cultivated through learning.

However, it must be cautioned that before basic education can be provided to a population, there has to be a gestation period of a few decades in order to form a working population. If one recognizes parental and sociocultural influences on child education and learning, the lead time has to be much longer. Unfortunately, many proponents of human resource development often overlook this important timing consideration and prescribe impatient measures, the consequences of which are often disappointing.

Indeed, Korea's economic development since the early 1960s is primarily attributable to its human factor. In view of the evidence presented here, its initial effort in human resource development has deep roots. From a historical perspective, Korea's initial development of basic education has been shown to be sui generis and to have adopted a basic needs approach. Due recognition of the contribution to basic education by traditional and indigeneous *Seodangs* may shed some light in explaining the human dimension of Korea's rapid economic growth and development since the early 1960s.

Notes

1. For examples, see Edward Mason et al., *The Economic and Social Modernization of the Republic of Korea,* (Cambridge: Harvard University Press, 1980), chapters 1 and 13, and Parves Hasan, *Korea: Problems and Issues in a Rapidly Growing Economy* (Baltimore: Johns Hopkins University Press, 1976), p. 29.

2. Basic education as referred to here means a minimum level of education sufficient to place a person beyond the threshold of illiteracy, rather than a complete program of elementary education.

3. Manabu Watanabe, *A History of Modern Education in Korea* (Tokyo: 1969), chapter 1 [in Japanese].

4. The expression used by Watanabe is "a reform directed to convert the bones by depriving the umbilical cord." Ibid., p. 77.

5. *Gye* is a traditional, informal financing scheme used in Korea. *Hak-gye* is that for financing education.

6. This was a formal requirement for entering higher level public schools under the Yi Dynasty and served as a general guideline for the *Seodang.*

7. Office of the Governor-General, *Three-Year Accomplishments In Korea* (Keijo: 1914), and Kenichi Ono, *Issues in Korean Education* (Keijo: 1936) [all in Japanese].

8. D. Tanaka, *An Overview of Education in Asia* (Tokyo: 1982), and J.S. Gale, *Korea in Transition* (Toronto: W. Briggs, 1909), p. 46.

9. Helen K. Kim, *Rural Education for the Regeneration of Korea,* unpublished doctoral disseration, Columbia University, 1931.

10. *Myun* is the administrative unit in use since colonial rule, covering an area bigger than a township, but smaller than a county.

11. H.H. Underwood, *Modern Education in Korea* (New York: International Press, 1926), p. 174.

12. According to Prof. H. Matsudaka's estimation, the number of *Seodangs* in Korea at the turn of this century is estimated to be about 30,000 for some 13 million people, as compared to the number of similar institutions in Japan, called *Terago-ya,* estimated to be about 12,000 for 30 million people before its modernization. See Watanabe, p. 541.

13. Won-Ik Yi, *Ori-Jungyo* (Guidelines for Governing), 17th century.

14. *Chigun-yokyul,* (Essences of Governing a County), early 18th century.

15. Yak-young Jung, *Mokmin-shimseo* (Thoughts on Shepherding People), Yejon Section 65.

CHAPTER 11

The Human Element in India's Economic Development

Sudipto Mundle

Paradoxes of Indian Development

News items about India's recent advances in nuclear energy technology or space research jostle for space with stories of drought and hunger. Statistics about the vast numbers of students graduating from scores of Indian universities, institutes of technology, medical schools and management schools come along with statistics about high levels of unemployment, low per capita availability of food or the abnormally low average calorie consumption. India today has a very large and diversified industrial economy, along with the third largest stock of scientists and engineers in the world, after the United States and the Soviet Union. But it also has millions of people surviving below the poverty line in a state of permanent hunger and gradual starvation.

These paradoxes of India's development experience force us to ask how we should view the human element in our perceptions of development. Should it be viewed merely as an input to be used more efficiently, a means to an end, or should it be viewed as an end in itself? The question is not purely rhetorical, for our assessment of the Indian experience could be very different depending on which view we choose to adopt. By one reckoning, planned development in India is, on the whole, an impressive success. By the other reckoning, it is a sad failure.

India's planners were, of course, as sensitive to the problems of stark poverty and severe unemployment as their colleagues elsewhere. Indeed, raising the level of per capita income and reducing unemployment have always been the central objectives of India's five-year plans. It was assumed that if suitable strategies could be devised for ensuring a high rate of real per capita income growth, this would automatically take care of both unemployment and poverty. Accordingly, plan strategies were worked out aimed at achieving particular target rates of growth. In the technical planning exercise, the human element came to be treated by and large as an input, a means to an end. This was consistent with the main traditions of modern analytical economics, i.e., neoclassical production theory, or Leontief's input-output analysis and Von Neumann's balanced growth theory. Unfortunately, the assumption that the benefits of growth would "trickle down" to all sections of the population turned out to be not entirely warranted.

With regard to overall growth, it is always possible to quibble about this or that plan target not being achieved. But, in fact, India's growth performance has been reasonably good by international standards. The World Bank's *World Development Report 1985* indicates that India's GDP grew at an average rate of 4 per cent per annum for the decade 1973-83. This is lower than the growth rate for middle-income countries and high-income oil exporters, but it is well above the 2.4 per cent average growth rate of industrial market economies or the 3.3 per cent average growth rate of low-income countries – the group to which India belongs.[1]

After allowing for a deplorably high population growth rate of 2.3 per cent and other adjustments, the per capita real income growth over the whole period 1965-83 works out to only 1.5 per cent per annum. However, this is still much better than the group average of 0.7 per cent for low-income countries. Moreover, this trend rate of growth of 1.5 per cent in per capita real income, maintained now for a period of over thirty years, should normally have eliminated the most intense layers of poverty – or at least curbed it. But this has not happened. By conservative estimates, well over 200 million Indian people, roughly comparable to the total population of the United States or twice the population of Brazil, survive below the poverty line, in conditions of chronic hunger and wretchedness.

Quality of Life and Basic Needs

Clearly, growth alone cannot serve as a proxy for development. If we agree, as we surely must, that human well-being is the goal of development, then we must abandon a functionalist view of the human element, which tends to see it merely as an input and goes on to calibrate development performance by the achieved rate of growth. Instead, we must follow the now well established tradition of evaluating development by variables which more directly reflect the material quality of the life of ordinary people.[2]

Hunger and longevity would appear to be the most appropriate measures of development from this point of view. Of the two, the measurement of undernourishment is extremely complicated.[3] Longevity, the expectation of life at birth, is more easily measurable, but unfortunately, it does not reflect suffering from hunger in the same way that it reflects suffering on account of early death.[4] We must, therefore, retain both these indicators of development and along with them consider other basic needs, such as access to education, health services and housing. Together, they serve as a reasonable set of reference variables to measure how the human element itself has been developed in the process of development.

Longevity and Hunger

Between the mid-1960s and the mid-1980s, infant mortality (age under 1) in India declined from 151 to 93, while the child death rate (age 1 to 4) declined from 23 to 11. There has been a corresponding improvement in life expectancy at birth, from 46 to 56 in the case of males and 44 to 54 in the case of females. These are significant improvements, and the average life expectation of Indians in 1983, at 55 years, is somewhat better than the group average of 51 for the World Bank group of low-income countries. On the other hand, it compares rather poorly with a host of other developing Asian countries, led by Sri Lanka and China, where life expectancy is now approaching 70 years.

This longevity data also has to be seen alongside the evidence on hunger. Of the more than 200 million hungry Indians who live below the poverty line (2,435 calories), the large majority belong to rural households dependent on agriculture. Studies show that in both dynamic agrarian regions such as Punjab-Haryana and backward regions such as Bihar, the incidence of poverty does go down with a rise in agricultural output.[5] Nevertheless, an analysis across fifteen states shows that barring such exceptional cases as Punjab and Haryana, there is no trend decline in rural poverty despite sustained agricultural growth.[6] This peculiar situation is explained by an amazing balance between agricultural growth and population growth which has left the per capita availability of grain static at a little under 450 grams per head per day for nearly thirty years! Between 1973 and 1983, for instance, agricultural output grew at an average rate of 2.2 per cent per annum, according to World Bank estimates. This was offset by population growth of the order of 2.3 per cent.

The phenomenon of agricultural output growth being offset by extra labor absorption in agriculture is again reflected in productivity trends. According to a recent study, aggregate labor productivity in Indian agriculture has tended to decline over time.[7] However, the same study also highlights significant interregional variations which have major welfare implications for the future. The disaggregated analysis shows that out of 281 districts, there are 109 slow or negative-growth districts, where labor productivity has declined significantly, and another 72 medium-growth districts without much change in productivity. As against this, there are 100 high-growth districts where labor productivity has improved significantly, i.e., output growth has outpaced extra labor absorption. In view of the earlier cited evidence that poverty incidence in Indian agriculture does decline with per capita output growth, it would appear that the question of eliminating hunger in India turns largely on the question of whether or not the performance of the hundred high-growth districts can be replicated in the rest of India.

Expenditure on Basic Needs

In our welfarist view of the human element in development, longevity and hunger are followed closely by a range of other basic needs, such as health, education and housing. These variables are themselves strongly correlated with longevity, even more so than per capita income, as indicated by the estimates for a sample of sixteen major Asian economies presented in table 1.

TABLE 1
Coefficient of Correlation with Expectation of Life at
Birth for Sixteen Major Asian Economies

Infant mortality	−0.976
Percentage enrollment of primary school age children	0.792
Population per medical person (doctor and nurse)	−0.760
Daily calorie availability	0.749
Share of government expenditure on health, education and housing	0.680
Per capita income	0.631

In a state-controlled economy such as that of India, public expenditure gives a fair measure of the emphasis laid on such basic needs program. Data for a succession of five-year plans covering thirty-five years since the inception of planning are presented in table 2.

TABLE 2
Plan Outlay on Selected Items 1951-85

| Five-Year Plan Period | Total Plan Outlay (Rs. millions) | Per Cent Share | | | |
		Education	Housing, Urban Development and Water Supply	Health, Family Planning, Nutrition	All Basic Needs (2 + 3 + 4)
(0)	(1)	(2)	(3)	(4)	(5)
1st Plan (1950-51)	23,560	5.7	2.1	5.9	13.7
2nd Plan (1956-61)	48,000	4.3	2.5	4.7	11.5
3rd Plan (1961-66)	75,000	5.9	2.7	4.6	13.2
4th Plan (1969-74)	159,020	5.2	1.5	7.3	14.0
5th Plan (1974-79)	393,030	3.3	5.2	3.3	11.8
6th Plan (1980-85)	975,000	2.6	6.6	5.2	14.4

SOURCE: Five-Year Plan documents, Planning Commission, Government of India.

From the First to the Fifth Five-Year Plan, the total plan outlay increased from about 20 billion rupees to 970 billion in nominal terms. This represents an increase of over five times in real terms after allowing for the rise in prices. The outlay on basic needs also increased over five times, having maintained its share at about 14 per cent of total outlay. Since population doubled during the period from 363 million in 1957 to 733 million in 1983, it follows that the per capita investment on basic needs has actually tripled in real terms during the period of planned development. In absolute terms, there thus appears to be an increasing emphasis on the human element in

India's development plans. This general proposition must, however, be qualified by a more disaggregated examination of the allocation of basic needs expenditures.

Housing, Urban Development and Water Supply

The allocation of plan outlay on housing and related expenditures has tended to increase over time, not only in absolute terms, but also as a proportion of total outlay. Its share has tripled from a little over 2 per cent in the early 1950s to over 6.5 per cent in the early 1980s. However, it is the allocation of resources within this general category which leaves room for considerable improvement. Breakdowns available for the just-ended Sixth Plan period show that out of this, a mere 3.5 billion rupees, or 5.5 per cent, was made available for rural housing. In this particular plan, another 21 billion rupees was allocated to a very major rural water supply program. But this still meant that over 60 per cent of the funds have been allocated to urban housing and urban development programs, which cater to just one-quarter of the total Indian population. This continuing urban bias in the delivery of basic services such as housing and water supply is clearly a serious impediment to the development of the human element in a society which is still predominantly rural.

Health, Nutrition and Family Planning

Total expenditure on health and related programs has been maintained at about 5 per cent of the total plan outlay, as shown in table 2. Given the increase in plan outlay, this implies that per capita outlay on health services has tripled in real terms over the period covered. But once again, the detailed allocations are critical. As shown in table 3, India's family planning program, which initially had only a nominal claim, now claims about a fifth of all health service allocations, without any clear evidence that the program has actually curbed population growth.

TABLE 3
Allocation of Plan Outlays on Health and Family Planning

	Health and Nutrition		Family Planning/ Family Welfare		Total Outlay on Health, Nutrition and Family Planning	
	Rs. Millions	%	Rs. Millions	%	Rs. Millions	%
1st Plan (1951-56)	1,393	(99)	7	(1)	1,400	(100)
2nd Plan (1956-61)	2,220	(99)	30	(1)	2,250	(100)
3rd Plan (1961-66)	3,148	(92)	270	(8)	3,418	(100)
4th Plan (1969-74)	8,410	(73)	3,150	(27)	11,560	(100)
5th Plan (1974-79)	7,974	(62)	4,974	(38)	12,948	(100)
6th Plan (1980-85)	40,530	(80)	10,100	(20)	50,630	(100)

SOURCE: Five-Year Plan documents, Planning Commission, Government of India.

The position was particularly serious during the Fifth Plan. The share of health services as a whole was reduced to only about 3 per cent of the total plan outlay, while the family planning program was very substantially expanded, with the result that the total allocation for health and nutrition programs was cut down even in nominal terms. After allowing for inflation and population growth, this entailed a significant cut in real per capita health expenditure.

Fortunately, this misallocation was later rectified. But the urban bias noted above in the case of housing also applies to health services: the large bulk of health expenditure is used to subsidize urban consumers, who account for only a quarter of the Indian population. A serious attempt to bring the major part of India's population under reasonable health service coverage would entail a very substantial reallocation of resources within the health sector from urban facilities to rural services.

Education

Finally, we turn to public expenditure on education. It is here, more than elsewhere, that prevailing biases in the treatment of the human element show up most sharply in India. The need for education is so basic that it is reasonable to consider it a fundamental human right. Moreover, education is not only important to that perspective of development which sees the human element as an end in itself; it is also fundamental from the more technocratic viewpoint, which sees the human element merely as an input, and education as the activity of human capital formation. It is, therefore, quite disconcerting to find that the share of education in the total plan outlay has been as low as 5 to 6 per cent in India's five-year plans, and that even this percentage has been declining in recent plans. As indicated in table 1, the share of education has declined with every five-year plan following the peak share of 5.9 per cent in the Third Plan. It had fallen to less than half that share by the time of the Sixth Plan.

The changing pattern of resource allocation within the total outlay on education is even more disconcerting. Despite steady improvements recorded since political independence, there was only 36 per cent literacy in India in 1981.[8] As such, it would be reasonable to expect that while the overall share of education in plan expenditure has been declining, at least allocations to basic education should have been protected. Instead, it is precisely the allocation to early and elementary education which has been most severely squeezed. In the First Five-Year Plan, 64 per cent of all educational expenditure was devoted to elementary education, while university and higher education got only around 10 per cent. As shown in table 4, the relative share of the latter category was more or less doubled from

TABLE 4
Allocation of Plan Outlays on Education

	Early and Elementary Education		University and Higher Education		Total Outlay on Education	
	Rs. Millions	%	Rs. Millions	%	Rs. Millions	%
1st Plan (1951-56)	850	(64)	140	(11)	1,330	(100)
2nd Plan (1956-61)	870	(42)	450	(22)	2,080	(100)
3rd Plan (1961-66)	2,090	(50)	820	(20)	4,180	(100)
4th Plan (1969-74)	2,347	(29)	1,835	(22)	8,230	(100)
5th Plan (1974-79)	4,100	(32)	2,920	(23)	12,850	(100)
6th Plan (1980-85)	9,054	(36)	4,858	(19)	25,237	(100)

SOURCE: Five-Year Plan documents, Planning Commission, Government of India.

the Second Plan onwards, while the share of elementary education has slowly declined over the different five-year plans. In the just-concluded Sixth Plan, the share of elementary education was brought down to only 36 per cent.

This unfortunate trend in plan fund allocations notwithstanding, the level of literacy has been improving. The most heartening feature in this is a certain equalizing trend, both across regions and between sexes. Table 5 gives a detailed breakdown of literacy rate changes by states, along with ranks. It will be noticed that generally, the rate of improvement in literacy is inversely related to the base literacy rate in a given state, such that interstate literacy rate disparities are declining. Similarly, it will be noticed that while female literacy is lower in every state, the improvement in female literacy between 1971 and 1981 is higher than the improvement in average literacy, such that literacy disparities between the sexes are now declining over time.

TABLE 5
Interstate Variations in Literacy Rates

	Literacy Rate 1981		Literacy Rate 1971		% Change 1981/1971		Female Literacy Rate		Female Literacy % Change 1981/1971	
Kerala	69	(1)	60	(1)	14.5	(15)	64	(1)	18.7	(15)
Maharashtra	47	(2)	39	(2)	20.9	(13)	35	(2)	32.7	(9)
Tamil Nadu	46	(3)	39	(2)	16.0	(14)	34	(3)	27.0	(14)
Gujrat	44	(4)	36	(4)	22.2	(10)	32	(5)	30.6	(12)
Himachal Pradesh	42	(5)	32	(7)	31.2	(2)	31	(6)	55.7	(1)
West Bengal	41	(6)	33	(6)	23.1	(8)	30	(7)	35.3	(7)
Punjab	41	(7)	34	(5)	21.0	(12)	34	(3)	31.8	(11)
Karnataka	38	(8)	32	(7)	22.9	(9)	28	(8)	32.7	(9)
Haryana	36	(9)	27	(9)	33.3	(1)	22	(9)	49.3	(4)
Orissa	34	(10)	26	(10)	30.3	(4)	21	(10)	51.7	(3)
Andhra Pradesh	30	(11)	25	(11)	21.9	(11)	21	(10)	30.3	(13)
Madhya Pradesh	28	(12)	22	(12)	25.7	(7)	16	(12)	42.3	(5)
Uttar Pradesh	27	(13)	22	(12)	26.1	(5)	14	(13)	36.7	(6)
Bihar	26	(14)	20	(14)	30.4	(3)	14	(13)	55.7	(1)
Rajasthan	24	(15)	19	(15)	26.1	(5)	11	(15)	33.8	(8)

SOURCE: Census of India (1981).
NOTE: Figures in parentheses indicate ranks.

Conclusion

Viewed from a "human capital" perspective, which sees the human element essentially as an input in the development process and not as an end in itself, the very large numbers of doctors, scientists, engineers, managers and lawyers in the country would lead us to believe that the human element has been central to India's development strategy. But this would be very misleading, for alongside this huge stock of highly skilled manpower, India also has what is perhaps the world's largest stock of chronically hungry and malnourished people — over 200 million, as we have seen. Under these circumstances, the human element in development can only legitimately be viewed from a humanistic perspective — as an end in itself.

Basic needs such as food, shelter, health and education are the crucial elements by which to measure India's development performance in this view. On the food front, the worst famines have been eliminated. Beyond that, it is a close race between output growth and population growth, the outcome hinging on whether or not the performance of the hundred high-growth districts can be replicated elsewhere. For the rest, we have the very real growth of per capita public expenditure on programs of housing and drinking water, health and education. However, we have also seen the various policy biases which persist — biases in favor of the elite against the rest, the urban sector against the rural, toward higher education and against elementary education and the like. These largely account for the miserable quality of everyday life that the majority of Indians have to suffer. Without a major change in these biases, the human element will remain incidental in India's economic development.

Notes

1. Low-income countries implies all countries in this group other than India and China, which are also shown separately in this report.
2. M.D. Morris, *Measuring the Condition of the World's Poor: The Physical Quality of Life Index* (Oxford: Pergamon Press, 1979).
3. See F.V. Sukhatame, "Malnutrition and Poverty," Lal Bahadur Sastri Memorial Lecture, New Delhi, 1977; "Assessment of Adequacy of Diets at Different Income Levels," *Economic and Political Weekly* 13 (1978); and T.N. Srinivasan, "Malnutrition: Some Measurement and Policy Issues" (mimeo), World Bank and Yale University, 1979.
4. A K. Sen, "Levels of Poverty: Policy and Change," World Bank Staff Working Paper No. 401, July 1980.
5. See S. Mundle, "Land, Labour and the Level of Living in Rural Punjab" in A.R. Khan and E. Lee, eds., *Poverty in Rural Asia* (Bangkok: ILO, 1985), and "Recent Trends in the Condition of Children in India: A Statistical Profile," *World Development* 12:3 (1984).
6. See S. Mundle, "Effect of Agricultural Prices and Production on the Incidence of Rural Poverty: A Tentative Analysis of Inter-State Variations," *Economic and Political Weekly* 18 (1983).
7. See G.S. Bhalla and Y.K. Alagh, "Labor Productivity in Indian Agriculture," *Economic and Political Weekly* 18 (1983).
8. See S. Mundle in Khan and Lee, *Poverty in Rural Asia.*

CHAPTER 12

Human Resource Development: The Jamaican Experience

Headley Brown

The current disequilibrium in the Jamaican labor market is reflected in a surplus of labor, largely unskilled, on one hand and a shortage of professional, technical and managerial manpower on the other.

A number of factors have given rise to this situation. In the first place, the economy has been characterized by a low and unstable level of job creation, which has been largely insufficient to absorb the growth in the labor force. In the period between 1973 and 1981, for example, while the growth in employment was only 15,400, or 2.2 per cent per annum, the labor force grew at an average of 26,100 persons, or at a rate of 2.9 per cent. Naturally, this led to a growth in unemployment levels. It is interesting to note that the increase in employment in this period was due in large measure to the increase in own-account workers, and that the growth in self-employment occurred against a backdrop of a trend of declining GDP. Between 1973 and 1981, the employment of own-account workers increased by 80,600, which represented 65.6 per cent of the total growth in employment, while between 1974 and 1980, the GDP declined by 14.8 per cent in real terms.

Second, there has been a failure to adopt a consistent and coordinated approach to manpower planning. An indication of this lack of sustained effort is given by the fact that very few resources have been committed to the process in the past. Thus, despite the fact that most major HRD studies/plans have pointed out the fragmented approach to HRD, the absence of adequate mechanisms to match the supply of labor with existing demand, and the dearth of labor market information to guide training institutions, the required levels of investment needed to correct the situation on a sustained basis were never made.[1]

The most recent case in point is the GOJ/USAID Manpower Planning, Training and Employment Project, which had the objective of upgrading and coordinating all manpower planning, training and employment service activities, eliminating duplicative functions and increasing the relevance and efficiency of its manpower-related services. The success of this project was limited during its lifetime, and after, by a lack of adequate resources. In most of the agencies involved in the project, activities were assigned low-priority status, and staff had minimal time available to spend on these activities. After the completion of the project, very few of the activities were institutionalized; that is, neither funding nor adequate levels of staffing were made available to follow up on the activities. Consequently, much of the experience gained during the project was lost, and there was another "break" in the operation of the system. While admittedly, financial constraints contributed to this situation, part of the problem was the failure of the relevant authorities to accept the importance of some of these activities.[2]

Third, and as a direct consequence of the above, there has been an absence of the type of information needed to inform education and training policies. The limited coordination between education authorities and employers, both private and public, has led to a situation where feedback of information from employers and the labor market to the education/training system has been scanty or nonexistent. Thus, while there has been massive and growing unemployment of school-leavers, there has also been a shortage of qualified manpower for jobs requiring basic vocational skills or skills at the junior technician level.

Fourth, the situation has been exacerbated by the migration of highly-trained labor from Jamaica, particularly during the 1970s. In the subperiod 1977-1980, the loss of professionals, managers and other high-level technical persons was estimated at 9,500, with that of skilled workers, craftsmen and operatives estimated at 9,100. It is noteworthy that during the decade, there was a shift in the occupational composition of migration to North America as the proportion of upper white collar workers increased from 16 per cent in 1970 to 27 per cent in 1980. The magnitude of this outflow can be better assessed when it is noted that the migration of trained persons between 1977-1980 was the equivalent of over 50 per cent of the output of local training institutions during those years.

A Comprehensive HRD Approach

It is now recognized that a "piecemeal" approach to HRD is inefficient and ineffective, a fact which is of increased significance in the current economic scenario. Further, and more specifically, the structural adjustment program for the economy needs to be complemented with an adjustment program in the education and training system to provide an adequate flow of the requisite skills into the economy. Indeed, the economic adjustment program itself makes specific demands on the training system. For example, the restructuring and streamlining of public administration, with its emphasis on greater efficiency and effectiveness in the management of the economy, implies a demand for skills in such areas as fiscal and monetary policy formulation, "early warning systems" and macroeconomic planning.

The government has, therefore, determined that HRD will be the centerpiece of its planning over the next three years. The specific strategies to be pursued will be undertaken within the context of the government's economic program. To this end, a comprehensive HRD plan is being prepared.

In formulating the HRD program, however, a number of issues need to be resolved. Three major ones are explored below.

Relative Emphasis on Different Levels of the System

In the first place, what should be the relative emphasis on the different levels of the education and training system? In the period 1981/82-1983/84, it is estimated that 31 per cent of the national recurrent budget was spent on primary and preprimary education (with an enrollment of 525,990), as against 34 per cent on secondary education (enrollment 165,156) and 26 per cent on tertiary and higher education (enrollment 14,312). Given this pattern of expenditure, it is not surprising that approximately 50-60 per cent of students leaving primary school are functionally illiterate. This severely restricts their capacity to be absorbed into further training programs.

To the extent that success at the upper levels of the educational system depends on the quality of education received at the primary level, it is imperative that in the development of the HRD program, continued focus be placed on improving the quality of primary education.

The need for an emphasis on good primary education is also indicated by the fact that the majority of the population may receive only primary education, and they have a high probability of employment. In October 1981, it is estimated that 71.4 per cent of jobs in the economy were held by persons with primary or pre-primary level education.

Such statistics, of course, beg the question whether employers are making the best of a bad situation by recruiting what is available in the labor market, or whether in fact it is the structure of demand (i.e., the types of jobs which are available) that dictates the employment of persons with these levels of education.

The question can be put into some perspective by exploring the following argument: If one accepts that there is a positive relation between levels of education and employment (levels of training are also important, but in the Jamaican labor market, the vast majority of the labor force — 80 per cent in October 1981 — received no training), then one can conceptualize the labor market as a long queue of persons, with those with postprimary education at the front of the queue and those with primary and preprimary education at the back. If employers had a preference (as dictated by the structure of demand) for those with higher levels of education, then it would be expected that those at the front would have a higher probability of selection for employment. The data are not consistent with this. In October 1981, for example, while the rate of unemployment was 39.1 per cent among persons with postprimary education, it was only 21.1 per cent among those with primary and below. This suggests that persons with primary and lower levels of education may stand a greater chance of being selected for employment. There are three possible explanations for this occurrence. First, employers may in some cases find it less expensive to recruit persons with lower levels of education. This implies some degree of substitutability between persons with postprimary education and those with primary education. Second, persons with this level of education have a high rate of own-employment creation. Indeed, the data indicate that over 53 per cent of employed persons with primary and lower levels of education were self-employed or in independent occupations. Third, it is possible that even if employers wanted to recruit persons with postprimary levels of education, such persons would prefer unemployment to working in the jobs offered, for which they may consider themselves overqualified.

However, whatever one concludes regarding the relationship between levels of education and the job market, the fact is that the majority of jobs in the economy are at present held by persons with primary and lower levels of education. Further, there is a high rate of own-employment creation among such persons. Hence, every effort must be made to provide the best quality education at this level in an attempt to improve overall productivity levels.

Role of Higher Education

A second major issue to be resolved in the design of the Jamaican HRD program is the role of higher education. Should it be regarded as investment or consumption? Should the demand for places be determined by projections of demand by the economy for qualified manpower or by the projected demand for places by individual students? This is an important consideration, since higher education makes very heavy demands on the country's resources. The issue is whether it is efficient, and equitable, to treat higher education simply as a luxury consumption good for a relatively small number of people.

This issue needs to be analyzed in light of the fact that government bears the major financial responsibility for the provision of higher education, private institutions at this level being virtually nonexistent. This it does by (i) providing direct financing to institutions, (ii) pursuing its policy of free education for all up to the higher levels, and (iii) providing board stipends for all students at the tertiary level without the application of a means test.

Since government's resources are limited, they must be utilized efficiently. In such an environment, it is imperative that government opt more for an investment role than for a consumption role for higher education. This has implications not only for the provision of training in institutions offering higher education, but also for their research programs, which must be geared to focus on current issues facing the economy.

But there is a second reason why government must think of the provision of higher education in terms of investment — that is, the provision of higher education on the basis of manpower needs. Given the current state of disequilibrium in the labor market, every effort must be made to effect a greater balance between the demand for and the supply of skills. Thus, the output of the higher education system must be geared towards meeting the perceived needs of the labor market. To do otherwise would imply training for export — or for frustration.

The choice of this role for the higher education system does not ensure its automatic implementation. There are a number of practical considerations which must be taken into account :

a) A considerable amount of information is required for this type of planning, which in turn implies that considerable financial and human resources will have to be invested in the process.

b) Great flexibility in the programming of higher educational institutions is required to accommodate the frequent changes which will be brought about by economic and social change and by technological progress.

c) Substitution possibilities between different categories of manpower do exist and need to be accommodated in the planning.

Impact of the Migration of Skills

A final issue to be considered in the development of the HRD program is the impact of the migration of skills. This can be analyzed from two points of view.

In the first place, the migration of skills from the public sector must be considered. The evidence suggests that shortages exist in a number of professional categories within this sector. They result not from an inadequate output of the local training institutions, but from the migration of these skills from the sector. The major factors contributing to this outmigration are the relatively low levels of remuneration and unattractive working conditions. The former consideration looms large, especially in the current climate of rising prices and falling real wages.

The strategy to be pursued by government to help bridge the gap is of critical concern. On one hand, the government could attempt to do nothing about the leakages and try to keep ahead of the situation by deliberately oversupplying the market with the needed skills. This is, of course, very costly, since it implies that public funds are being channelled into investments from which little or no returns can be expected. In addition, the high turnover rates which will result if nothing is done to stop the leakages will lead to low productivity levels. This will only aggravate the situation, since the public sector is already characterized by a persistent high turnover, especially of those in the 35-44 age bracket. The loss of these workers at the height of their capacities may open opportunities to younger, more qualified and perhaps more talented personnel, but it also robs the public sector of its more experienced staff.[3]

Alternatively, government could consider improving the conditions of service for public sector workers. Given the current economic constraints, it is not possible for the government to address the needs of all its workers at one time. However, it is possible that it could engage in a phased program of salary upgrading, starting with those skills which pose the greatest constraint to the successful implementation of its policies.

Secondly, the issue of the migration of skills from the country must be considered in terms of its possible impact on HRD. As mentioned previously, there was a significant outflow of professional, technical, managerial and skilled labor to North America during the late 1970s — the equivalent of more than 50 per cent of the output of training institutions during the period. The loss of the professional and highly skilled represented a serious drain on the country's resources.

On the other hand, however, is the fact that during the same decade, there was also an outflow of domestic and general service workers estimated at 28,000, or approximately 28 per cent of the total migration during the period. There is no denying that the departure of domestics, laborers and general service workers from the labor force had a positive impact on the economy, since it helped to relieve unemployment. But there is some controversy regarding the role of the migration of the professional, technical and managerial groups. It is generally agreed that Jamaica's development efforts were adversely affected by the outflow of these groups. However, it has been suggested that there was and still is a lack of effective demand for these skills in the economy, and particularly in the public sector, since the country is unable to employ these workers at levels of remuneration which repay their investment in their own training. This is an even greater problem in an environment of steeply rising prices.[4] Hence, the actual loss of workers would be less than that suggested by the data. In addition, the movement of these persons from the Jamaican economy made room for younger persons.

The issue can be put in some perspective by asking what would have occurred in the labor market had these persons not migrated. Higher unemployment levels is a strong possibility. However, to the extent that some of these persons were entrepreneurs, they would have created their own employment, as well as some possible employment for others.

The government now finds itself in a dilemma regarding the retention of skills in the economy. If it attempts to restrict the movement of persons in whom considerable investment has been made, this would be seen as a threat to basic freedom and could have an adverse impact on the stability of capital flows. On the other hand, government must continue its training programs to provide the skills required by the economy. The question to be answered in framing its HRD progam is, therefore, how can government maximize the returns from its investment in human capital? The solution, which is certainly easier to articulate than to implement, lies in creating those conditions which facilitate the retention of skills in the economy. One possible strategy to be adopted is to reduce training for export by:

   a) Gearing the content of training programs specifically to the development objectives of the economy, i.e., making trained persons less attractive to the export market.
   b) Where possible, substituting local training for training in foreign institutions.

Objectives of the Human Resource Investment Program

Based on a consideration of the issues outlined above, a Human Resource Investment Program has been designed which will provide the financing for HRD. The broad objectives of the program would include the following:

   a) To fill the vacancies which currently exist and/or at least balance annual output with annual demand in respect of certain critical skill areas.
   b) To rationalize the secondary school system through implementation of a common curriculum in Grades 7-9 of the five types of secondary schools.
   c) To expand the capacity of the secondary school system so that the intake from the primary school system can be increased.

d) To increase significantly the output level of the post-secondary and tertiary institutions, including UWI, and to make
their training programs relevant to the skills demand profile,
thereby further bridging the skills gap. Tertiary institutions
will be expected to be more flexible in their research and
development programs, and in their programming in general,
in order to meet the needs of the productive sectors.

e) To expand, refurbish and generally strengthen the primary
school system.

Conclusion

Given the size and potential scope of the HRD program, it will be
essentially long-term. Some aspects of the program are, however,
already in place. The establishment of a Human Employment and
Resource Training Trust to coordinate, fund, monitor and promote
skills training activities, especially among youth, is one important
component of the program.

Nonetheless, in the short to medium term, complementary
strategies to help fill the skills gap are being explored. The establishment of the focal point for a short-term advisory service under the
umbrella of the UNDP is one measure which is of critical significance
to Jamaica.

Notes

1. See, for example, the *Jamaica Education Sector Study* prepared in 1973 which
states, inter alia, "Development of the total human resources of Jamaica and the education
and training of all segments of the population to more fully meet human needs and aspirations, as well as to support the economic and social development of the country, are highly
fragmented at present... A major constraint to the achievement of the country's development regulations is the almost complete lack of coordination of education/training activities... The overall HRD effort is splintered, inefficient and ineffective."

2. It may be noted, however, that since 1984, a Population and Manpower Planning
Division has been created within the Planning Institute of Jamaica to play a focal role in
the coordination and management of the Jamaican labor market.

3. A study of the civil service in 1983 by Green, Gordon and Jones shows that
because of the attrition of more experienced workers, there is a bulge in the age group 25-35
years (42 per cent) and a contraction in the older age groups (21 per cent).

4. Patricia Anderson, "Migration and Development in Jamaica," *ISER* (1985).

CHAPTER 13

Human Resource Development: The Benin Experience

Zul-Kifl Salami

The development strategy of the People's Republic of Benin is based on self-sufficient and self-maintained development as defined in the Second Development Plan (1983-1987).

Regarding the self-maintenance concept, it should be noted that there is no economic development without an extended reproduction of the material basis of the community. Benin's development strategy aims to create a domestic market large enough to constitute a sound basis for the mobilization of consumption and to bring about the installation of industrial enterprises capable of manufacturing consumer goods under conditions of economic viability. The objective is to gradually create an extended demand for processed farm products, finished industrial goods and semifinished industrial goods. This domestic market will give the national economy the weight it needs in order to make it the focal point of economic growth.

The major part (71.2 per cent) of the Beninese population lives in the rural sector. The extension of the domestic market should aim at increasing the purchasing power of these people. The strategy of development must thus revolve around activities centered on farming, fishing, cattle raising and forestry.

Concerning the industrial sector, it is the mainstay of this strategy of development. It will have to ensure an expansion of the marketing of goods in the agricultural sector, bring about increased productivity in this sector, and make processed agricultural products available to consumers and input available to farmers. It should, finally, meet the growing need among farmers, whose purchasing power is ever-increasing, for finished consumer goods.

To attain such objectives, the following provisions have been made:

a) Measures required to improve the farmers' contribution to development and to increase their incomes include instruction in functional literacy, the creation of farmers' cooperatives and the development of integrated rural development projects.

b) A readjustment in the industrial sector will make it possible to abandon industries that are of unsuitable size to promote, on the one hand, labor-intensive small and medium-sized industries, and craft and microtrade on the other. The enactment of new legislation on investments, and the recent meeting between the Head of State and national and foreign economic operators working in Benin, constitute incentives for investment.

c) Finally, the effective implementation of the staff regulations for government employees (releasing of increments, widening of the salary brackets, etc.) will enable a smoother functioning of the domestic market.

In the light of the preceding, human resources emerge as the essential factor and the most precious resource to ensure self-sufficient and self-maintained development. In full awareness of this, Benin supports and finances activities related to training, executive training, follow-up training and social well-being, as well as pre-schooling, primary, secondary and vocational education for the nearly 50 per cent of the population below 15 years of age.

This report on the role of human resources in development will focus on:
a) Population and work force.
b) Education and literacy training.
c) Employment.
d) Problems and prospects of human resource development.

Population and Work Force

The March 1979 general census of population estimated the population of Benin at some 3,338,240, inhabitants with a density of 30 inhabitants per square kilometer. In 1985, the population is estimated to be 3,800,000 inhabitants, with a density of 34 inhabitants per square kilometer. The population is unevenly distributed, with over 50 per cent concentrated in the three southern provinces (Atlantique, Oueme and Mono), which cover only 10 per cent of the total surface area.

Furthermore, this population is very young, with nearly half (49 per cent) being less than 15 years old. This has a direct consequence on demographic investments (schools, health, etc.).

According to a recent fertility survey, the average age for first marriage is 16 years. Infant mortality is 14 per cent. The dynamics of the Beninese population are revealed through its growth rate of 2.7 per cent, which doubles the number of the population every 26 years. This rate will remain high for a long time to come, since the country is now in a transitional phase of increasing its population until the total population nears 10 million inhabitants.

Among a work force of 1,493,097 persons according to the 1979 census, 1,063,401 (71.2 per cent) are employed in the primary sector (farming, forestry, fishing and animal husbandry), 100,310 (6.7 per cent) in the secondary sector (mining, processing, building and civil engineering), and 317,407 (21.3 per cent) in the service sector (trade, transport and services), with 11,979 (0.8 per cent) unofficially employed. While the work force remains the main element in the implementation of a strategy for self-sufficient and self-maintained growth, it must be noted that this strategy confronts an employment structure characterized by abundant manual labor in both rural and urban areas coupled with high levels of underemployment, unemployment and rural exodus. The mobilization of the population to attain the stated objectives of development requires the setting up of education and training facilities based on the guidelines described below.

Education and Literacy Training

The reform introduced in 1975 according to the National Education Guidelines is part of a comprehensive policy of human resource development and constitutes an essential dimension in Benin's economic and social development strategy. The guidelines are based on the following principles:

a) Equal opportunity of education, with the aim of reaching every school-age child by the end of the century.

b) Putting the educational system at the service of national independence by having it countribute to the gradual creation of an adequate technology and by orienting it toward the development of national culture.

c) Gearing the educational system toward the economy through the promotion of scientific, technical and economic training.

Through its policy of universal schooling, the People's Republic of Benin has experienced a genuine increase in school enrollment in recent years. From 1970 to 1983, the number of primary school children rose from 155,225 to 428,185. In the secondary schools there were 17,243 children in 1970 and 99,295 children in 1981, showing an average growth rate of 17.25 per cent. The growth of enrollment in technical and vocational schools is more modest — from 6,810 in 1980 to 6,877 in 1982.

As far as higher education is concerned, the National University of Benin has developed quickly. In 1971-72 it had only 580 students, a number which reached 6,000 in 1985. Added to these students trained in Benin are those who have been trained in foreign universities.

In 1981, a presentation for public inspection made it possible to conduct a first stock-taking which, while confirming the fundamental principles of the new guidelines, revealed some shortcomings and suggested a few improvements.

The curricula have undergone important modifications with the introduction of productive activities, which have made room for school cooperatives within which the youth are encouraged to train themselves in democracy and management.

Alongside conventional training, Benin has developed extramural education in literacy. This is meant for those who, for various reasons, have not been able to enjoy the conventional type of education. Literacy education is paramount, since its target is the rural population, on whom is focused the strategy of the Second Development Plan. The political authorities very quickly understood that it is by trying to raise the standard of living of the rural population, by improving their working conditions through advisory services and by instructing them in functional literacy that it will become possible to mobilize them for national development programs. This education receives the same emphasis as the conventional type, extending its activities throughout the country. It is conducted in the local languages in order to facilitate the assimilation of these techniques by the population.

Apart from keeping pace with the increase in population noted earlier, Benin is confronted with the difficult problem of making optimum utilization of its human resources. The objective is, in fact, to ensure harmonization between the efforts made toward the promotion of individual human beings through education and training and the possibilities of making use of their abilities in the structures of national production.

Employment

The employment situation will be reviewed in the structured as well as the nonstructured sector.

The Structured Sector

The number of persons employed in the structured sector has grown from 70,993 in 1980 to 86,443 at the begining of the Second Plan period and stood at 98,414 in 1985. In 1990, the number of workers in this sector will increase to 139,659 if the employment growth rate observed between 1970 and 1980 is maintained (6.7 per cent). Job opportunities between 1983-1990 will theoretically rise by 26,846. These figures accounted for only 4.6 per cent of the working age population in 1980. According to a recent estimate, the structured sector will employ only 6.4 per cent of workers in 1990. Thus, in spite of the investment efforts which it enjoys, this sector will not be in a position to meet the demands of the Beninese youth. The remaining workers (93 per cent) will have to be employed either in agriculture or in the urban nonstructured sector (crafts and microtrade).

TABLE 1
Growth of Employment in the Structured Sector

Sectors	1977	1980	1983	1990
Farming, fishing and forestry	2,740	5,012	5,525	6,935
Mining	90	96	130	265
Electricity, gas and water	470	717	973	20,576
Manufacturing	5,810	6,450	9,135	1,982
Building and civil engineering	3,910	8,311	11,153	22,152
Trade and tourism	6,870	7,870	9,294	13,700
Transport and communication	6,100	12,669	14,961	22,054
Banks and insurance	2,960	2,733	3,227	4,758
Services	27,150	27,135	32,045	47,237
Total	56,100	70,993	86,443	139,659

SOURCE: "Training-Employment Connection", a quantitative study conducted by *MPS/DPE/SHR.*

The evolution of employment in the structured sector should not be allowed to veil other realities, among which are the quantitative and qualitative inadequacies between supply of and demand for employment. A review of the employment situation in this sector shows an oversupply of unskilled labor in the urban areas coupled with high levels of underemployment and unemployment, as well as a lack of middle management personnel and specialists. The situation is aggravated not only by the rural exodus, but also by the influx into the labor market of academic graduates with no professional qualifications.

In fact, from 1976 to 1980, the annual demand for jobs has increased from 7,300 to 10,300, making a growth rate of 9 per cent per year. Meanwhile, job openings have increased from 6,000 to 9,500 over the same period, providing a cover ratio of 88.6 per cent. In other respects, it should be mentioned that for 1983 and 1984, the labor and employment bureaus have registered, respectively, 21,496 and 16,222 applications. In the employment bureau, of over 399 candidates retained on the national short-list in 1983, 267 could not be recruited, while for 407 candidates short-listed for 1984, the cover ratio of employment barely exceeded 25 per cent.

Thus, in the modern or structured sector of the Beninese economy there is a permanent abundance of labor looking for a job. This is an obvious waste of human and financial resources in this period of international economic crisis.

The Nonstructured Sector

This sector is of particular importance, because on the one hand, it embraces agricultural activities and urban nonstructured activities (crafts, microtrade), and on the other, because it represents a future salvation for those who cannot find employment in the modern or structured sector.

Farming, Forestry, Fishing and Animal Husbandry

It will be recalled that these activities employ 71.2 per cent of the work force, with 68.1 per cent in farming, 1.5 per cent in animal husbandry, 1.55 per cent in fishing and 0.05 per cent in forestry. Activities in the sector are dominated by traditional methods of farming, characterized by allowing the ground to lie fallow for long periods under a system of crop rotation. Little importance is accorded to salaried agricultural work, so its potential is negligible in the present phase of the development of employment possibilities in this sector.

Moreover, an analysis of the economic activities of the sector cannot be carried out without considering unemployment, under-employment and the rural exodus. The rate of unemployment evaluated at the national level varies from 40 to 60 per cent from south to north, with considerable regional discrepancies according to periods of farming, but sometimes reaching 100 per cent in the slack season. Underemployment observed at this level is due not only to an insufficiency of cultivated acreage compared with farming areas, but also to a scarcity of labor linked with the rural exodus.

Living conditions in the rural areas periodically motivate the able-bodied to leave in search of employment in the urban centers. As a result, villages suffer from a shortage of workers to participate in labor-intensive production, while in the urban centers, the arrival of rural youth raises serious problems of housing and employment.

Crafts and Microtrade

This sector employs migrants from the rural areas and graduates of the conventional education system.

Craft workers account for 7 per cent of the total work force. Various studies carried out (1980, 1981) revealed that the number of people working in the sector totalled 100,000, with 50.3 per cent in production-oriented crafts, 30.7 per cent in service-oriented crafts and 19 per cent in art-oriented crafts. Thanks to its labor-absorptive capacity, this sector ranks third after agriculture and trade. The possibilities for growth of this sector are enormous and can be pursued by means of comparatively small capital investments for a proprotionally greater contribution in terms of job opportunities. This is a priority sector for the development of employment oppor-tunities, particularly for youth and women. Furthermore, this sector represents a basic stage in the process of industrial develop-ment, promoting the transition toward small- and medium-scale enterprises.

As far as trade is concerned, it employs 21.3 per cent of the work force. It is advisable to note that on the grounds of its transient, elastic nature and its size, trade is a difficult sector to assess as to the exact number of people employed, employment trends and employ-ment potential. Nevertheless, concurrent information collected from the 1979 census and other sources (such as the Memorandum of Benin presented at the United Nations Conference on the Least Advanced Countries) shows a rough count of 478,000 in the commercial sector, including wholesalers, dealers in small quantities and retailers. The trade sector stands out as an asylum for school-leavers, young people coming from villages, and women.

Above and beyond employment in the major sectors of the Beninese economy, the permanent mobilization of the population for development constitutes another opportunity for Benin. This process is carried out through mass organizations such as the Organization of the Revolutionary Youth and Benin (OJRB), the Organization of the Revolutionary Women of Benin (OFRB), the Defense Committee of the Revolution (CDR) and cooperative institutions. The target populations are periodically mobilized to participate in large numbers in the attainment of such objectives of the National Development Plan as reafforestation exercises, swamp drainage and urban sanitation campaigns.

In a program worked out to the control the rural exodus, many cooperatives have been created in urban and rural centers, among them the Benin Cooperative Board of Agricultural Equipment (COBEMAG), the Socialist-Type Experimental Farm Cooperative (CAETS), the Cooperatives-Oriented Revolutionary Group (GRVC), the 4-D Clubs, committed to supporting cooperative institutions, and furniture cooperatives, tailoring cooperatives and the like.

Problems

The mobilization of human resources for development is not without difficulties linked with demography, education and the coordination of education with employment.

Demography

Inhabited by nearly four million people today, Benin will shelter about six million people in the year 2000, with significant consequences for education, health and food security policies. The under-15 population will rise to about 2.9 million, an addition of 980,000 over the 1985 figure. As it is in a phase of demographic transition, the country will continue to grow at a high rate until a projected drop beginning in the year 2020.

The sociocultural behavior of the population, the high rate of infant mortality and the low level of female education are obvious causes of such demographic pressures. In order to reduce the consequences of such demographic pressures on the standard of living of the Beninese people, planners and policymakers should make it a priority to maintain an annual economic growth exceeding in real terms that of demographic growth.

Education

Despite efforts made in education and training, the country still suffers from a shortage qualified professionals, particularly in middle management. There is a scarcity of supervisors, skilled labor and skilled and semiskilled technicians, while at the same time, emphasis is placed on training school and university graduates already holding their master's degrees, bachelor's degrees, vocational training or school certificates. In industry, the shortage of skilled manpower is reflected in poor production management and difficulties in ensuring international standards of profitability.

The reorientation of the educational and training system, together with the creation of polytechnic schools and colleges embarked upon in the previous plan, is continuing in order to supply the country with qualified professional staff.

In other respects, the 1975 educational reform, in making education available to the entire school-age population, has created a real educational boom that has brought with it a number of difficulties:

a) The rapid growth of the educational system has not made it possible to ensure a balanced coverage of the various regions and categories of school children. Fewer girls are being reached than boys.

b) Not enough qualified teachers are available, making it necessary to rely on inadequately trained staff.

c) The educational system relies heavily on the state budget; 37 to 40 per cent of this budget is allocated to education. It becomes practically impossible to release new resources for schooling while the needs of the existing educational institutions are not yet totally met (equipment, furniture, teaching materials, etc.).

Apart from these internal problems, there are others related to the connection between the educational system and its environment. The contents of training have been inadequately adapted to the socioeconomic environment, resulting in quantitative and qualitative maladjustments between training and employment.

In an attempt to find a solution to these problems, it is imperative to develop appropriate means to monitor both the educational and training systems.

Optimum Utilization of Skills

The orientation law on national education specifies in Article 8: "At all levels of education, theoretical education should be linked with production. The state is supposed to provide job prospects at the end of a course of instruction and therefore to prepare reception structures."

Though the new school system makes production activities an important priority, the problem of transition from school into working life is crucial. There is a glut of unskilled labor on the labor market. At the production unit level, underemployment affects all sectors.

In its current stage, the Beninese economy is not in a position to provide all job applicants with employment. Young people graduating from primary school and those with secondary school certificates should be oriented toward the nonstructured sector.

The number of commercial trainees is also greater than the needs of the country. The glut of graduates in this sector is ascribed to private institutions, which have considerably increased their enrollment in recent years.

The third area of tension is university graduates. Their number greatly exceeds the absorptive capacity of the job market.

Prospects

This decisive role played by human resources in development is nowadays appreciated by all planners and policymakers. In Benin, efforts are being made to set up a coherent system for the planning of human resources. The creation of a National Committee on Human Resources, which constitutes a privileged forum for discussion and suggestions, has closed an institutional gap felt by all the economic partners of Benin. The smooth functioning of this institution will play a decisive role in the orientation of school children and students and will also bring about the setting up of a reliable data bank for employment, training and health.

Committed to universal education, but faced with a serious shortage of all categories of teaching staff, the Beninese authorities have appealed to the World Bank for the creation of three integrated teacher training colleges within the framework of Education Project II. These colleges, which will be in charge of the training and in-service training of the teaching staff in both the general and technical schools, will bridge the gap of qualified staff in the sector.

In order to bridge the statistics gap noted in recent years, it is imperative to set up a permanent system for the collection and processing of data on employment and training for the reinforcement of the national teams responsible for them. To this end, a Human Resources Planning Project has been prepared by Beninese executives, but due to a lack of financing, this project to study the connection between training and employment has not yet been implemented.

Finally, the forthcoming inception of population planning activities will facilitate the consideration of demographic variables in the elaboration of development plans and strengthen the gradual integration of human resource planning into economic planning.

Conclusion

To improve the role of human resources in the development of Benin, it is imperative that measures be taken to improve their quality and to ensure their utilization. To this end, it becomes urgent, on the one hand, to set up a coherent system of human resource management to support the National Committee and, on the other, to carry out a number of essential studies, namely :

a) Occupational mobility of workers, in order to better assess training needs.

b) Professional qualifications, which will allow an analysis of specific employment requirements with a view to improving training and in-service training programs.

c) Labor migration and the rural exodus.

d) Preparation of a dictionary of occupational titles.

CHAPTER 14

The Human Role in the Development Process: Experiences of Japan and Singapore

Ryokichi Hirono

There are a number of similarities between Japan and Singapore. During the last two decades or so, in spite of difficulties arising from energy crises twice during the 1970s, the two countries have exhibited remarkable development performances, with real per capita GNP rising annually at rates of 6.3 per cent and 7.4 per cent respectively during the period 1960-81. The unemployment rate has been kept to the minimum in both countries, while inflation rates were restrained at 5.2 per cent and 7.4 per cent respectively during the 1970s.

There was a decline in the rate of economic growth in both countries between the 1960s and the 1970s. In Japan, the annual rate of real GDP growth halved from 10.4 per cent during the 1960s to 4.5 per cent during the years 1970-81, while in Singapore it declined, albeit slightly, from 8.8 per cent to 8.5 per cent between the two decades. The high rate of increase in manufacturing value added during the 1960s, i.e., 13.6 per cent for Japan and 13.0 per cent for Singapore, was moderated in real terms during the years 1970-81 down to 6.5 per cent and 9.7 per cent respectively. These rates, however, constituted nearly the highest in their respective groups of countries. The largest decline took place in the rate of increase in gross domestic capital formation, i.e., from as high as 14.6 per cent to 3.1 per cent in Japan, and from 20.5 per cent to 7.2 per cent in Singapore.

Similarities between Japan and Singapore are observed not only in economic performance, but also in resource endowment and noneconomic aspects. Lacking the natural resources necessary for industrial development, the two countries have relied continuously upon imports of raw materials from abroad to process and export them in finished form. The only abundant economic resources available to both countries are human resources, skills and technologies. While the annual rate of increase in the labor force went down during the last two decades in both Japan and Singapore, i.e., from 1.9 per cent to 1.3 per cent in Japan and from 2.8 per cent to 2.7 per cent in Singapore, the quality of the labor force has been maintained and even improved. There has been a remarkable increase in the proportion of the school-age population going to middle schools, i.e., from 74 per cent to 91 per cent in Japan, and from 32 per cent to 55 per cent in Singapore. During the same period, the proportion of the 20-24 age group going for higher education rose from 10 to 30 per cent in Japan, while increasing only slightly, from 6 per cent to 8 per cent, in Singapore. In 1980 the adult literacy rate reached as high as 99 per cent in Japan, against 83 per cent in Singapore. There has also been a relatively long period of political stability in each country under a single political party's regime.

Differences

There are also major differences between Singapore and Japan. Singapore was a British colony and remained undeveloped for a long time before gaining political independence. There is still a colonial mentality, and many residues of colonialism in political, legal, social and educational life are finally giving way before the changing needs and requirements of a politically independent and economically industrializing country. Except for a brief period of Allied occupation after World War II, Japan has never been a colony of any western power, taking pride in maintaining for centuries its own indigenous culture, traditions and social institutions. Singapore is a multiracial, multilingual and multicultural society, making it more difficult for Singaporeans to remain both united and dedicated to their national interests. On the other hand, Japan has a relatively homogeneous population, speaking a common mother tongue and sharing similar social values.

Economically, contrary to Japan, Singapore has a small domestic market, which has compelled Singapore to adopt an export-oriented industrialization strategy and to become even more dependent upon the rest of the world economy in terms of both productive inputs and product markets. Merchandise imports and exports were both rising faster during the 1970s than during the 1960s, i.e., from 5.9 per cent to 9.9 per cent per annum for imports, and from 4.2 per cent to 12.0 per cent per annum for exports. Unlike Singapore's performance, Japan's rate of increases in merchandise imports and exports went down from an annual average of 13.7 per cent and 17.2 per cent respectively in the 1960s to 3.9 per cent and 9.0 per cent in the 1970s. As a result, in 1981, merchandise imports as a per cent of GDP were 213.8 per cent, and merchandise exports as a per cent of GDP were 162.4 per cent in Singapore, whereas the respective figures for Japan were 12.7 per cent and 13.5 per cent. While Japan has in recent years been a perennial payments-surplus economy, Singapore has constantly been a payments-deficit country, running in 1981 a deficit of US$ 1,750 million against Japan's surplus of US$ 5,117 million. Singapore's deficits have been financed in the main by both private direct investment and borrowing from overseas, and to a small extent by public borrowings from multilateral and bilateral sources, including Japan.

In terms of economic structures, Singapore has been moving away from a traditionally service-oriented to an increasingly manu-facturing-oriented economy. During the period 1960-81, GDP originating from the service sectors declined from 78 per cent to 58 per cent, while GDP originating from the manufacturing sector increased from 12 to 30 per cent. Japan has been moving in just the opposite direction, with the service sectors rising from 42 per cent to 53 per cent of GDP and the manufacturing sector declining from 34 per cent to 30 per cent during the same period. Partly reflecting this trend towards a larger manufacturing base, Singapore, unlike Japan, has become a very energy-intensive economy, with per capita energy consumption in 1980 reaching as high as 8,544 kilograms in coal equivalent, against 4,649 kilograms for Japan.

Requirements of Industrialization and Modernization

Singapore and Japan were in a similar predicament at the time of launching their respective national industrialization and modernization programs, although the time of launching was nearly a century apart.

Confronted with the military threat of western imperialist powers, but with a strong sense of nationalism among the population, the newly created Meiji Government had to fully mobilize domestic financial and manpower resources for achieving the two overwhelming objectives of the nation, i.e., the enrichment of national economic power and the strengthening of national defense capability. Since

Japan's was a predominantly agrarian economy with a low level of per capita GNP, a large reservoir of unskilled manpower resources and a keen shortage of risk-taking capital, the difficult task ahead compelled the government to take an initiative in the provision of economic and social infrastructures essential to the national economic and military buildup and, in addition, to set up critical manufacturing industries which would lay down the industrial, technical and financial foundations of modern industry. The government also encouraged the private sector, then composed of merchant capitalists and artisans/craftsmen, to establish modern industrial, financing, wholesale and shipping companies and move into the production of goods and services required by industrialization and modernization programs.

Japan was fortunate that at that juncture in history, all the feudalistic ideologies and institutions preceding the Meiji Restoration helped the government to maintain tight control over the population. It allowed the government to tax the people, particularly on the farm, to channel public savings into the new industralization and modernization programs, to induce people to maintain plain living as a traditional virtue of life so as to moblize private savings for national priority programs, and to educate people to improve on their relatively high literacy rate and favorable work ethics.

The government introduced a compulsory national education system whereby all children were compelled to go to primary school and study for four years at the outset and for six years under the later educational reform in order to cope with the general requirements of modern industry and administration. Since workers had to be mobilised predominantly from the rural areas to work away from their homes and families in modern industrial mills, employee residence halls were set up on or near the factory compound, and further education and training were given after work by factory management. Emphasis was laid not only on enlightening employees on new techniques and methods of production, but also on maintaining and improving their team spirit.

Many technical schools and colleges were set up to train primary and secondary school graduates to take up technical and specialized jobs in modern factories and workshops. To meet the increasing demand/supply gap for qualified skilled workers and technicians and to improve on the technical and human relations quality of these crucial workers, both public and private sector companies set up in-house training facilities and institutions. Engineering universities were later introduced to develop the engineers increasingly required by the rapidly expanding metal industries and machinery industries. As part of such technical and engineering capacitation programs, both government and private sector companies invited, at high cost, a number of engineers from overseas in an attempt to speed the transfer of technology to their Japanese counterparts. They also sent thousands of engineers and other professional personnel abroad to learn about technology alternatives being used in the industrially developed countries.

Though surrounded by a much more fortunate international political and economic environment than Japan, Singapore was confronted, in launching its industrialization and modernization programs after World War II, with a similar set of internal constraints. Although better educated and more literate than the average workers in neighboring developing countries, Singapore's work force was predominantly unskilled and industrially untrained because of its high concentration in entrepot trade and related servicing activities prior to political independence. With the adoption by the British government of the East-of-Suez policy and the separation of Singapore from the Federation of Malaysia in 1965, there was a rising level of unemployment in Singapore. The business mentality and practices of merchant capitalists in the country were such that they were not willing to take a risk in such long-term investment ventures as manufacturing activities. And there was little tradition of developing manufacturing technologies among the government bureaucracy and business entrepreneurs.

Confronted with these domestic constraints, the Singapore government had no choice but to expand education and training facilities and programs to meet the critical shortage of industrially trained manpower necessary for industrialization. Other than initiating some public sector enterprises in certain limited sectors of the national economy, the government relied in the main on foreign investors willing to bring in risk capital, technology and management knowhow, as well as overseas markets for their output. Fortunately for Singapore, by the early 1960s there were plenty of American, Japanese and European manufacturing investors seeking viable investment opportunities overseas. Because of its strategic location, well-developed harbors, warehousing, road network, financing, communications and other servicing activities, the availability of trainable and hard-working labor, and favorable prospects for political stability and bureaucratic efficiency, Singapore was a logical choice for many foreign investors. The only critical problem was the small size of its domestic market , which would compel foreign investors to market their products overseas. As foreign manufacturing investments became larger and more diversified, domestic merchant capitalists joined in these new, longer-term manufacturing ventures and contributed to the further industrialization of Singapore.

Dual Role of Education in Industrializing and Modernizing States

In any industrializing and modernizing state, education, whether public or private, has a dual role to play. On the one hand, to meet the objective of the state to industrialize its national economy, education has to be geared and dedicated to the continuous development and improvement of the quality of manpower so that workers can both adapt themselves to the changing technical and mental requirements of advancing technologies and increasingly complex social organization, and still work efficiently on the jobs assigned. On the other hand, to meet the objectives of the state to modernize its society and social institutions, education has to be geared to the continuous upgrading of the human quality of individuals so that the individual citizens can both better appreciate such virtues as faith, love, honesty and beauty, and also discharge their social responsibilities to make their community a more pleasant and livable place.

To facilitate the process of industrialization and modernization, both the Japanese and Singaporean governments expanded their primary, secondary and tertiary education programs and reoriented them toward the production of industrial manpower, including skilled technicians and engineers, and clerical and professional manpower, including secretarial, accounting, sales, administrative, legal and managerial staff. The expansion and improvement of general education was emphasized in both countries to involve the masses in their respective industrialization and modernization programs. The people were to provide the semiskilled labor increasingly required in modern factory production and office work. There was also a prerequisite of technical and more specialized education at the secondary level for the limited number of people who would provide supervisory labor in modern mills, and at the tertiary level for the selected few who would become top management personnel in government and various private sector organizations.

In manning the secondary and tertiary schools, particularly in technical and professional areas, liberal use was made in both countries of teachers and instructors from many European countries and the United States to meet the critical shortage of well-educated and well-trained teachers at home. Thousands of teachers and potential teachers over a few decades were sent overseas for further training in teaching methods and for advanced courses in specialized subjects.

In-house training for company employees received greater emphasis at that time in Japan than in today's Singapore, partly because the quality of general and technical education available to employees prior to joining companies was inferior to present-day Singapore's and partly because corporate management in Japan found it profitable in the long run to invest in human capital in a social milieu where workers tend to be less mobile between different companies. The Japanese corporate system of rotating workers from one job to another, from one department to another and from one location to another, including overseas assignments every three or four years, also requires a much more intensive in-house training program so that the workers are able to work more efficiently as a team in any job, department or location assigned. In-house training programs are thus well tailored to the requirements of different jobs, departments, locations and levels of management.

In Singapore, both production and nonproduction workers tend to move from one company to another in search of higher pay, faster promotion and greater job challenge, which understandably does not induce corporate management to invest in company employees through intensive and extensive in-house training programs. When, as is usual in Singapore, a company is small, less diversified and less dispersed in the country, an employee's chances for exposure to different jobs and people within the same company are limited, forcing those who seek such opportunities to move from one company to another. That the mobility of workers in smaller firms·is greater than that of workers in larger firms in Japan attests to the universal preference among workers, irrespective of nationalities, to be exposed to different jobs and people, as well as to respond rationally to economic incentives. Workers in larger, diversified, multiplant companies in Japan are provided with such opportunities not only without making intercompany moves, but through regularized intracompany rotation programs.

To the extent that Singaporean mentality was affected by British and western individualistic values, particularly among the educated and top-to-middle-class layers of society, the organizational culture and philosophy in government and private sector enterprises are based on an individualistic orientation, where creativity and competitiveness are the basic criteria for judging individual and corporate performance. Although the extremes of western individualism are moderated in Singapore by the predominance of a lower-middle-class Chinese population, among whom Confucian respect for family and hierarchy still predominates and by the surrounding Malay population, culture and traditions, the individualistic values and orientation among the elite are widely shared by the middle-class segment of the Chinese, Malay and Indo-Pakistani population aspiring to join the elite. The high interfirm labor mobility among educated Singaporean workers must certainly have a great deal to do with such a value orientation.

In spite of exposure since the Meiji Restoration to western individualistic ideology, education, technology and culture, and in spite of the brief but active intervention by the Allied occupation forces after World War II, groupistic values have remained characteristic of Japanese individual and corporate behavior. Under Japanese groupism, creativity and brilliance of individuals are less important than cooperation and harmony among individuals in running corporate and other organizational activities. Individual interests are integrated into group interests, and individual employees identify their interests and objectives with those of their respective work groups, workshops and corporations. While individual employees' performance is crucial to corporate success, their devotion and dedication to corporate objectives and interests are considered vital. In fact, individual employees are appraised on the basis of their devotion and dedication, assessed by their superiors in consultation with coworkers, as much as by their work performance. This explains why Japanese employees tend to stay at work for long hours every day and take as little paid leave as is socially condoned and practiced.

In Japanese corporations, human resources are considered the most vital element, and human resource management is accorded the highest priority. Corporate management is deeply concerned with the well-being of individual employees and their families, as is exemplified by a wide range of corporate welfare schemes, including family picnics and athletic meetings sponsored and attended by all the top management of factories and corporate offices. Wages and salaries tend to move up with the age and the length of service of individual workers and in accordance with their families' increasing financial requirements. Corporations often provide their employees with either low-rent housing facilities or low-cost housing loans, as well as low-cost education loans for their children. Incentive schemes are usually provided on a group basis, and workers bear collective responsibility for their performance. The group approach to work and responsibility is conducive to higher efficiency and productivity among workers because of their devotion and dedication to corporate objectives and their insatiable zeal for self-improvement and higher efficiency. These qualities, in turn, are the result of corporate incentive schemes and prevailing social values.

Education at home, school and in corporations, which in itself is the cause and effect of prevailing social values, has thus contributed in a substantial manner to the rapid economic development of Japan and Singapore.

CHAPTER 15

Human Development in Jordan

Crown Prince Hassan Bin Talal

As we all know from introductory economics, development brings about integrated socioeconomic structural change with a view to mobilizing and utilizing resources in such a way as to achieve the highest possible level of welfare in a given society. In economic jargon, development implies more output and changes in technical and institutional arrangements, as well as changes in the allocation of inputs by different sectors. However, the whole process must reflect on the individual human being in producing a better quality of life, whether this is judged by higher income levels, satisfaction of basic needs or other criteria. In some cases, this may be a theoretical objective beyond the reach of a given generation. Hence, greater emphasis is placed on the other side of the relationship, namely, on making human resources the vehicle for further national development. In this sense, they are looked at as a means to a desired end.

Some renowned economists who have spoken on the subject include Fredrick Harbison, who said that human resources are the ultimate measure of the wealth of nations; Alfred Marshal, who said, "The most valuable capital is man"; and Karl Marx, who postulated that the human being is the element which gives the cosmos its value.

Whether the objective of development or its tool, the quality of human resources determines the efficiency of mobilizing other factors of production and the priorities of their use. We know that in a static condition, production depends on labor, capital, land and entrepreneurship. However, development cannot proceed except in a dynamic society where two other factors come into play: technology and time. In certain instances, it appeared that some factors were more significant than others. Thus, after World War II, capital accumulation was thought to be the key to development. A long time ago, the Physiocrats considered land or natural resources as the only source of production. But in the last two decades, human resources, which include both labor and entrepreneurship, have been given due consideration, with emphasis on training, education and management.

The role of the human element in development cannot be divorced from the notion of investment in human capital, which comes via education. Hence the quality of education plays a paramount role in this issue. Investment in human capital is cybernetic in nature, and a substantial segment of it, in Jordan's case, is directed to regional development.

As we all know, the role of investment in the education and training of human beings has begun to be better understood in many countries. The human element can and should be upgraded in such a way as to suit development needs. In retrospect, its role can be clearly traced if we consider what happened in countries devastated by war. Taking Japan and Germany as examples, we can easily discern that they were virtually rebuilt through human ingenuity. By the same token, we should bear in mind that human deviations and misguided human judgment have themselves instigated the plight of many nations during two world wars.

Jordan is not rich in natural or financial resources. Luckily, however, it enjoys a high quality of manpower. In the words of His Majesty King Hussein, "Man is our most valuable possession." Jordan's human resources have played an important role in the development not only of Jordan, but also of many other states in the region.

Socioeconomic Progress

Right from the beginning of its modernization and development drive more than thirty years ago, Jordan has held firmly to the conviction that the Jordanian citizen was the means, as well as the beneficiary, of our national development. This conviction was translated into a strategy affecting the speed and nature of our development process. Apart from making eminent sense in human terms, it also emanated from the difficult constraints that Jordan faced, particularly in the early phases of its socioeconomic progress.

The Jordanian economy is small in size, whether judged by geographical land mass (90,000 square kilometers), GNP (JD 1.9 billion) or population (2.7 million in 1985). Close to 83 per cent of its area is arid, with irrigated farming accounting for only 1.5 per cent of the total. Phosphates, potash and limestone are abundant, but other natural resources are scarce. For our energy needs, we depend almost entirely on imported oil, which amounts to 20 per cent of the import bill and inflates our production costs. Oil exploration has been under way for some years now, but so far with limited success as far as prospects of economic utilization are concerned. Other serious constraints and challenges were the Israeli occupation of the West Bank, including Arab Jerusalem; the threat of further Israeli military expansion; political instability in the region, coupled with violence and ideological upheavals; and the vacillating character of regional cooperation.

Against this not-so-favorable climate for development, Jordan has achieved remarkable progress. The growth rate of our national income was among the highest in the developing world and was sustained for relatively long periods in the 1960s and 1970s (10 per cent annually in real terms). A modern infrastructure was built across the country: roads, telecommunications, electricity, water and so forth. University enrollment is the highest among developing countries. Institution-building spanned all areas of public services, private concerns and banking facilities. With the exception of a few years in the mid-1970s, growth was achieved with bearable inflation, contributing to economic stability and a strong Jordanian dinar.

True, because of scarce financial resources, Jordan succeeded in avoiding social unrest. The distribution impact of development, though difficult to measure, was always carefully monitored by policymakers. Social harmony has been maintained among workers, employers and the government. Opportunities have been open to any individuals willing to improve their skills or to seek social, occupational or geographical mobility. Islamic values are upheld without rigidity or closed-mindedness. Private ownership is protected, and private initiative is encouraged. All in all, our development has not been a purely economic exercise, but also a truly humane experiment.

Labor Mobility

Regional and local demands on Jordanian human resources are such that there is always a pressing need for increasing and strengthening the educational and vocational training facilities of the country. Hence, the successive five-year plans have placed a special emphasis on the upgrading of human resources, including not only adult education and literacy programs, but also an expansion of training opportunities in management and administration.

It is worth mentioning in this specialized context that Jordan has stressed the role of women in development, although their participation in the labor force remains fairly low. To rectify this situation, and to increase the scope and effectiveness of available human resources, the current five-year plan has addressed the role of women in the development process, with encouraging results. This is all the more pressing given the fact that, besides the fundamental role of human resources inside Jordan, about one-third of the Jordanian labor force is contributing to the development of neighboring Arab countries.

We recognised at an early date that the economic boom in the Gulf during the middle and late 1970s was bound to generate inflationary pressures in Jordan, causing real wages to remain below their nominal level. But because of limited resources, Jordan was unable to compensate its workers for the shortfall in wages, with the result that they were impelled to seek higher pay in neighboring Arab countries, especially in the Gulf, which has buoyant economies. This labor drain had the effect of reversing the traditional picture, and we found ourselves in dire need of labor, where previously, Jordan had enjoyed a surplus. In turn, the ensuing shortage of necessary skills had its impact on the country's ability to implement national development plans. On the other side of the coin, and as a result of this brain drain, there was significant internal migration from the rural to the urban areas.

In recent years, the international migration of labor has been prevalent and has acquired a position of utmost importance. Like many other countries, Jordan has also been an exporter of trained labor to developed countries. This movement of labor has benefited both the exporters and importers of human resources, but at different net levels. Not only does this form of brain drain inflict economic losses on the exporting countries, but it also decreases their scientific and technological potential. Labor-exporting countries should turn this situation to their advantage by formulating policies aimed at utilizing the experience of their nationals abroad.

The Jordanian government has consistently paid special attention to the upgrading and management of manpower. The main objective is to deal with labor imbalances by creating jobs for new entrants into the labor market and meeting labor shortages through education, training and a judicious importation of workers. Jordan has experienced both situations, unemployment and a tight labor market. In order to achieve the desired flexibility, we have adopted a range of policies on manpower management, as described below.

Manpower Management Policies

a) Investment in education has become a national priority. Before 1962, there were no universities in Jordan. Twenty years later, we have 3 universities and 46 public and private community colleges, with a total enrollment of 50,000 students. In addition, there are 60,000 Jordanians studying in higher educational institutions abroad. The rate of return on education has been high, particularly with regard to employment in the Gulf Cooperation Council (GCC) states.

b) Jordan has a liberal policy on the outflow of its manpower to the GCC states, where 270,000 Jordanians work at the present time. Jordanian workers have taken up professional, technical and skilled jobs in an essential process of regional cooperation. Even when Jordan faced labor shortages in the late 1970s, the door was kept open for Jordanian workers to leave for the Gulf.

c) The remittances of Jordanian workers abroad have been an important source of foreign exchange and savings contributing to the financing of the country's development plans. In 1984, JD 485 million was received in remittances through the banking system, with an estimated 50 per cent of that total additionally coming in through other channels. The government refrained from enacting restrictions on the individual use of these funds, preferring recourse to investment incentives to determine their allocation.

d) With the development boom in the region and in Jordan since the mid-1970s, Jordan was obliged to import foreign labor from neighboring and other countries, particularly Egypt. Currently, there are 125,000 foreign workers in Jordan, mostly engaged in semiskilled and manual jobs in construction, agriculture and services. The inflow of foreign labor has been under government scrutiny with regard to both numbers and occupations in order to minimize competition with Jordanian workers. Though manpower projections in Jordan indicate a general labor surplus and a concomitant rise in unemployment in the coming years, there will be a continued need for more than 50,000 manual workers from abroad due to mismatches in required skills.

e) The government sends promising young administrators for further training and education abroad, thus providing the civil service, particularly in new institutions, with qualified and high-level manpower. Realizing the important role of the civil service in furthering development, the government introduced a set of policies aimed at improving working conditions and personnel management.

f) Jordan has been persistent in seeking an increase in the participation of women in the labor force. Starting from a low rate of 4.8 per cent in 1974, female participation rose considerably, to about 15 per cent in the last decade. Women workers are no longer confined to traditional jobs in agriculture, teaching and nursing, but have branched out into most occupations. Females account for 55 per cent of all teachers, 31 per cent of bank employees, 23 per cent of the total staff in tourist firms and 9 per cent of industrial workers. Their enrollment rate in higher education is now close to that of males — more than 40 per cent overall, and exceeding 50 per cent in several fields of specialization.

g) Jordan's liberal economic policies have encouraged the promotion of private sector entrepreneurs and activated the role of voluntary institutions in social and economic development. Investment by the private sector has consistently surpassed the levels in successive development plans. Private investors have significantly contributed to the rapid expansion of the last decade by investing in modern agriculture, new industrial ventures, hotels, real estate, transport and other economic activities. In addition, institutions of the private sector are invited to take part in the preparation of development plans and in drafting new laws and regulations — for example, the Amman Chamber of Industry, the Federation of the Chambers of Commerce, the Association of Banks, the Federation of Trade Unions and others. There are more than 350 voluntary societies providing social services to the poor, the retarded, the handicapped and broken families, as well as underprivileged geographical communities.

h) Finally, Jordan's income policy has made it a priority to improve the real wages of workers with a view to ensuring that nominal wages increase faster than inflation. Other benefits are extended to workers, including social security, housing at reasonable cost and medical care. There are seventeen trade unions representing the various occupations, in addition to a number of professional associations. These are entitled to engage in collective bargaining with employers and the government to improve working conditions.

PART IV

CONTRIBUTIONS OF DIFFERENT SECTORS

CHAPTER 16

Women, Institutions and Development

Mercedes Pulido de Briceno

Development is commonly described as a process in which the changing of certain conditions leads to an improvement in the quality of life in societies. What are these conditions? How can these conditions be influenced, and in what manner should they be evaluated? These are crucial questions. Depending on the answers given, different development models will result, with different emphasis in their plans of action and with results that are not always predictable.

The United Nations has thrice declared a special decade dedicated to development since the 1960s in response to the needs formulated by the community of member states. Important changes occurred throughout these decades. For example, during the first decade, economic growth seemed to be the key objective of development, on the assumption that economic indicators such as housing, food, health and education, among others, would move in harmony with this rate of growth. It is clear from the documents of this decade that the economic planners of the period "saw the development problem almost entirely in terms of building domestic capacity within the developing countries to achieve a self-sustained growth in the long run." [1] As a consequence, the local capacity to save, capital inflow, education and technical assistance became essential factors in achieving the desired range of growth.

Although the importance of economic growth was maintained during the 1970s, emphasis was directed towards a more egalitarian distribution of wealth, and in particular, to the least-developed segments of the population. Writers of the period called attention to the unequal relationships between countries and to "the need for special measures in favour of the least developed and land-locked among the developing countries, to offset the persistent bias in the world economic system against such countries." [2] In these cases, the achievement of a global strategy was dependent to a large extent on the degree to which the objectives of the decade coincided or maintained a relationship with the national objectives of member states.

The inequalities and imbalances in international economic relations stand out very clearly in the literature of the 1980s, when the problem of development is described as conditioned by factors other than those of a mere economic nature. The political situation begins to form part of the analysis of the problem, basically through an analysis of North-South, East-West and South-South relationships. On the other hand, a series of objectives is being established, among which it is very difficult to find an order of priority. They seem, however, to point to one central problem — the lack of world peace — and to identify two groups of the population whose conditions call for immediate attention: women and youth.

The fact that youth represents a high proportion of the population in both the least-developed countries and the developing countries explains the special attention that youth is given throughout the present decade. For instance, according to statistical information available from the United Nations, in 1984 the youth population, that is, those under fifteen years of age, represented more than 46 per cent of the total population in twenty countries, including Kenya, Botswana, Nicaragua and Bangladesh. [3]

Women, on the other hand, represent half the world population, and their situation as the procreating part of the human species has given rise to conditions that affect them in a very special manner. This explains the interest of many different social groups in addressing this issue.

The decade of the 1980s presents a rather complex panorama at the global level which provides the background for each and every development process. Many countries of the global community have recently felt the impact of an economic crisis that brought up such problems as external debt, inflation, deflation, increasing unemployment and similar afflictions.

The consequences of such processes differ for every region. The developed countries can count on flexible productive machinery and on important technological innovations for their production; their service sector allows them to respond in a relatively efficient and positive manner to any crisis. It is foreseeable that "the need for financing in . . . industrial countries would absorb a substantial share of the available resources in the world financial markets. On the other hand, it is estimated that official aid for development will not grow in real terms or it will only do so in a small scale."[4]

The developing countries face great difficulties with changes in international trade. The limited ability of their productive machinery to respond appropriately, and the relative weakness of their service infrastructures, create a difficult outlook for these countries. They are obliged, then, to look for innovative alternatives on the basis of their local resources — those which are productive, as well as those provided by nature or by their populations.

The role of women as an active element in the development process must be studied in light of all these variables. Policies and programs that have been implemented up to now have made it possible to bring women into this process. However, their specific conditions have been given little consideration. This has created a series of obstacles and limitations that become apparent by analyzing some available data.

Women and Development: Basic Assumptions

In reality, the status of women, as well as the development process, are matters of enormous complexity and variety. Countries and regions show basic differences in their conditions of development. At the same time, the status of women varies within the borders of one and the same country. However, some general observations may serve as a basis for discussion on the subject.

Concern for the status of women is a relatively recent phenomenon within the framework of the global community. It was only in 1975 — through the world conference and the declaration of the Decade for Women — that institutional mechanisms were set up to deal with this specific area.[5] The situation of women should be seen within the framework of development that we just finished reviewing, that is, linking it with the need to achieve a better quality of life through the three fundamental principles of the world conference: equality, development and peace.

Within this context, the integration of women in development implies specifically:

a) Equality in opportunities for education.
b) Equality in employment opportunities.

c) Equal access to health services.

d) Full participation in public service.

The basic assumption underlying these priorities is the following: To the extent that countries develop their internal capacities, women will have greater possibilities to participate in the educational process and the labor market, have access to better services and enjoy higher standards of health.

The situation of women has changed during the past few years, partly because of progress made in the development process in many countries and partly due to initiatives taken during the Decade for Women. However, as will be shown later, the scarcity of women participating at the highest decision-making levels, their partially self-induced exclusion from less traditional fields of work and the burden of their double role (at home and outside the home) are some examples of the need to introduce certain changes to ensure an improvement in the terms under which women are brought into the development system.

Women, Institutions and Development

The presence of women in institutions linked to critical areas of development constitutes an important prerequisite for their assumption of a major role in this process. Education, work and health are aspects that have traditionally been linked to possibilities of improving the quality of life, and the status of women in these areas has shown significant advances in the last decades. At the same time, women have entered the world of political organizations in an active manner. Below are some facts to illustrate this.

Women and Education

This is one of the areas in which the participation of women has been very important during the decade. It can be reviewed from two perspectives: formal education (the educational system) and informal education (literacy campaigns and other types of training).

In the formal educational system, two situations shed light on the participation of women: their access as students and their access as teachers. In spite of the difficulty of presenting precise statistical data from so many different sources, and in spite of problems in comparing different educational systems, the publications of UNESCO provide a data base that allows us at least to identify the main trends. Table 1 provides the estimated percentages of female enrollment in education by main regions. It show that :

a) Female enrollment exceeds 40 per cent of the total in all regions of the world.
b) Among the regions, Europe, the Americas and Oceania show the highest proportion of women enrolled in formal education.
c) There are important differences between the developed countries, where women represent half (49 per cent) of total enrollment, and the developing countries, where the highest proportion was 42 per cent in the years 1980 and 1981 and 40 per cent in 1982.
d) For 1982, Asia and the Arab states are the regions which showed the lowest proportions of female enrollment.
e) The transition from primary to tertiary education is characterized by an important reduction in the proportion of female enrollment.
f) Europe has the highest proportion of enrollment at the tertiary level, while the lowest percentages are found in Africa.
g) The general trend shows an increase in women's participation in education between 1970 and 1982.

Therefore, in spite of major differences from region to region, education has been one of the main factors bringing women into the development process. On the other hand, when women enter the educational system to teach, they are found mainly at the primary and secondary levels. Their access to teaching positions at the tertiary level is very limited. Notwithstanding the difficulty of comparison inherent in the data, tables 2 and 3 show some situations that illustrate this.

TABLE 1
Estimates of Female Enrollment by Level in Respect to
Overall Enrollment
(Percentage)

		Total	1st Level	2nd Level	3rd Level
World total	1970	–		–	–	–
(including China)	1975	44	45	44	40
	1980	44	45	44	42
	1981	44	45	44	43
	1982	43	44	40	43
World total	1970	44	45	44	38
(excluding China)	1975	44	45	45	40
	1980	45	45	45	43
	1981	45	45	45	43
	1982	43	45	40	43
Africa	1970	39	40	31	23
	1975	40	42	35	25
	1980	42	43	37	26
	1981	42	43	39	27
	1982	43	45	39	27
America	1970	48	49	49	40
	1975	48	49	49	44
	1980	49	49	50	49
	1981	49	49	50	50
	1982	49	49	50	50
Asia	1970	39	41	35	27
	1975	40	41	37	29
	1980	41	42	38	32
	1981	41	43	38	32
	1982	37	41	27	32
Europe	1970	49	49	51	43
(including USSR)	1975	50	49	52	45
	1980	50	49	52	47
	1981	50	49	52	47
	1982	50	49	52	47
Oceania	1970	47	48	48	33
	1975	47	48	48	40
	1980	48	48	49	44
	1981	48	48	49	44
	1982	48	48	49	44

– Continued

TABLE 1 – Continued

		Total	1st Level	2nd Level	3rd Level
Developed	1970	49	49	50	41
countries	1975	49	49	51	44
	1980	49	49	51	47
	1981	49	49	51	48
	1982	49	49	51	48
Developing	1970	40	42	35	29
Countries	1975	41	43	37	32
	1980	42	43	39	34
	1981	42	44	39	35
	1982	40	43	31	35
Africa	1970	40	41	33	20
(excluding Arab	1975	42	43	36	20
states)	1980	43	44	37	20
	1981	43	44	38	20
	1982	44	45	37	20
Asia	1970	39	41	35	27
(excluding Arab	1975	40	42	37	29
states)	1980	41	42	38	31
	1981	41	43	38	32
	1982	37	41	27	32
Arab states	1970	35	36	30	24
	1975	37	38	34	28
	1980	39	41	37	31
	1981	40	41	40	32
	1982	40	41	40	32
North America	1970	48	49	50	41
	1975	49	49	50	45
	1980	50	49	50	51
	1981	50	49	49	52
	1982	50	49	49	52
Latin America	1970	48	49	48	35
	1975	48	49	48	42
	1980	49	49	51	44
	1981	49	49	50	44
	1982	49	48	51	45

SOURCE: *UNESCO Statistical Yearbook 1984,* Table 2.4, pp. II-17, 18.

TABLE 2
Estimated Female Teaching Staff by Level of Education
(Percentage)

		1st Level	2nd Level
World total	1970	—	—
(including China)	1975	52	—
	1980	52	39
	1981	51	40
	1982	52	40
World total	1970	58	45
(excluding China)	1975	58	45
	1980	57	44
	1981	57	43
	1982	57	43
Africa	1970	31	31
	1975	32	30
	1980	33	32
	1981	33	32
	1982	44	32
America	1970	82	47
	1975	80	46
	1980	79	46
	1981	79	46
	1982	79	46
Asia	1970	36	27
	1975	37	30
	1980	40	30
	1981	40	30
	1982	39	30
Europe	1970	70	56
(including USSR)	1975	70	57
	1980	71	56
	1981	71	56
	1982	71	56
Oceania	1970	63	46
	1975	65	46
	1980	64	46
	1981	64	46
	1982	63	45

– Continued

TABLE 2 – Continued

		1st Level	2nd Level
Developed countries	1970	72	51
	1975	72	51
	1980	72	51
	1981	72	51
	1982	72	51
Developing countries	1970	45	33
	1975	47	34
	1980	47	34
	1981	47	34
	1982	48	34
Africa	1970	28	36
(excluding Arab states)	1975	31	33
	1980	31	33
	1981	31	33
	1982	45	32
Asia	1970	36	27
(excluding Arab states)	1975	37	29
	1980	40	30
	1981	39	30
	1982	38	30
Arab states	1970	37	27
	1975	37	30
	1980	42	32
	1981	43	33
	1982	45	33
North America	1970	84	45
	1975	82	46
	1980	81	45
	1981	81	45
	1982	81	45
Latin America	1970	81	49
	1975	78	46
	1980	77	47
	1981	77	47
	1982	77	47

SOURCE: *UNESCO Statistical yearbook 1984,* Table 2.5, pp. II-20, 21.

TABLE 3
Estimated Female Teaching Staff in 3rd Level in All Institutions
(Percentage)

		3rd Level
Africa		
Congo	1970	21
	1975	15
	1979	7
	1980	9
Malawi	1970	13
	1975	9
	1979	13
	1980	20
Mali	1970	7
	1975	–
	1978	12
	1979	10
Niger	1975	15
	1979	11
	1980	13
America, North		
Canada	1970	–
	1975	–
	1979	21
	1980	24
	1981	21
	1982	21
El Salvador	1970	17
	1975	23
	1979	20
	1980	23
	1981	24
America, South		
Argentina	1970	31
	1975	39
	1979	40
	1980	43
	1981	44
	1982	44

– Continued

TABLE 3 — Continued

		3rd Level
Colombia	1970	—
	1975	14
	1979	19
	1980	20
	1981	21
	1982	21
Peru (universities and equivalent)	1970	10
	1975	12
	1979	16
	1980	16
	1981	17
	1982	18
Asia		
Bangladesh	1970	8
	1979	11
	1980	11
	1981	12
	1982	11
China	1970	—
	1975	24
	1978	—
	1979	26
	1980	25
	1981	26
	1982	26
India	1970	—
	1975	17
	1978	18
	1979	18
Iraq	1970	9
	1975	20
	1979	16
	1980	17
	1981	16
	1982	18
Europe		
Bulgaria	1970	26
	1975	32
	1979	36
	1980	39
	1981	34
	1982	37

— Continued

TABLE 3 – Continued

		3rd Level
Norway	1970	17
	1975	16
	1979	19
	1980	19
	1981	26
Portugal	1970	19
	1975	32
	1978	33
	1979	34
	1980	32
Oceania		
New Zealand	1975	23
	1979	–
	1980	25
	1981	26
	1982	27

SOURCE: *UNESCO Statistical Yearbook 1984*, Table 3.11, pp. III-254, 283.

Although information about the participation of women at the management level in educational institutions is scarce, one may suppose that something similar to what we observed before happens: as the level rises, women's participation decreases. Some regional and national studies show that women who rise to the highest levels of education mainly choose professions that are closely linked to the traditional concept of the female role. This may be seen as self-discrimination, but nevertheless, it is a step towards better conditions of life.

With regard to informal education, two types of problems are usually approached jointly: literacy campaigns and vocational training programs. In some regions and countries, serious efforts have been made recently to bring down the level of illiteracy, which seems to go hand in hand with the level of poverty and the distribution of the rural population. These efforts seem to have been more successful where they were linked to some form of training aimed at increasing labor productivity. In such cases, literacy training does not take the form of an isolated program, but rather of a useful and indispensable tool that makes it easier to carry out economic activities which are normally linked to basic subsistence needs.

Women show high levels of illiteracy in all regions. Certainly, this presents an important restraint to their integration into the development process, because apart from the factors already mentioned, illiteracy in women can also be associated with a particular view of their role as mother and wife, in which the lack of reading and writing skills is not seen as a problem.

Women and the Labor Market

Paid labor, or employment, is usually seen as one of the direct way in which women are linked to the development process. Statistics in this area may, however, be misleading. First of all, it should be clear that the work women do in the home takes place outside of any economic category; therefore, it should be stressed that most societies do not place any economic value on caring for a family when this is carried out by housewives. The moment that an outsider takes on these responsibilities, however, domestic labor is considered employment and normally included in the service sector. Efforts have been made to establish a methodology to quantify the work of housewives. For example, studies done in Venezuela, Poland, the USA and Canada show that the contribution of such work to the GNP reaches a very high level if it is accounted for as productive work or employment. The work of rural women also presents serious problems when considered from an economic or statistical perspective, since in many instances it is considered an extension of their domestic duties. These facts indicate that there is a certain neglect or lack of appreciation for this type of work, though by its very nature it makes a fundamental contribution to society.

It is particularly difficult to make general statements concerning women and the labor market, not only because situations can be so diverse, but also because the methodologies are lacking that would allow a comparison of data. However, some trends can be described on the basis of information provided by the ILO and INSTRAW. Table 4 shows how the participation of women in the work force has increased in the various regions since 1950. The developed areas show the highest levels of participation. With regard to the regional distribution of working women, "in 1975, women workers of Asia, Africa and Latin America accounted for 68.5 per cent of the total... Asia alone accounts for more than half of all 'economically active' women."[6] For 1985 these same regions accounted for 70.4 per cent of all female workers. The distributions across the different occupational sectors vary substantially from one region to the next. For example, in Africa, women are mainly found in agriculture, while "the industrial sector offered relatively little opportunities for women during the 1950-1970 period."[7] On the other hand, during the past few years, the participation of women in the service sectors has increased significantly.

TABLE 4
Labor Force Participation of Women by Region: 1950-2000

Region	Year	Female Labor Force Participation Rate (%)	Female Share of Total Labor Force (%)	Female Labor Force Distribution (%)
World				
	1950	27.5	31.3	100.0
	1975	29.1	35.0	100.0
	1980	28.6	34.8	100.0
	1985	28.2	34.6	100.0
	2000	28.2	34.5	100.0
Asia				
	1950	26.0	29.0	50.2
	1975	29.2	34.3	56.0
	1980	28.4	34.0	56.1
	1985	27.9	33.8	56.5
	2000	28.2	33.6	57.6
USSR				
	1950	48.1	51.8	14.1
	1975	46.2	49.7	11.0
	1980	46.2	48.7	10.6
	1985	44.9	47.7	9.9
	2000	43.8	46.9	8.1
Europe (socialist economies)				
	1950	39.8	40.9	6.4
	1975	43.9	43.7	5.1
	1980	44.2	43.7	4.9
	1985	44.9	43.8	4.7
	2000	46.2	44.7	4.0

– Continued

TABLE 4 – Continued

Region	Year	Female Labor Force Participation Rate (%)	Female Share of Total Labor Force (%)	Female Labor Force Distribution (%)
Europe (market economies)				
	1950	25.6	29.6	11.0
	1975	26.7	32.7	8.1
	1980	27.5	33.3	7.9
	1985	28.5	33.7	7.7
	2000	29.6	34.8	6.6
North America				
	1950	24.0	28.3	5.8
	1975	32.2	37.4	6.8
	1980	33.7	38.1	6.9
	1985	34.3	38.4	6.8
	2000	37.2	40.2	6.4
Latin America				
	1950	12.7	18.0	3.0
	1975	14.1	22.3	4.0
	1980	14.6	23.2	4.3
	1985	15.4	24.2	4.8
	2000	18.3	27.4	6.5
Africa				
	1950	28.0	32.9	9.1
	1975	24.4	32.4	8.6
	1980	23.6	32.2	8.8
	1985	22.9	32.0	9.1
	2000	22.0	31.7	10.3
Oceania				
	1950	22.7	25.9	0.4
	1975	27.9	32.3	0.5
	1980	28.3	32.7	0.5
	1985	28.3	33.0	0.5
	2000	30.3	34.5	0.6

SOURCE: OIT and INSTRAW, "Women in Economic Activity: A Global Statistical Survey (1950-2000)," pp. 18-19.

While for some countries in Asia, agriculture also provides the main source of employment, the service sector brings together the major proportion of female workers for the region as a whole. In Latin America and the Caribbean, female workers are found mainly in the service sector: "The agricultural sector absorbs the smallest number of women workers... Perhaps the most salient fact about women's employment is the low occupational status of the majority."[8] These data coincide with the presence of an important proportion of unpaid family workers in regions where agricultural activities are of major importance. Therefore, in Africa, such workers represent 23 per cent and in Asia 23.5 per cent (figures for 1980-1983), while in Latin America, they represent only 5.4 per cent of the economically active female population.[9]

Some indicators concerning unemployment may help us understand, to a certain extent, how this crisis affects working women. In accordance with statistical information presented by the International Labor Organization and INSTRAW, "In 1981, seven out of twelve selected developing countries indicated that women's share of unemployment was higher than their share of employment. Among twelve other countries for which data are available, five indicated that the percentage of women in the category of unemployed is higher than men."[10] This phenomenon also occurs in many developed countries, where very high levels of participation in the work force can be observed, but where, nevertheless, unemployment seems to affect women in larger proportion than men.

Women and Health

Important efforts have been made in most countries to improve the quality of health services and to expand their network. Women have recently found themselves favored by the special attentions of hospital and ambulatory services. Studies and proposals that came to the fore during the Decade for Women made it possible to place special emphasis on primary health care and on programs for mothers with young children. These innovations in the field of health, on the one hand, have made it possible to obtain more information about the situation of women, and on the other, have facilitated the integration of women as workers into the primary health care services.

Serious problems of sexual discrimination in health care remain, above all, in Asia and Africa, especially since malnutrition in those countries where the problem is most serious seems to affect mainly young girls. A report prepared for the Nairobi conference stated that "infant girls were 21 per cent more likely than boys to die in their first year of life."[11]

Women and Political Organizations

The recent trend toward the integration of women in the fields of education, health and employment also occurs in political organizations, though with less intensity. In most countries, women have joined political parties as active members, which has given them access to public positions previously closed to them. They have reached important positions in local and national governments, and they are visibly present in parliamentary bodies.

It is difficult to obtain comparable data about the integration of women into political organizations for all regions. Some general trends, however, can be illustrated. In Europe, for example, a region where women have made great progress with regard to education, labor and access to services, the data indicate a slow but increasing participation of women in politics, albeit with important variations from country to country. The highest proportion of political representation can be found in the Scandanavian countries and the Netherlands, while elsewhere, proportion is rather lower, as table 5 indicates.

With regard to their representation in political groups, women exceed a proportion of 20 per cent in virtually all of them, as table 6 demonstrates. On the other hand, women's participation is higher in local political bodies than at the national level, as shown in table 5.

In supranational bodies, such as the European Parliament, women have begun to show their presence, but they are usually found in fields of work considered "feminine." This is the case, for example, in the commissions that address women's rights, the environment, health, consumer protection, youth, culture, education, sports, social affairs and employment.[12]

TABLE 5
Political Representation of Women in Parliament and in
Local Assemblies in 8 Countries of the European Council
(Percentage)

Countries	Parliament		Municipal Councils		County Councils	
Sweden	1945:	7.8	1946:	12.5	1946:	5.8
	1979:	27.8	1980:	29.8	1979:	31.1
	Increase:	+ 20	Increase:	+ 17.3	Increase:	+ 25.3
Norway	1945:	4.7	1945:	3.4		
	1981:	25.8	1979:	22.8	—	
	Increase:	+ 21.1	Increase:	+ 19.4		
Denmark	1950:	8.0	1946:	3.0	1946:	3.0
	1979:	23.4	1974:	18.0	1974:	7.6
	Increase:	+ 15.4	Increase:	+ 15.0	Increase:	+ 4.6
Netherlands	1946:	4.0	1946:	1.6	1946:	3.5
	1982:	18.0	1978:	12.5	1978:	16.0
	Increase:	+ 14.0	Increase:	+ 10.5	Increase:	+ 12.5
Federal Republic of Germany	1949:	6.8	1951:	9.9		
	1980:	8.7	1979:	11.4		
	Increase:	+ 1.9	Increase:	+1.5		
Italy	1948:	7.8	1956:	1.6		
	1979:	8.4	1975:	3.8	—	
	Increase:	+ 0.6	Increase:	+ 2.2		
France	1946:	7.0	1947:	3.1	1945:	0.8
	1981:	5.3	1977:	8.3	1982:	3.8
	Decrease:	− 2.3	Increase:	+ 5.2	Increase:	+ 3.0
United Kingdom	1945:	4.0	1964:	12.0		
	1979:	3.0	1976:	16.0	—	
	Decrease:	− 1.0	Increase:	+ 4.0		

SOURCE: "Situation of Women in the Political Life of Europe," Council of Europe, p. 17.

TABLE 6
Proportion of Women in Each Political Group in the European Parliament
after Elections of 1979
(Percentage)

Political Parties	Women Enrolled in Each Party	Women Elected from Each Party
Communist	22.7	10.7
Socialist	21.2	27.5
Liberal and Democratic	20.0	9.7
European Democrats for Progress	22.7	5.4
Christian Democrats	9.3	26.1
European Democrats	9.3	16.6
Independent	36.3	2.7
Nonregistered	22.2	2.2

SOURCE: "Situation of Women in the Political Life of Europe," Council of Europe, p. 32.

Conclusions and Recommendations

One conclusion seems clear from an analysis of these data: women have now become visible in areas which may be considered to have priority in the development process. In fact, in spite of their high level of illiteracy, women now have better access to education. Although their work as housewives does not gain recognition, they are more frequently integrated into the labor process. They have better health care opportunities. And, although their access to decision-making levels and to mechanisms for eligibility are still limited, they participate actively in political organizations.

The permanent ambivalence in the status of women leads to the thought that there are certain specific elements in their situation which, since they are not taken into consideration, have become obstacles to equality of opportunity. The development process, as it has been understood until now, does not take women into account as such, but addresses the whole population. Therefore, women benefit only indirectly and partially; they can also contribute only partially.

However, at a time when the global context of development requires special efforts to mobilize all resources, especially in the least-developed and developing countries, it is important to introduce innovations that will permit the full utilization of the potential offered by both women and men. Here, women appear as a crucial variable, which makes it necessary to examine anew the relations within families and within institutions in order to ensure a real equality of options by giving a new shape to the development process. From this perspective, it becomes imperative to take actions that will allow women to take up decision-making roles at both the national and the international level. Policies for better utilization of human resources may become of great importance in this area.

International organizations have a unique opportunity in this context to take on a leadership role when it comes to integrating women into the institutional framework of development. They can do so by ensuring that the dimension of women's experience is fully reflected in the policies and programs they develop, and even more convincingly, by integrating women into the decision-making process where such policies and programs are formulated.

Only when women can be seen in leadership positions in the international context will their leadership role at the national and local level be fully accepted. The international organizations can become a role model to accelerate social change by their own example, as well as by their efforts to institutionalize the integration of women in the economic and social arena. In this manner, the potential of the world's human resources can truly be realized to its fullest extent.

Notes

1. Antony Jennings and Thomas G. Weiss, *The Challenge of Development in the Eighties: Our Response*, (Pergamon Press, 1982) p. 16.

2. Ibid., p. 17.

3. See *World Population Prospects*, ST/ESA/SER.A/86, p. 19.

4. CEPAL, 1985, p. 44.

5. Even though the Interamerican Commission on Women was then functioning, its sphere of interest was restricted to the countries belonging to the Organization of American States (OAS).

6. International Labor Organization/INSTRAW (1985), p. 21

7. Ibid., p. 47.

8. Ibid., p. 26.

9. Ibid., p. 26

10. Ibid., p. 32.

11. Background information for the Nairobi Conference, "The State of the World's Women 1985."

12. See "Situation of Women in the Political Life of Europe," Council of Europe, pp. 30-31.

CHAPTER 17

Employment and Human Development

Francis Blanchard

Two key elements among the human factors in development are employment and training for employment. Through employment, workers are productive members of society and fully participate in development. The background paper to this meeting states that the human element is both an objective of development and a means to achieve it. To overlook this basic truth is not only socially unjust; it is irrational in economic terms, too. Yet the current crisis in the world economy has resulted in a sad neglect of the basic importance of the human element — in large-scale unnecessary human suffering which is socially unacceptable in itself, but which also could have incalculable consequences for future development efforts.

The World Employment Picture

Today, we experience a hesitant recovery. Paradoxically, as this happens, unemployment, stagnant wages and job insecurity persist and even worsen. The combined gross national product of the industrialized market economy countries grew by almost 5 per cent in 1984 — the best result since 1976 — and inflation was reduced at the same time. But unemployment has continued to increase in many OECD countries, particularly in Europe, and it now affects more than thirty million workers. Youth unemployment is generally twice the average, and the duration of the period a worker is unemployed has become longer for young as well as for adult workers.

In order to arrive at an unemployment figure equivalent to 1979, before the recession set in, 20,000 additional jobs would have to be created every day in the OECD countries between 1985 and 1989. Few are optimistic about the chances of achieving this. The experience of the United States, which has had apparent success on this score, is not easily transferable to other OECD countries and even less so to developing countries. In many developing countries, the benefits of strong growth in the 1960s and 1970s have been largely wiped out by rapid population growth and by reductions in incomes following drastic measures taken to improve the balance-of-payments situation, to tackle debt problems and to halt the deterioration of export earnings. Unemployment and underemployment have grown considerably over the last few years. The problem has reached catastrophic proportions in the least-developed countries, particularly in Africa, where fragile economic structures and extreme dependence on external aid and trade have made these countries and their populations extremely vulnerable to an unfavorable world economic environment. All this underscores the fact that the fight against unemployment in the North and poverty in the South continues to be a major challenge for us all.

The developing countries, paradoxically, face serious shortages of skilled manpower, as well as widespread unemployment and underemployment. Much has been done over the past three decades to develop human resources and prepare people for work through training. National programs have been set up, as well as enterprise-based schemes, rural training activities and programs for the improvement of managerial skills. But by and large, such programs reach only the ten per cent of potential trainees who seek regular, salaried jobs in industry rather than the masses of rural workers and the self-employed most in need of training.

Priorities

How can employment be promoted and human resources development enhanced through training? There are a number of priorities.

First and foremost, governments should adopt and follow a macro policy framework which explicitly includes social goals on a par with economic objectives. Such a macro policy should be anchored in a basic needs philosophy. Since the beginning of the 1980s, the consensus on this concept has gradually faded. Yet it would ensure that adequate weight is given to longer-term goals for nutrition, health, education, poverty eradication and employment promotion and guarantee that none of these factors would be unduly sacrificed for short-term economic considerations, emergencies or stabilization. At the recent Society for International Development conference, a number of speakers advocated a more human-focused approach to adjustment. While adjustment to the crisis is inescapable for years to come, and while it necessarily involves sacrifices, ways must be found of ensuring that the burden of adjustment does not fall – as it tends in most countries to fall – on the working people, and in particular, on those who are unprotected in terms of labor legislation and social security coverage. Adjustment programs inspired by the advice of the international financial institutions and supported by them should be linked to national development plans and not implemented in such a way as to destroy or seriously compromise the attainment of the longer-term social objectives that a country has fixed for its population.

Second, such a national policy framework must be supplemented by micro policies and programs, soundly managed and targeted on the groups most in need. In this connection, experience gained with job creation schemes provides useful insights. For instance, the ILO has been instrumental in setting up labor-intensive public works in a number of least-developed countries. We were able to demonstrate in those cases how job creation can be combined with development of infrastructure, and we could prove, in addition, the economic viability of this approach.

Third, in order to promote productive employment, investments in education and training are essential, and not only formal training programs catering for the modern industrial sector. New approaches to training should be sought, such as self-instruction and training through radio, television and correspondence, and programs should be especially designed for groups such as women and youth. Training programs must become much more sector-specific and enterprise-based and directed to a greater extent at self-employment. Finally, training should be linked to employment opportunities, as well as to systems of incentives and rewards.

Last, but not least, special efforts should be made to expand the social protection of vulnerable groups in society. This definitely applies to children and young people, to women at work outside or at home and to the large numbers of unorganized workers in what is often referred to as the informal sector. It is, first of all, desirable that self-employed artisans and farmers and salaried workers outside the mainstream of the formal sector find productive and gainful employment. This requires judicious intervention of government in favor of the informal sector, including, wherever possible, measures to extend the scope of social protection and income security for these groups.

Beyond the national level, there is a grave responsibility for the international community to facilitate human development by way of financial assistance and technical cooperation, as well as through the opening up of markets and increased trade and sectoral specialization in the South and the North alike. Specialized agencies in the United Nations system can make their contribution to this endeavor, offering to the developing countries their expertise and experience on such issues as employment, health and education. I have myself taken the initiative of proposing that the ILO Governing Body and Conference convene a high-level meeting of ministers of finance and ministers of labor, employers' and workers' leaders and executive heads of international financial and economic institutions such as the IMF, the World Bank, GATT, UNCTAD and the OECD. In this meeting, the employment consequences of international, commercial, financial and monetary policies will be examined. We will try to explore together how the longer-term goals of employment, social progress and human development can be protected and promoted in the difficult environment in which we live today, and how the human dimension of development can be safeguarded in drawing up adjustment programs. My hope is that this meeting will contribute to a dialogue and a better understanding — which is, in my view, urgently needed — between those responsible for economic and financial policies and those responsible for the social and human aspects of development, and thus to a search for a more just and rational solution to the problems with which this world is confronted.

CHAPTER 18

Employment as an Aspect of Human Development

A. M. A. Muhith

Economic development seeks improved conditions of life. In most developing countries, living conditions improve with the availability of more goods and services. Production of more goods and services depends very heavily on the quality of the human input in the production process. The better the quality of this input, the higher the productivity, and thus the more goods and services obtainable from a given combination of physical resources. Thus, while improvement of the conditions of life may be the ultimate objective of development, in the process of reaching that objective, it is also necessary to improve the quality of human existence. Such quality improvement is both an intermediate product and the ultimate objective.

Somehow, this perception has not always dominated all development efforts; there has been neglect of the intermediate product. This neglect has resulted in the slow pace with which we are moving toward the ultimate objective of development.

When we complain about unfavorable incremental capital/output ratio, we are really referring to human failure to make the right combination of physical resources, or to exercise the right choice in technology or mode of production. When we regret that the production of goods for mass consumption has been neglected, once again we are referring to our failure to manage the human dimension of development. In this case, demand generation has perhaps lagged behind because more people could not participate in the development process and thus earn incomes to spend on consumption goods. Or, it may also be that skills dissemination and training have not been right, so that the production process has remained confined to enclaves of capital-intensive technology. The inputs of labor, technology, management and innovation make a great difference in the efficiency and productivity of a production process. These inputs are all human inputs, whose quality can be improved.

This is one aspect of the human dimension of development, and we try to pursue it through investment in social services. We provide for education and training, for health services, for family planning, for nutrition or for recreation. Unfortunately, these services do not receive adequate attention, and in a situation of resource squeeze they bear the brunt of all reductions. In the last four or five years of nearly universal adjustment efforts that developing countries have made, the biggest victim has been investment in the improvement of human resources.

There is another aspect of the human dimension of development. The production of more goods and services ministers to the needs of the greatest number of people. This objective can be achieved if control over assets can be widely distributed, or if large numbers of people are enabled to participate in the production process. After years of experience with planned development, we find that without an employment strategy, the fruits of development cannot be extended to large groups of people. Whether planned development refers to central planning, administrative planning in limited sectors, planning by direction or planning by inducement, it is true that the employment question has become a matter of serious concern. Because without the creation of enough employment opportunities, in the context of limited asset holdings in most developing countries, it is not possible to provide for the most important aspects of the human dimension of development.

This paper discusses the employment issue in search of an appropriate employment strategy that should govern development efforts. The pivotal position of labor in the creation of wealth is beyond question. Even if Marxist doctrine is not fully accepted, or Schumpeter's innovator is honorably acknowledged, it seems that the profoundest truth on the subject was given out by Adam Smith over two centuries ago: "The annual labour of every nation is the fund which originally supplied it with all necessaries and conveniences of life." The available fund of labor, its utilization and its productivity are what provide for growth of output. It has been believed for a long time that the alleviation of poverty comes along with growth of output, i.e., with the availability of more goods and services. In the postwar period the global product has increased enormously, and yet both poverty and unemployment have grown, in the sense that there are more poor and unemployed people on earth than ever before. In recent times, therefore, attention is being paid not only to output growth, but also to empowering people with command over the growing output. And unemployment — the nonutilization of the fund of labor — is perhaps the most serious problem before us. In its eternal search for betterment of the conditions of life, the biggest challenge that mankind faces in the next twenty to seventy years is that of gainfully employing the available manpower.

Measuring Unemployment

The labor of man and, of course, his ingenuity have been manipulating the physical environment since the descent of Adam and Eve from the garden of Eden. In fact, we are given to understand that this manipulating instinct, the capacity to maneuver, caused the expulsion of the species from Paradise. Human ingenuity is what can be economically termed as skills, as well as enterprise. Skills can be acquired from experience, from observation or, as we understand it in modern times, from studies and apprenticeship. Enterprise is essentially a mental spirit — call it innovation, courage or risk-taking — and this, too, can be helped by enrichment of mind or conduciveness of the environment. Manipulation of the physical environment began the economic process — i.e., the creation of goods and services, or the wealth of nations. Increasing specialization provided for the division of labor, greater utilization of manpower and thus the creation of more and more wealth. With the application of tools and energy, the capacity to create wealth naturally multiplied. Capital and energy, therefore, became the engines of the industrial revolution that multiplied the global product enormously in the last two centuries.

In manipulating the physical environment, however, man has been consuming the resources of the planet earth both ceaselessly and a little callously. We have been exploiting both renewable and exhaustible resources. The speed with which such consumption increased in the postwar period is indeed phenomenal. In ten years, between the late 1950s and 1960s, we consumed as many resources as mankind had consumed throughout its entire history until then. Wealth creation shifted from primary production to secondary and tertiary production processes. Increasingly, manufacturing and services became more important than agriculture and mining.

Labor input has been closely following these changes in the pattern of wealth creation. However, for reasons we need not explore here, this forward march has been uneven between regions and countries. In fact, the world is now divided into developed and developing nations, which is perhaps a euphemism for a more devastating real-life characterization. Again, developing nations are not all equal in their stages of development. Various categorizations are commonly made, e.g., high-income oil-exporting countries, middle-income newly industrialized countries, lower-middle-income countries, low-income countries and the least-developed countries. Nor is it true that the developed countries are a homogeneous lot, even if the centrally planned economies are clearly differentiated.

In developed economies, unemployment can be easily measured. A potential wage-earner or self-employed person without any income is considered unemployed. In most of the postwar period the unemployment rate in the developed world hovered around 6 per cent of the labor force.[1] In the developing countries, on the other hand, open unemployment does not tell the full story. There is considerable underemployment in diverse forms. There is the known case of seasonal employment. There is nonwage employment that does not fully meet subsistence needs and hence creates a situation of unemployment. There is employment not providing adequate income and thus camouflaging unemployment. There is employment that neither utilizes the skills of the worker adequately nor engages his time fully and thus makes for unemployment. All of these, combined with open unemployment of about 6 per cent, used to account for about 25 per cent of the labor force in the 1960s and into the 1970s.[2]

Today, the situation is very grim. Even though the average unemployment rate in the developed world is below 8 per cent, mainly because of good performance in Japan and the USA, the U.K. and Italy show unemployment rates as high as 13 or 14 per cent. In the developing countries the extent of unemployment is well over 30 per cent, and in some countries it is as high as 40 per cent.[3] At the very outset, it is important that we follow this definitional distinction of unemployment in the developing countries.

In traditional societies there is generally no problem of unemployment. There are problems of poverty or productivity, along with those of famine, disease, war or shelter. In African tribal societies or Asian feudal estates, everyone has a defined role to perform and thus remains occupied. In an ILO publication, it is stated, for example, that at independence, Ivory Coast had no unemployment problem; it began to be noticed only after 1965.[4] As labor specialization moved in its stride following the industrial revolution in Europe and as the monetization of economies expanded in the developing countries, problems of unemployment appeared. From subsistence agriculture, labor started moving into commercial agriculture, industries and services. Unemployment as well as underemployment in developing countries intensified as the duality between the traditional and modern sectors expanded. A large proportion of the labor force in developing countries is still engaged in agriculture, where unemployment, and especially underemployment, do not show up easily. Subsistence farming and the joint family system disguise many of the facts as well as the pangs of unemployment. Let us, at this stage, note the magnitude of labor distribution between types of economic activities in the world. In meeting the challenge of unemployment, this information will be of great significance. The position in 1950 and as it evolved by 1980 is shown in table 1.

TABLE 1
Composition of Labor Force
(Percentage)

	Agriculture		Industries		Services	
	1950	1980	1950	1980	1950	1980
Developing countries	80	60	8.5	18	11.5	22
Developed countries	38	6	30	38	32	56
Asia	79	64	9	17	12	19
Africa	80	70	7	14	12	16
Latin America	53	30	19	24	28	46

SOURCES: ILO, *Labor Force Estimates and Projections* (Geneva, 1977); World Bank, *World Development Report 1984* (Oxford University Press); and P. Bairoch and J. M. Limbor, "Changes in the Distribution of the World Labor Force by Region, 1880-1960," *Essays on Employment* (Geneva: ILO, 1971).

It should be observed that differences between the developing and the developed world are indeed very great. But simultaneously, it should be noted that disparities between regions and groups of developing countries are even greater: Nepal and Bhutan each have

93 per cent of their labor force in agriculture and only 2 per cent in industry, while Chile and Lebanon have 62 per cent in services, and Ivory Coast, Central African Republic and Lesotho have 4 per cent in industry. Again, the country with the largest concentration of its labor force in industry – some 57 per cent – is a developing country (Hong Kong), and a good number of such countries have more than 50 per cent in this sector (Egypt, Tunisia, Cuba, North Korea, Syria, Hungary, Yugoslavia, Iran, Singapore, Trinidad and Tobago, and Kuwait).[5]

Problems in Employment Creation

The postwar period is generally marked by great success in development efforts. It is relevant, therefore, to wonder aloud what went wrong with employment creation. With hindsight, it can be said that we were beguiled by some rather simplifying assumptions. First, it was felt that the traditional sector, which meant low-level subsistence agriculture, had an unlimited labor supply, and workers could be easily withdrawn to the modern sector to push output growth. Second, a large part of development efforts would involve construction work, which would draw labor out of the traditional sector and add to its productivity and, hence, its income-earning capability. Third, as output growth took place, the service sector would develop to absorb more labor. Fourth, the withdrawal of labor from the traditional sector would be accompanied by increased productivity in agriculture, which would meet the demand for food of the modern sector while improving the earning capability of those engaged in the traditional sector. Simultaneously, it was naively believed that the pursuit of growth through expansion of the modern sector – essentially manufacturing – would be beneficial to society as a whole and bring about an alleviation of poverty. Such a belief, perhaps, numbed the International Labor Organization, the oldest thriving international body, which was established in 1919, into caring only for conditions of employment, and not at all for opportunities for employment. It was only in the 1960s that employment issues came to the fore, and employment was recognized as an objective to be pursued in its own right.[6]

The fact of the matter is that many of these assumptions misfired. The ability of the modern sector to open up employment opportunities turned out to be very limited, as capital intensity and new technology acted against labor absorption. Construction did not prove to be that much of a dynamic activity for employment purposes. Lack of vitality in agriculture constricted demand on the one hand and failed to generate surpluses for modernization on the other. Labor productivity in the absence of proper education and training relied primarily on capital intensity, and hence, employment opportunities remained limited. Social and political institutions appeared to have conspired against sharing in growth by the weak and the depressed of society. Underutilized labor being a lost opportunity, it symbolized the deficiency and weakness of the process of economic development. With this experience of frustrated expectations, we turned full circle. In the late 1960s and early 1970s, the raging fashions in development mythology became: (i) the concern for employment, leading to the World Employment Conference in 1976; (ii) population planning, culminating in two world conferences a decade apart – in 1974 (Bucharest) and in 1984 (Mexico City); and (iii) programs for poverty alleviation, as reflected in the slogans like "growth with redistribution" or "distribution from growth" or "target-oriented rural development."

The challenge of creating employment opportunities has become overriding. Poverty alleviation depends on opportunities for income earning by more and more people. It has been contended that the key to the success of South Korea or Taiwan in handling the poverty problem lies in their growth strategy, providing for large-scale employment expansion.[7] Mexico, on the other hand, with a consistent record of good growth for decades (until the 1980s) and strong population planning policies, did less well because of inadequate attention to employment generation strategies. While the economy in the 1950s grew at 6.5 per cent per annum, labor absorption grew by only 0.4 per cent.[8]

Why has the employment situation deteriorated so badly? A combination of many adverse factors can explain the current situation; but first of all, let us assess the size of the problem, summarized in table 2. The labor force of the developing countries in 1980 totaled 1,250 million, or about 39 per cent of their population of 3,200 million. Moreover, about 430 million of the labor force was unemployed or underemployed. In the developed world, on the other hand, the labor force was about 550 million out of a population of 1,180 million, with about 45 million unemployed. In the remaining two decades of this century, developed countries are likely to add 180 million more people and 90 million more laborers to the world rolls. The developing countries, however, are likely to increase their population by 1,700 million and their labor force by 650 million. The rates of growth are staggering in their differences. Population will grow at 1.0 per cent in the developed countries and at 2.2 per cent in the developing countries, while the labor force will grow at 0.7 per cent and 2.1 per cent respectively. In the subsequent fifty years, assuming great progress in population planning, the population will grow at .05 per cent in developed countries and at 1.0 per cent in developing countries, labor growth being .018 per cent and 1.33 per cent respectively.

To appreciate the meaning of these statistics, it is worthwhile to look at developments in the immediate past. Between 1950 and 1980, years marked by dramatic growth in the wealth of the world, population in the developing countries has grown at an annual rate of 2.2 per cent and labor at 1.9 per cent. In the developed world during this period, these rates of growth have been only 1.07 per cent and 1.0 per cent respectively. For a hundred years, from 1800 to 1900, in the early days of the industrial revolution, it was the developed world whose population and labor growth rates were almost double those of developing countries, i.e., 0.8 per cent and 0.9 per cent, as against 0.4 per cent and 0.4 per cent respectively. In the first half of this century, the picture began to change. The developing countries' population was growing at a rate of 1.1 per cent and the labor force at 0.8 per cent against comparable rates of 0.8 per cent and 0.7 per cent respectively for the developed countries. This historical perspective points out the difficulties of absorbing the additional labor that is expected in the next seventy years. In the two decades of the 1980s and 1990s, the developing countries have to find jobs for a billion people. It is worth remembering that in the previous three decades, they could create only between 260 to 300 million jobs.

TABLE 2
Growth of Population and Labor Force

	1900	1950	1980	2000	2050
			Population		
Developing countries (millions)	1,120	1,650	3,200	4,900	8,400
Annual growth rate	0.4	0.78	2.21	2.16	1
			Labor Force		
Millions	470	700	1,250	1,900	3,700
Rate	0.4	0.8	1.9	2.15	1.33
Activity ratio	42	42.4	39	38.7	44
			Population		
Developed countries (millions)	580	860	1,180	1,360	1,400
Annual growth rate	0.8	0.8	1.07	0.7	0.05
			Labor Force		
Millions	280	400	550	640	646
Rate	0.9	0.7	1	0.75	0.018
Activity ratio	48	46.5	46.6	47	46
			Unemployed Labor		
Developing countries (millions)			430		
Rate			36.4		
Developed countries (millions)			25		
Rate			8.2		
			New Job Opportunities Needed		
Developing countries				1,080	1,800
Developed countries				135	6

SOURCES: ILO, *Labor Force Estimates and Projections*, (Geneva, 1977); World Bank, *World Development Report 1984* (Oxford University Press); Lyn Squire, *Employment Policy in Developing Countries*, World Bank Publication, (Oxford University Press, 1981), p. 16; and P. Bairoch and J.M. Limbor, "Changes in the Distribution of the World Labor Force by Regions, 1880-1960," *Essays on Employment* (Geneva: ILO, 1971).

The Industrial Sector

Undoubtedly, the size of the problem of unemployment is staggering. We may now return to the question of how it happened. We may look at the labor problem from both the demand and the supply side. Let us first look at labor absorption during the last three decades. Why and how did we fail to create sufficient job opportunities? Why did demand lag behind supply so very much? We had very high hopes for labor absorption by industry, which is not as fast as one would like it to be. Noble Laureate Sir Arthur Lewis tells us that it cannot grow at more than 4 per cent a year. Japan in the 1960s achieved a 3.6 per cent growth rate. Only the USSR in the 1930s achieved a higher growth rate − 4.6 per cent − but that was because of a special emphasis on the manufacture of armaments.[9] In the developing countries, the rate of absorption has been even lower, mainly because of their preference for capital-intensive and sophisticated technology. Exchange rate and interest rate distortions, devotion to import substitution through protective walls, as well as the desire to catch up with modern technology have fostered capital-intensive over labor-intensive employment. Perhaps the demonstration effect of the ILO's labor welfare conventions has also contributed to the discarding of labor-intensive technologies. There are some industries which are highly labor-intensive, such as textiles and clothing, footwear, plywood and furniture making.[10] But market access in these industries is not so easy. Of the US$ 95 billion trade in textiles and clothing, developing countries account for only US$ 30 billion, of which one-third is traded within the Third World.[11] And yet you hear so much about quotas, fiber agreements and protection. There are resolutions and bills before the U.S. Congress, there are special television programs or full-page advertisements in the *New York Times* demanding protection for the textile industry.

Technological innovations and rapid productivity increases in the manufacturing industry have prevented even historical levels of labor absorption by industry. In the 1880s, the developed countries of today absorbed 42 per cent of the incremental labor force in the industrial sector. The industrial sector in the developing countries in the 1960s, on the other hand, absorbed only 22 per cent of the incremental labor force. The economic conditions in the developing countries in the 1960s were about the same as those in developed countries in the 1880s, with a few significant differences.[12] In the developing countries in the 1960s, there was certainly a higher level of education and literacy. The growth of industrial output in the developing countries was taking place at a much faster rate. And finally, technological fixes perhaps needed less labor input, even though robotics was still on the drawing board. Two of these differences should have had a positive influence on the extent of labor absorption, while only one could be held to have had some negative influence. In areas such as technology choice and free trade based on comparative advantage, much can be accomplished by both developing and developed countries in promoting the employment of more workers. Developing countries, however, must consider unorthodox and novel policies. Capital concentration for job creation is not a viable option for many countries, even though this is the current practice. Capital available per new entrant into the work force is in fact less than US$ 10 in most developing countries. For Colombia it is US$ 10, for Egypt it is US$ 9 and for Bangladesh it is US$ 1 only.[13]

Of necessity, therefore, the developing countries must opt for less capital-intensive and more labor-absorbing technologies and techniques for industrialization as well as for infrastructure works. The four-day week, at least for the modern sector, should also be an option to consider in order to provide jobs for more people. The twelve-hour, six-day week was decreed by King Henry VII in 1495. Three hundred and sixty-two years later, in 1857, the U.S. federal government introduced the ten-hour workday. It required the ingenuity of Henry Ford to start the forty-hour, five-day week almost a century later in 1956.[14] It is not wild or unusual to expect the developing countries to jump steps and move to the four-day week now.

The Service Sector

The growth of the service sector in the developing countries has not followed the historical path. In these countries the service sector, even at a lower stage of economic development, has absorbed more labor. In the service sector there are clearly two types of demand. First, there are the traditional services, such as petty trading and domestic services, where scope for expansion is limited. Yet in a sample of the developing countries, as per estimates made in 1975, traditional services accounted for 8 per cent of employment, even though in the developed countries it accounted for only 5.5 per cent.[15] This is perhaps because, labor productivity being low and labor remuneration being inadequate, more laborers are employed to do the same work.

But the modern services, both of consumption and intermediate value, are altogether different. The demand for education, health, tourism, entertainment, transport and communication, commerce, banking and finance, professional services and government services goes up with growth in output and incomes. While these services accounted for about 21.5 percent of employment in the sample of developing countries, they accounted for 39 per cent in the developed countries.[16]

The high growth of labor absorption in the service sector in the developing countries can be partially explained by two developments. First, there has undeniably been a massive growth in government and parastatal services in many developing countries. In Guinea-Bissau, 80 per cent of all wage earners are public servants. In Benin it is 50 per cent, in Malawi it is 33 per cent and in Gambia it is 25 per cent. In Egypt and Somalia, the government is obliged to employ all school graduates. Second, the rate of urbanization has been very high in the middle- and higher-income developing countries, and urbanization surely creates a demand for services. In Latin America employment in the service sector has gone up in thirty years from 28 to 48 per cent, and urbanization in the same region has covered about half the population, growing from around one-fifth. On the other hand, in India and China, where urbanization has grown from about 18 to 22 per cent in twenty years, employment in the service sector has only risen from 8 to 13 per cent.[17]

Though the service sector in the developing countries has grown fast, without output growth it is not likely to grow fast enough in the coming years. However, in the already expanded service sector, it seems that the lifestyle in the developing countries is conducive to higher labor absorption. The only way this trend can be maintained is by deliberately patronizing the informal service sector through the provision of credit and upgradation of skills and techniques.

Emigration provided an important outlet for the European labor force when it was expanding fast in the last century. Between 1850 and 1940, Europe exported some 10 to 15 per cent of its incremental labor force to the Americas and Oceania. During the same period, Asia could only export a paltry 0.1 to 0.5 per cent. Today, the annual legal outflow from the developing countries to the developed world is about 500,000 a year. Some of the more developed countries among them, such as the Gulf countries, Venezuela, Ivory Coast and Nigeria, have absorbed about five million people. Guest workers in Europe and illegal immigrants to the USA in particular probably number about 10 million.[18] These figures taken together are of no consequence to an unemployed labor force of 430 million. Immigrants are not welcome in the known habitats of man. Of course, luring away experts and geniuses is a game which has been played skillfully since the days of the Ptolemies of Egypt.[19] However, unless massive export to other planets or space becomes feasible, emigration holds out no hope for labor absorption in the future.

Agriculture

Agriculture in 1950 employed 80 per cent of the labor force of the developing countries, as against 38 per cent of the labor force of the developed countries. In thirty years, the developed countries have reduced the agricultural labor force to a mere 6 per cent, while the service sector has absorbed 24 per cent more and the industrial sector, 8 per cent more. During the same period, developing countries barely managed to expand industrial employment by 9.5 per cent and service sector employment by 10.5 per cent, still leaving 60 per cent of the labor force in agriculture. Contrary to historical experience, it seems that it is in agriculture that the bulk of future job openings have to be found. Bringing more land under the plough is no longer a viable option, and therefore, the intensity of cultivation has necessarily to be expanded. Fortunately, an increase of intensity by 10 per cent increases labor absorption by 3 to 4 per cent.[20] Denudation of forests has gone on so rampantly that reafforestation cannot but be a compulsion for ecological balance. Again, to sustain the capacity for work, more and more energy needs to be harnessed, and in large areas, woodlots and forest products have to provide that energy. Social forestry, fortunately again, is a labor-intensive venture, as can be verified from the experience in the Indian subcontinent. Aquaculture today provides only 8 million tons of fish against a total supply of 75 million tons per year.[21] Sea fishing is not expanding at all, while aquaculture has quite a potential. Again, this is also a labor-intensive investment, as is so amply demonstrated in China, which accounts for half of the industry's production. Livestock farming by small and marginal cultivators has shown great promise, particularly in rural employment and rural development programs in India. Rural works programs contributing directly to agricultural productivity, as well as to rural capital formation, have transformed the countryside as well as the employment scene in China. Various other experiments in this regard have been less successful, mainly because of lack of continued commitment and weakness in rural organization. Rural works programs, however, hold the key to the immediate problem of providing income to the rural unemployed. Many off-farm activities go along with increases in agricultural productivity, provided there is credit and organization. In Nepal and Bangladesh, a spurt of such activities is changing the face of selected areas. Thus, there are ways for absorbing labor in agriculture and yet increasing productivity. This, however, is not in keeping with historical evidence in the developed counrries.

Meeting the Challenge

So far, we have considered the question of labor absorption. What about the supply side of the labor force? How did it become so abundant? How did we come to this stage where we have to create four times the job opportunities that we have been able to create in the past? The answer is simple and obvious. The population explosion is the villain of the piece. In telescoping the development process, the developing countries have been quite successful in most endeavors. They have successfully eradicated epidemics. They have adjusted more easily to an industrial ethos. But such successes have caused an imbalance of gigantic proportions. Mortality rates have dropped dramatically, but birth rates have either gone up or remained unchanged. The normal process through which demographic transition has taken place in developed countries has become ineffective in maintaining the historical level of population balance. The growth of population in the postwar era has taken place on an unprecedented scale.

To underscore the situation, let us note that in the wake of the industrial revolution, the U.K. population required seventy years (from 1781 to 1851) to double to 27 million.[22] But the population of the developing world doubled to 3.2 billion in just thirty years — from 1950 to 1980. Modern practices were emulated too rapidly in some areas and not so rapidly in other areas, thus causing the population explosion. Fertility rates went up as breast-feeding and child spacing were abandoned. As the nuclear family system made inroads, and sex education was no longer taboo, reproduction accelerated. For a while, the conviction that demographic transition would come about automatically with economic progress stunted state or community action on population planning. Fortunately, such a view is no longer held with any conviction in the developing countries. No one is prepared to wait for the downward slope of the Kuznetian U-curve, even though a large number of countries have yet to undertake positive population control measures. The world indeed has moved a long way from Bucharest to Mexico City in ten years. But the havoc caused by the population explosion is going to haunt the employment scene for almost a century more. The proportion of children below 15 years is still 40 per cent in the developing countries, as against about 23 per cent in the developed world.[23] Compared with the working age population, the labor force is still quite small in most developing countries. So even with a fall in the population growth rate, labor force expansion will continue at a phenomenal rate well toward the third quarter of the next century. This is the most mind-boggling challenge of the employment creation problem of the future.

Let us look at the statistical import of the issue. Taiwan has the best record in labor absorption in the nonagricultural sector, initially growing at 3 per cent per annum and then reaching 6 per cent per annum.[24] In a country where 75 per cent of the labor force is in agriculture and the population growth rate is 2.5 per cent, the nonagricultural sector will have to absorb 10 per cent more workers each year merely to prevent the growth of the labor force in agriculture beyond 75 per cent. Even the Taiwanese experience suggests that this is not simply a tall order, but indeed an impossible one. This, however, is the predicament of most developing countries. Even with the best of known and tested development strategies, it is difficult to go too far. But there are ways of trying, and try we must.

a) Slowing down the rate of urbanization will help. Urbanization calls for larger investments, as well as larger agricultural production by fewer people on less land. Some of the Latin American countries, such as Argentina, Uruguay, Chile, Venezuela, Brazil and Mexico, have nearly 70 per cent of their population in urban centers. Even a large number of poor African countries, such as the Central African Republic, Ghana, Somalia, Zaire, Ivory Coast, Zambia, Egypt and Senegal, have about 40 per cent of their population in urban areas. The demand for urban investment leaves little to invest in agriculture, and job creation in the urban environment costs more in capital investment. The Philippines in the mid-1970s clearly represented the dilemma of urban investment. The diversion of resources to urban development was stopping the generation of the surplus so badly needed to sustain it. And again, stagnation of demand in the countryside was retarding the growth of the modern sector.[25]

b) The elimination of factor price distortions through a realistic exchange rate regime and positive interest rate policies will help.[26] A situation in which Argentina in the 1950s grew at an annual rate of 4.4 per cent while labor absorption declined by 2 per cent, or where Kenya grew at 7.6 per cent while labor absorption declined by 1.1 per cent, can surely be avoided and reversed. By contrast, India in the same decade experienced a growth rate of 6.8 per cent, accompanied by growth in labor absorption of 3.3 per cent.[27]

c) Remodeling the educational facilities will certainly help. Up to now, a focus on formal education, primarily oriented toward the liberal arts, and high priority to higher levels of education have made educational investments more of a consumption expenditure. In many societies a school-leaver is a loss to the productive process because of cultural attitudes towards manual labor. A corps of disgruntled educated people, either unemployed or not-so-gainfully employed, is a problem in many countries. Again, as more students enter the educational system, resources for other productive investments are shrinking. Community schools, education for self-employment and nonformal basic education are measures being tried in such countries as Bangladesh or Ivory Coast in order to reduce the cost of meaningful education and improve the environment of direct production.

d) Above all, redirecting resources toward agricultural and rural development, as already discussed, is a must. For well over a decade, African countries have produced less and less food, although the demand for food for new mouths alone has gone up. There is no harm in reiterating that buoyancy of agriculture is a sine qua non for industrial growth. It should be noted, however, that once again, it is desirable to be aware of a possible misadventure. The choice of labor-intensive technology coupled with an attempt at greater labor absorption in agriculture and rural development may land the developing countries in a low-level technology trap. But perhaps this is only an unwarranted anxiety. In today's world of fast communication, this may be only a bad dream.

The population explosion has not only engendered a mind-boggling problem about the creation of opportunities for employment; it has also raised another frightening problem — that of the limits to output growth. We can sidestep the controversy over the ice-age syndrome versus the greenhouse syndrome, but it cannot be denied that the food/energy balance and the man/resource balance are under considerable strain in most developing countries. Unexploited resources are there, but their exploitation demands capital and energy, both of which are hard to come by. The destruction of forest lands, erosion of topsoil, desertification, cultivation of marginal lands, shortage of sweet water, lack of fuelwood and other energy resources are systematically plaguing most developing countries and holding back economic progress.[28] The debt crisis has exacerbated the situation by reversing the process of capital flow, thus making capital even more scarce. In 1800, in the early days of the industrial revolution, the developing countries of today hosted 74 per cent of the world's less than a billion people but had command over 44 per cent of the world's product. In 1980, while representing 78 per cent of the global population, these countries commanded only 21 per cent of the global product.[29] In another twenty years, they will account for 85 per cent of world population. How much of the global product will they command at that time? If their share in global manufacturing product stays at 9 per cent, as it is now, how are new job openings going to be created for even a fraction of one billion new workers? Population planning, no doubt, is a top-priority issue, but this will do very little to meet the immediate challenge of unemployment. Even half a billion unemployed people without hope can make the sustenance of life on a stable basis highly problematic, to say the least.

The handling of the unemployment problem is not a matter of quick fixes. Policies of population control and deliberate employment generation have both national and international dimensions. For population control, we do not have to follow the path of demographic transition experienced in the developed world. Japan took 40 years to halve the crude birth rate, but Korea achieved this in a little over half that period, and China did it in less than two decades. The monetary investment for population control measures is not very high. Per capita expenditure on population control today is quite low, from 3 cents in Bolivia to 177 cents in El Salvador. Good, strong programs in China are run at an expense of 100 cents per capita; in Korea it is 71 cents, and in India it is even less — only 34 cents.[30]

The crux of family planning programs is motivation and organization. First, there has to be an awareness of the gravity of the problem at both the government and community level, something that is uniquely lacking in many countries. This is a typical area where private loss is certainly a social gain. Perhaps land use planning is the only other comparable area where public and private perceptions of what is desirable and profitable are so very different. It is in these selected areas that action cannot be left to market forces; strong public or community intervention is required. It is in the areas of policy and strategy that public intervention has to be made. In the provision of services, however, much can be done by the private sector. In fact, a great deal of investment in population planning is community-generated, as well as community-managed.[31] Second, the organization of both motivational work and service delivery has to be largely decentralized. Without local management, family planning programs face an uphill task. Third, population planning has to be integrated into an overall development strategy. Health care, education, infrastructure development — all such activities must promote family planning. Finally, technological breakthrough has to be maintained, at least at the existing level.

Hand in hand with population control policies, employment generation policies have to govern the entire economic life of nations. It is in the weakest and the poorest of countries that such action has to be primordial. Even in Latin America, however, where growth has been significant until the recent past, deliberate population and employment policies are essential for the upkeep of their societies. The growth rate of the labor force in the next seventy years will be the world's highest in Latin America. The region has the additional handicap that service sector aborption there cannot increase much. The challenge of employment is an area where historical experience may not be of much avail, except to suggest changes in strategy. Confucius thought inequality should be lamented more than scarcity, but the challenge of unemployment does not provide any option between these two lamentable choices. Unemployment breeds both inequality and scarcity, and it also flourishes in such an environment.

In the foreseeable future, the challenge of unemployment has the aspects of a nightmare in virtually all developing countries. Unless we believe in social Darwinism, it is inconceivable that the world as a whole can escape its catastrophic consequences. Bold and unorthodox, and at the same time imaginative and compassionate, measures are required to meet this challenge. The efforts must focus, on the one hand, on removing both inequality and scarcity, and on the other, on severely limiting population growth. Concerted and timely action is not only essential; it is urgent. The alternative is simply unthinkable. After reaching such heights of accomplishment, we certainly cannot countenance a relapse into a state of nature.

An employment strategy is needed not only to bring the fruits of development to more people, but also to avoid the disaster and chaos that many societies may face on account of unemployment. In some countries, the growth process can be sustained by generating sufficient domestic demand. But the success of an employment strategy will again depend on corollary investments in the social services. The productivity of labor is very important, as we do not want to land ourselves in a low-productivity, high-employment poverty trap. For this reason, careful social investment is of very great importance. Nutritional levels and health conditions must improve for labor productivity to improve; but because these services must have wide coverage, they have to involve limited capital investment. The production of wage goods must be given priority. Primary health care giving greater attention to the preventive aspects of public health has to receive priority. Literacy and numeracy are required to make unskilled laborers more productive. Skills improvement is needed to upgrade traditional technology and, hence, the income-earning capacity of more people; the priority in education thus shifts from university education to the spread of numeracy, literacy and basic skills training. For the service sector and rural economy to be more productive and more labor-absorptive, community schooling, training for self-employment and upgradation of indigenous technology become crucial. Thus, in the pursuit of an employment strategy, it is also necessary to attend to the intermediate product of development objectives: improvement of the quality of the human aspect in the development process. Concern for employment, therefore, cannot be oblivious to the other human dimensions of the development process.

A Case Study : Bangladesh

Let us now sketch the difficulties, as well as the hopes, of an individual nation to try to appreciate the applicability and desirability of the strategy discussed so far. The nation has a labor force of about 29 million, of whom perhaps 40 per cent are unemployed. The population is growing at a rate of 2.5 per cent. The working-age population by the end of the century will be 84 million, but the actual labor force will go up to 50 million only. About 48 per cent of the domestic output is generated in the agriculture sector, while industry and mining contribute only 13 per cent. Of the labor force, 74 per cent are in agriculture, 11 per cent in industry and 15 per cent in services. The urban population is only 15 per cent and the literacy rate only 26 per cent. About 80 per cent of the population lives below the poverty line, although they account for 58 per cent of the GDP. That is to say, the nation is very poor indeed. Although 65 per cent of the land is arable and crop intensity is over 150 per cent, there is tremendous land hunger, an average holding being of the size of 0.3 acres. Exports account for less than 6 per cent of the GDP and remittances by workers abroad for around 4 per cent. But imports account for a little less than 20 per cent of GDP. The country depends heavily on external capital flows, up to about 10 per cent of GDP, usually obtained as grants or on concessional terms.

This is a picture of total despair. The duality of the economy is very pronounced. Economic developments over the last forty years have been very uneven. Periods of comparative growth have invariably been followed by great upheavals, stagnation or even retrogression. In the early 1960s, good progress was made in building infrastructure, both physical and institutional, and setting up industries. Then there was a period of civil disorder, followed by a brutal war of liberation that took a toll of nearly one-third of the GDP. Reconstruction efforts occupied the first half of the 1970s. During this period, the terms of trade deteriorated very adversely. A trade gap of about $100 million in 1969 U.S. dollars turned into a gap of one billion in 1974 dollars, primarily on account of food and petroleum imports. The second half of the 1970s registered a growth rate of about 5.2 per cent a year. But then came stagnation, with only a weak pick-up now. A purchasing power loss of about one billion dollars in 1981 and 1982 precipitated the recent deterioration. Domestic political changes and inflexibility of policies are no doubt at fault every now and then, but external conditions are a basic source of periodic destabilization.

This nation needs to pursue sound economic policies for an extended period of time, but it also needs strong resource support. It has carried out successful programs in rural development. Despite political vicissitudes and the endless search for an ideal implementation mechanism, the works program has survived as an effective mechanism for employment generation, capital creation and agricultural productivity drives. Agriculture, particularly the food production program, is on the right track: the expansion of an effective input package is receiving due attention; pricing and stocking policies are complementing this effort; subsidization has virtually been phased out in order to find resources for the expansion of coverage; irrigation possibilities are still not fully exploited; ecological conditions augur well for a substantial increase in yield per acre from the present low level of about a ton; rural forestry has picked up momentum and has immense potential; and aquaculture and backyard livestock farming are being emphasized. The community schools program also has considerable promise. The population program is designed neatly and well, but the problem is one of efficient implementation: coordination, supervision and monitoring are complicated and weak. Fortunately, motivation is not a problem in a country where the population bomb is slowly exploding. Delivery services, however, are inadequate and inefficient. All these programs, and others of similar quality, have two things in common: they have high labor inputs, and they are closely linked with output growth. The rural thrust of the programs is intended to defuse the urban push and resist the urban pull, mainly to conserve resources for investment with a favorable incremental capital/output ratio. Coupled with the special programs detailed below, it looks like a revolutionary development.

Two new programs – one for a new institutional structure and another for off-farm activities in rural areas – deserve special mention. The institutional structure is designed to overcome the ineffectiveness of all decentralization measures. Decentralization seldom works, because every now and then there is central intervention, or usurpation of decentralized powers and functions. It is also handicapped by the inefficiency of the process of supervision and monitoring. The remedy is total devolution of functions and powers, along with financial resource support. A population program or a rural works program becomes the responsibility of a community of between 200,000 and 500,000 people. The basic education program would be run entirely by the community. Agricultural production programs would also be a local responsibility. The central government, in fact, sheds its powers and functions in favor of the local governments of small communities. It is said that NGOs succeed in their programs because they operate on a limited scale, and in a target area. It is similarly maintained that managing a Singapore or a Hong Kong is much easier because of their size.

These examples have also prompted the experiment in institutional restructuring that is taking place now. It may lead to some resources being frittered away. There may be cases of wrong planning or misplaced priorities. But they will be less harmful than national mistakes and wastages. The only real fear is of overbureaucratization in rural centers, and the only antidote is vigilance.

The other program is very simple, and its effects are already visible. Land hunger is so great, and agricultural productivity still so low, that almost half of the rural labor force must engage in some kind of off-farm activities on either a full-time or a part-time basis. Individuals under the Grameen Bank Program are encouraged to get into trade or other services and simple processing or production activities. Tending a milch cow, looking after a backyard duckery, vending sweets, husking rice, collecting fuelwood for sale, sewing carrying bags, hawking utensils in the village, growing saleable vegetables in a courtyard, running a blacksmith shop, operating a potter's wheel —these are the kinds of jobs that people take up. They get credit and guidance and are organized into mutual help groups to ensure continued good work. I have personally observed the progress of such programs. And I have felt Adam Smith in action: how labor specialization adds to the total wealth of the community and creates earning opportunities for all! Perhaps all this is taking place in an environment of low technology and low levels of productivity; but it is a change, and it promises hope.

The issues of low technology and low productivity have naturally drawn the attention they deserve. There is now a new program for the establishment of rural resource development center to promote off-farm activities, and perhaps also to upgrade the skills level in farm

activities. These centers, which are likely to be set up in rural administrative centers or rural primary marketplaces, are designed essentially
to provide training in skills. But they will be much more than mere
training centres. They will help in processing activities that cannot be
organized on a cottage industry basis. They will help open up opportunities for marketing by providing links with urban or foreign
buyers. They will help with the dissemination of designs and patents
suitable for larger markets outside the rural areas. It will be necessary
to establish close coordination between these centers and credit
institutions in order to add to wealth creation in rural areas. One
indirect, but healthy, effect of this program will be the resistance it
will offer to the urban push. This activity, however, is still in the
planning stage, and its impact can be judged only after it is put into
practice.

In a situation where statistical reality and historical precedent,
instead of inspiring hope, spell disaster, these programs and experiences provide a welcome relief. This is the scenario in Bangladesh,
a country that holds out the spectre of unmitigated suffering and
presents a canvas of all conceivable difficult development problems.
But unorthodox strategy and novel measures give rise to a vision of
vibrant rural centers numbering some five or six hundred, teeming
not only with thousands of people, but also with produce and
commodities. Utopia it may be, but where else do you flee, confronted by angry young millions demanding jobs and incomes? In
the next fifteen years, in a 14-billion-dollar economy with a very
poor resource base, jobs must be found for 30 million additional
people. The state of nature is certainly no option at all !

Notes

1. ILO, *Employment, Growth and Basic Needs* (Geneva, 1976).
2. ILO, *Essays on Employment* (Geneva, 1971), pp. 25-26. Sabola's estimates in
"Sectoral Employment Growth: The Outlook for the '80s" are on the highly conservative
side.
3. Some of the current unemployment rates are as follows: Italy 14.2 per cent, U.K.
13.0 per cent, Federal Republic of Germany 9.4 per cent, France 10.6 per cent, Canada
11.2 per cent, USA 7.3 per cent, Japan 2.6 per cent, Bangladesh 37.0 per cent.
4. Philip Ndegwa and John P. Powelson, eds., *Employment in Africa* (Geneva: ILO,
1973), p. 1.
5. World Bank, *World Development Report 1984* (Oxford University Press), table
21, pp. 258-9.

6. ILO, *Employment, Growth and Basic Needs.*

7. A. K. Sen, "Levels of Poverty: Policy and Change," World Bank Staff Working Paper, 1980, p. 36.

8. Karl Wohlmuth, ed., *Employment Creation in Developing Countries* (New York: Praeger, 1973), p. 43.

9. Sir W.A. Lewis, *Evolution of the New International Economic Order* (Princeton: 1978), p. 42.

10. H.F. Lydall, *Trade and Employment* (Geneva: ILO, 1975).

11. United Nations, *Yearbook of International Trade Statistics 1982* (New York: 1984), pp. 1174-1216, combined total of fabrics and clothing.

12. Lyn Squire, *Employment Policy in Developing Countries*, World Bank Publication (Oxford University Press, 1981), pp. 25-6.

13. World Bank, *WDR 1984*, p. 87.

14. For a detailed discussion of the short work week, see S.M.A. Hameed and G.S. Paul, eds., *Three or Four Day Work Week* (Edmonton: University of Alberta, 1974).

15. Squire, *Employment Policy*. p. 137.

16. Ibid., pp. 137-9.

17. World Bank, WDR 1984, pp. 67, 258-61; ILO, *Labor Force Estimates and Projections* (Geneva, 1977).

18. World Bank, *WDR 1984*, pp. 68-9. Illegal immigrants to the USA are estimated at three million in this report, but the ILO estimates between seven and twelve million in *Employment, Growth and Basic Needs.*

19. See Walter Adams, ed., *The Brain Drain* (New York: MacMillan, 1968).

20. World Bank, *WDR 1984*, p. 92.

21. Lester Brown, *State of the World 1985*, Worldwatch Institute Report (New York: Norton), pp. 74, 84, 85.

22. Phillis Deane and W.A. Cole, *British Economic Growth 1668-1959* (Cambridge University Press, 1976), p. 27.

23. World Bank, *WDR 1984*, p. 67.

24. Gustav Ranis, John C.H. Fei and Shirley W.O. Kuo, *Growth With Equity: The Taiwan Case*, World Bank Research Publication (Oxford University Press, 1979), pp. 28, 31.

25. For a more detailed discussion, see "Sharing in Development," ILO Report on the Philippines (Geneva, 1974).

26. For more details, see "Matching Employment Opportunities and Expectations", ILO Report on Ceylon (1971), and "Employment, Incomes and Equality," ILO Report on Kenya (1972).

27. Wohlmuth, *Employment Creation*, p. 43.

28. Brown, *SW 1985*, pp. 3-22.

29. World Bank, *WDR 1984*, p. 6.

30. Ibid., p. 149.

31. Ibid., p. 151.

CHAPTER 19

Health and Human Development

Hakan Hellberg

In dealing with the health of people, it is difficult to ignore the human dimension: it is brought close with every patient or client contact. But in terms of overall planning, resource allocation and infrastructure development, it is nevertheless easy to develop health systems based largely on the terms of the providers. "Statistical compassion" is necessary for an overall view but may be insufficient to fully realize the human element both as an input and as an objective of development. A result of this process, there is an overemphasis on medical repair services to passive recipients in institutions developed and functioning on the terms of the providers, be they doctors, nurses, administrators or political decision-makers.

The inadequacy, as well as the inhumanity, of this approach becomes evident when it is recognized how little our medical repair services can do to cure the results of chronic disease, whether of infectious or noninfectious origin. Of course, we need acute, curative, medical care and should be grateful for its capacity to relieve human suffering and restore health. But the human dimension is tragically missed when resources are used in such a way that the prevention of disease and the promotion of good health for individuals, communities and society at large are neglected. Inadequate nutrition or outright starvation, irreversible results of environmental hazards to individuals and large population groups, or consequences of inhuman conditions in settlements and communities cannot be repaired with drugs or surgeon's scalpels.

Health for All

It was the realization of the human dimension in health that led the member states of WHO in the 1970s to give the global health development process a new emphasis and direction. Putting international health activities and WHO's program under the social goal of

Health for All by the Year 2000 was based on an awareness of the existing inequalities and injustices in the level of health between and within countries. The "for all" is really a symbol of the human dimension, emphasizing the need for universal access to the possibilities of health and, through knowledge, individual initiatives and support from others, arrive at the minimal requirements for a socially and economically productive and satisfying life. It is, therefore, not a matter of sophisticated health or medical services for all, although some level of such services is naturally one element of any health-for-all approach.

Focusing on "the year 2000" is also based on concern for the human dimension in order to underline the urgency of dealing with unnecessary suffering and death. It is also to focus attention on prospective action and emphasize management by goals and objectives. The latter is important in an area where the traditional approach is very much a reactive and retrospective one, i.e., dealing with already manifest disease. In view of the risks and dilemmas people are facing, it is simply inhuman not to point out the need for and the possibilities of preventive and promotive action.

This brings up the issue of "health" as a combination of promotive, preventive, curative and rehabilitative action. Taking the human dimension in health development seriously means striving for the right balance and proportions between these elements of health for individuals and communities.

Primary Health Care

During the years following World War II, there have been different phases in the health development process. During the 1950s, community health aspects were emphasized to balance the individualistic approach. Man is not alone in either health or disease. In the 1960s, basic health services were underlined to balance the dominating role of large hospitals, where curative medical possibilities were rapidly increasing.

The primary health care movement of the 1970s brought to the forefront two elements of great importance for a discussion of the human dimensions of health and development, namely, people's participation or involvement, and the need for intersectoral understanding and action.

The participation issue focused on the need to take people seriously as a resource as well as an objective. Methods of self-care have developed, as well as participatory mechanisms and experience in understanding one's own health or disease. People participate in different ways in planning and implementing interventions aimed at health promotion, illness prevention and rehabilitation. The process of people taking their health more and more into their own hands is continuing all over the world. It is not an easy one; it meets with suspicion and resistance from health professionals and politicians, as well as from a public that has become too passively dependent on the provision of medical repair services from above.

The intersectoral approach to development has been discussed for many years, and it is generally recognized as both important and difficult to implement. In terms of the human dimension, inter-sectoral vision and action for health and development means taking seriously the complexity of the human situation. People do not divide their existence into watertight compartments of health, education, social action, economics etc. Their reality is one complex whole, and their dilemma very often is to cope with compartmentalization introduced by the authorities, who thereby dominate instead of serving and supporting. Taking people seriously means accepting their terms instead of forcing our terms on them. In practice, this means administrative flexibility instead of rigidity, and openness to renewal instead of dogmatic defense of the status quo.

Essential Elements of Primary Health Care

The Alma-Ata Conference of 1978 outlines the essential elements as at least:

a) Education concerning prevailing health problems and the methods for preventing and controlling them.
b) Promotion of food supply and proper nutrition.
c) An adequate supply of safe water and basic sanitation.
d) Maternal and child health care, including family planning.
e) Immunization against the major infectious diseases.
f) Prevention and control of locally endemic diseases.
g) Appropriate treatment for diseases and injuries.
h) Provision of essential drugs.

Even the order of these elements emphasizes the essential human dimension, beginning with the most important aspects — knowledge, food, water — and then the different interventions as needed. Each of the eight elements provides for the human dimension to be taken seriously, but may also be misused by overpowering or remote professional and political leaders preventing real participation.

As countries struggle to implement primary health care, they recognize many obstacles based on both national and external constraints, both in administrative procedures and attitudes. Giving priority to the human dimension helps to alert those concerned to the pitfalls and to remedial action.

Are We Achieving Health for All?

The inbuilt monitoring and evaluation process for the Health for All movement enables us to look at failures, weaknesses and achievements. The results from 1983, and now in 1985, reveal three main areas of weakness. Behind these weaknesses lie a disregard for the human dimension, the selfishness of certain groups and also managerial inadequacies. First, regarding *resources,* not only is there an absolute lack of resources, but there is also a failure to use existing resources optimally. The second area of weakness is a low level of technical performance, with an underlying cause of insufficient *administrative and managerial capabilities.* Third, one finds inadequate ability or willingness to *communicate* among various groups in society and different levels of the administration; again, a sign that the human dimension is not taken seriously enough. There is a need for a mature handling of relationships instead of primitive attitudes of dominance and subservience. Or, in simple words, for people to take each other seriously.

The Health for All process is very much a matter of relationships: sharing information about health and disease in a responsible, i.e., an understandable and meaningful, way; tackling problems of food and nutrition, water and waste, starting with people's agenda; developing health and medical interventions so that they are accessible, acceptable and affordable. Human growth and maturity is also the goal with regard to the realities of unavoidable suffering and death.

At this stage we are in a "Yes — BUT" phase of the health-for-all process. Yes, there are positive results that are improving the human condition, but there are also many constraints and obstacles to be tackled.

Among the constraints related to the human dimension are the resistance and suspicion of ordinary people to the plans and projects developed by the authorities. These authorities, national or international, tend to blame lack of success on the people instead of reviewing their own attitudes and actions. It is easy to blame the victim. But, perhaps people hesitate because they have been disappointed too often, and their survival may have depended on a certain need for traditional conservatism.

Realizing the importance of the human dimension in health and development presupposes the motivation to do something for other people, caring for what happens to others and drawing the consequences of such humane attitudes into everyday work. Unfortunately, these elements are too often lacking at all levels of society, as well as in national and international agencies. A major challenge is, therefore, to discover and use ways of inculcating such motivation and dedication at all levels.

Development means reinforcing the existing positive elements in the human situation and taking incremental steps toward change based on that situation. Sometimes only the change aspects are underlined, with an automatic assumption that all change is not only good, but also understood and accepted. A high degree of rationality is assumed which does not exist (in any society); and one neglects to note that there may not only be an inability to change, but a feeling of lack of authority to change. In many cultures, the prevailing view of reality does not give people an automatic legitimacy to introduce change, because they see themselves as the victims or objects rather than as agents of change. This aspect of the human dimension may too often have been neglected in development efforts.

In our day and age, a dominating aspect of the human dimension is the longing for security and survival: survival in the microcosm of one's own situation, and in the macrocosm of our shared human existence. The threat to that existence through nuclear holocaust is today the ultimate public health hazard. We owe it to our fellow human beings, as well as to ourselves, to prevent that catastrophe, which would negate all development efforts everywhere. Working for peace and prosperity, we are well aware that the eradication of evil and human selfishness is not possible, but we must do everything to balance and control conflict at reasonable levels and by reasonable means. This is a lesson we learn in health development, where disease eradication is seldom possible, but control must always be strived for. For the sake of people.

CHAPTER 20

The Role of Primary Education

Just Faaland

Our thinking about the role of primary education in development has changed a great deal in the postwar period. We have come a long way from the view that development could be brought about by the simple act of creating infrastructure, or by industrialization, or even by increasing output. We have begun to learn that much more importance must be attached to the quality of development, to whom it serves, and to the nature of the contribution that it makes to human welfare.

An important indicator of the quality of development is the extent to which it meets basic human needs. I will not linger on the definitions of such needs, but amongst the many competing ones, education is never omitted, at least at the primary level. Its contribution is direct insofar as it meets the needs of individuals, whether felt or not; it is also indirect in being an ingredient for meeting basic needs in the future and, eventually, in going far beyond that.

Justifying Primary Education

In economics, we are always concerned with choices, and early approaches to the provision of primary education were concerned with this too. In the 1960s, for example, education became a prominent aspect of the provision of human capital and was researched intensively in order to establish its investment yield. Many different conflicting and contrasting results emerged from the numerous studies that were carried out. This is hardly surprising: the methodology was difficult to apply, and the data very uncertain. Moreover, as education spread, yields changed, sometimes quite sharply. Analyses and facts were advanced showing that income distribution affects the apparent yield on investment in education, and that income distribution itself is dependent on the supply of educated people.

Reviewing these studies today, it is clear that they did not always, nor even predominantly, provide justification for the extension of primary education to every boy and girl in the primary age group. Often they tended to support the contention that the value of education was more a matter of ensuring that just enough educated people were provided to meet the needs of development. This was often shown to be far fewer than universal primary schooling. The phenomenon of the redundant university graduate that attracted so much attention in relation to India was not confined to higher education in the minds of many, who, like the British Raj, envisaged education as only a means to meet their own ends of providing sufficient clerks or artisans. Taking as an example the work carried out by O.D. Hoerr in the early 1970s, the return on secondary education, given the existing level of primary education (and income distribution), was greater than the return on primary education itself.[1] This might be construed as indicating that within budgetary constraints, any additional resources might be better devoted to secondary rather than to primary education. Other analysts and other decision-makers took this argument even further, concluding that investment in industry with a yield (in some cases) of 15 per cent should have preference over investment in primary education, with its yield sometimes of 10 per cent or less.

Not all econometric work concerned itself with rates of return. It was also possible to relate education to income distribution. The relative neglect of primary education in the distribution of educational resources is a factor making for inequality in the distribution of income generally, and in the fruits of development in particular; increased educational opportunities at the early stages of education may help to redress the imbalance. For example, using regression analysis, M.A. Ahluwalia has suggested that increasing the primary school enrollment rate appears to improve the income share of the poorest 40 per cent of the population, while increasing the secondary school enrollment rate improves the position of the middle 40 per cent in income distribution.[2]

An analytical approach which is directed to social concerns rather than to straight economic cost/benefit considerations comes much closer to my own feelings on this subject. I say feelings advisedly, because I am expressing a belief and a conviction about human values rather than conducting an argument about economic optimization. We may not be in a position to show conclusively that a country moving rapidly toward universal primary education will also grow more rapidly in terms of GDP than one that does not; nor can we demonstrate convincingly that national welfare will be enhanced by pursuing the first rather than the second path; nor, for that matter, can we indicate with any precision the other and accompanying conditions that would influence the outcome. No doubt, positive economics must always be respected, but only if it maximizes the right things, and in this case accepts that to move toward primary education as rapidly as possible is an end in itself, to which priority consideration is due.

Primary education, effectively organized and consistently pursued, can be a successful way of reaching the poor and a relatively cheap and practicable way of benefiting them. However, as I see it, universality is a necessary condition for ensuring that the poor, and *all* the poor, benefit. Anything short of universality does not leave out the rich; it will be the poor who will be excluded.

Country Performance

It is instructive in this connection to look at the wide disparity evident in the provision of primary education. Great progress has been made in the provision of primary education in recent years. Even amongst the poorest countries there are well known, and not quite so well known, examples of universal or near-universal primary education. China and Sri Lanka come quickly to mind; but Tanzania, Togo, Madagascar, Kenya, Lao PDR, Mozambique and Vietnam are almost, if not quite, there, judging by World Bank statistics. Others, including Zaire, Ghana, Burma, Nepal and India, are well advanced in their programs. Table 1 summarizes the position for low and lower-middle-income countries.

TABLE 1
Percentage of Age-Group in Primary School
1982 (when available)

Percentage	No. of Low-Income Countries	No. of Lower-Middle-Income Countries
20 - 30	4	–
30 - 40	4	1
40 - 50	3	1
50 - 60	1	1
60 - 70	5	4
70 - 80	5	3
80 - 90	1	2
90 - 100	3	5
* 100 +	7	17
Total	33	34

* Children at school may include some outside the standard age-group.

It is interesting to speculate about the variations in performance. How is it that out of roughly the same number of countries, seven of the low-income countries should have achieved universal primary education, while only 17 of those in the lower-middle category have done so? It is clearly not a question of income levels alone : witness Oman and Saudi Arabia, amongst the high-income oil exporters, which have not so far come close to universal primary education. In their case, it appears that female education lags behind and brings the average down. Of course, this is often true in the case of other countries, but it is far from a complete answer. The overwhelming factor determining progress toward universal primary education is political commitment and political systems. It is not just the fact that India is poorer than China that determines the difference in their performance in primary education. It is no accident that the more strongly socialized countries have moved faster than others along the lines of universal primary education.

Many people argue that primary education has to be constrained because it can cost so much. Amongst the poorest countries, as much as 20 per cent of the central government budget may go for education, as in Kenya and Togo[3]. The figure is often less, but it is generally quite high and would be greater still if all children were included. As is commonly known, the costs of education increase progressively as further stages are ascended on the way to the university level. But universal primary education need not be expensive, or beyond the reach of all but the poorest countries. For primary education of five years, perhaps 15 per cent of the population would need to be in school. With a pupil/teacher ratio of 20:1, this would mean that no more than the equivalent of perhaps 2 per cent of the working population would need to be engaged in primary teaching. In addition, of course, provision has to be made for buildings and equipment. Often these can be locally provided, and fairly economically, using local and voluntary effort. Again, of course, there is a need to train teachers, but here one can make do without insisting that everyone should have a gold-edged certificate to display. However, when self-help is not forthcoming and available resources are too meager, the international community might step in.

In such circumstances, it is natural to ask what role the international community might take in supporting educational efforts. I have been asking myself about the scale of the task of completing the provision of universal *world* primary education. How might the failure to provide universal literacy be erased in the way that smallpox has faded from the scene?

World Primary Education

The cost of a program of universal primary education would be large, and it would need to be sustained for a decade or two to be firmly established. Yet, the value of additional resources required over and above the present level of effort is well within the financing capacity of the world. In fact, given the fact that we are directly concerned with the quality of life of hundreds of millions of individuals, the cost is trivial, perhaps on the order of $10 to 15 billion per year equivalents. (The higher figure in this range would allow for significant improvements in the average quality of education as well.) If half of this were to be provided as aid from industrialized countries, the sums involved would be equivalent to two to three times what DAC countries now provide for all education (about $2.5 billion). Many donor programs are unimaginative and lack any expression of solidarity. Here is an opportunity to remedy that and make assistance available at the grassroots, where it is so badly needed.

What might universal primary education be expected to accomplish for those who receive it? Functional literacy and numeracy should still be at the head of the list, and I would go so far as to say that the multiplication tables learned by rote still have a part to play in areas of the world that are unlikely to be governed by pocket calculators or computers for some time yet.

Even at the elementary level, some effort must be made to get pupils to think; learning by rote, necessary though it may be, is not enough. A scientific outlook needs to be instilled, as well as an elementary understanding of nature. Still another aspect is the imparting of family and domestic skills. Skills of civic participation are also important, as well as political awareness. How far, in other ways, primary education should attempt to provide vocational skills has always seemed to me to be uncertain. There is a limit to what can be done in five years or so, and a general education focused on the three R's must remain the first, if not the only, aim.

It is now more generally appreciated that it is necessary to look at the curriculum critically to ensure that it is not undesirably academic and that the system of primary education is complete in itself, and not designed essentially as a passport to higher education. Problems remain about the languages of instruction; in Africa for example, more than 2,000 languages are in use. Whatever language is chosen as the medium of instruction, appropriate textbooks have to be prepared in the countries that are to use them. Books inherited from a colonial past are seldom suitable and often many years out of date.

The development of a satisfactory standard of primary education should probably be approached in several stages. Given the emphasis placed on universal primary education, the first priority should be to bring all children to school and to retain them there for the full course of primary education, say, five years. Granted, teaching skills are likely to be of a low average standard initially, and steps will need to be taken to enlarge and improve teacher training. How quickly this can be done will depend on the provision of training facilities and the finances to run them. After that, standards may be improved in other ways.

Conclusion

Universal primary education would fundamentally enhance the capacity of individuals to realize their inherent potential. With less than universality, primary education is generally denied to the children of the poor and weak in society, and in particular to girls. The quality of education needs to be enhanced generally. This would have a high cost/benefit ratio, both in terms of the realization of human potential and (arguably) in terms of economic growth and social development. Moreover, improvement in standards is needed in order to reach and retain all children of school age.

The resources needed to provide universal primary education within a decade or so are of an order of magnitude well within the capacity of the countries directly concerned to mobilize and, as needed, of the industrialized countries to finance.

Notes

1. "Education, Income and Equity in Malaysia," *Economic Development and Cultural Change* 21:2 (January 1973), pp. 247-273.
2. See "Income Inequality: Some Dimensions of the Problem" in Hollis Chenery et al., *Redistribution with Growth* (Oxford University Press, 1975), p. 17.
3. World Bank, *World Development Report 1985*, p. 224.

PART V

IMPACT OF SCIENCE AND TECHNOLOGY

CHAPTER 21

Of Science and Human Development

Abdus Salam

It is axiomatic that without highly motivated and highly trained manpower, no lasting development can take place. My purpose here is to try to highlight the role of a much-neglected community, that of scientists — so highly neglected that they did not figure in the first draft of the U.N. Development Programme. Technologists did, but scientists did not.

My own experience of dealing with development-related science derives from directing a United Nations-run International Center for High-Level Physics located in Trieste, Italy. Since its inception in 1964, this center has had the privilege of hosting on the order of 25,000 visits by experimental and theoretical research physicists, nearly 13,000 of them working in developing country research institutes and universities.

Since I am speaking in Turkey, I wish to relate my remarks to the situation in Turkey, to that in nearby Egypt and to my own country, Pakistan. These three are all small countries, with population levels ranging between those of France and Japan, but five to ten times larger than Sweden's. During the last 15 years, we at Trieste have welcomed 325 physicists from Turkey, 375 from Pakistan and around 600 from Egypt.

Let me begin by recalling the year 1799. Against the opposition of the *ulema* — and, surprisingly, even of a section of the military establishment — Sultan Selim III introduced the subjects of algebra, trigonometry, mechanics, ballistics and metallurgy in Turkey. He imported French and Swedish teachers to teach these disciplines. His purpose was to rival European advances in gun-founding. Since there was no corresponding emphasis on research in these subjects, Turkey could not keep up with the newer advances being made elsewhere. The result was predictable: Turkey did not succeed. Then, as now, technology, unsupported by science, will not flourish.

As my second example, take the situation in Egypt at the time of Muhammad Ali, thirty years after the episode with Selim III. Muhammad Ali had his men trained in the arts of surveying and prospecting for coal and gold in Egypt. This attempt was unsuccessful, but it did not occur to him, nor to his successors, to train Egyptians on a long-term basis in the basic sciences of geology or in related environmental sciences. Thus, to this day, there is not one high-level desertification research institute in the entire subcontinents of North Africa or the Middle East (except in Israel). When we recently organized a course on the physics and mathematics of the desertification process, we had to import teachers from Denmark — with their experience in the wastes of Greenland!

My third example is again from Egypt, where 30 million dollars was reportedly spent in setting up a factory for the manufacture of thermionic valves. The factory was built in the same year that transistors were perfected and began to invade the world's markets. The recommendation to set up the thermionic valve factory was made by foreign consultants. It was readily accepted by Egyptian officials, who were not particularly aware of the way science was advancing, and who apparently never consulted the competent physicists in their own country.

The Neglect of Science

Why do we neglect science for development? First and foremost, there is the question of national ambition. Let me say it unambiguously: countries of the size of Turkey or Egypt or Pakistan have no scientific communities geared to development because we do not *want* such communities. We suffer from a lack of ambition toward acquiring science — a feeling of inferiority toward it, bordering sometimes on hostility.

In respect of ambition, take the example of Japan at the end of the last century, when the new Meiji Constitution was promulgated. The Meiji Emperor took five oaths. One of these set out a national policy towards science: "Knowledge will be sought and acquired from any source, with all means at our disposal, for the greatness and security of Japan." And what comprised "knowledge"? Listen to the Japanese physicist Hantaro Nagaoka, specializing in magnetism — a discipline to which the Japanese have contributed importantly, both experimentally and theoretically. Writing in 1888 from Glasgow — where he had been sent by the Imperial Government — to his professor, Tanakadate, he expressed himself thus: "We must work actively with an open eye, keen sense, and ready understanding, indefatigably and not a moment stopping. ... There is no reason why the Europeans shall be so supreme in everything. As you say, ... we shall... beat those *yattya bottya* (pompous) people [in science] in the course of ten or twenty years."

Among the developing countries today, from our experience in Trieste, we can name just five which do value science: Argentina and Brazil in Latin America, and China, Korea and India in Asia. Barring these five, the Third World, despite its realization that science and technology are the sustenance of progress and the major hope for economic betterment, has regarded science, in contrast to technology, as only a marginal activity. Unfortunately, this is also true of the aid-giving agencies of the richer countries and also of the agencies of United Nations, including the UNDP.

Assuming that science has a role in development, why has science in developing countries been treated as a marginal activity? There are two reasons.

Fisrt, policymakers, prestigious commissions (even the Brandt Commission) and aid-givers speak uniformly of the problems of technology transfer to the developing countries as if that were the only thing involved. It is hard to believe, but true, that the word "science" does not figure in the Brandt Commission report. Very few within the developing world appear to stress that *for long-term effectiveness, technology transfer must always be accompanied by science transfer*. The science of today is the technology of tomorrow. And when we speak of science, it must be broad-based in order to be effective for application. If one were being Machiavellian, one might even discern sinister motives among those who try to sell to us the idea of technology transfer without science transfer. There is nothing which has hurt us in the Third World more than the recent slogan in the richer countries of "relevant science." Regrettably, this slogan was parroted in our countries unthinkingly to justify stifling the growth of *all* science.

Second, science transfer is effected by — and to — communities of scientists. Such communities need building up to a critical size in their human resources and infrastructure. This building up calls for wise science policies with four cardinal ingredients: long-term commitment, generous patronage, self-governance of the scientific community and free international contacts. In addition, the high-level scientist in our countries must be allowed to play a role in nation-building *as an equal partner along with the professional planner, the economist and the technologist.* Few developing countries have promulgated such policies; few aid-giving agencies have taken it as their mandate to encourage and help with the building up of the scientific infrastructure.

Building Up a Science Infrastructure

Why science transfer? What is the infrastructure of sciences I am speaking about, and why? First and foremost, we need scientific literacy and science teaching at all levels, and particularly at the higher levels – at least for the sake of the engineers and technologists. This calls for inspiring teachers. No one can be an inspiring teacher of science unless he has experienced and created at least some modicum of living science during some part of his career. This calls for well-equipped teaching laboratories and, in the present era of fast-moving science, the provision of the newest journals and books. This is the minimum of scientific infrastructure any country of any size must provide for.

Next should come demands on their own scientific communities from the developing country government agencies and their nascent industries for discriminatory advice regarding which technologies should be acquired.

Then, for a minority of the developing countries, there is the need for indigenous scientists to help with their applied colleagues' research work. For any society, the problems of its agriculture, of its local pests and diseases, of its local materials base, must be solved locally. One needs the underpinnings of a first-class base in science to carry out applied research in these areas. The craft of applied science in a developing country is made harder simply because one does not have available next door, or at the other end of a telephone line, people who can tell the applied scientist what he needs to know of the basic principles relevant to his applied work.

I spoke earlier of indifference toward science. When I was recently consulting my Turkish colleagues, I was told that this came sometimes even from the engineering community — a community which, in Turkey, enjoys a good reputation and high status. Some Brazilian scientists also told me the same thing. I was surprised by this for many reasons. First, in Pakistan, my experience is that a lack of appreciation of the possible role of scientists stems from the short-sightedness of planners and economists, not of engineers. Second, I was surprised because in the history of recent fundamental advances in physics, a crucial role has been played by engineers. Thus, for example, Y. Nishina, the man who first brought high-level physics to Japan and who was the teacher of the two Japanese Nobel laureates in physics, H. Yukawa and S. Tomonaga, was an electrical engineer by profession. P.A.M. Dirac, the creator of quantum mechanics, who, in my opinion, is the greatest figure in physics of the twentieth century, was trained as an electrical engineer. Eugene Wigner, who won a Nobel Prize for physics, started out as a chemical engineer.

To reinforce my remarks, let me recall that in 1961, I attended the centennial celebrations of the founding of Massachusetts Institute of Technology, perhaps the most important technological school in the United States. To my surprise, it was the engineers at this school who wanted the quantity of science to be increased in their curricula.

But there is one aspect of the neglect of science that one cannot gainsay: the neglect demonstrated by numbers. In the whole Arab world, there are altogether around 1,500 scientists. Of these, 55 per cent come from one country, Egypt. Of these, one-quarter are physicists — altogether some 150 individuals. About two per cent of these will be very good; and during their youthful working life, this two per cent will wish to go where their work will flourish and be appreciated. Do you blame them? The same type of figures obtain in Turkey and in Pakistan. Extrapolating from international norms — which prevail in Japan or Israel — the number of scientists in Turkey should be on the order of 6,000. Believe me, Turkey or Egypt or Pakistan will not go bankrupt if they each produce, say, 1,000 physicists, provision them, and equip research institutions for them.

The Potential

But before I speak of these, I should perhaps speak of the situation in neighboring Greece — until recently a developing country, according to the definition of the UNDP, but now in the category of the developed. Greece has recently applied for, and secured, membership in the Center for Nuclear Research in Geneva — Europe's largest and most prestigious organization for particle physics research. Greece displayed the ambition of joining the big leagues in science, and one can see as a result the maturity which Greek physics has acquired and its transformation year after year. How this maturity will reflect itself in the area of development will, of course, depend on the policies Greece pursues in employing these physicists; the physicists will be there, at any rate.

Let me come back to Turkey and discuss the development of institutions which can be created and which will need Turkish physics manpower. I know from the personal experience of working with them that Turkish physicists are some of the most imaginative physicists in the whole developing world. They consciously undertake difficult problems in physics — and this is something I respect. I had the privilege of visiting this country a short while back, when I was honored to be received by President Kenan Evren. I suggested to him that, in my opinion, what Turkey needed in its national plans and priorities was something analogous to the Bell Telephone Laboratories in the United States in the field of communications. That laboratory has produced six Nobel laureates who have contributed to basic physics, besides including transistors and transistor technology in their roster of inventions.

I estimate that the Turkish, Egyptian or Pakistani analogue to the Bell Laboratories would cost forty million dollars to build and around four million dollars yearly to run. I believe it can be done with the highest level of quality, and that one can find those capable of creating it in Turkey. May I hope that this and similar science projects will soon come to fruition in the developing world?

CHAPTER 22

Technological Change and Human Problems in the Developing World

Mihaly Simai

Technological transformation has its quantititive and qualitative aspects in every society. Human beings as biological and social units and the societies in which they live are influenced by both aspects of the transformation process. It is, however, the qualitative aspect of the technological transformation which is more important and more difficult to deal with from the point of view of individuals and societies.

Some of the most important qualitiative factors which are relevant in the process of technological progress from the human point of view are the following:

a) Changes in occupations and changes in the distribution of wealth and income influencing social stratification.

b) Education and training, which improve the quality of labor.

c) Public health and medical services, which contribute to the effective performance of the working population.

d) Changes in living conditions and cultural amenities, which influence the values of the population.

e) Industrial relations, which influence a wide range of attitudes in a society.

f) New tensions and conflicts resulting from technological change and social innovations.

g) Improvement in the media of communication, sometimes including modernization of the language.

In the process of global technological transformation, the quantitative and qualitative aspects are interconnected, bringing new economic and social forces into action continuously.

Technology: Effects and Side-Effects

Technology has always been two-sided. On the one hand, it has promoted man's mastery over his physical environment and increased his ability to achieve certain human goals, such as an improved diet, better shelter, more rapid transport and communications, prolongation of human life via more sophisticated medicine and medical instruments, the prevention of the formation of new lives by improved contraception technology, etc. On the other hand, technologies also produce or are accompanied by different negative effects or unfavorable side-effects.

The capacity of technology to make weapons more effective is certainly an adverse consequence. Negative side-effects are often not visible until the diffusion of the given technology is widespread, when their identification is often a posteriori.

Where new technologies have been introduced, the less developed the countries have been, the more difficulty they had in dealing with the side-effects. Sometimes the side-effects are very direct; sometimes they are indirect.

One of the distinctive characteristics of modern technology has been its association with new kinds of human interactions. Sometimes these interactions are the direct consequences of certain peculiar characteristics of modern technology, such as environmental pollution. In other cases, the interactions flow from the social organization required by or connected with the technological change, such as urbanization, which may generate important benefits, but at great cost to society. There are some historical interactions which gained greater significance in the past few decades, such as mass migration from the rural areas or the brain drain.

Technological change on our globe has always been a highly unequal, extremely differential process. While in the late twentieth century the differences among countries, regions and functional areas of economic and social activity resulting from technological transformation are caused by both traditional and new factors, both types of factors are interacting in an unprecedented way and setting new forces into motion within the given societies.

The rapid entry of transistors, television, electronic games and other products of the information revolution into societies on a lower level of economic development speeded up the impact of the demonstration effect and contributed not only to consumption patterns which otherwise would not have emerged, but also to migration. The spread of the use of modern medicine, including vaccination, led to declines in mortality rates in the poorer countries while those countries were still at a much lower level of development — sometimes centuries behind the more developed regions. The impact of this change contributed to faster population growth, which in turn resulted in new requirements in economic and social policies. The proliferation of modern military technology in the developing world before these countries developed their overall technology-absorbing capacities takes its toll not only in more and more victims of "small wars," but also in diverting funds and the talents of the best experts away from economic and social development and toward unproductive purposes.

The socioeconomic implications in the interaction of traditional and new factors will become stronger in the coming decades, and they are going to lead to new opportunities, as well as many new conflicts, within the developing countries and on an international scale. The sources of potential progress and conflict are found in the nature of the present technological transformation on the one hand and in the characteristic features of the socioeconomic environment, including the system of international cooperation, on the other.

Immediate and Long-Term Problems of Technological Change

The world is at an early stage of a new scientific and technological revolution, the implications of which can be much more far-reaching than those of all previous changes. The information revolution, the biological revolution, the revolution in the field of materials and the changes in the field of energy are, first of all, opening up an unprecedented double perspective for humankind: the possibility of global annihilation or a chance to solve many of the problems which have been sources of suffering and misery throughout human existence. The technological revolution is also the source of many immediate and longer-term problems due to a number of reasons.

First, the process of technological transformation has been initiated, and is still highly concentrated, in a few industrial countries, and it is tied to a great extent to the defense sectors. A large part of this technology has a potential for double use: civilian and military. These factors influence the conditions and channels of the international diffusion of those technologies and build new inequalities into the international system, together with new sources and forms of dependency. While many developing countries are not idle bystanders to change but are actively working to build up their own research and development capacities — some of them with spectacular results in certain fields — the gap is still widening in the command, control and use of new technologies.

A second, very important characteristic of technological transformation is the speed of the process. Many studies have presented data documenting the speed of the invention and diffusion of new technologies. While the rate of change has not been independent of world market conditions, it is important to note that technological transformation in the highly industrialized countries continued at a relatively rapid rate even during the global recession of the early 1980s. Only countries and sectors having the necessary research and development background, the capital, the required mix of skills, entrepreneurship and a strong domestic and/or export demand, together with marketing potential and, often, substantial government support, are able to maintain a swift pace of technological change. There are very few countries where these factors are present on an optimal scale. Even in those developing countries which are better off than others, it is important to establish the required factors in the framework of a comprehensive national program and, if possible, within a structure of national cooperation.

The third important feature of the technological revolution is its relative complexity. While earlier technologies have been such direct extensions of nature through human activity that they were easily understood by literate persons, today's great technological leaps in almost every important field occur through the link-up of creative minds with computer systems. Due to the speed of creating and introducing new technologies and the accelerated obsolescence of the existing ones, the general human capacity to understand and control the new technologies has been substantially reduced, and the role of the technological elite has been expanding.

As a result, the vast majority of human beings are more ignorant of the nature and functioning of the new technologies than ever before. This general ignorance is much greater, of course, in countries at a lower level of economic and technological development. The task of expanding technological literacy and, within this field, computer literacy is becoming a vital problem in every society. It makes new demands on the educational system — demands which, in turn, can become important sources of new inequalities within the countries themselves.

The increasing pervasiveness of the new scientific and techno- logical revolution is a fourth important source of problems. Since these new technologies are able to revolutionize almost every area of human activity, they are able to produce far deeper and wider socioeconomic effects than the previous technological revolutions. In the highly industrialized countries, these effects are increasingly felt in process technologies, in the entry of new products into the market, in office work, in different services, etc. Industries which were traditionally considered labor-intensive are increasingly becoming highly capital-intensive. Patterns of demand for labor are thus chang- ing; while the demand for cheap unskilled labor is on the decline, for example, the demand for cheap skilled labor is on the rise. This is eroding the competitive advantage enjoyed up to now by some countries with an abundance of cheap unskilled labor.

Human Resource Implications

Modern industry at various, but mostly intermediate, levels of technology provides the bulk of the industrial output in Third World countries. Large-scale, modern, capital-intensive technologies (with elements of peak technology) are, of course, also present. In some branches, this technology represents the only possible alterna- tive in a given industry. Industrialization based on modern large-scale establishments has a significant impact on society and is the single most important source of social transformation, with the strongest human implications.

Industrialization influences, and often determines, the techno- logical transformation of other sectors, such as agriculture and the services. The contribution of industry to the GNP in the developing countries stood at almost one-third in the middle of the 1980s, higher than the global average. There is, of course, a wide scattering from the average in different countries. Industrialization strongly influences changes in social stratification, in income distribution and in the pattern of settlements. It is also a major force in shaping new consumption structures. Expectations concerning the favorable impact of industrial transformation have been among the strongest motivations in the development strategies of most countries.

There are important human implications to all the economic issues which could be raised in connection with technological trans- formation in the developing countries: how and from where modern technology can be acquired; how the necessary experience is gained to use the technology; how to promote the national diffusion of a new technology; how a strategy for the technological transformation of the developing countries could be formulated and implemented. This is not peculiar to the developing countries; but these issues and their human implications have different dimensions in the developed and developing countries, and the same issues very often require different solutions.

Acquisition of Technology

Acquiring modern technology in most cases requires imports from the more developed parts of the world. Successful technology import depends on bargaining power and on local expertise in the public and private sectors. An important human component is the quality of local engineers, managers and experts who screen technology imports. National legislation concerning the conditions for technology import must be well prepared to cope with the issues involved. In the present structure of the world economy, the conditions of technology transfer also have an important effect on the distribution of global income in favor of the richer countries.

The character of the imported technology — its sophistication, capital or labor intensity, input requirements and possible ways of utilization — is closely connected with the human factors in decision making. It is generally recognized, for example, that many developing countries import technologies which do not help in the solution of their domestic problems; they tend to purchase labor-saving, capital-intensive technologies. Sometimes there is no technological alternative; sometimes this technology is the one most readily available on the market, or through foreign assistance programs.

There is in general very little research, even within Third World countries, aimed at the development of alternative technologies. Transnational corporations are eager to introduce their sophisticated technologies into a new environment. Sometimes even Third World decision-makers do not want smaller-scale or intermediate technologies; they want the best available, regardless of the local consequences. Business leaders also think in terms of international standards and international competition; they are not primarily interested in technologies which would help, for example, to increase industrial employment within their own countries. In most cases, it is only the public sector which can plan to acquire technologies appropriate to national employment and savings policies. But sometimes even the public sector disregards these issues in selecting technologies.

The issues concerning product technologies are even more complicated. If the products are sold mostly for export, it is of course the foreign customer who determines the patterns. However, in cases where new products are only, or predominantly, for domestic consumption, a very important long-term question is emerging (which has often 'been discussed in economic literature by such distinguished personalities as Raul Prebisch): is it advisable to import western consumption patterns and values into a developing society at all, or at the rate which has characterized the last three decades? Such issues also figured in discussions about the "strategy of basic needs."

It is quite possible, however, that in a world which is increasingly interdependent and connected through many channels of mass communication, the demonstration effect in consumption patterns will prove stronger than efforts to organize a more rational development of consumption. In this context, the issue of incentives also emerges. Some experts consider the modernization of consumption patterns via consumer goods of western origin to be an important source of incentives in the less-developed countries.

Utilization of Technology

The effective utilization of modern technologies is another very important issue which binds technological change to human factors and values. The social efficiency of the use of modern technologies depends, essentially, on the rate at which the more highly productive layers of technology are absorbed from the lower layers. There are, however, important factors influencing this process.

The ability to adapt a technology to local conditions is a fundamental and very difficult task in promoting efficient utilization; it also requires special skills that are very difficult to obtain. The greater the gap between the technological levels of the exporter and the importer of a technology, the more important this task will be. Enclave industries are often the consequences of nonadaptation. Developing technological capabilities, which include production, investment and innovation capabilities, depends to a large extent on skill formation. This is, in general, a long-term process; but in connection with a particular technology, it can be a shorter-term training process which may take different forms.

A fundamental task and condition of technological transformation, therefore, is to raise the quantitative and qualitative levels of human skills. It is a well-known and well-documented fact that trained and skilled manpower is still a scarce resource in many developing countries. There are also countries where many skilled people are unemployed or underutilized due to the fast growth of the educational sector and the slower increase in the demand for highly skilled labor due to structural disharmony.

It is also well known that the developing countries often do not need many highly qualified experts, but they do need many middle-level technicians who contribute most to the utilization of new technologies, whether imported or locally generated.

The need for organizational and managerial capability in connection with the efficiency of technological transformation must also be strongly emphasized.

Another extremely important factor in developing countries is their local research and development capabilities. About six developing countries account for almost all the R & D expenditure in all developing countries.[1] R & D activities in the developing countries could be more relevant than in the developed countries for such tasks as making better choices for investment decisions, making more efficient purchases of foreign technology, adapting the new technology to local conditions, improving the absorption and diffusion of technology, reducing technical vulnerability and developing indigenous technological capabilities. Greater efforts are needed to establish and utilize the national R & D manpower and to create stronger ties between the research and productive sectors. Better utilization of researchers and the creation of more appropriate conditions for them would certainly reduce the "reverse transfer of technology" process – the brain drain.

Traditional vs. Modern Technologies

Relations between traditional and modern technologies in developing societies have become an important issue in the process of technological transformation, both in industry and in agriculture. The issue has been raised in different forms and at different times, and on various levels – the ideological, the practical, etc.[2]

A forceful defense of traditional technology appeared in the ideology of Gandhi during the struggle for the liberation in India, where the demand for industrialization was also forcefully expressed. Gandhi formulated the dilemma in the following way:

> Mechanization is good when hands are too few for the work intended to be accomplished. It is an evil where there are more hands than required for the work, as is the case in India. The problem with us is not to find leisure for teeming millions inhabiting our country. The problem is how to utilize their idle hours, which are equal to the working days of six months in the year. Dead machinery must not be pitted against the millions of living machines represented by the villagers scattered in the seven hundred thousand villages of India. Machinery to be well used has to help and ease human effort.[3]

The idea of using traditional technologies parallel to modern ones to speed up economic growth also influenced thinking in China during the "Great Leap Forward" period, and to a certain extent in the practices of the communes. Mao Zedong was a firm believer in China's endogenous technology, and he wanted to use its full potential by encouraging the spread and improvement of traditional forms of production. He disregarded, however, the idea of integrating the new and the traditional, and the possible linkages between endogenous and imported technologies.

The problems of the relations between traditional and modern technologies are difficult human issues and not just reflections of the struggle between the traditionalist and the modernist views, even though in many countries they originally appear that way. There is no question that the survival of a large, may be the greater, part of the population of our globe will depend for many more decades on traditional technologies because of the lack of material and human resources to purchase and use more modern technologies, or because of the rigidity of existing structures. However, it is also a fact that modern industries are spreading; they are creating most of the new industrial jobs in many countries while traditional technologies and their products become increasingly obsolete and antiquated.

The quality, and often the price, of urban and foreign products are often more attractive to consumers than the price and quality of local products. Traditional operations with their traditional technologies cannot compete, because they are locked into inflexible, inefficient structures often incapable even of maintaining the mere subsistence of their owners or workers.

In many developing countries, new solutions must be found, since it will be necessary to maintain and promote small- and medium-scale local and rural industries. This is dictated by many economic and social factors. The modernization of agriculture is increasingly reducing the labor requirements of that sector, pushing out tens of millions to other areas, often forcing them to migrate to already overpopulated cities. The number of landless agricultural workers is on the increase in villages, while urban employment in modern industries and services is not expanding at a rate which can absorb all the job-seekers. There is a demographic factor involved too: the growing proportion of people in the working age groups will reach its peak in the coming decades. Rural industrialization on the basis of technologies which can integrate traditional and modern processes and upgrade local industries seems to be one of the most important instruments for dealing with these problems. The task is far from being an easy one. It requires a new approach to community development which includes changes in local training and a significant modification in the allocation of financial resources.

Often, new structures in national and export marketing must also be developed in order to channel local products into other regions and countries. Another fundamental task is to conceive and develop the required technologies. It is often possible to upgrade traditional methods with the introduction of one or two modern pieces of equipment or a new machine, which may lead to substantial increases in productivity and to the improvement of the quality of the products. Not only crafts, but also services can be modernized and upgraded in local communities. This could be especially important from the point of view of finding new job opportunities for women.

In many cases, a new type of international cooperation will also be needed to achieve the above goals. The UNDP and NGOs in particular must pay greater attention to the type of cooperation required to foster the above-mentioned changes. New relations — subcontracting, for example — between small-scale local industries and larger modern industrial firms must also be promoted. One can strongly endorse a statement made in one of the UNIDO documents:

Small and large industries are in fact interdependent. Large industries depend on small feeder industries. Small industries require intermediate products to process them into finished products. The technology for small industries requires in many cases special attention, hence, the small industry promotion and training organization needs to examine carefully traditional technologies and give appropriate advice to the small industrialists to use modern technologies with the proper selection and adaptation as to the size of operation, availability of materials, suitability to local marketing and relatively scarce high skills.[4]

The ILO also published a very important volume recently about the possibility of using new technologies in traditional sectors.[5]

Different case studies illustrate that the process is far from being an easy one. It requires a very good understanding of both the new and traditional technologies, and it presupposes that traditional technologies and productive activities can be really intergrated — that such capacities exist on both sides. It also needs active local initiative, participation and, of course, funds.

Social Transformation

It is extremely difficult to analyze and generalize the process and implications of social transformation taking place as a result of technological change in the developing countries. From the point of view of social transformation, progress in technology must be understood in a broader framework including institutional changes, diversification of demand patterns, etc., only some of which I will touch on here.

a) Technological change influences entrepreneurs and shapes the face of the emerging middle class in a given sociopolitical environment. In the developing market economies, the process differs from that which takes place in countries of socialist orientation. This paper deals more with the former. In most cases, in the earlier stages of development, the entrepreneur and the owner are still one and the same person. The "barefoot businessman" still represents the greatest number of entrepreneurs in the developing countries; small- and medium-size establishments are managed by the owners. But in larger and more complex enterprises, there are many owners who no longer perform entrepreneurial functions. Joint ventures with transnational corporations often speed up this process. Large business groups like those of the industrial West are emerging in certain countries, exposing small entrepreneurs to increasing competition.

b) A small proportion of the labor force can meet the requirements of the new technologies in respect of skills. They are usually in a better position in the structure of income distribution. There is a more or less permanent demand for this stratum of people. Lower down on the scale of skills, demand is rapidly diminishing, and those lower layers represent the great majority of the labor force. They are struggling for their daily survival, and technological change contributes to the marginalization of these people. Hundreds of millions of them live in the slums and shantytowns of big cities, and their numbers are permanently increasing due to rural migration and population growth. High rates of urban unemployment and underemployment are the increasing social cost of technological change.

c) Unutilized and underutilized skilled or highly educated persons are another important source of social tension in certain countries. Society is wasting a large proportion of its capital as a result of this phenomenon. These problems are also connected with the process of technological transformation. Sometimes they are caused by the copying of the educational systems of more developed countries, thus creating disparities between the demand for and the supply of skills. In other cases, the development of the educational system outpaces the growth of the absorbtive capacity of a given society. Much more concrete research is required to reveal the extent of interrelations between technological and social transformation and their implications. A very important special issue is the role of the army in the field of technological and social change.

d) Technological transformation is also a major issue in shaping the structure of the rural population. In many parts of the developing world, such transformations have increased the number of landless agricultural workers. The better-off landowners and the richer peasants were the chief beneficiaries of the process, and the gap between them and the rural poor has widened.[6] The speed of the transformation, and the social conflicts emerging in the process, are other important issues in the rural environment.

While there may be some similarities in the social impact of technological change in countries of socialist orientation and in the developing market economies, it is evident from socialist practices that deliberate social policies may change the process, especially in areas such as the nature and structure of the middle class, the rural population or industrial workers.

e) Among the negative consequences of technological change is environmental degredation. This must be dealt with separately, since it is a growing problem in the developing as well as the developed countries. It is best defined as a growing pressure on the human and animal population and on natural resources. There is a real and far-reaching conflict between the genuine attempts of governments and peoples to create more jobs and to banish hunger, undernourishment and disease, and some of the results of these efforts: the destruction of forests, the erosion of soil, the loss of wildlife, the accumulation of wastes in urban areas and the impact of industrial pollutants on the population, especially chemical toxins. The tragedy which recently occurred in India proved that in the environment of the urban slums, people are extremely vulnerable, and the damage can be vast.

The same is true in the field of water pollution. In most developing countries, the major source of pollution of natural waters, including costal waters, is the discharge of city waste, since most of them do not have sewerage facilities, and where they exist, there is no system of waste treatment. The urban waste problem is aggravated by agricultural run-off containing pesticides, herbicides and other hazardous chemicals contained in fertilizers. In many cases, irrigation water also serves as a discharge channel for municipal waste.

Measures or laws concerning the protection of the environment in most developing countries are weak, and they are often disregarded in the struggle for faster industrialization or more food production. In the majority of these countries, environmental accountability is a vague category which is disappearing in the division of responsibilities between different branches and levels of public administration, or between public and private firms.

Environmental issues represent a grave and multidimensional danger to human beings in poor countries, where the great majority of the people are directly exposed to all sorts of pollutants. Not just the right choice of a technology, but a whole range of economic, institutional and educational measures are required to mitigate the situation.

There are other important areas, such as the educational system or the problems of families, especially of women and children, which require serious efforts to analyse the negative side-effects of the technological transformation, including such specific issues as breast-feeding.

Conclusion

This paper has dealt with some of the human problems of technological transformation in the developing countries. In the coming decades, processes which bring about major technological changes will continue to be introduced in the Third World. It is necessary to be more conscious in understanding the nature of these changes and their consequences. It is also very important to develop comprehensive national policies and planning frameworks which anticipate some of the most serious problems and deal with them in time. This requires not only more effort, but specific expertise in social engineering.

It is also necessary for the more developed world to pay greater attention to the development of new technologies appropriate to the specific environments of developing countries.

In the framework of international multilateral cooperation, the issues on the human side of the development process, including the technological transformation, should be more widely discussed; national experiences in connection with problems, as well as their resolution, must be made available. On this basis, much more comprehensive international cooperation would be possible. Indeed, it is becoming indispensable.

Notes

1. UNCTAD, TD 277, Rev. 1, 1985, p. 13.
2. "Traditional technologies were defined as the ones which are used in crafts and small scale enterprises and have deep, well established roots in indigenous economic development. They have evolved over considerable periods of time to suit local conditions and purposes. Traditional technologies are so well fitted to local skills and available resources that they are literally the social pivots of many populations." M.S. Swaminathan, Introduction, *New Frontiers in Technology Application* (Dublin: Tycooly Int. Publ. Ltd., 1983).
3. M. K. Gandhi, *Rebuilding Our Villages* (Ahmedabad: Navajivan Publishing House, 1952), p. 32.
4. UNIDO, ID 6WG 391/lo. 1983, p. 37.
5. *New Frontiers in Technology.*
6. See, for example, M.N. Srinivas, *Science, Technology and Rural Development in India* (Puna: Gokhale Institute of Politics and Economics, 1977).

CHAPTER 23

Introducing Advanced Technologies:
The Human Implications

Omer Akin, Raghu Nath and Raj Reddy

Development through technology has a long and less than illustrious history. Understanding the problems involved requires the consideration of three key subjects: technology transfer, knowledge-based societies and human resources. The solutions to the present problems of development through technology will no doubt be forthcoming from many sources in the immediate future. A most promising avenue is the use of advanced technologies to develop self-improving technologies which, when transferred, can adapt to local and regional conditions. In order to meet this challenge, we propose the creation of a World Center for Development Through Technology. The center would be responsible for making advanced technologies available to developing countries, in addition to addressing the many complex issues involved in the transfer of new technologies, such as identification of relevant technologies, preparation of the infrastructure for transfer, training and education of the local population in order to improve skill levels and to create informed consensus about the new technologies, alleviation of the ill-effects of migration and displacement, development of strategic niches in the universe of advanced technologies, and elimination of technological colonialism and dominance.

Developing Advanced Technologies

In the 1980s, technology, particularly advanced technology or "high-tech," has become a primary determinant as well as a measure of progress. Nations with world supremacy see it as insurance for maintaining their role. Others aspiring to become world powers see it as their primary alternative. Developing nations see it as a salvation and yet do not know how to approach it.

On the other hand, recent world history is full of examples of failures in "transferring" (to use a dated term) technology for the purpose of bringing technologically backward nations up to par with the more advanced ones. Excluding the few and remarkable instances of success (such as Japan), all of these efforts have failed miserably. In transporting, installing and assimilating technologies that are imported from the "outside," there are serious problems, most of which are unresolved even today.

These problems have been identified and documented numerous times in the past. Often the lack of "western" work ethics, skilled labor, capital and industrial infrastructure are blamed. To date, there are no known solutions to these problems, anywhere. Furthermore, we now witness the failure of technological developments in strongholds of "high-tech" (such as the USA), where the factors purported to be the cause of failure in developing countries do not exist. It is clear that the introduction of new technology into any society is a complex problem to which no nation of the world is immune, and which will be solved only if explicit strategies to address these issues are developed and implemented. This paper will argue for some of these strategies.

Before we present these strategies, however, let us review some experiences with technology transfer from the recent past.

Egypt and Industrialized Building

Beginning in the late 1950s and early 1960s Egypt, in an effort to solve its housing shortage, imported a high-tech solution. A total of nine prefabrication plants were purchased from the West and installed in Egypt in a span of about a decade and a half. The combined yearly production capacity of these plants exceeded 100,000 units. To date, the total number of prefabricated units built in these facilities does not exceed several hundred.

The problem is not unique to Egypt, where local industries and trade are fiercely competitive and protect their markets from intrusions, namely, government-sponsored prefabrication. Other examples of imported high-tech solutions to housing shortages can be cited in many other locations in Africa, the Far East, the Middle East and the USSR, where the results were also unsatisfactory. The causes of failure are not limited to the protectionist behavior of local industries, but are far-reaching. They include (i) lack of appropriate distribution systems, (ii) lack of fair and accessible subsidy programs, (iii) inappropriateness of the product to regional lifestyles and values related to conventional housing, and (iv) lack of provisions in the technology for self-correcting behavior (many of these systems were discards from the West supplied to Egypt under the guise of international subsidy).

These factors, while prevalent in technologically unsophisticated nations, are also valid even for centers of advanced technology. In the 1930s and 1940s, pioneers of prefabrication (such as Walter Gropius and Konrad Wachsmann) came to the U.S. and developed effective and efficient technology for prefabricated housing. Their efforts were technologically sophisticated, yet unsuccessful, due to the lack of marketing and distribution systems and to the inappropriateness of the product to consumers' lifestyles and values.

A lesson to learn from all this is that technical sophistication is necessary but not sufficient for bringing advanced technology to a new location. A critical step in the process is the assimilation of the new technology into the fabric of the location's existing culture, economy and infrastructure.

USA /Japan and the Micro- Chip Industry

The technological war between the USA and Japan in the production of computer chip or "super-chip" technology has been going on silently for several decades. Now that the spoils of the apparent winner, Japan, are coming home to roost, the story is being told with a degree of historical confidence and accuracy.

In the most advanced areas of technological development, Japan, whose national economy was a shambles after World War II, has swiftly and decisively taken the lead away from the all-time leaders of recent history. Both the U.S. and West Germany, in spite of their undisputed role of leadership in world technology, have surrendered one industrial product after another to Japanese industry. The last in this series (computer chips) is the most significant. It represents, for the first time, a product which cannot be called old-hat but is in fact at the cutting edge of high-tech production. How did the U.S. end up in this position? Or rather, how did Japan manage to pull it off?

The answer, when simplified, points to automated industrial production. The Japanese, in assimilating robotics technology in their industrial production, have attained a level of technological and industrial superiority which can hardly be matched by any other nation. This underscores the significance of high technology as a key to twenty-first century industrial development and the compounded acceleration of progress expected to result from it.

India and the Steel Industry

India has some of the world's finest deposits of iron ore and coal, found in close proximity to each other. A study by the MIT Center for International Studies in the early 1950s concluded that India has a comparative advantage for establishing an indigenous steel industry. India, therefore, decided to import steelmaking technology from the USSR.

In spite of the comparative advantage based on the availability of first-grade raw material resources and cheap labor, India today produces steel at about twice the cost of more efficient mills, such as those of Korea. A closer examination reveals, first, that the technology imported by India was neither the latest nor the most efficient. Second, in contrast to Japan and Korea, the steel industry in India is ridden with bureaucratic management that stifles productivity. Third, while new technologies and processes have developed, India has failed to update its imported technology, because there was no appropriate arrangement built into the technology transfer agreement for the continual updating of imported technologies. Fourth, there has been minimal development of human resources to manage and improve the imported technologies. Though some technical people were trained in the country from where the technology was imported, other types of skills, such as improving on the technology, were not developed.

Finally, the plants were located in areas where skilled labor was not available, and insufficient attention was paid to developing the required labor skills prior to the installation of plants. As a result, a nation that had a clear comparative advantage in steelmaking is now unable to meet its internal needs, particularly in high-grade steel.

Another example of outmoded imported technology is that of the automobile industry. Until very recently, the two types of cars manufactured in India (Ambassador and Fiat) used technology imported in the 1950s. In recent years, the government of India entered into a joint venture with Suzuki Motors of Japan and started manufacturing the Maruti, which utilizes modern Japanese technology. This has forced other manufacturers to update their technology and bring out much-improved new models.

Sudan and Milk Processing

Yet another example was the setting up of a large milk processing plant in northern Sudan. This area of Sudan is inhabited by nomadic tribes. A modern milk processing plant built in northern Sudan used the latest western technology and was intended to process milk for distribution to the rest of Sudan. However, the planners of this project (primarily western technical experts) failed to take into account local customs and culture. It was later discovered that nomadic tribes living in this area had a taboo against the selling of milk. As a result, these tribal people refused to supply raw milk to the plant. The huge plant stayed inactive without any milk to process. Finally, the entire project was declared bankrupt.

Ethopia's Transportation System

A final example of a failed project was an attempt to build a modern highway system in Ethiopia. This elaborate system was designed for Ethiopia by western experts in the early 1960s. The technology used in the West to build modern highways was employed. Since this technology was ill-suited to the local geography and climate, the road system started deteriorating rapidly. Also, local people were not trained to repair the road system. Foreign technicians and experts had to be invited back, and this involved expenses which were not budgeted for in the original plan. Above all, the local traffic comprised very few motor vehicles and consisted mostly of rural transport vehicles, which accelerated the damage suffered by the modern road surface. The need for continual repairs, combined with limited utilization, soon led to the abandonment of the system. As a result, this road system now lies in ruins.

As can be seen from the half-dozen projects reviewed above, effective technology development in developing regions requires very careful planning, as well as adaptation to the local culture and conditions, particularly when the new technology is imported from developed countries. Most importantly, the appropriate infrastructure needs to be developed and human resources trained to maintain and improve the technology.

Knowledge-Based Society

In order to understand the complex reasons for, and solutions to, the problems illustrated above, we must first acknowledge some fundamental changes taking place in the technically and industrially sophisticated societies.

Product-Based vs. Knowledge-Based Societies

Until recently, the development of nations was measured through industrial production. The products of a society — cars, TVs, dialysis machines, nuclear warheads, submarines, etc. — were the primary indicators of technological supremacy. Today, these kinds of product-based measures fail to reflect the actual potential of nations or societies for technological supremacy.

Instead, knowledge (both technological knowhow and information storage, manipulation and access capabilities) and industries revolving around knowledge engineering have become significant indicators of progress. Since products and production means are relatively easy to transfer across national boundaries, we have discovered the inadequacies of merely using products and production to effect positive changes in society. As a measure of progress, product is no longer a credible commodity. Instead, knowledge, the ingredient which seems to make the difference between Japan and the U.S., for example, is the prime commodity of our time.

Humans are producers, disseminators and consumers of knowledge. Knowledge, in turn, determines how humans interact with technology, independent of how advanced or primitive this technology may be. In all instances which we can call progressive, there is an understanding of the limits of societal knowledge and how technology can best be integrated in this knowledge. In cases where advanced technologies are successfully assimilated in the industrial production of a society, there have been deliberate efforts to develop knowledge (both at the technical and cultural levels) for integrating new technologies with the society as a whole. These efforts invariably start from an understanding of the needs of a society before any goals are defined. Often, when goals are identified without an understanding of needs, the result, as we observed in the examples above, is the wastage of human resources.

Rate of Growth and the Widening Gap

One of the innocent culprits in the identification of improper goals for national development is the urgency of narrowing the ever-widening gap between developed and developing nations. This urgency, while acknowledged by everyone, has often been translated into shortsighted strategies. Generally, these strategies argue for the development of products that are "like" those of the developed nations, independent of their value and long-term impact on development.

While the solutions to this problem are not apparent, the problem itself, the widening gap, has profound implications.

Technological Dominance

Due to the development of technological and cultural knowledge by the nations of the world in a manner that is independent of one another, these nations face the prospect of further fragmentation of their shared human heritage. As this gap widens, communication and exchange of knowledge (the real cure for the problem) will become progressively more difficult, making the solution of the problem very difficult, if not impossible.

Today, technological colonialism has replaced other forms of colonialism. Time and time again, supremacy in technological terms has meant the exercise of power of the "haves" over the "have-nots" and the tightening of the lines of alliance within each group. Today, more so than in the past, we can identify hard boundaries between nations: the West, the East, the developing nations, the Third World, Muslim countries, oil producers, members of the economic summit, the socialist countries, the Common Market, NATO countries, and so on.

Long-Term vs. Short-Term Measures

The history of remedies for the widening gap is full of "quick fixes" which provide the *appearance* of solutions, of stopgap measures which do not solve long-term problems. It is obvious to all involved in international exchanges of this kind that real solutions do not come about by remedies aimed at the symptoms of problems, but through well-thought-out, long-term planning, nurturing and commitment from all involved. Resorting to short-term remedies may thrust a society into irrevocable conflicts from which they may never be able to emerge without experiencing massive damage.

Centralization vs. Decentralization

One of the factors contributing to the difficulty, and often the demise, of efforts to develop new technologies has to do with centralization. Since central governments play key roles in spearheading efforts of technology exchange, planning and implementation efforts are often controlled centrally. This removes the element of local and regional input and stifles private initiative, further curtailing the possibility that the new technologies will truly solve the problems of the local people.

Fear of the New

Natural resistance to the introduction of new technology largely stems from lack of knowledge. The various elements that introduce a distance between the deliverers and the recipients of technology prevent the would-be benfactors from coming into contact with the new technology and the knowledge that surrounds it. This curtails the assimilation of the new knowledge into existing local knowledge. The result is fear of the new and the unknown.

Human Resource Implications

The issues we cited above — in the context of both introducing new technologies and the knowledge-based nature of today's societies — point to important concerns about the availability, use and advancement of the most important resource of any nation: humans.

Let us now highlight some of the demands and pressures placed on this precious resource and identify some of the current trends.

Impact of the Demand for Higher Skills

Each new technology introduced means that new skills have to be acquired by the consumers of that technology, whether they are the recipients of its products or the actual producers. Also, each group of consumers of technology has a certain capacity for absorbing new technologies without any ill effects. As the automobile replaced the cart or carriage and the TV replaced the radio all over the world, a human ability to adapt to the new and acquire new skills has been clearly demonstrated. Problems arise with this absorptive capacity when it falls short of the demands of the new technology, as we have seen in the examples introduced earlier. In order to solve such problems, it is critical that this absorptive capacity be expanded through education, training and infusion of knowledge prior to, during and subsequent to the introduction of technologies.

Development and Quality of Life

Most new developments involving new technologies aim at improving the quality of life in some fashion through providing better health services, food, shelter or other human amenities or necessities. Well-conceived development efforts often lead to a well-adjusted infusion of technology, and the new function fits into the existing fabric of functions almost like the matching piece of a jigsaw puzzle. When this is not the case, the piece being lodged into place may dislodge other pieces that are already in place. The result becomes a diminishing of the quality of life rather than the intended improvement. We witness, for example, a drop in the quality of life of the underprivileged all over the world as they are placed in new housing situations suited merely to the biological needs for shelter and hygiene, but not to the psychological and cultural demands of a home — in the public housing slums of the USA, in prefabricated units in Egypt, in the squatter prevention areas of Turkey. A public housing development in the USA by Pruitt Igo, a prominent design award winner in the 1950s, is perhaps the best known testimony to this problem. After years of vandalism, crime and violence stemming from the cultural inadequacies of the housing scheme, the complex of high-rise apartments was demolished in the early 1970s. Hence, unless undertaken properly, the introduction of high-tech products does not guarantee an improvement or enrichment of human lives and may even mean the opposite. The recent Union Carbide disaster in India is further evidence of the importance of this issue.

Another aspect of the qulaity of life has to do with the demands of new working conditions on those employed in the new technology. Here exist similar concerns and dangers, as well as potentials for improvement.

Displacement and Migration

One of the pressures almost universally imposed on the human population due to the development of new technologies is the problem of bringing the technology and an appropriately skilled sector of society to the same location. This may assume different forms: migration towards technology, migration of technology, displacement due to upward mobility or devaluation of human labor, and displacement of humans by automation.

a) One solution to the problem of matching skills with advanced technology is the migration of labor to where the technology happens to be located in the first place. A widely recognized example of this is the migration of workers between the Eastern Mediterranean nations and the Northern European countries, between Mexico and United States, between the Far East and Arab countries. These kinds of moves result in a complex of problems, the mention of which will suffice for our purposes here: problems of the labor population in adapting to the new setting; social rejection of the foreign population by the host country; problems in workers' readapting to their home setting after contact with the high-tech culture; and the infusion of foreign values in both settings.

b) A more recent solution to the problem has been the migration (not transfer) of technology as a complete production operation to locations where appropriate labor or consuming populations exist. We can cite various examples of this is transactions between Japan and the USA, the USA and Brazil or the USA and Taiwan.

c) The introduction of new technologies generally results in a demand for the improvement of human skills. Resources are made available to provide training programs. As a consequence, a segment of the population becomes more skilled. For this segment, some upward mobility is realized in social, economic and physical terms. A side-effect of this is the loss of value of their labor experienced by segments of the population outside the affected segment as a result of the relative decrease in their skill levels. This is an unavoidable consequence which awaits a remedy.

d) Even in labor-intensive and capital-poor circumstances, automated forms of technology or production means are a valid alternative. New forms of automation have enabled the creation of relatively inexpensive "intelligent" systems where automotion, rather than resulting in the displacement of labor, ensures the healthy adaptation of technology in a new context, and vice versa.

For example, the introduction of computers in many instances has resulted in the increase of job opportunities because of specialization. Numerous support mechanisms are needed for the computer's use — software creation, maintenance, etc. The introduction of intelligent computers in the service of automated production is likely to add to this demand due to the further specialization of support functions that it requires over time — installation, training, diagnosis, repair and improvement. For the reasons cited in the previous section, the net result of this, however, may lead to problems of displacement.

Further Problems

Along with the more problematic trends cited above, there are positive motivations for aspiring to obtain advanced technology, besides the obvious goals of development. One of these is the idea that a society with little or no advanced technology can import advanced forms of technology and avoid the difficulties, detours and costs of development normally involved if similar developments were undertaken from scratch: that is, leapfrogging from their backward position into a position at par with the advanced countries of the world. The problem with this theory, which after numerous trials remains unresolved, is that the prediction is not borne out by practice. Imported technology does not go through the natural evolution of home-grown technology and thus suffers from a lack of adjustment to indigenous conditions. The motivating value of this theory, however, is still relevant in many instances where technology changes hands.

We alluded earlier to the power implicit in technological supremacy. This provides another motivation and a hope that, by carefully planning, a developing country can carve out an appropriate niche in the complex world of technological development and dramatically improve its own position. The strongest example of this is the movement of Japan into the driver's seat of world technology. Even today, Japan continues to pursue its research and development efforts by exploiting its strategic advantages in the field of technological supremacy.

We have reviewed some of the important circumstances and consequences of technological development, knowledge-based societies and human resources. Before we begin discussing some of the viable solutions to the problems presented, let us, by way of review, cite the questions we must face in responding to these problems.

A fundamental question is: How to narrow or eliminate the ever-widening knowledge gap between the technologically advanced and the technologically backward nations? This, in turn, raises many more specific questions: How to eliminate total dependence on advanced nations during and after technology transfer? How to maintain a common knowledge base for all nations and societies of the world? How to prevent the many ill-effects of displacement and migration? How to overcome the fear of accepting new technologies? How to positively influence the quality of life?

As one strives to solve these problems, it is important to keep the primary purpose of introducing new technologies in mind : that is, to solve basic human and societal problems. The only way to solve these problems of universal scope — medicine, agriculture, housing, education, etc. — with limited resources is to employ new technologies in efficient and effective ways. Thus, we must ask a host of questions in this regard : How to make effective and efficient use of existing human resources in the introduction of new technologies? How to alleviate the ill-effects of new technologies on existing human resources? How to balance these two objectives?

Finally, questions regarding the future of these efforts must be asked : How to produce long-term (lasting) improvements? How to ensure self-preserving and self-improving results?

World Center for Development Through Technology

The questions we have posed are complex. The solutions, more than likely, will emerge from actions which demonstrably solve problems and improve our knowledge about the nature of both the questions and their possible answers. Here, we can only put forward suggestions as to how this may come about and provide the initiative for turning words into actions. What is needed is a set of strategies to research and to fashion new ways of introducing new technologies in developing countries. A continuous, concerted and intelligent effort is needed in order to eliminate political and economic exploitation. We see this as the role of a World Center for Development Through Technology. Below, we provide a blueprint for such a center.

Rationale

Successful technology transfer requires a broad base of knowledge and tools at the hands of the deliverers and recipients of the new technology. A thorough understanding of the needs needs of the ultimate recipients of the technology, including local infrastructure, skill levels, values and traditions, is critical. In addition, it is necessary to be knowledgeable about how technologies may fail during and after transfer, what are the ways of taking corrective measures, and how one might develop self-correcting situations.

In short, the process of technology transfer is itself a technological problem which must be approached with the same intensity and vigor with which sophisticated technological questions are approached by advanced nations. This issue is no different in magnitude from the issues of the conquest of space, of cancer, or of energy; it requires recognition, planning and adequate resources. Special technologies suitable for driving the process of technology transfer are essential.

The knowledge developed in this center would aim to place the most advanced technological knowhow at the service of basic human needs, including education, health, nutrition, housing, security and communication. Nations or societies with specific problems would be able to receive guidance and supervision from the center in order to diagnose their own problems, to determine what they need, to prime their existing infrastructure for receiving new technologies, to install these new technologies, to assimilate them in their existing infrastructure and to continuously monitor and improve them over time.

If the center functions as a mere pusher of new technologies, it is doomed to fail, as did earlier attempts. The center must develop and monitor its own activities through explicit policies designed to protect the interests of its clientele.

A critical policy the center must promote is the networking of a locale designated to receive a new technology. This includes the creation of channels of communication between groups and institutions that are expected to play key roles in the reception and assimilation of the new technology. Development of a climate of informed consensus is one of the first things needed for technological development.

Another important area for policy development is in relation to the ill-effects of displacement and migration. Here, in addition to proper information networks, a massive educational effort is needed. The only known precaution against social alienation and displacement is to educate the workers, their families and their social cohorts about the difficulties that should be expected alongside the benefits. Counseling programs and mechanisms for information dissemination must be developed to inform as well as modify attitudes. Also, it is necessary to retrain displaced persons and develop programs to facilitate their adaptation to new jobs and locations.

The use of portable, intelligent technologies also provides advantages. By bringing technologies to people instead of bringing people to technologies, the adverse affects of migration and displacement can be minimized.

Self-Directed Installation of New Technology

The center would advocate the self-directed installation of a given new technology by the recipients. This requires a participatory process in which the recipients, under the guidance of the center, identify the technology needed, develop plans for assimilation, monitor implementation and operation and evaluate future development.

Each venture of the center would be approached by the examination of problems in a deductive manner, starting with the most general issue, i.e., the needs of society, and following a step-by-step approach to more specific problems as determined by general ones. Ultimately, a technological innovation best suited to the needs of the society would be identified.

We know from past experience that approaches where solutions are identified before the parameters and context of problems are understood have all resulted in such disastrous failures as prefabrication in Egypt, the Pruitt Igo housing in the USA or the highways of Ethiopia.

Selection of the relevant technology involves more than a rational analysis of problems; often, human customs, traditions and taboos, as in the case of Sudan, play important and unexpected roles in the acceptance or rejection of innovations. For example, a structural column placed quite accidentally in the center of the living area in a "modern" housing complex in South America becomes the informal family "shrine" and unexpectedly contributes to the success of the development. The reinforced concrete floor finishes in housing developed specifically for earthquake resistance in Turkey, on the other hand, have a less fortunate fate; local residents prefer earth or wooden floors over the more sturdy concrete floors. They also have no use for bathtubs, other than for storing grain. In the history of technology transfer, one can cite at least ten unsuccessful instances for every successful one when it comes to matching human values with new technology.

Successful assimilation of new technologies into existing conditions is a rare occurrence. Even when all precautions are taken to compensate for potential problems emanating from human needs and values, success is not guaranteed. Other sectors of a society not directly related to the new technology may come into direct conflict with it.

Examples can be found in the saga of the steel and automobile industries in the U.S. and the improper use or disuse of computing hardware in technologically backward countries. In losing the leadership in automated manufacturing to Japan, U.S. companies displayed a lack of initiative in developing new technologies due to complex interactions between government, labor, market and economic conditions. Recently, numerous developing or wealthy and technologically underdeveloped countries have been acquiring excessive quantities of computing hardware. Normally, the routine use of these tools is expected to improve efficiency and productivity at the workplace or complement the network of information systems already in place. However, neither of these conditions is present in these countries. The scale of efficiency obtained with the computer is inconsistent with the magnitude of efficiency norms found in these countries, and the realistic prospects for any kind of information networking are nonexistent.

The center, then, in response to the problem of assimilation would require the priming of a host of complex factors that make up a context for the new technology, in addition to human needs and values.

Self-Monitoring and Evaluation of Progress

Technology transfer is a long and involved process. There are ample opportunities to guide the assimilation of technology during the course of its introduction. Corrective measures, as well as improvements, can thus be interjected. The center would require the monitoring and periodic evaluation of a phased implementation plan. The recipients of the technology would undertake these under the guidelines and criteria developed by the center. As these criteria were satisfied, the implementation plan would advance from one phase to the next, eventually completing its ultimate objective.

Self-Insured Packaging of New Technologies

Advanced technologies are dynamic entities. They evolve, break down and behave in other unpredictable ways, particularly when introduced in new contexts. For example, no region of the world has exactly the same set of building materials. Any building technology introduced from the outside has to be adaptable to changing conditions. Similarly, no group of people has the same behavioral patterns as any other. The Union Carbide disaster in India would not have occurred if it were not for a particular combination of corporate attitudes and local conditions.

A viable remedy for the problem is to equip the technology itself with self-monitoring capabilities: guiding, tutoring, warning and interacting with its users. The knowhow necessary for the development of such intelligent tools is no longer the subject of science fiction literature alone. The fields of artificial intelligence and robotics have started to deliver the goods. Today, it is conceivable to create the "electronic village" of tomorrow, where computer networking, automated manufacturing and data processing capabilities can assist the 1,000-5,000 inhabitants in solving their basic problems effectively and efficiently.

Such an environment would require and support technologies for production and other prupose which possess a minimum of five basic functionalities: (i) self-describing, (ii) self-training, (iii) self-diagnosing, (iv) self-repairing and (v) self-improving.

The critical function in this sequence of functions is the fifth one, the ability to be self-improving; that is, it should be able to improve its performance with respect to conditions that are external and dynamic. For any entity to be self-improving, it is necessary for it to be self-repairing; that is, it should be able to modify its structure according to certain performance criteria, which it can develop by itself. This requires the ability to self-diagnose; that is, based on observations about its own behavior, it should be able to deduce standards of acceptability. This requires the technical ability to describe itself and to instruct itself on its own operations. Thus the five functionalities listed above constitute layers of prerequisites which, when combined, constitute an ultimate ability for self-improvement.

The center would promote the development of technologies which are self-improving in this sense, thereby providing a technological solution to the problem of reliability and suitability of technologies that are imported or transferred.

International Assistance

A center of this kind can be created only if international agencies such as the United Nations, the World Bank, etc., collaborate in supporting the objectives outlined here. In addition, technologically strong regions and institutions of the world must play a leadership role in bringing together the resources needed to develop such a center. As we look at the excruciatingly pessimistic track record of technology transfer of the past, we should have a well-founded optimism in such new prospects for development as the World Center for Development Through Technology and the possibility of using technology in the service of humanity.

Summary

Development through technological innovation is an old problem in a new guise. Numerous past experiments with the problem inform us of the difficulties, as well as the possibilities, that await us. In searching for new solutions, it is critical to recognize the changes in how we measure progress. Advancement in today's society is more readily explained through the commodity of information and knowledge than through product, which has been the prevalent measure in the recent past.

Development, particularly through the importation of technology, has profound interactions with the human dimension. Technology starts with humans as an extension of their human capabilities and comes back to humans as a partner, or sometimes as a threat with which to contend. Several dimensions of these interactions are important for understanding the technology transfer process: human skills, the quality of life, displacement and migration, leapfrogging and international dependence.

A review of these factors reveals the magnitude and scope of the enromous problems raised during the process of development through advanced technologies. Our considerations have focused on several key questions:

a) How to identify those technologies most appropriate for the development of a particular society?

b) How to prepare the society, its infrastructure and its inhabitants for the successful reception, acceptance and assimilation of new technologies?

c) How to package new technologies so that there are built-in mechanisms for improvement and adaption over time?

Any solution to these problems must include a concentrated and concerted effort between the deliverers of technology and the international political bodies. A formally established World Center for Development Through Technology could choreograph the total process of technological development for nations seeking its guidance, from identification of their needs to implementation of the various stages of their development process.

CHAPTER 24

Technology and the Human Factor:
The Uses of Microcomputers

Dan Resnick

Just as the vast inequality among nations is reflected in indicators of wealth per capita, education and human services, so is it also seen in access to new technology. But because the developing world remains overwhelmingly rural and agricultural, advanced technology may appear as a trap to avoid rather than a gap to narrow; for with new technology, there is the fear of unemployment, conflict between generations, foreign dependence and the devaluing of traditional village life. Can computer technology be any different?

All nations now have access to the technology of hand tools for human pursuits that range from agriculture and construction to music and pictorial art. In some areas, the hand tool, the symbol of artisanal production, enjoys a merited reverence. In other areas, it is correctly seen as an instrument of crippling labor. The short hoe has bent and twisted enough farm workers for it never to be the subject of an elegy.

Almost all nations in some sectors of their economic activity have access to the technology of power tools. Motors come in all sizes, shapes and applications, suitable for particular agricultural, industrial and domestic purposes. There are lathes for production, generators for power and tractors for a variety of farm and construction work. From aircraft engines to tiny fans, the motor in various shapes and sizes has gained wide acceptance. A few people reject motors on principle, a few more on their days of rest; for most, however, the question is not whether motors in general are an appropriate technology, but whether a particular tractor, processor, or generator is right for a particular project.

Only a few nations are rich in computers, which are still expensive acquisitions. These tools have in the past forty years undergone a remarkable transformation. The replacement of vacuum tubes first by transistors and then by integrated circuits has reduced size and price while increasing speed and memory. The maxi mainframe that once required an air-conditioned presidential suite is ceding its market to powerful minis that can fit on desktops; and the micros, some nearly as powerful as the minis, have found a place in the household. But computers have not yet had the opportunity to evolve into the varied pieces of relatively low-priced equipment that now characterize motor-driven tools. The consumer does not expect to use the same motor both to drill a hole through metal and to whip up a chocolate mousse; but with computers, the buyer still risks having to purchase expensive all-purpose equipment for which, as an add-on, special applications software must be purchased.

The microcomputer has become an appropriate tool for human resource development projects. Small units with eight, sixteen or thirty-two-bit microprocessors, in modest configurations of less than a megabyte of memory, with monochrome screens, can be purchased for prices that range from $300 to $3,000. A few are available as battery-powered instruments that also resist dust and high temperatures. They are powerful enough to handle a variety of functions, from data collection and analysis to instruction. Because they allow data to be collected, stored and analyzed without reference to centrally controlled data banks, they are an excellent development tool for rural areas.

Nonetheless, there are very few micros in the developing world. There are mainframes in the capital cities of even the poorest countries in sub-Saharan Africa, serving the interests of large state agencies, but very few smaller machines to serve the interests of cooperatives, small universities, schools, health centers and isolated branches of public administration. Because the number of micros available to developing world users has been very limited, the range of possible uses has not been well explored.

The question of how microcomputer technology can be appropriate for development purposes needs to be examined in the light of all current knowledge. Given the small amount of experimentation that has taken place to date, what has been learned in the trial programs of the World Center for Informatics in Paris is of special interest.

The World Center for Informatics (Centre mondial informatique) was created four years ago by President Francois Mitterand to address the development and diffusion of computer technology for

France and the developing world. From the beginning, our interest has been in the human factor — the training of people to deal with the possibilities presented by this new technology. Both our first president, Jean-Jacques Servan-Schreiber, and our current president, Jean-Louis Funck-Brentano, have called the improvement of human skills and talents an economic and moral imperative.

What have we done, and what have we learned? Software and some hardware development was undertaken for programs in three human service areas — education and training, agricultural management and planning, and medical diagnosis and treatment. The material developed was used in various trial programs within France and in parts of the Third World. In the course of our experimentation, we have learned a great deal about how users relate to computers, but also about ways in which the technology needs to evolve. Some of our experiences with different uses for microcomputers in the areas of education and medicine will be described below.

Informatics and Education

The notion of what should be learned as a part of general education continues to broaden and deepen in modern societies, at the same time that methods for making that learning more efficient receive more attention. Some of the work by pedagogues and subject area specialists in teaching basic literacy skills — reading, writing and numeracy — has been done with computers. At the center, we have been especially interested in computer-aided basic literacy programs for very young children.

Computers for the classroom, starting with the earliest grades, are a priority public school investment in the developed market economies and are becoming so elsewhere. The school landscape is now dotted everywhere with experiments of various kinds to see how the technology can be best adapted, and with what software, for children of different ages, studying different kinds of subject matter in different cultural settings. The center has participated in this experimentation, encouraging a national plan for computer workshops in France *(Plan Fabius)* based in the schools.

The printing press, generating inexpensive and standardized text, made possible Martin Luther's mass literacy movement, the first in the modern period. What, then, can computers be expected to contribute to the growth of literacy skills in our own century? Most computer programs are designed for the already literate. Interaction with the computer takes place almost everywhere in the West through the medium of alphabetic text. The means of access to the screen is most frequently a keyboard, with the same letter-face that was introduced on typewriters a century ago. The ability to read at some level is a prerequisite for all but the most routine of instructional programs. Progress on many programs demands the skills of a touch typist.

We have found, however, in trial programs with children aged 4-7 that it was possible to design programs that used the keyboard and screen graphics to make learning and manipulating words easier. Learning goals could now be extended from the reading of unfamiliar text to writing stories. Access to interesting teachers and good written materials helped make this growth possible, but the computer played an essential role. Children enjoyed working with attractive graphics and screen text. Especially appealing was a nearby printer attached to the computer which gave the child the experience and satisfactions of an author.

Those who have had experience with children from poor and immigrant neighborhoods in these trial programs are enthusiastic about the human possibilities opened up by this technology. Of course, this computer software is an aid to teachers, not a replacement for them; it is also an additional expense, above and beyond textbooks. But it does permit skill development that was not possible under other conditions. Developing countries can allow their interest in this kind of program to grow as the price of hardware drops. We are currently discussing with educators from countries in the South the codevelopment of software in other languages to teach reading and composition in ways appropriate to other cultural traditions.

Adult Technical Programs: Training Computer Educators

Computers, unlike humans, are capable of working day and night, and benefit from installations where they can receive round-the-clock use. The center has been an advocate of computer practice centers in public buildings, where heavy investments in equipment can be justified by equally heavy use. This formula for grouping machines, software and printers was adopted for France on a national scale in the Prime Minister's program, *Informatique pour tous*. With our encouragement, a program of public computer centers has also been launched by Colombia, which now has at least eight centers in operation.

Computer literacy centers require trained personnel to run them. At the handsome Bourguiba Center in Tunis, inaugurated in 1985, we ran our first technical training program outside France for prospective computer center directors. Our staff, in cooperation with computer scientist-educators from Tunisia, ran a six-week program for trainees from Tunisia, Senegal and the Ivory Coast.

We agreed with our hosts in Tunis that such centers, to assure their viability, would have to provide instruction for three different groups — government employees interested in the processing, filing and retrieval of information; students and researchers in universities and schools with specific instructional or programming needs; and a wider public interested in gaining some hands-on experience with different kinds of software. The instructional program was thus centered on application software for text editing, budgeting and planning, and less heavily on programming languages.

What does a computer center manager need to know? Our answer was that in addition to center management issues and some primary maintenance on the machines, the training program should cover software applications of interest to prospective users.

It is likely that such centers will grow in appeal, because they make efficient use of both machines and software libraries and can meet the needs of many different sections of the public. A booklet on the running of such a center, including a recommended syllabus for training managers, is now being prepared by the center, drawing on the experience with our latest training program in Tunis.

Videodisks for Instruction

Visually interesting programs for instruction can be run interactively with computers without recourse to the alphabetic keyboard. Such programs are accessible even to illiterate audiences. We have become aware of the extent to which the capacity of the alphabetic keyboard to define responses far exceeds the needs of certain learning programs. For many uses, even the small key-set of a telephone — ten to twelve keys — is more than sufficient. In some instances, a lightpen, mouse or finger touch is enough. A videodisk program can work with the simplest of interfaces for programs of great density.

About the size of an LP record, the videodisk has great storage capacity: 54,000 images on one side, enough to hold all the volumes of a great encyclopedia. The stored information is not useful for instructional purposes unless it can be accessed rapidly, under various headings, and properly displayed. A microprocessor unit is needed for access to the images and soundtracks, and a television screen for display. Very shortly, it should be possible to place the microprocessor controls within the videodisk player and to have a work station that consists of only the screen and player unit.

No more skill is currently required to begin to learn from a videodisk program than is needed to listen to a television program, change the station, raise and lower volume. Instructions about what questions the viewer would like to have answered, what sequences should be shown again, what areas of knowledge should be opened up, can be given by nonalphabetic screen control devices like the mouse. Text messages do appear on the videodisk programs we have produced because we found them useful, but they can be replaced by voice and icon cues.

We have been producer or coproducer of three videodisks, one in the field of public health and the other two in the area of farm management. The first of these, and the only one that has had a year of trials in different settings, won a prize for its quality as a teaching program in emergency medical care. The other two will soon enter their trial phase. In each of these cases, our use of the videodisk is an experiment to explore educational uses of the medium, to encourage investment in this technology and to produce programs of high quality.

Interactive videodisks are a useful device for conveying visually interesting educational material even to illiterate viewers. But without experimentation, there will be little pressure for the improvement of technology, and in a commercial sense, little priming of markets. Production costs are high. The authoring of software that places images and soundtracks in particular sequences, and the graphics card hardware that permits the user to access the sound and images, are an investment whose cost can be recovered from royalties. But the storybook, production and pressing costs are specific to each videodisk.

Portable Microcomputers in Rural Areas

Most makers of portable microcomputers have addressed themselves to the market offered by executives and other professionals in the developed world. They have created a briefcase tool, like a dictating machine or a calculator, that can be carried home or taken on business trips. To meet the needs of this market, attention has been paid to size and weight, the number of lines on the screen, memory, the readability of the screen, and easy linkage to other computers, telecommunications and printers. Some of the needs of developing areas are reflected in these features, others not at all. Although the capabilities of the portable continue to evolve, and prices are declining even as improvements appear, the specific needs of the South have not received adequate attention.

The environment of the developing world is not that of the executive in the industrial North. Machines in the North can live in power-rich and often air-conditioned comfort, traveling in automobiles with shock absorbers on smooth road surfaces. In the South, those machines must live in a ruder, less accommodating environment. They must be able to survive very high temperatures for long periods; they must resist the penetration of dust and moisture; they must be able to resist shock; they must generate very little heat themselves; and they must be easily rechargeable.

Some of the improvements in the portable over the last three years will benefit North and South alike. Relatively large internal memories, readable screens, rechargeable battery units and communication with larger standard machines are now possible on many models. What has not received adequate attention is how to make the machine more rugged, dust-resistant, shock-proof and impervious to moisture.

The center has been a pioneer in the development and trial of medical software that can serve health needs in developing areas. For this purpose, we needed a very rugged portable computer with good battery life that would function well in high temperatures, rough terrain, dust and sand. We identified only one machine that met our specifications and have continued to work with it in field trials. It now offers up to 352K of memory, an eight-line LCD screen and safe data storage. A bottom-of-the-line model with 80K of memory sells for about $1,600; the 352K model is available at $5,000. Such machines have a variety of uses for data collection and analysis in field studies.

The computer, equipped with appropriate software and data banks, can be an important way to bring expert knowledge into "bush" areas for the training of health workers, the gathering and maintenance of patient files, and the diagnosis and treatment of diseases. Experiments are needed, however, to establish the quality of what has been produced, its relevance to the user and its effectiveness in altering health care.

For Chad, our group designed software programs to create and access a data bank containing the symptoms of about 500 tropical diseases. To this was added a data bank of medicines recommended by the World Health Organization. The program proposes a step-by-step procedure for diagnosis and relates diagnosis to recommended medicines for treatment, where appropriate. The rural health worker thus has an opportunity to model his own procedure and judgment on that offered by the program, which tries to offer expert medical consensus, where this exists.

Devices of this kind can be excellent aids in the training of medical and paramedical personnel in developed and developing sites, but we recognize that a good deal of human resource development in the health area may be necessary before they can be effective in saving lives. It is easier to reduce error in diagnosis than it is to make treatment more effective. More error-free diagnosis may call for special medication, hospital procedures and medical expertise. But if the medication is not available or is past its shelf life, if the hospital is too distant or expensive and the medical expertise absent, better diagnositic aids can do little to improve treatment.

Micros and Human Development in the South

Health and education investments have no short-term payoffs and are difficult to justify in terms of two- or three-year perspectives. It is evident from World Bank statistics that central government expenditures for health and education have been declining as a portion of total expenditures in developing countries over the past decade. Fiscal constraints imposed by international lending agencies have contributed to the scarcity of funding. How, then, can we expect microcomputers, which will add to the cost of health and education spending, to assume a place in human resource programs in the developing world?

Funding for investment in computer technology is likely to become available before the larger issues of priorities for human resource development are resolved. The largest single explanation for this is to be found in the current near-saturation, at least in the short term, of markets for microcomputers in the developed world and the intense competition for new outlets that has developed among the major producers in the U.S., Western Europe and Japan. The competition for new markets has brought pressure on development agencies to favor computer-aided development programs. In some cases, manufacturers are negotiating directly with foreign states and agencies; in other cases, they are working through their governments and international agencies. In all cases, there is interest in stimulating the growth of markets in developing countries, particularly those that are middle-income.

Receiving unwanted, unnecessary or poorly chosen technology can launch national computer development on an irrational and unproductive course. It is not simply that the recipient country may have to work with outdated models and inappropriate equipment; the larger problem is that each piece of computer equipment (gift or purchase) entails an investment in collateral costs at least equal to the value of the machine. These costs will develop in the area of maintenance, personnel training, software acquisition, site and power source preparation, and communication with other computers.

Moreover, because the operating systems are not yet standardized, it is conceivable that public administrations may find themselves with different systems, accepted in part as donations, which cannot communicate with one another. Files developed on one may not be transferable to the other, and training programs developed for one machine may not be appropriate to others. Although this problem is on its way to resolution, the question of compatibility must be considered from the moment the first investments are made.

A number of developing countries addressed this issue in meetings as early as 1978. The clearest policy statement, with recommendations for practical action, comes from a report published just three months ago of a conference held last year in Colombo, Sri Lanka. Two groups organized in 1982-83 funded this gathering, one Sri Lankan and the other American. The Sri Lankan group was the Computer Information and Technology Council, responsible for computer and informatics policy. The other patron and organizer was the Bureau for Science and Technology of the U.S. Agency for

International Development, which funded the Board on Science and Technology for International Development (BOSTID) of the National Research Council, National Academy of Sciences, to discuss the place of this technology in international development.

Technology gap or technology trap? The authors of the Colombo report are convinced that micros are coming, and that they will greatly benefit developing countries. The hardware is likely to be produced outside the country by foreign suppliers, but if the terms of access are monitored, national computer industries will also develop, especially in software production and hardware maintenance.

Gap or trap? The historical experiment that will allow us to answer this question may never be completed. Protectionist strategies and donor agency resistance, both tied to the current economic crisis, may have the last word. But the industries that make computers are tapping at the door — sometimes pounding — in the search for new markets. If they succeed in opening the door, it will be up to watchdog advisory commissions in international agencies and developing countries to see that the benefits return not only to the exporters of the North, but also to the peoples of the South.

References

1. Georges Broussaud, "Les Videodisques: Histoire, Principes de Fonctionnement et Principaux Domaines d'Application" (submitted to the Centre National d'Etudes des Telecommunications for publication).

2. Centre Mondial Informatique et Ressource Humaine, "Rapport d'Activities 1984," Paris, 1985.

3. Jean-Louis Funck-Brentano, *Technologies et societe: Rapport au Premier Ministre* (Paris: La Documentation Francaise, 1985).

4. Harold Goldberger and Peter Schwenn, "Man-Machine Symbiosis in the Assistance and Training of Rural Health Workers: A Proposal," in J.-C. Pages et al., eds., *Meeting the challenge: Informatics and Medical Education* (Elsevier Science Publishers B.V., 1983).

5. Mohan Munasinghe, Michael Dow and Jack Fritz, eds., *Microcomputers for Development: Issues and Policy* (Sri Lanka: Computer and Information Technology Council of Sri Lanka and the U.S. National Academy of Sciences, 1985).

6. Edgard Pisani, *La main et l'outil: Le developpement du Tiers-Monde et l'Europe* (Paris: Editions Robert Laffont, 1984).

7. Proceedings of the Second World Conference on Transborder Data Flow Policies, Rome, 26-29 June 1984.

8. Raj Reddy, "Technologies for Learning," in Alan Lesgold and Fredenck Reif, eds., *Computers in Education: Realizing the Potential* (Washington, D.C.: U.S. Department of Education, 1983), pp. 49-60.

9. Daniel P. Resnick and Lauren B. Resnick, "The Nature of Literacy: An Historical Exploration, *Harvard Educational Review* XLVII: 3 (August 1977), 370-85.

10. Daniel P. Resnick, ed., *Literacy in Historical Perspective* (Washington, D.C.: Library of Congress, 1983).

11. Jean-Jacques Servan-Schreiber, *Le defi mondial* (París: Artheme Fayard, 1980).

CHAPTER 25

Applications of Artificial Intelligence in Agriculture

Dominique Peccoud

A short examination of the origin of a word can often be a revealing starting point. The word "development" first appears in English in the sixteenth century from the French *developper*, which appeared in the French language in the twelfth century. Its etymology goes back to the agricultural practice of wheat threshing: the *faluppa* in low Latin meant "chaff," i.e., the successive layers of membranes enveloping the grain. To develop originally meant to free the grain, making it fit for consumption. Development encompasses the revelation of the heart or core, a meaning which is found today in the use of the world in photography. The same should apply to the meaning of human development: the revelation of the dynamism rooted in the heart of each human being, each family, each tribe, each nation and the human race as a whole within the scheme of the unive se.

Such is, in fact, not the case. The more developed countries suffer an inhumanity crisis wherein the most sophisticated technology has been used to rid society of the outer envelopes of malnutrition and sickness, but seems at the same time by some perverse effect to have given rise to multifarious impediments, encumbering man and making him incapable of competing in life's race in harmony with his fellows. At the same time, the less-developed countries are prey to sickness and famine; yet he who penetrates the heart of their misery shall discover what richness of humanity pervades in their midst.[1]

With this as a starting point, an attempt will be made to demonstrate what role the kind of artificial intelligence technology that the World Center for Informatics in Paris is trying to apply in agriculture plays in the development of mankind. This will lead us to see that the specific example under examination is paradigmatic of all new technology, from which we shall then be able to draw some more general conclusions.

The World Center's Agricultural Projects

In June 1984, the World Center's Agricultural Department launched its ARPEGE Project (Aid to Solving Problems in Agricultural Holding and Stock Breeding Management).[2] The aim of this project is to examine the feasibility and production of an archetype for an Interactive System for Decision-Making Assistance[3] in polyculture-animal breeding holdings. This type of production is the most common in France and in all countries where breeding is of reasonable importance. The aim of the project was to solve the underlying computer problems for an overall system for decision-making assistance in agriculture. But we did not want to add to these difficulties those originating from a production system about which we knew too little. However, as the word "archetype," which was the chosen objective, would suggest, the proposed study, once completed, would enable the fairly quick creation of prototype interactive systems for decision-making assistance applicable to other types of farming.

In order to quickly launch prototypes which better correspond to the commonest forms of agricultural production in their countries of origin, foreign engineers were and will continue to be involved in the project. Their involvement also complies with the center's mission to transfer technology to developing countries.

At the same time, another team from the same department will produce two interactive videodisks for basic agricultural training. One will deal with the management of an agricultural holding in France and the other with basic crop practices in moist equatorial climates. This new technology involves the use of a videodisk player, a TV display unit and a control computer. The training program is followed interactively on the screen. The program often pauses, calling on the learner to answer questions displayed on a specific area of the TV screen by using either a light-pen or a mouse. The program then continues as a function of the answer given. The aim of the project is twofold : in the short term, to develop increased mastery of interactive videodisk technology and test different ways of presenting knowledge to various target learners; and in the long term, to integrate the interactive videodisk into machine-user interfaces for decision-making assistance systems developed separately.

This twofold project calls for a description of the consideration given to the human element in the problems under examination.

They will be dealt with in the light of the notion of an interactive system for decision-making assistance.

A System

An agricultural holding is a complex system and an element in a yet more complex system — the economy of which it is a part. The greater mastery a farmer wants to have over his holding, the more competent he must be, both to have a sufficiently clear view of the parameters of his holding and to conjugate them with constraints which are imposed from without.

In this field, current techniques of artificial intelligence, widely distributed through *expert systems,* do provide very precise advice in well-determined areas. The same can be said of automatic diagnosis systems for agriculture, one of which was developed by the French National Institute of Agronomy, which brings top-level tomato phytopathology specialists closer to the terrain, as it were.[4] The undeniable utility of this type of expert system to give broad circulation of a sophisticated technique does not, however, correspond to the objective which we set ourselves: to assist the farmer in running his holding by himself. The use of such a system requires the presence of a competent site technician who is able to adapt the advice to each individual farmer and to each type of holding — to each field. Moreover, this type of system is suitable for providing the solution to an individual crisis situation, of which phytopathology is an example. On the other hand, they are not able to provide overall assistance in *forecasting* crop growth. Since they only take into account individual aspects of the holding, they would eventually provide the farmer with contradictory information without his being able to choose, except by chance, the best solution. In fact, it is well known that in system theory, local optimum can lead to the worst in the development of the total system. The farmer should not, therefore, be forced into a line of conduct that he thinks the right one because it has been laid down by a machine and which, in reality, would result in a catastrophe.

This necessarily led to our integrating:

a) A detailed description of the agricultural holding concerned.

b) An estimation of the technical qualities of the farmer to be advised so as not to aim above his initial technical level.

c) Basic knowledge, provided not only by experts, but also by site advisers or farmers themselves, making it possible to provide more precise advice as a function of the problems to be solved.

In order to achieve this aim, it is necessary to combine representation technology and information processing of a much more diversified nature, such as:

a) Relational and deductive data bases.
b) Inference motors type 1 or 2, with which it is possible not only to carry out propositional calculations, as in the case of diagnosis, but also to predicate calculations, including variables and definitions of flow strategies for the activation of rules concerning these same predicates.
c) The general resolver of combination problems, with which it is possible to simulate various overall solutions for the management of the holding under consideration.

Interactivity

For a long time, computer programs were black boxes into which data was entered and which spewed out results. These results were applied with an excessive aura of technological magic, by virtue of which no error was conceivable. This practice – insane from a human point of view – by which data processing was handed over in toto and in blindness to a machine was a reasonable makeshift at a time when the decentralization of data processing was still technologically impossible.

Today, there is an increasing need for the user to be involved in real time in the use of programs. In this way, in a system for decision-making assistance, unlike conventional operational research programs, the user is able to interact frequently to select one direction of research rather than another, or to go back over the management of any hypothesis. Such an aim is extremely costly in the development of a system, especially if it is to be accessible to the greatest number of users possible: the man-machine interface will have to be as near as possible to natural language, or use graphic or image display to communicate even more efficiently with the user – which explains the use of an interactive videodisk, for example. It is, however, only at this cost that computers can become an active tool in training and not just an object of a magic cult (or total rejection).

The problems encountered herein are not only those of computer technology. The experience we have gained in the production of an interactive videodisk in Ivory Coast has taught us with what care the image must be manipulated in this domain, for its meaning is highly dependent on the cultural context of its use. It has become apparent, for example, that a well-defined content is poorly perceived in a filmed sequence during which irrelevant details in relation to the item of knowledge to be transmitted will uselessly capture the attention of the learner. Also, the reduction of a photographic image to a graphic form, pertinent in relation to the information to be transmitted, will have to be accomplished according to well-defined rules which we may find disconcerting; for example, the conventional perspective of our diagrams will have to be replaced by an elevation superposed by a plan view.[5]

The minimization of basic problems of human communication linked to a specific cultural environment has until now often been the source of failure in a vast number of recorded training projects.

An Aid in Transmitting Knowledge

The system which it is our intention to create is not one in which decisions presumed to be the optimum ones are imposed, but rather a system to *assist* in decision making.

The most important assistance we propose is undoubtedly the improvement of farmers' knowhow, which is the only way to help them to make better-informed decisions. Any improvement in knowhow obviously depends on the transmission of knowledge. The conventional method for transmitting knowledge consists in presenting the learner with treatises, books or pamphlets, all more or less based on theory, to encourage learning of the contents of these works, and only then to put the theory into practice. Artificial intelligence and expert systems offer a considerable innovation in offering the self-explanation of each step in the learning process. The system is used very practically and concretely; then, if required, it can be requested to explain the process. If the field of expertise is only of occasional use to someone, then the person will not be inclined to request such an explanation. If, on the other hand, it covers a field of frequent use for someone else, then that person will be likely to seek to know more and to gradually go further into the expertise — even as far as the creation of the expert system itself.

"The farmer should always have the possibility of reading in an expert-system like in a book that is always open at the right page."[6]

For a Decision by the Farmer

The final aim is *decision making* by the farmer. What category of person do we mean by "farmer"? What is the scope of meaning covered by "decision making"?

The farmer is the head of an agricultural undertaking, that is, the person who is reponsible for the decisions concerning the management of the undertaking he controls at the moment when these decisions will have a concrete effect on the finality of the crop campaign. He may operate alone on his holding or have wage-earners under his charge. In the latter case, why do we not refer to these wage-earners as "farmers"? For the simple reason that in exchange for a wage, they carry out a task with well-defined responsibilities, whereas the head of the holding (or sector in a developing country) must answer for the decisions taken.

The term "decision making" is taken to mean the location of a choice among several possibilities, none of which is obvious from any rational determinism in relation to the objectives that the farmer sets himself. In this respect, there are two comments which need to be made, one concerning the choice of objectives and the other concerning the actual decision itself.

Many existing programs designed to assist farmers contain veiled and inaccessible optimization, and very often, productivity maximization strategies which underlie their process, such as cattle feed or fertilization programs. The original feature of the system that we intend to create is to explain the way in which optimization strategies are created so that the farmer retains mastery of his decision. One may want to increase his income; another may want to reduce his work-time at a given period of the year, even if that implies a reduction in productivity on his holding. Whatever the reason, the computer system must not impose a specific strategy on a blindfolded user, who must retain the ability to obtain an explanation and to criticize the strategies proposed.

As far as specific decisions are concerned, it can be said that they are usually not the result of the optimization of strategic objectives. In this, we are reiterating a position adopted by H. Simon (Nobel

Prize for economics) in his theory of limited rationality: man does not seek the optimum solution, but stops at the first solution he encounters which satisfies certain explicit or implicit criteria he has set himself. M. Crozier has adopted the same view by rejecting the old idea by which an undertaking is managed as the adequation of means to objectives and subscribing to the more recent one, which considers the company as being an entity subjected to constraints, and to which certain opportunities are presented. Advantage is either taken of these opportunities, or it is not: the decision lies with the company manager. So, we make no pretension of proposing solutions to the farmer, but rather give him the possibility of analyzing the situation and of predicting the possible consequences of one decision or another.

As we come to the end of this introduction to the ARPEGE system, it can be seen that there are four elements to be retained concerning technology transfer if the human factor in development is to be taken into account:

a) Technology always penetrates a preexisting human reality. This reality is never simple, but it is still a *system* composed of simple elements, and itself a component of a more vast network that could be called a suprasystem.

b) The assimilation of a new technique by man, which he takes further, presupposes that he *interacts* with it. It is for this reason that we must study closely the language, images and customs that compose the culture into which the technique is to be introduced so that it can be transmitted in as pertinent a manner as possible.

c) The most basic *aid* that can be furnished by a given technique is not in the realm of finalized knowhow, but the stimulation of the knowhow of the person who will use it, through his knowledge having been broadened. Here, we are speaking of a true sharing of knowledge whose vocation is to remain open; to state clearly its bases, and not just to deliver a "package deal" technology that will remain complete and hermetic to the user.

d) The aim of technology transfer is to give greater freedom of *decision* to those who use the technology, demanding that they formulate the problems and participate in solving them. The aim is not to serve them with deterministic solutions (founded on reasoning which sees itself as purely scientific) to problems they had not even considered.

Four Comments Concerning the Development of Man

These four statements are worthy of further development in the form of comments regarding man in the process of development, if not in the form of irrefutable arguments.

The Notion of System

A system is the result of certain elements entering into relation. "Might the following not be suggested? For a given field of reality, in a specific activity, the sights of understanding seem to open up, in relation to this field, to a horizon of structuring."[7]

In such a perspective, there is no systemic approach which overrides all others in the name of a single necessary scientific reasoning. A clear example of this would be the difference between the ecosystem of a partisan of fast energy growth applying nuclear energy and that of a "green" ecologist, a partisan of the minimum use of energy. Each is as rational as the other, but they have not set their sights on the same understanding of man in his universe. Each has his own view rooted in an ideology or religious conviction from which springs his conception.

The Notion of Interactivity

The greatest obstacle confronting the interactive transmission of technological knowledge no doubt lies in very widespread illiteracy. Illiteracy should be understood not only as the lack of knowledge of how to read or write, but also the lack of a continuous relation with communication and reflection for a person who is familiar only with the transient nature of oral communication. This type of illiteracy is not so much the result of any intellectual inability to grasp a written code as of the desire to remain in the realm of the oral. Indeed, it is much more difficult to bring into play the learning process for the articulation of sounds to gain access thereby to the articulation of the phonemes of a language than to teach someone to recognize and even reproduce letters. Still, no one can escape oral communication, which is of prime necessity for survival and expanding into the life of a human group, while it is totally conceivable that one could spend an entire lifetime not knowing how to read or write. Therein lies a problem of extreme interest, which the remarkable work by Seymour Papert and his experiments with the LOGO system have highlighted.[8] A child of three and a half is perfectly capable of learning to use a keyboard and to read, providing he has some interest in doing so. One might cite the growing illiteracy in developed countries, where contact with the transient world of film, television and music — in the form of an incessant musical background, and not as work listened to for its own sake — goes hand in hand with a loss of interest in reading, except for comic strips.

It is true that reading is a "style of being"[9] in which man finds himself halfway between the passiveness of the dream and the activeness of the creative imagination, without which the text would remain unheeded. It is the point where personal thought evolves in a dialectic between the ideas suggested by the text and actually perceived and those already existing and which are brought into question by the text's implacable materiality. Hence, the promotion of reading and writing or, on the contrary, the choice of transmitting a tradition through the spoken word and initiation rites, is the result of the ideology or religious convictions on which a society founds its style of communication.

The Notion of Knowledge

The different types of knowledge which underlie the various technologies we want to transfer are based in a more fundamental knowledge that could be covered by the term "physics-mathematics." "It is sufficient to note the incredible expansion of contemporary technology which obviously presupposes a theoretic science of Universal vocation. It accepts to present all phenomena perceptible to the human eye or those reinforced by visible manifestations of those phenomena which are not visible but which correspond in an absolutely strict sense not to any form of speech but to mathematical functions which relate thereto with extreme precision."[10]

The association of the two terms "physics" and "mathematics" is an attempt to account both for the progress of mathematical abstraction and for the conviction that it is applicable to the observable "reality" in which we live. No one disputes the fact that this school of physics-mathematics first appeared in the sixteenth century in Western Europe. It is true that the Greeks, Chinese and Arabs contributed greatly to mathematics, whether pure or astrological, but it was not they who gave it this new impetus which we have called the expansion of physics-mathematics. It may be wondered whether this would have been possible without the bounds of a basic ideology or religious conviction which holds that the meaning of existence in an absolute sense is manifested in man's duty toward the universe.

The Notion of Decision

To give man the ability to make a decision, whether as an individual or in an increasingly large group, is the true meaning of human development. Man is not man, that is to say, the smallest entity, until he can commit and bind himself by a decision-making process for which he is prepared to answer to his fellow man. All processes of material development are aimed at surmounting the stage of survival, the perpetual anguish in which all decision is impossible.

One might then wonder what is meant by the "human factor" in the development process. To speak of the human or any other "factor" in the analysis of a system is to objectivize it as one element among others in the system. In the process of development, the aim is for man to become a *subject* of decision, with all that this implies of the inescapable unforeseen, so it is not possible to speak of the human "factor" without actually compromising the aim of development itself. To speak of the human "dimension," on the other hand, is perfectly acceptable, provided that it is understood not to stand in the way of all other dimensions of development.

Such reasoning is not based on pure rational analysis, but on an idea of man and humanity in the universe that can only be perceived in terms of metaphysical convictions of a religious or ideological nature.

Conclusion

Let there be no illusions: modern technology offers very powerful advantages in terms of the means which can be made available for development. But the aim of this development is not of a technological nature. As soon as one speaks of man in his most basic freedom of decision, one necessarily reaches a metaphysical level of reflection, of which religious conviction is born or ideologies are formed. Communication and exchange in this field of ideas does not function at all in the same way as scientific discussion; it presupposes a quite different style of training of the intelligence and memory, as has been discussed elsewhere.[11] It should not be forgotten in this respect that the sixteenth century, in which modern science and technology came to the fore, was one of the most philosophical and theological in history — one in which convictions played against one another with an extraordinary diversity. The hypertrophy of science and technology today has relegated all reflection on the meaning of human existence to a secondary level, and the training dispensed usually aims only at achieving specific technical competence.

There can be no doubt, when confronted with the failure of development so far, that a way will have to be found to invest in long-term education (more than one generation) in varying cultural contexts which will make it possible to find the way to achieve free decision making. Small-scale operations carried out by nongovernmental organizations associated with material development operations are likely to be more successful than vast, overencompassing projects operating from the top towards the bottom of the hierarchial tree, in which the leaves are likely to be considered as just so many objects among others.

To thresh wheat to make the grain fit for consumption is an easy task. Man's development is a somewhat more difficult task, as he must be helped to shed the chaff by himself, not with a view to simply consuming, but to free the grain unharmed so it may bear ever more humanity.

Notes

1. Dominique Lapierre, "La cite de la joie," Robert Laffont, 1985.
2. Paul Bourgine and Dominique Peccoud, "The ARPEGE Project: An Overview," CMI, 1985.
3. Paul Bourgine, "La MAO, Modelisation Assistee par Ordinateur," Interfaces, July 1984.
4. Ste Cognitech, "Demonstration d'un systeme-expert en diagnostic et traitement des maladies et accidents culturaux de la tomate," 4emes Journees ADI-AFCET systemes-experts, Avignon, Mai 1984.
5. Alain Killmayer, "Rapport de mission en Cote d'Ivoire," CMI, 1984.
6. M. Roux, "L'objet des systemes experts," Journee I.A. et medecine, Marseille, 1984.
7. Jean Ladriere, "L'articulation du sens," CERF, 1984.
8. Seymour Papert "Mindstorms," traduction francaise: "Jaillissement de l'esprit," Flammarion, 1981.
9. Emmanuel Levinas, "Ethique et Infini," Fayard, 1982.
10. Alexandre Kojeve, "Melanges Alexandre Kojeve: L' Aventure de l'Esprit," Hermann, 1964.
11. Dominique Peccoud, "Discours scientifique et parole politique," Economie et Humanisme, Fevrier 1985.

CHAPTER 26

The Informatics Revolution and the Third World: Leapfrogging

Henri Hogbe-Nlend

Informatics is neither a scientific discipline nor a particular technique. Informatics is by its very nature interdisciplinary; it is the crossroads, the meeting point of all the sciences and techniques that contribute to the automatic processing of information — not raw information, but information in the sense of knowledge and ability. Wherever there is knowledge and a need to process this knowledge automatically, there is a need for informatics.

The basic tool for processing this knowledge is the computer. The computer is only a machine, yet it is an extraordinary machine, one quite out of the common; indeed, it is the Proteus of the machine world, capable of assuming an infinity of forms and of accomplishing an infinity of functions. The discovery of the computer, especially of the personal computer, is the most important discovery man has made in the five centuries since the invention of printing. It will lead mankind to the third great revolution of history, the informatics revolution, which in turn will pave the way for a new world civilization based on the universal outflow of human creativity — the civilization of human resources.

Far from being a prolongation of the present industrial revolution, this civilization is in fact the negation of it, in the sense of a refusal, a rejection, a challenge.

As paradoxical as it may seem, this new civilization will display traits closer to the agrarian societies of the Third World, or the "South." Herein lies the basis of our central theme of "leapfrogging": there is a real possibility for the Third World to make a qualitative leap from the agricultural age to the new postindustrial age.

This does not mean that the Third World will not industrialize; the process of its industrialization, however, will not be simply to

This is a summary of the basic theses contained in a larger report on "The Informatics Revolution and the Problems of Global Development" which the author prepared for the United Nations Intergovernmental Committee on Science and Technology for Development.

copy the "North" (Europe and North America). It will be entirely new and will form an integral part of the thrust of the new civilization.

The great conflict of this century is not that between the left and the right, between socialism and capitalism; it is the conflict between those who desire progress, who seek to speed up the birth of the new civilization, and the selfish, privileged members of the declining industrial civilization, who seek to keep it alive. It is to this supreme conflict that history calls our generation.

Thesis 1 : Failure of Development Strategy in the South

The former development strategy of the South failed because it tried to imitate and catch up with the North. The outcome was the development of *misdevelopment*, typified by islands of prosperity in an ocean of misery.

Thesis 2: No Mass Development Currently Possible in the South

It is impossible to envisage mass, endogenous industrialization in the countries of the South within the framework of the present world economy, dominated as it is by huge capitalist monopolies. In this economic structure, the South has no other function than to provide raw materials and cheap labor. Children no more than five years old work fourteen hours a day in some countries of the South.

At the most, the South can benefit from a few basic processing industries for their raw materials before exporting them to the North to be transformed into finished industrial products and from a few substitution industries (e.g., assembly lines) using obsolete technologies.

Thesis 3: The General Crisis of the Industrial Age

The current world crisis is not only an economic and social crisis; it is a crisis of civilization. The root cause is the antagonism between the legitimate aspirations of the people of both the North and the South for a new lifestyle and the manifest inability within the framework of present industrial society, to satisfy the basic needs of the people.

Thesis 4 : The Agricultural South is Closer to the New Civilization

The new society that the people from the North hope for has certain characteristics that bring it closer to the agricultural society of the South than to present-day industrial society : harmony with nature; the depopularization and destandardization of communication and culture; the turning to new and renewable sources for the energy base of the future; new scope and importance for personalized work, for the invisible economy (production for consumption), for flexible working hours, for individual dwellings; the desire for a new kind of economic structure based on decentralization and deconcentration ("small is beautiful"); the desire for a customized education, one that is linked to real life, that is continuous and permanent (learning is a lifetime experience).

Thesis 5 : Leapfrogging

This analogy between the new basic aspirations among the populations of the North and of the South for a new world civilization has several notable consequences :
   a) Solidarity of long-term interests between the populations of the North and the South.
   b) Globalization of the problems of development.
   c) Appearance, for the first time, of realistic possibilities for the Third World to burn the conventional bridges of classical industrial development and to make a qualitative leap from the agricultural age to the new postindustrial age.
This is what we call leapfrogging. The new civilization rehabilitates the great values of the agricultural age and focuses on its strong points, not only on its retrograde aspects.

Thesis 6 : Mass Creative Development -- Five Principles

What development, and which development strategy? The development we need should be conceived of as a global outpouring of creative human activity with the aim of gradually transforming the natural, economic, social and cultural environment and the ultimate goal of satsifying the material and cultural needs of the vast majority of the people of the world. This kind of development must come from within. Further, it must be centered on, integrated with and undertaken by the people themselves. In short, it must be mass development.

The strategy for this development must be founded on the following five broad principles:

a) Breaking with the outmoded strategy of development based on imitating and trying to catch up with the industrialized countries of the West or the East.

b) Planting the firm conviction of the fundamental value of the culture and civilization of all peoples and regions of the world.

c) Opening up to the outside world on the basis of Senghor's principle of "assimilate without being assimilated," i.e., borrow from others without giving up one's own identity.

d) Promoting forward-looked vision in the working out of development plans. Emergency pressure should not lead to the "fire-brigade syndrome," thereby hindering preparations for the future on a more lasting basis.

e) Abandoning micro nationalism and following instead a strategy of systematic regional cooperation with a view to the creation of critical masses that are politically, economically and culturally viable in a world of broad entities.

Thesis 7: Creativity and Development – Human Resources

In the final analysis, to be developed is to be creative. This is valid at the individual level as well as at the level of nations, peoples and continents. The key to success in the global problems of development is to bring a creative spirit and intelligence to leadership. Thus, man is at the center, beginning and end of these problems. The only true development is the development of man, his intelligence, his creativity – the development of human resources.

Thesis 8: Computers for the Creative Development of Man

The computer is simply a machine, but a truly special machine that can be a powerful instrument to accelerate development and speed up the birth of the new world civilization. The bases of this conviction are the following:

a) The computer reduces the intellectual input of man and his creative faculties, contrary to the technological systems created thus far, which simply reduced the physical input of man and animals in favor of machines.

b) The computer is by nature universal. It is the Proteus of the machine world and has incomparable powers of simulation. It can, therefore, be adapted to every culture and every civilization.

c) The computer enables problems to be grasped and treated in an integrated fashion, and with several parameters (e.g., equation with several unknowns). This is a particularly positive element in dealing with development problems which are by definition multi-variable and interdisciplinary. The computer is the antidote for crumbling, compartmentalized culture.

d) The computer, particularly the personal computer of the future, which will be capable of establishing a dialogue with man, will enable the illiterate members of Third World countries to be rehabilitated into society. In present-day industrialized society, anyone who does not know how to read and write is cast out. The information age will favor a renaissance of oral culture. With the fifth-generation personal computer, it will no longer be necessary to know how to read and write in order to be useful, to do a job, to transmit knowledge from one generation to another.

In this sense, it is the rehabilitation of the knowledge of the "elders" of traditional Third World societies. *There is an African saying that when an elder dies, it's like a whole library burning down.*

e) The personal computer will favor the advent of a customized, decentralized education system — a particularly important point for the transmission of knowledge into the heart of the remotest villages of the Third World.

f) The personal computer will enable education to be more closely associated with life, work and pleasure and will allow us to reject once and for all the idea that education can only be acquired en masse, in classrooms. There will be a spectacular rehabilitation of the educational theories found in the traditional societies of the Third World.

Thesis 9: The Informatics Revolution and a New World Civilization

The informatics revolution is a revolution for the universal outflow of creativity and the birth of a new world civilization. It is the third great revolution in the history of mankind. The first, the neolithic revolution, gave birth to agrarian society. The second great revolution, the industrial revolution, gave birth to the industrial age, which is now in the process of decline. The third great revolution is the present informatics revolution. This will in turn give birth to a new civilization, one based on the development of human resources.

In the context of this new global civilization, the whole world is underdeveloped. Certain countries — those of the North — will become a part of it via the industrial age; others — those of the South — via agrarian society. As paradoxical as it may appear, agrarian society seems much closer to the new civilization. To enter the new age gradually, yet with no intermediary stages, the Third World must master the latest in modern technologies. Hence the following thesis.

Thesis 10: Modern and Traditional Technologies Hand in Hand

In order to speed up its development towards the civilization of the twenty-first century and the information age, the Third World must master the latest in modern technologies, especially those in the information and communication fields, biotechnology, micro-electronics, space technology, the technology for new and renewable supplies of energy, finished goods, the exploitation of undersea resources, etc. Since they are still new, these technologies have not yet been perfected and indeed are currently the subject of intense study, research and experimentation in the industrialized world.

The developing countries cannot remain outside the great move-ment to promote these technologies. In fact, because of the bias in their economic relations with the industrialized countries, notably from the transnational corporations, the developing countries have already been penetrated by some of these technologies (information systems, for example) in management, the economy and services. The developing countries must, then, take an interest in the latest of modern technologies and organize themselves at the national and regional levels so as to control, assimilate, tame and master them. At the same time, the developing countries must promote the tradition-al technologies which were created by their ancestors and which embody the values of their culture and civilization.

The developing countries did not come empty-handed to the meeting of civilizations. Indeed, within their geographical area lies the cradle of mankind, of world civilization:

Just as modern science and technology come from Europe, so in Antiquity did universal knowledge flow from the Valley of the Nile towards the rest of the world, and in particular towards Greece, which served as the intermediary link.[1]

Science and technology are thus the common inheritance of all humanity. No people, nor any race, can or should usurp for their own exclusive use the scientific and technological gains of mankind. No civilization is ill-suited, or by nature immune, to science and technology. A people that has life is a people that creates technology. Hence, it is of the utmost importance for a people to promote its own traditional technologies. This should not, however, entail the concept of utter self-sufficiency. Our countries must borrow from other nations what they have developed best and must try to absorb these gains.

Modern and traditional technologies are the two essential, complementary paths that will with certainty lead to the technological development of the Third World. These two types of technology are mutually enriching, and neither one of them can be underestimated without great danger. They must be wedded, integrated, mingled, blended, bound one to another. In other words, we must proceed hand in hand.

In this sense, the current concepts of "the transfer of technology," "intermediary technologies," "appropriate technologies," "soft technologies," are unacceptable as a sole, fundamental strategy for the technological development of the Third World.

Thesis 11 : No Rush Forward or Backward, No Royal Road

In tackling the overall task of mastering modern technologies and promoting traditional technologies for development, the Third World should not plunge blindly toward everything modern (the "rush forward"), nor toward everything traditional (the "rush backward"). A creative spirit of imagination, of sound judgment, is called for. There is no royal road to success that has simply to be copied.

More particularly, the mastery of modern technologies presupposes certain preliminary conditions, the most important of which are:

   a) A critical stable mass of upper and mid-professionals qualified for the technologies considered.

b) Substantial financial means.
c) Consideration of the general level of education, of the scientific and technological culture of the society, and of its technological permeability.

When these conditions are not fulfilled, the import of modern technology is nothing more than a technological graft, a technological excrescence; it is certainly not technological development. Such a graft can only aggravate the external dependency of the importing country and upset its internal sociocultural balance.

Thesis 12: Training the Trainers — The First Priority

It follows from everything above that the first priority in aiding the scientific and technological development of the Third World is to launch and promote a vast world program for the development of knowledge and creativity. In the developing countries, the program should have as its goal the accelerated training of a vanguard of professionals in the basic sciences (maths, physics, chemistry, biology) and in advanced technologies (automation, robotics, artificial intelligence and expert systems, biotechnologies and microelectronics, etc.). Training would take place in high-level international courses and seminars. Grants for excellence in achievement should be set up. Study and research visits should be encouraged, as well as the creation and promotion of international centers for research and training.

Thesis 13: New Jobs in Human Resources

There is a school of thought which believes that the introduction of informatics and its consequences (robots, automation in the tertiary sector, offices and services) aggravates unemployment. This is only partially true, and even then, only in the short term.

In reality, the introduction of automated information systems into society frees man from minor, repetitive tasks and allows him to devote himself to higher, more worthy undertakings based on creative imagination and intelligence — in other words, tasks using human resources.

The real problem is that of organizing man's ability to change activities throughout life by a speedier and more complete education of the young, by lifelong adult learning and by enabling so-called senior citizens to remain active and productive.

Thus, those who "lose their jobs" will be in a position to take up newly created jobs which are better than the ones they had, since they will have to be more inventive and use more imagination and creativity.

Thesis 14: Reliance on One's Own Strength: International Solidarity

In the gigantic task of modernizing their societies, developing countries face numerous difficulties. Despite these difficulties, the Third World must be determined to follow the path of its own technological progress. In the first place, it must rely on its own efforts at the national and regional level. It must also draw the benefits of an international solidarity that will strive even harder to complete these efforts and contribute to a more just, more brotherly world.

Notes

1. Sheik Anta Diop, *Civilization or Barbarity?* (Paris, 1981).

CHAPTER 27

Technological Change:
A Challenge for South-South Cooperation

Aurelie V. Wartensleben

Technology is a commercial asset commanding a price which reflects its relative scarcity or abundance on the market, as well as the cost of producing it. Technology comes in many forms and combinations: there are technological assets of a tangible nature embodied in capital goods, machinery, equipment, etc.; there are technological assets of an intangible nature protected by industrial property rights or secrecy and embodied in models, blueprints, plans, patents, etc.; and there are skills and knowhow as technological assets embodied in people.

Technology relates to each and every phase of the production-consumption system. Its human dimension is, therefore, vast indeed. It requires people to devise new products and to generate new technologies to make them. It requires people to produce fairly standard goods and services by efficiently utilizing relatively well-known technologies, adapting them to local conditions or improving on them to raise productivity. And even the most ancient or least sophisticated products or services call for adequate tools and skills for producing them.

Technological changes have their first impact on the production process, but they also profoundly affect the skill requirements of the consumer or user of the new or improved product or service offered on the market. Indeed, the human dimension of introducing a fully integrated computerized system in a bank in Manhattan is not altogether different from introducing modern, highly mechanized agricultural technologies in a least-developed country, or from introducing an electrical cooker to replace a wood-fuelled stove in a poor family unit. This is to say that what is well known and widespread in one society may look like a technological revolution in another context.

This paper reflects inputs from the UNCTAD secretarial staff, in particular, Mr. J. d' Oliveira e Sousa, Mr. Y. Soubra and Ms. V. Ventura.

The technological transformation of developing countries critically hinges on their capacity to improve upon traditional methods, to adapt and efficiently utilize imported technologies and to innovate or generate new technologies. While technological change has often been associated with inventions or innovations at the outermost frontiers of technology, incremental changes in methods of production, or innovations that extend a known principle to new fields of use are equally important to the development process of developing cou tries. In both cases, the human factor is of critical importance, and the challenge for developing countries lies in harnessing these capacities and skills so as to maximize and optimize the impact of technology on their development processes.

The first section of this paper briefly reviews current patterns of technology trade, including skill exchanges among developing countries. The second section refers more particularly to the incidence of newly emerging technologies on the trade and development patterns of developing countries. The last section attempts to delineate some of the prospects and possibilities of technological cooperation among developing countries. It refers to the human factor primarily in terms of technological skills or services exchanged commercially or traded in an imperfect and rapidly changing market. It is quite obvious that there are many underlying and resulting issues of a socioeconomic nature which would merit urgent attention elsewhere.

South - South Trade in Technology and Related Services

The advantages of the exchange of technology among developing countries originate from the fact that the technological capacity of the suppliers already encompasses a learning process, experience and adaptations relating to technologies transferred from the developed countries. With the development of a capital goods sector and skill formation, the more advanced developing countries have built up the ability to self-adapt and generate technologies suitable to their specific needs and circumstances. The experience gained in descaling, material substitution, adapting and recreating standard modern technologies in the context of their socioeconomic environment is specific to them. Their mastery over imported technology and their capability to introduce adaptive innovations have created the necessary potential to export technology-intensive products, knowhow and technical services of a specific variety to other developing countries and to developed countries as well. Inasmuch as factor conditions and demand patterns are similar, expanded commercial technology exchanges among developing countries can provide the importing countries with suitable standard-modern technology and products — which account for the bulk of their requirements. To the extent that trade and structural changes reinforce each other, the enlarged export of technology would not only reflect the exporting countries' technological capacity, but would also become a contributory factor to further structural shifts and domestic technology buildup. At the same time, importing developing countries would be benefiting from an adaptive effort inherent in the technologies supplied to them by other developing countries.

Apart from the direct market-determined benefits, there are various externalities associated with the increased technology exchanges among developing countries. For instance, the synergistic effect of expanded technology exchange on industrialization and technological progress in both exporting and importing countries would be substantial. The increasing industrialization aided by technology and related resource flows creates scope for increasing trade among developing countries in a wide range of commodities, primary as well as manufactures and services. The strengthening of technological capacity collectively would also have a positive influence in improving the bargaining position of developing countries with the developed countries in all exchange relations. The "learning effect" of technology exchanges among developing countries increases their capacity to absorb, utilize and fully benefit from technology transfers from developed countries as well. On the whole, the fostering of technology development and its exchange among developing countries has immense potential for self-sustained growth in factor productivity and income in the Third World.

In the last two decades, a small group of developing countries was able to diversify their production and trade, and through a complex mix of deliberate policies, to become successful exporters of a wide range of products, including capital goods, and also of technology and technology-related services. Detailed case studies have revealed that the process of establishing a diversified productive structure, in addition to government policies, was directly associated with the technological learning process developed over an extended period of years.[1] Manufacturing production, mostly for domestic or regional markets, entailed the accumulation of technological capacities at the enterprise level which were later used to serve foreign markets.

The establishment of an endogenous manufacturing sector involved a process of import, assimilation, adaptation and creation of technology, predominantly of a standard-modern nature. These technologies, in various forms and combinations, constitute the core of South-South commercial exchanges of technological assets.

There are several indicators to show that technology exchanges among developing countries have gained momentum in the recent past. The period since 1972 has witnessed an increasing number of commercial technology transactions encompassing: (i) simple direct sales of hardware technology, (ii) process packaged and project packaged sales and (iii) technological knowhow, skills and services.

South-South Trade in Capital Goods and Hardware Technology

The data on intra-developing country trade in capital goods, defined to exclude consumer durables and related parts, revealed that the oil-producing and exporting countries (OPEC) constituted a substantial market — around one-third of all intra-South exports in 1981. The share of developing countries in the world total exports of capital goods moved up from 1.7 per cent in 1972 to 3 per cent in 1975 and further to 5.5 per cent in 1981. Intra-South trade constituted its largest component, followed by exports to developed market-economy countries.[2]

Technologically more advanced developing countries, including countries and territories such as Argentina, Brazil, Hong Kong, India, the Republic of Korea, Mexico and Singapore, accounted for the bulk (67 per cent) of developing country exports in capital goods. Intra-South exports in those goods are largely concentrated within subregional/regional groupings, especially in Latin America. For intance, 70 per cent of Argentina's and 62 per cent of Brazil's capital goods exports to developing countries in 1981 were within the Latin American Integration Association (ALADI). The trade among technologically more advanced developing countries was not substantial.

However, around 90 per cent of developing country imports of capital goods originate from developed market economy countries. Intra-developing country trade in capital goods accounted for 50 per cent of total developing country capital goods exports in 1975, falling to 45 per cent in 1981. But South-South trade in capital goods supplied roughly 7 per cent of developing country imports in these goods in 1981, pointing to the magnitude of the potential for any significant substitution of North imports by South suppliers.

South - South Trade in Process and Project Packaged Technology

Process packaged sales of technology involve the supply of hardware technology combined with software elements and technological services ranging from preinvestment and feasibility studies to the installation and commission of plants through consultancy service contracts, engineering contracts, construction contracts, turnkey contracts and others. Project packaged exchanges in technology involve licensing agreements, management contracts, direct investments and joint ventures. The stock of developing countries' direct investment in other developing countries is fairly small in the global context. Yet the establishment of joint ventures is emerging as a significant phenomenon in intra-South technology exchanges.

It is mostly in the activities of design, management and implementation of specific investment projects that a few developing countries have built up a competitive edge and could provide such services overseas, particularly to other developing countries. These services are exported either as a package including equipment and construction (embodied technological service exports) or as a separate entity (disembodied technological service exports).

Although there is very little data on technologies available in developing countries, estimates based on World Bank project disbursements revealed that during the period 1971-1980, 31 per cent of total project disbursements by the Bank had accrued to local developing country suppliers of goods and services. These suppliers had been most active in civil works and construction supplies. The position of developing countries in the market for consulting services and equipment supplies was somewhat weak. Indeed, information contained in the *Engineering News Record* covering international contractors and foreign contracts shows that although several developing country firms ranked among the top turnkey contractors on projects other than power or process plants, these were projects involving a great deal of construction works.[3]

In the developing countries, technology-related services have evolved along with the accumulation of industrial and infrastructure capital as a process of learning-by-doing, often on the basis of technology transfers from abroad. Foreign turnkey contractors set up continuous process industries and equipment plants which were later monitored by local engineers. As industrialization proceeded and the number of local engineers increased, developing countries tended to rely less on turnkey contracts and more on licensing agreements in order to acquire foreign technologies. Government procurement methods and public sector investments also call for the acquisition and utilization of vast amounts of technologies, skills and services. This could form the basis for increasing intra-developing country transactions.

Further research will be needed on the determinants of the technological transformation of the developing countries. While the impact of technological change on the development perspectives of developing countries is quite far-reaching, relatively little is known concerning the resulting shifts in production and trade patterns, including South-South commercial technology transactions.

Technological Knowhow, Skills and Services

Knowhow and skills constitute important producer goods or technological assets embodied in people resulting from a longer-term investment in human capital. Heavy investments in the developing countries over the last thirty years have brought about major structural changes in the skill and knowhow profiles of these countries, with consequent impacts on their socioeconomic structures, as well as on their trade and development patterns.

Technological knowhow, skills or services are commercially hired or rented on national and international markets, singly or in conjunction with more complex technological process or project packages or sales of capital goods, machinery and equipment. The closer the knowhow, skills or services are to frontier technologies, the higher their price on the internal or international market. The differentials in skill requirements, availabilities and costs arising between servicing a computer and servicing a standard tractor perhaps illustrate more expressively the technoeconomic bases on which intercountry transactions involving knowhow, skills and services would take place.

Whether such transactions take place directly among public or private enterprises in the form of management or service contracts, design, engineering or consultancy arrangements, contractual provision of knowhow, projects or process packages, etc., or are provided/ financed through technical assistance, aid or cooperation programs of a bilateral or multilateral nature does not alter the economic value of knowhow, skills and services as technological assets. But the human dimensions of creating these assets, utilizing them productively and exchanging them internationally through a variety of commercial and noncommercial channels are all-pervasive.

Three different forms of intra-South flows of human resources or *skills* can be distinguished: (i) the flows that take place between skill-endowed, capital-deficient countries and capital-endowed, skill-deficient countries in response to conditions in their respective markets; (ii) similar movements from skill-endowed, capital-deficient countries to other skill-endowed, capital-deficient countries in response to maladjustments in the markets of the receiving countries (replacement migration); and finally, (iii) from skill-endowed, capital-deficient countries to those countries which are deficient in both capital and skills, predominantly through bilateral and multilateral technical assistance programs.

While data on South-South commercial exchanges of knowhow, skills and services is very scanty, intra-developing country migration of personnel could be used as a proxy in examining the present patterns and prospects for future cooperation. Most intra-South migration has been intraregional rather than interregional. Capital-deficient, skill-endowed countries in the Arab region and Asia, for instance, constituted the major sources of migrant flows to five Arab countries (Saudi Arabia, Libyan Arab Jamahiriya, Kuwait, United Arab Emirates and Qatar) in 1980. In Africa, a sharp rise in the outflow of migrants from Ghana to the neighboring oil-producing countries of Nigeria, Liberia and Libya was noted beginning in 1975. Developing countries experiencing strong economic growth tend to pull skilled and semiskilled labor from stagnated economies in the region. Available information indicated that migration from developing to other developing countries tended to be for "fixed periods," responding to economic considerations and presupposing the return of migrants to their countries of origin.

Although there are gains involved in the intra-South skill flows, they also raise many questions. The skill-importing country has the benefit of access to skilled manpower on substantially better terms than those offered to the equally skilled personnel from high-cost developed countries; access to skill experience more relevant to the economic and cultural basis of their societies; greater choice in the selection of skills and sources; and, more importantly, an assured supply of a variety of skilled people required for the implemetation of their industrial programs.

For the skill-exporting developing countries, possible advantages would include, inter alia, short-term relief from unemployment or underemployment and the generation of much-needed foreign exchange from remittances. The effect of unemployment on migration is, however, double-edged. Skilled and semiskilled workers who leave their countries in search of improved opportunities may not be necessarily and adequately replaced by others from the reservoir of the unemployed because of difficulties in occupational mobility in the labor market, often closely related to quality and levels of skills or types of specialization. The need for a more organized cooperative exchange of skills among developing countries in order to maximize benefits to all concerned is, therefore, of prime importance.

New Technologies: A Challenge to South - South Cooperation

The world is witnessing rapid technological developments in various fields, such as microelectronics, biotechnology and materials technology. A host of new products is appearing on the market — computers and software packages, new seeds or hybrids, new materials, etc. Their applications are affecting, or have the potential to affect, a wide range of economic sectors and have profound implications, both positive and negative, for the developing countries.[4] At present, it is the exchange of new products that predominates, whereas the technologies for making these products are only rarely the object of international commercial transfers, except perhaps in the form of subcontracting and back-buying of a limited number of components or elements of the final product. The benefits for developing countries arising from the application of new products to meet developmental needs may be considerable. They would be even greater provided that the technologies themselves were to be transferable or endogenously reproducible in these countries.

The picture is far from clear, however. First, some of these technologies, such as numerically controlled machine tools and computer-aided design, which embody skills in the equipment itself, make certain required functions more readily accessible or less time-consuming to the user, economizing on both skilled and unskilled labor. At the same time, these technologies may be creating the need for new skills that are in scarce supply in developing countries. Second, several of these technologies are in fields of primary interest to developing countries. For example, the use of recombinant DNA for the production of vaccines and drugs needed in tropical medicine, or the development of new seed varieties suited to arid zone agriculture and for improved recovery of ores in mining operations, could be made to boost international trade and development.

The transfer of these technologies to the developing countries could in principle make a positive indirect contribution to the export capability of these countries through improvement in the overall productive efficiency of the domestic economy. Of particular relevance are the possibilities afforded by the application of microelectronics and computerization technology for streamlining a host of services related to management, informatics, design and engineering, insurance, etc. Transferred to developing countries, the advances in information technology, including telematics, could help to improve the state of knowledge of world market conditions and decrease the distance between developing country suppliers and their customers, thereby improving their capacity to service overseas markets efficiently. It should be borne in mind, however, that the managerial and decision-making skills and the infrastructure required for exploiting and assimilating these advances remain to be developed in many countries.

Some of the new applications of microelectronics, information and, to a lesser degree, telematics and biotechnology have already begun to spread to the developing countries and are to be found in a variety of uses in a number of economic sectors. Little is known about the effects of this diffusion on socioeconomic and technological development in developing countries, with the result that no basis exists for promoting their rational use, apart from considerations of private commercial profitability. This is all the more critical if the new investment necessary for the utilization of these techniques is quite large on account of their "systemic" or "packaged" nature. Microelectronic-based applications are associated with the introduction of systems to replace a series of older and mainly discrete electronic, electromechanical and mechanical equipment. The scrapping of such equipment could be quite costly, especially if investment in existing equipment has not been amortized. In addition, microelectronics often requires system compatibility within the firm, and it requires the enterprise to modify not only production methods, but also management and marketing practices, after-sales service methods and personnel policies, including retraining programs.

For the majority of developing countries, the level of technological advance is quite low, and these technologies have proven to be highly research and development-intensive in the industrialized countries. Although developing countries are hardly likely to make major innovations in these technological fields in the foreseeable future, the fact remains that they will also need to devote resources to R & D for adaptation and even minor modifications if they are to be able to assimilate the technology. Moreover, a small number of the more industrialized countries have already embarked on the production of some of the key components of these technologies in, for example, microelectronics. For the latter countries, the R & D commitment would seem to be even more strict than for developing countries as a whole and would require larger financial resources. Because of the newness of these fields and the rapidity with which technological changes are taking place throughout the world, the problem of rational allocation of R & D resources — whether in enterprises or in public institutions — is a major one. It encompasses not only policy decisions concerning the distribution of financing, but also manpower development and the organization of skills from various disciplines.

It is almost certain that the ongoing wave of technological change, which has only recently become pronounced and the effects of which have just begun to appear, will remain for some time in the center of attention, particularly for policymakers in the developing countries. For them, the phenomenon acquires special relevance because of their efforts to elaborate and implement a strategy for their technological transformation constrained by severe financial difficulties.

Prospects for South - South Cooperation and Joint Activities

Developing countries differ very widely in terms of size, population, resource endowments, production structures and technological capacity. This very heterogeneity provides numerous opportunities and immense possibilities for exploiting actual or potential complementarities among them. There are indications that developing countries are increasingly taking advantage of these complementarities in terms of growing trade in capital goods, expanding flows of skills, knowhow and services, and larger investment, credit and aid flows among themselves.

While constituting a heterogenous group, developing countries share a number of similar conditions and are confronted with similar types of problems. A situation of complementarity arises not only out of the differences among countries, but also out of the very similarity of the nature and content of their economic, commercial, technological and developmental problems. Again, there are a number of indicators to show that intra-developing country linkages and cooperative arrangements are being established as a means of maximizing benefits from economies of scale, minimizing costs in areas of common interests, or deriving benefits from each other's differing experience or capacity.

A large part of intercountry technology transaction takes place through commercial channels. Multilateral policies and programs could be identified to create the necessary favorable conditions for interactions between developing country suppliers and buyers of technology. Supportive policies and measures in this regard could concentrate on (i) strengthening technoeconomic and commercial information flows, (ii) establishing preferential arrangements for the development and transfer of technology on equitable terms and (iii) evolving special arrangements for the exchange of software technologies and related transactions.[5]

Preferential arrangements, for instance, could be established to remove the barriers in the technology market and facilitate better interaction between developing country firms on the basis of their real competitiveness and the appropriateness of their technologies to economic and social requirements. Suitable policies could help shape entrepreneurial decisions in favor of local or developing countries' sources of supply of technologies.

South-South technology transactions and cooperation among enterprises are progressively increasing. The public sector is not only an important user of technologies, but also a prime generator of commercial technological assets, particularly in the form of high-level skills, applied R & D results and innovations of relevance to economically productive activities. Suitable interlinkages need to be established in the developing countries between the generators and users of technologies in the public and private sectors.

Technological cooperation among developing countries can also be pursued through arrangements, interlinkages and joint actions aimed at pooling resources to supplement each other's shortages, to derive economies of scale or to avoid repetitive investments in the adaptation, improvement, upgrading, generation and subsequent utilization or commercialization of technological assets. The main areas of joint cooperative action could include the following: (i) joint technological research and development, (ii) joint activities in sectors and areas of critical importance, (iii) joint procurement, production and commercialization, and (iv) skill cooperation and the provision of services.

Joint R & D activities are progressively taking place. Among some examples are the Andean Technological Development Projects (PADT) or those of the Asian Regional Institute of Technology. Institutions such as the Agricultural Machinery Center in Asia or the International Rice Research Institute in the Philippines provide examples of joint sectoral R & D activities.[6] Greater efforts are called for in order to utilize productively or commercialize the technologies, innovations and results of R & D emanating from these joint endeavors.

Human resource development is a critical factor in the technological transformation of developing countries. It calls for an integrated approach to manpower planning, education and training, the development of advanced and specialized technical institutions and research centers, and the provision of suitable links with productive activities. At present, there are a series of mismatches between skill formation and skill utilization, with surpluses, shortages or irrelevant specialization being some of the most patent manifestations of the problem.

There are also avenues for combining the acquisition of technology from other developing countries with cooperative arrangements in the area of human resources. For instance, the acquiring country can provide a conducive environment for the employment of highly skilled personnel from other developing countries who would be responsible for the training of local personnel in detailed engineering, installation, operation, maintenance and management, with a view to accelerating the process of indigenization and technological adaptation.[7]

Some advanced developing countries — mainly those that have upgraded the skills of their labor force and estabished a fairly well developed infrastructure — have been able to make inroads into the areas of high technology. The countries that have succeeded in building a technological capacity in this field could play a leading role in the rational diffusion of their technological strategies to other developing countries. The transfer of technology on equitable terms can be achieved through cooperation among developing countries involving both governments and enterprises. The development of the required skills, the strengthening of R & D facilities and the promotion of adjustment programs on the basis of monitoring international trends are potential areas that lend themselves to subregional, regional and interregional cooperation.

South-South cooperation in areas such as microelectronics may also be instrumental in improving the collective bargaining power that could enable developing countries to obtain more favorable terms and conditions from technology suppliers than they could by negotiating individually. Such collective bargaining could be justified by the vast potential market for this technology in the South and the fierce competition prevailing in the industry in the North, whose future growth very much depends on the internationalization of its activities.

The fairly rapid rate of technical change taking place in microelectronics and other new areas such as biotechnology and materials technology makes it essential that developing countries cooperate among themselves to monitor and take advantage of new developments in these areas in order to maintain and strengthen the competitiveness of their industries and to adapt their economies to the changing pattern of international comparative advantage.

The accumulation of physical, human and institutional capital associated with an increasing mobility of factors of production, including skilled labor, has contributed to the expansion of exchanges of skill-intensive products and services among developing countries for the last decade. These exchanges have laid the foundation for more complex forms of cooperation in the future. The emergence and progressive diffusion of research and skill-intensive technologies will challenge developing countries to formulate an integrated strategy for their technological transformation, including skill formation and utilization. International cooperation is certainly called for in support of these endeavors.

Notes

1. Simon Teitel and Larry E. Westphal, Editors' Introduction, *Journal of Development Economics* 16 (1984): 1-11, and Morris Teubal, "The Role of Technological Learning in the Exports of Manufactured Goods: The Case of Selected Capital Goods in Brazil," *World Development* 12 (1984): 849-65.

2. The data quoted in this section comes from UNCTAD, "Interregional Linkages and Cooperative Arrangements among Developing Countries for their Technological Transformation," TD/B/C.6/118 (1984).

3. Andre Sapir, "Trade Among Developing Countries in Investment-Related Technological Services" (Paper submitted to the informal symposium on South-South Trade: Obstacles to its Growth, UNCTAD, Geneva, 26-29 June 1985).

4. UNCTAD, "New and Emerging Technologies: Some Economic, Commercial and Developmental Aspects," TD/B/C.6/120 (1984).

5. UNCTAD, "Interregional Linkages," pp. 10-13.

6. See also UNCTAD, "Report of the Meeting of Government Experts on the Transfer, Application and Development of Technology in the Capital Goods and Industrial Machinery Sector," TD/B/C.6/82 (1982); "Report of the Meeting of Governmental Experts on the Transfer, Application and Development of Technology in the Energy Sector," TD/B/C.6/94 (1982); and "Report of the Meeting of Governmental Experts on the Transfer, Application and Development of Technology in the Food Processing Sector," TD/B/C.6/78 (1982).

7. See also UNCTAD, "Cooperative Exchange of Skills Among Developing Countries: A Case for Technical Cooperation among Developing Countries," TCDC/2/INF/3 (1981).

PART VI

CONTRIBUTIONS OF THE PRIVATE SECTOR, NGO'S AND INSTITUTIONS

CHAPTER 28

People: The Key Resource in Industrial Development

Ernst G. Knappe

People have the potential to offer much more to our organizations. This is the most encouraging possibility the company is faced with today. It shows there is enormous loyalty and willingness on the part of people to achieve more. It is only due to our poor leadership that this potential is not developed in a sensible way. Although much has been achieved, much remains to be done. At Volvo, we have gained great experience over the years in upgrading our performance by working through people.

New technology is playing an increasing and important role for companies and people. The application of technology has to be handled carefully and demands new competence. High technology in the true sense is not necessarily good; it needs to be wisely applied. The technology of the automotive industry, for instance, allows it to run competitively the most complex industrial system found anywhere in the world.

The more sophisticated the technology, the more important people become. Increased complexity also means that some people within the organization need to have ever greater command of the sophisticated systems put at their disposal. This clearly indicates that the successful application of technology depends on people and not on equipment. It is our ability to *use* the equipment — which we can define as skills — which we must continually measure against that of the competition.

We should be concerned about defining skills and technologies clearly so that people both within and outside the organization understand what we want to achieve.

The Dialogue Program

People and their aspirations are important. That is why Volvo is now investing heavily in a corporation-wide program geared to training every employee to understand the overall activities of the group in order to start a dialogue with them. Over the past few years, Volvo has carefully developed a real commitment to giving all employees a true stake in the corporation, based upon the belief that people with a knowledgeable insight and commitment can help build a successful company. The aim is to involve the employees more deeply in helping to shape and steer both their own and the corporation's future.

The program, called Dialogue, is geared to increasing employees' knowledge about Volvo's activities and business environment, goals and basic values, products and markets, organization and guidelines. It also increases knowledge and awareness about Volvo's role in society. A dialogue is started within each Volvo company and department around specific work tasks and the conditions for doing a satisfactory job.

On the subsidiary level, each company is designing an in-depth program to focus further on specific and local issues. When people can relate their work to a larger perspective, true achievement and an increase in competence are realized.

The continuing challenge is to develop the kind of leadership that keeps this process moving. It requires leaders who know how to harness the potential of the whole organization.

At the heart of Volvo's organization development efforts at the plant level during the 1970s and 1980s has been the pursuit of two simultaneous objectives: to increase efficiency and to improve the quality of work life. Many means have been used, as the following examples show.

Kalmar

The Volvo plant at Kalmar was revolutionary when it began operating in 1974. For the first time since the traditional assembly line was devised by Henry Ford, an automobile plant had been designed without a rigid machine-paced line for final assembly.

"We orginally planned a facility capable of producing 30,000 cars annually on a one-shift system and with the capacity to double that turnover if required," recalled Karl-Eric Nilsson, Senior Vice President of the Volvo Car Corporation. "The first·blueprints showed a fairly conventional, albeit modern, auto plant. But Pehr G. Gyllenhammar felt a more farsighted production layout should be developed, and therefore, we launched a study to look into how best to meet his belief that the focus should be on the people working in the plant, with humans running the machines and not vice versa."

The ideas that evolved from the study, combined with Mr. Gyllenhammar's own ideas, resulted in a document calling for the creation of a production facility that boosted efficiency by enabling workers to work in teams. Through job rotation and breaking of their routine, workers would more easily identify themselves with the product and feel a greater sense of responsibility for its quality.

Work progressed fast on planning the novel plant. One stumbling block was how to transport the car through the facility if one did away with the traditional assembly line. The solution proved to be a mobile assembly platform on which each car body could be carried from one work station to the next. Thanks to computer technology, these platforms or carriers, as they have now come to be called, could be steered by electrical impulses from contoured loops in the floor. Work on a prototype quickly revealed the advantages that would be gained by installing a device that tilted the body at 90 degrees, thus easing assembly work under the vehicle body.

In 1983, the Kalmar plant management and unions jointly requested an independent labor-management body, the Swedish Efficiency and Participation Development Council, to evaluate the factory. The final report of the council focused on the evolution of Volvo/Kalmar over a ten-year period, evaluating the extent to which it has fulfilled its original business goals.

The authors of the study note that the most interesting aspect of the Kalmar plant is the way new technology and new organizational patterns have been combined to create an entirely new type of working environment. This has made it possible for every employee to have meaningful work, personal involvement in his or her day-to-day activity and a high degree of job satisfaction. They note that this has been done with no sacrifice of efficiency, profitability or competitiveness, and that the Kalmar plant is a dramatic demonstration of the feasibility of achieving extremely positive production results in an unusually favorable working environment.

How do the employees feel? According to the study, the overwhelming majority of employees at Kalmar feel that the work organization is either "good" or "fairly good." Jobs are deemed better than those on a traditional assembly line, although there is still a belief that there is too little room for initiative and personal growth on the job.

Financially, too, Kalmar has proven to be a success. Assembly costs are the lowest of all the Volvo Car Corporation's plants, and the facility shows the lowest figures for office employee man-hours per car produced. There seems little doubt that these positive results have helped contribute to the creation of a favorable climate in the plant, with employees increasingly displaying an interest in learning more about production factors.

The study also reached some conclusions that could be drawn from Kalmar's first decade. Amongst other things, the study said, new technology changes the basic conditions that determine the design of organizations and jobs. Radical technological changes, purposefully carried out, can create opportunities to expand job content and simultaneously improve efficiency.

Also, the division of a large organization into several independent production facilities makes the pressures exerted by the external environment much clearer to the small units. It also intensifies the employees' awareness of the total context of which their units are a part. Volvo has found this lesson supported in many other cases, especially if the unit produces a complete product.

Leadership styles and information policies are of great significance for the employees' commitment. By adapting the technology and the work organization to the people, the often hidden resources of employees to develop and grow can be liberated.

Torslanda

Volvo's largest production unit, and the largest workplace in Scandinavia, is the Torslanda plant of the Volvo Car Corporation. Built in 1964 and employing around 8,000 people, the Torslanda plant is a complete car factory with pressing plant, body plant, painting plant and final assembly. But Torslanda is a very different workplace today than it was two decades ago.

Torslanda is one of the most technically advanced facilities in Europe, especially regarding the utilization of industrial robots. Yet because Volvo stresses that its most important resource is the people working at the plant, employees at Torslanda have direct access to facilities such as a day nursery, health care facilitates, and study and recreation premises.

Naturally, over a twenty-year period in such a huge plant, a variety of different employee management schemes have been tested. For instance, there was the original "time and motion" method, which involved measuring the amount of time it took a person to perform a specific action. Volvo's pragmatic commitment to implementing researched solutions has gradually evolved into the current guidelines for industrial engineering, which take a more holistic view of human resources in productive work.

Production at Torslanda starts in the press shop. The four lines shear, punch and press the sheet metal to form roofs, floors, fenders, sides and more — in all, forty different parts being worked in twenty presses. Production is very highly automated, and the only manual job is taking out the parts after the final press. Previously, there were two men between each pair of presses moving the sheet metal — a tough and noisy job. Today, the sheet metal is moved with the help of a Doppin feeder, which was invented by Volvo.

The Doppin feeder was the key to transforming the work for humans from a backbreaking ten-second lifting cycle a decade ago into a more enriching work function providing greater intellectual stimulation. Previously, the team was highly segregated into specific job tasks, with little or no interaction due to the physical impossibility of communication. Not only were the groups too large, with fifteen members or more, but management added to the communication problem by streaming workers into jobs according to their educational backgrounds.

Today, all that has changed. Automation has not only removed boring jobs and helped improve the working environment, but Volvo has also added a new dimension demanding a greater integration of worker skills. Based on experience gained from its Olofstrom plant, Volvo chose this option rather than going the route of adding more specialists to the organization.

That is why Volvo has retrained its workers into highly educated "mechanical engineers" with a much higher degree of responsibility. The main benefits include higher productivity resulting from minimized losses that stem from the interaction within the team and their commitment to efforts arising from the perceived improvements in the quality of their work life.

Being part of a team that is successful in itself adds to the feeling of satisfaction. The evidence also underlines that correct use of modern technology can greatly assist or spark the motivation to change, while deeper employee involvement creates a potential readiness for change through greater awareness.

The experience gained at the press shop has been utilized in developing new working techniques at the innovative TAO body and white plant and the KBS body assembly plant.

At TAO, employee skills have been maximized with adoption of production groups comprising ten people sharing full responsibility for activities within their own spectrum, including quality, quantity and financial control. Technical training is high and job rotation the rule. Workers are not only responsible for production itself, but also for service and maintenance of the machines and robots, inspection, material handling and much more.

Considered one of the most advanced users of industrial robot technology in Europe, the Torslanda plant utilizes robots and automatic welding machines to carry out 98 per cent of all welding. The recently developed KBS body assembly plant represents a complete departure from the line system.

All assembly work is carried out on a stationary body, which is transported on automated guided vehicles from one work station to the next. People work in pairs on jobs that would in traditional situations have been divided up into several short procedures. It takes roughly one hour before the body moves on from each work station to the next.

Developing good work organization in an existing large-scale plant calls for other approaches than the above-mentioned investments. In the assembly plant, where some 3,300 employees work, major efforts have been made to streamline production flow and involve personnel more deeply. For example, quality circles were first launched in 1977 at Torslanda. Today, there are well over 80 meeting regularly. One clear bonus of Volvo's commitment to its human resources has been that many of the changes at the Torslanda plant have been implemented during normal running production.

Some Lessons

What has Volvo learned from its experience in bringing about change at the plant level? Certainly, its efforts have not been an unalloyed series of successes. There were false starts, errors, outright failures and, periodically, brilliant breakthroughs.

There seem to be several conditions which must be present if change is to be introduced successfully. First, the value system of top corporate management must wholeheartedly support the overall goals, and this support must be communicated broadly both within and outside the organization. These values should also reflect the values of the broader society.

A second condition is that management must be willing to support organization development efforts both during prosperous periods and when there are downturns. An on/off approach results in lack of confidence and impedes further opportunities for gaining support.

Third, open communication on all matters related to the change is required — not only between management, the unions and the workers, but also among individuals in each of the groups involved.

A fourth condition is that the responsibility for implementing change must be assigned to the line organization, not the staff specialists or the consultants, who can at best be only advisers. The roles of all actors have to be defined in unambiguous terms.

Fifth, extensive support systems are required, not the least of which is training. Wage schemes must keep pace with changes in job requirements; otherwise, the effort to change will be impeded.

A sixth condition, particularly given the industrial relations situation in Sweden, is that the unions must support the change process or at least take a neutral position.

Last, solutions to problems must be tailor-made to each situation. These are no panaceas, no theories or practices which can be imported uncritically. Each work team has its own particular characteristics. Thus, goals, means and timing must be adapted to the local situation.

The Need for Leadership

Volvo has been very much in the limelight both in Sweden and abroad for its efforts to introduce new production technologies and to humanize the workplace. Some critics have taken the company to task on the latter, accusing it of being too "soft" and lacking "hard-headedness."

Volvo profoundly believes that it is not a question of "either/or" but of "both/and." It assumes that a company of its size — relatively small on a world scale, though large in Scandinavia — must do everything in its power to increase its international competitiveness. One fundamental tool for accomplishing this aim is to ensure that it stays on the cutting edge in terms of production technology. This is the sine qua non of survival. However, the introduction of technology is not merely a matter of installing hardware. That hardware requires compatible "software," and the most important element of this software is the social system within the plant. These are the people who are charged with designing, implementing and maintaining the hardware. In other words, introducing technological change is a sociotechnical process.

Volvo's assumption has been that without the total involvement of plant personnel, the probability of successful introduction of new production technology in a cost-effective way is reduced significantly. The "socio" part of the equation in fact is the key *means* to achieve the "technical" goal. Thus, rather than being "soft," Volvo's emphasis on people turns out to be very hardheaded and bottom-line oriented, as the Kalmar success has shown.

The continuing challenge for Volvo is to develop the kind of leadership that can keep this process moving. It requires leaders who know how to harness the potential of all employees, from worker to plant manager, not simply for humanitarian, quality-of-work life reasons, but because the company's future is at stake.

CHAPTER 29

The Human Element in the Private Sector: A Turkish Experience

Rahmi M. Koc

Turkey started industrialization some eighty years later than the western world, yet today, after only twenty-five years, it can compete with the long-industrialized western countries in certain areas with certain goods and services. Turkey has changed its industrialization strategy by shifting the base of its industry from import substitution to an export orientation that can compete on the international market. Twenty years ago, industrial products accounted for only 15 per cent of Turkish exports. This percentage did not improve dramatically until five years ago. With a new outward-looking economic program, Turkey has since then increased the share of industrial products to 75 per cent of total exports. The export of traditional agricultural products has also continued to increase during this period.

This change in the industrial structure has highlighted the significance of the human element.

Structure of the Labor Force in Turkey

The population of Turkey presents an ironic situation: not only does it grow at 2.1 per cent per annum, but also it gets younger at the same time. Half of the population in Turkey is aged 20 years and under, while in Germany and France, for example, half of the population is 50 years or older. The elderly account for only 13 per cent of the total in Turkey. There are 600,000-700,000 new job-seekers joining our market each year, and yet there is still an acute shortage of trained and qualified personnel.

Structure of Turkish Industry

Industrialization first started in Turkey, as in some other countries, with state enterprises. This was because the private sector had neither the funds nor the knowhow to build industry. At that time, the capable minority sector preferred trading. In fact, the private sector did not go seriously into industry until the late 1950s. However, this late entry brought one advantage: the latest technology and equipment was adopted.

There was also a division between public and private sector industries. The government produced mainly primary and secondary materials, whereas the private sector preferred lighter and finished products. The private sector started from assembly, then moved into manufacturing and is now busy adjusting to more sophisticated, exportable, industrial goods. The public sector, on the other hand, unfortunately could not keep up with the rapid changes and was unable to seriously restructure itself. It is my firm belief that the strength of the private sector comes from its ability to adjust to changing conditions.

The one thing that the private and public sectors had in common was the shortage of qualified mangerial skills, middle management and supervisory people. This arises from the fact that the manpower policy of Turkey is closely related to its macroeconomic objectives. These are:

a) Rapid growth.

b) Full employment.

c) Price stability.

d) Export-oriented industries.

e) Accomplishing equal balance of payments.

The approach to the human element in Turkey must therefore be examined within the scope of these objectives.

Importance of the Human Element in the Private Sector

Although the private sector in Turkey started its industralization much later than the public sector, it made a fantastic effort and achieved maturity in certain areas that took the western countries some 150 years. Today, Turkish industry and its products can compete on the lower end of the market with the products of the industrialized western and eastern countries. The stability of the human factor has played a prominent role in this struggle.

Turkey currently has a fair industrial base, does not lack capacity and can find financing. It does, however, feel a serious shortcoming in the incorporation of managerial techniques into its untrained but abundant manpower.

The Human Element in the Growth of Koc Holding

Koc Holding, with 46 industrial and 61 commercial and service companies, presently employs 33,000 people. It is the oldest and largest industrial group in Turkey. Starting out as a general store 60 years ago, it is a fine example of how the private sector has developed. It went into industry in the 1950s as a result of changing conditions and since then has been serving the economy in 11 different sectors.

Our basic philosophy is: *The human element is the most important single factor in an operation.* The group's success is closely related to this philosophy. We operate on a totally decentralized system, where individual managerial skills become more important than ever.

Every single one of the 117 companies is run by managers who feel that they own the business, that the business is their responsibility and that their welfare is closely related to its success.

Each company works within a planned discipline of one- to five-year short-term and ten-year long-term objectives. As long as the subsidiary companies operate within their objectives, they are managed without interference from the parent company. Of course, individual company programs are first consolidated into various groups and then combined as a whole to make up the Koc Holding master plan. Being able to operate independently motivates company managers to take a strong interest in the motivation and well-being of their employees.

Two other main factors in the Koc Holding personnel policy are the importance of seniority and the system of rotation. A person who works loyally and has not changed jobs for a year or two is a superior candidate for promotion. Rarely does an outsider obtain the top position in a major subsidiary. Rotation is of utmost importance, and a subject which has caused many differences of opinion in policymaking. Some argue that successful personnel should not change positions just because of the passing of years. Others insist that rotation brings vitality, whereas duration causes stagnation. At the moment, a key manager can expect to change position after five years, and certainly before ten years. This policy makes our most senior managers aware of the challenges and problems inherent in managing a diverse group of businesses.

The evaluation and remuneration of the individual are other important ingredients of our personnel policy. Each of the 7,500 white-collar workers in the group is appraised by his immediate supervisor and by the general manager of the company. Every worker is individually evaluated, these evaluations are checked against the Koc Holding department records and a final consensus on the person is reached.

Middle and top management are also evaluated by the Koc Holding management. In this case, we check the company management against the objectives of the companies they run. None of these evaluations are carried out as mere reasearch exercises; their results reflect heavily on individual promotion and remuneration in the group. The top managerial forces in the group have annual earnings very closely related to their companies' profitability, because only 30 per cent of their total earnings represent their salaries — the rest comes from bonuses. There is therefore a close correlation between managerial manpower and the performance of the company.

Not only do we use modern techniques and systems to employ qualified personnel; we also educate and train them ardently. In addition to the training that our industrial companies offer on an ongoing basis, we also train top, middle and supervisory management in "Kogem" (Koc Improvement and Education Center). This system has been adapted from similar centers, such as those at Siemens, Fiat and General Electric. Kogem operates in close coordination and relation with the universities and thus has access to the latest educational methods, whether for training a foreman or a top manager. We also have training programs outside the country, either in international training centers or in the companies that we do business with.

All thése programs, unfortunately, bring with them a disadvantage. Since it takes years to train personnel properly, our competition and newly formed companies — with neither time, patience nor funds — prefer to take a short-cut and hire our personnel away from us at exorbitantly high transfer payments and monthly salaries. The offers are so lucrative that when our employees break the news of their departure to us, we have no choice but to agree with them.

In an attempt to safeguard ourselves against this situation, we have adopted a system whereby each year we take 20-40 promising young students with top performances and inject them into our system. They receive six months of training for higher managerial posts in various companies and positions. Their progress is very closely and personally monitored by the managers and assistant managers of the company. They are excluded from the group's white-collar personnel figures. Twenty per cent of these trainees make it to the top; the rest are grabbed at various stages by the competition.

Of course, there is no limit to the amount of training a person can receive, but then there emerges a cost factor. Sometimes it costs so much to train a person that eventually it does not prove worthwhile, since we train and invest in our personnel with no strings attached.

As the Chairman of Koc Holding, I personally see all top managers and their assistants who resign after working for a group for more than twenty years. I do not try to convince them to stay, but rather to ascertain the underlying reasons for their resignation.

There are always areas that can be improved in our personnel policies. Nevertheless, I am very happy to report that we are still the leaders in recognizing the importance of the human factor in private sector success. Indeed, our systems have been widely copied by our competitors.

CHAPTER 30

The Human Element :
A Gap Between North and South

Nemir A. Kirdar

Human resources are the most critical component in any economic environment. It is the human dimension that commands, directs, organizes, plans, controls and optimizes the utilization of all other factors of production in any economic endeavor. No success has ever been accomplished without the existence of a capable, driving force of human effort behind it.

At macro levels, the development process of any country is by definition dependent on the degree of productivity and creativity of its human resources. Since the ultimate objective of the developing world at large is to achieve progress towards narrowing and eventually eliminating the productivity gap that exists today between the North and the South, it is indeed time that we took a fresh look at this most vital subject.

The organization with which I am now associated, known as Investcorp, was established as a sophisticated investment bank in the South that would operate as closely as possible at par with the very best industry anywhere in the world. Its full name is the Arabian Investment Banking Corporation E.C. It was established in the State of Bahrain, which has emerged as one of the major banking centers of the world, and certainly the most prominent in the Arab world. Investcorp was established in 1982 and has shown a successful performance to date.

In this paper I would like to discuss three points :
a) The significance attached to human resource development in the corporate planning process in the North.
b) Highlights of the human element deficiencies in the South.
c) The recent experience of creating Investcorp and the critical importance we attach to the element of human resource management.

I do not believe there should be any significant generic difference or distinction between the planning processes applied by the world's leading corporations and those pursued by most developing countries. Both wish to optimize the utilization of their available resources to generate greater wealth through increased efficiency and productivity. The ultimate objective of any developing country is to utilize its incremental wealth to upgrade the standard of living of its citizens. Corporations are no different: their aim is to utilize their net earnings either for expansion or for the enrichment of their stock-holders. Most corporations use any newly created "wealth" for both objectives.

Therefore, in this paper, while I will attempt to focus on the direct relationship between the degree of importance attached to human resources and the ultimate success of any corporation, I would certainly hope that the same linkage applies in the case of the economic development of any country. The interpendence of the human element and the successful implementation of any development plan in either sector is not dissimilar.

Corporate America

Over the years, it has repeatedly become evident that some companies do extraordinarily well, while the performance of others in the same line of business, operating in an identical environment and with similar resources, falls far behind, and they cannot achieve more than mediocre results. Upon closer examination of the underlying facts and analysis of the fundamental reasons, the prime difference can often be traced to the question of how well the organization has been able to bring out the great energies and talents of its people.

People are the root source of productivity. They are at the core of all development efforts. Today, one can hardly come across an annual report of any major U.S. corporation without finding a prominent pronouncement of the fact that the ultimate success of the corporation and its growth is directly related to the talent and training of its people. Thus do corporations justify the large sums they invest annually in the further development of their future manpower. Most large corporations recruit a number of graduating students and run them through highly extensive and extremely expensive training programs with the expectation that the payoff from their contributions will come in five to ten years. Top-management of these corporations consider such investments in human resources similar to funds earmarked for research and development or large-scale capital expenditures.

The purposes of human resource planning in U.S. corporations are to :

a) Identify and acquire the right number of people with the proper skills.
b) Train and develop them for filling future positions.
c) Motivate them to achieve high performance.
d) Create interactive links between business objectives and people-planning activities.

A company's skills and staffing forecasts are set by both its organizational structure and its business goals. Business goals generate requirements that are translated into performance objectives for the individuals and organizational units. Corporations that have the people in place to meet their performance objectives are well equipped to implement their business plans successfully.

The basic philosophy for managing people in most of the successful corporations in the U.S. is to assure their employees that they will be respected, treated as individuals and enjoy individual dignity at all times. This declaration of what employees can expect of their corporation is paralleled by an equally clear declaration of what the organization has a right to expect from its employees in return. This kind of mutual understanding is fundamental to effective human resource management.

The human resource question has increasingly become a major issue in corporate strategic planning. With greater emphasis, corporations are viewing scarce management talent as a critical strategic resource that requires priority attention over money and technology.

Obvious Deficiencies in the South

a) *Education.* Experience has reflected that a significant number of countries in the South have suffered more by the quality of education imparted to their graduates than by a shortage of graduates, which is a separate drawback. This, in my judgment, is an extremely serious problem which will continue to be counterproductive and have a deleterious impact on the future.

The systems of schooling in most of the South are run by less than competent and socially and economically deprived teachers. The lack of adequate textbooks, laboratories, libraries and modern audiovisual aids adds to the list of disadvantages suffered by the South. Students are often expected to memorize, going through a set of rigid required programs and moving from one class to another until completing a certain number of years, after which they earn a certificate or diploma of minimum qualifications in comparison to what is being offered in the North.

After graduation, job and pay levels available to graduates are not related to the content of the education received, but are rather geared to the level of the degree that has been awarded. Thus, a large number of undereducated and overrated degree-holders flood the government job market annually, causing not only a negative impact on productivity, but also potentially explosive social and political difficulties.

b) *Training.* Schools do not normally develop skills, but rather prepare the mental capacity of the individual in order to enable him to acquire skills needed after graduation. In the North, the enterprise which the individual joins after graduation normally invests a great amount of time and money in him to ensure his productivity in the right job.

The availability of such training has been rare in the South. Those institutions that offer skill development programs have not always scored high in quality. In an attempt to save time and money, training in the South often lacks the depth and breadth of comparable programs offered in the North.

c) *Decision making.* Most enterprises in the South are government owned or related. This breeds bureaucracy and discourages initiative, creativity and entrepreneurship. Furthermore, because of the rigidity of the system, an individual is seldom rewarded for making the right decision but can be severely reprimanded for any slight misjudgment affecting public sector-owned interests. Therefore, the individual is perpetually motivated toward indecision and passing on the responsibility to someone higher up in the organization. This type of environment is the number one enemy of productivity, prosperity and progress, generating eventual frustration and disappointment for both employer and employee.

d) *Critical mass.* It takes more than a single exceptional individual to run a productive unit, irrespective of his outstanding qualifications. Often, a successful unit is composed of a "critical mass" that provides the unit with the required momentum, vitality and continuity. By "critical mass" I mean a collection of diversified talents with the opportunity to interact regularly with one another in the accomplishment of the organization's goals, as opposed to an exceptionally brilliant individual who is operating alone.

It is imperative that this "critical mass" is supported by an effective and highly motivated infrastructure and totality, all of which make the attainment of superior quality production possible.

Most companies have either lacked the above conceptual approach or have failed to implement it. They may have been able to attract capable individual talents but have often failed to organize a totally capable infrastructure and an effective critical mass.

e) *Compensation.* There is a major disadvantage in most of the countries of the South that needs urgent attention. To be able to have what is by western standards a normal, middle- class standard of living often means seeking luxury standards at exorbitant prices in most countries of the South. This factor has not only contributed to the "brain drain" from the South to the North, but also to the demotivation of the many qualified people who have chosen not to migrate. Therefore, unless the compensation system in the South is totally reviewed and reestablished around international standards, productivity and creativity will continue to suffer.

The Investcorp Experience

Investcorp was established in 1982. The founders recognized a need for a new kind of investment institution that would :

a) Focus its products and services on the very particular requirements of the Arabian Gulf investor.

b) Locate, structure and place high-quality international investments to suit the needs of its carefully targeted clients.

c) Enable local investors to participate fully in the type of prestigious investments available elsewhere in the world.

d) Channel the area's substantial economic resources into projects and investments which would foster regional economic development and truly represent the best interests of the region.

In order to be able to achieve these objectives, we were convinced that attracting and retaining professional talent of the highest quality would be crucial to our success. Accordingly, we conducted extensive studies on various human resource policies and compensation programs of the leading international investment banks and based the

Investcorp human resources approach on the most sophisticated and up-to-date standards.

The results have been gratifying. During 1983, which was our first fiscal year, Investcorp concluded US$ 58 million of investments in the U.S. and generated net earnings equal to a return of over 20 per cent on its paid-in capital (stockholders received 15 per cent as dividends). In 1984, we concluded over $250 million of investments in the U.S. and Western Europe and generated net earnings of over 22 per cent return on paid-in capital (15 per cent was again paid to stockholders as dividends). In 1985, we believe, our momentum is well on target, and we anticipate a similar level of performance.

Although, admittedly, three years might be too short a period to judge realistically the performance of any corporation, the initial takeoff of the business was highly successful. I attribute this early success to the accurate preplanning that preceded the establishment of Investcorp and to the human resources we have assembled to implement those plans. We have established a team of successful and experienced individuals, each possessing an outstanding background, energy and skills. Their expertise, enthusiasm, dedication, vision and creativity make them uniquely qualified to respond to our market needs.

From the very beginning, our primary objectives have been to create a performance-oriented and a people-oriented marketing environment that demands integrity and stimulates entrepreneurial spirit, productivity and a deep sense of commitment and responsibility to Investcorp and its shareholders and clients.

As a reflection of its commitment to attract and retain excellent human resources, Investcorp has allocated a sizable percentage of its equity for management options. Thus, the officers of the organization have a significant personal interest in the firm's long-term development and prosperity. Additionally, our staff has a direct interest in the ongoing profitability of the firm, as they participate in the annual profit-sharing through a well-defined formula that rewards each individual according to his initiative and the degree of his contribution.

Investcorp employs a partnership approach in decision making and management. Each of its executive directors operates as an equal. Each is responsible for a particular area of activity and is also a member of the firm's management committee, which makes all policy, procedural and investment decisions. The partnership concept encourages a free exchange of information and ideas between functional areas. This is particularly important in terms of Investcorp's market-driven philosophy and need for speedy decision making.

Conclusions: The North

a) There is a significant awareness in the North that human resource development management is the key to achieving greater tangible success in almost any line of business.

b) Employees are considered an investment, not a cost. The very purpose of such an investment is to tap the creativity and energy of people in order to maximize their influence on and contribution to the success of the organization.

c) The motivation and commitment of people to the organization is a primary factor in the success of an enterprise. In order to accomplish that, the organization must provide adequate long-term training, development and meaningful management participation.

Conclusions: The South

a) Totally insufficient attention has been given to the adequate development of human resources in the South. Accordingly, economic progress over the past forty years has been disappointing.

b) With the substantial and continuing emphasis on the importance of human resource development in the North and the lack of it in the South, there is a danger of an accelerating gap that needs to be seriously dealt with and closed.

c) Numerous experiments have proved that if we were to adopt the necessary ingredients and assemble the right human resources, we could establish models of successful enterprises in the South that are no less sophisticated and productive than their best competitors in the North. The challenge confronting the South is how to broaden the base of such successful experiments so that they are constantly duplicated and would eventually become the rule, not the exception.

CHAPTER 31

NGOs and Human Development:
The ASEAN Experience

Lim Teck Ghee

One of the most striking developments in the recent history of countries in the Asia/Pacific region has been the emergence of nongovernmental organizations (NGOs) as articulate and organized critics of the prevailing political, economic and social systems in their respective countries. Initially attracting only a small membership from the literate and middle-class segment of society, these organizations have rapidly proliferated in the past decade and attracted a larger and more diversified membership.[1] More importantly, they have been able to assert themselves in the forefront of public articulation on many crucial questions, including those related to the broader issues of democratic rights and freedom traditionally articulated by political parties, as well as a host of newer issues related to the development goals and strategies of their societies.

The growth and increasing importance of what we might characterize as interest groups or issue-oriented organizations might appear surprising, as it comes at a time when there has been a hardening of centralizing and authoritarian political tendencies in the region. The period after World War II initially saw a wave of decolonization followed by the unshackling of social restrictions, but this soon gave way to increased pressures towards concentration of power, attempts to form single political parties and encroachments on oppositional politics. In many countries, moves by the parties in power to enforce "national solidarity" largely through local and national level institutions and organizations under their control have been supplemented by a weakening of the legislative and judicial process. At the same time, the number of military and authoritarian regimes has grown. The position of political democracy in one of the ASEAN countries described below can be taken as a fair reflection of the regional pattern:

The increasingly dominant position of the executive branch of government is one of the two general characteristics of the decline of freedom... The other is the curtailment or even elimination of the rights of participation in the democratic process for a whole variety of social groups. This does not mean that political freedom does not exist anymore. It does, in a severely limited form.

The most dangerous consequence of the decline of freedom in any society is the emergence of authoritarianism. The overwhelming dominance of the executive and the emasculation of public participation can lead to this, just as it can produce an "administrative state" where none of the fundamental issues in nation-building are discussed or dealt with.[2]

NGOs in the Asia/Pacific Region

Given the unconducive environment, how and why have NGOs spread? What and who do they represent? What has been the impact of NGOs on the socioeconomic processes in their countries and the region? To what extent do NGOs facilitate growth toward more participatory forms of planning and administration or presage the emergence of more pluralistic tendencies? What are the social forces that promote or limit NGOs? These are some of the major questions that will be addressed in this paper.

NGOs have long been an integral part of the West European and North American democratic tradition, where they are regarded as characteristic of urban industrial societies where interests are differentiated, stratified and wide in their range. Among these interests are consumer organizations, trade unions and women's groups, which had their origins in the nineteenth century cooperative, labor and women's suffrage movements. Their development in the West, although within a different historical and cultural context, offers some clues explaining the growth of NGOs in other parts of the world.[3]

On the other hand, there has been a paucity of serious writing on NGOs in this area of the world, in part because social scientists have regarded political parties, the bureaucracy and the military as the main political and social forces and concentrated on their study. In fact, the sum of serious writing on NGOs in this part of the world is confined to a small number of mainly journalistic articles that describe the activities of particular organizations, usually in relation to an item of news that happens to be in the immediate public eye, whether this is the environment, human rights, consumerism or lifestyles.[4]

Not only is the existing knowledge on NGOs limited by a lack of method and documentation, but also, the analytical tools applied have been deficient. In the West, NGOs differ from conventional political parties in that they do not participate directly in the political process by presenting candidates for election.[5] Also, they usually represent a narrower range of interests than political parties, which tend to have programs in every major sphere of life. Finally, they have been characterized as being rooted in middle-class ideology and interests, although this depiction is perhaps more correct in relation to NGOs today than in the past, since historically, the most dynamic NGOs in the West, such as the early women's suffrage and workers' movements, have offered radical (as opposed to the existing) viewpoints on crucial issues. In the Asia/Pacific region, NGOs cover a wide range of small and large social, religious, economic, cultural and political groupings and associations. In this paper, the focus is on those which, for want of a better term, are referred to as developmental NGOs. By this is meant that although the organizations might focus on a single issue, e.g., consumer problems or environmental degradation, unlike the traditional single-issue organizations such as trade unions or youth associations, they see their work as explicitly situated in the context of a wider concern for progressive social development and change in society. Developmental NGOs might also take up the cause of certain aggrieved groups or classes in society, e.g., slum dwellers or farmers, but their main concern is really with all the various groups and classes found in society and with wider social processes.

The Asia/Pacific NGOs share some of the characteristics of their western counterparts, but they have to contend with forces that operate at a different level and on a different scale. One of the most prominent activities they engage in is the monitoring of the state. In many Third World nations, governments exert a pervasive control over many sectors of life. As one paper on law describes it:

A bewildering variety of state and parastatal institutions (Ministries, boards, public corporations, regulatory bodies, co-operatives, courts and others) exercise a variety of powers (planning, rule making, licensing and adjudication, provision of goods or services) affecting land, credit, technologies and services, wages and prices. Different kinds of law (national legislation, administrative regulations, and often, settled, but uncodified practices) create these institutions and large realms of administrative power within them.[6]

The situation is no different in the Association of Southeast Asian Nations (ASEAN) countries, where the past decade has seen an unprecedented expansion of the bureaucracies and their rise to prominence as one of the main, if not the major, instrument of development. During this century, the number of goverment employees in Indonesia rose from 50,000 to over a million, and in Thailand, from 80,000 to a quarter of a million. In Malaysia today, government employees number about 15 of every 100 people employed. In all five countries, bureaucrats are in control of the burgeoning sectors of education, health, communications and defense and have even extended their control into the economic realm.[7]

At issue is not only the quality of the services offered, but the more important question of whether bureaucratization contributes to further dependency, domination and discrimination. Indeed, as pointed out by one critique, "the very assumption that governments should rely on bureaucracies (rather than community structures) as a means of distribution or redistribution of resources frequently needs critical examination and seldom gets it."[8] Among the severest critics of bureaucracy have been the NGOs. But to what extent they can actually persuade the power holders to decentralize authority toward community structures (including NGOs), or establish public control systems that ensure adequate social accountability, is an open question whose answer depends as much on the wisdom of the present power holders as on the skill of the NGOs in walking the tightrope between permissible and "subversive" or "anti-national" dissent.

Dimensions of the Development *Problematique*

It is not just the modernizing bureaucracy which is being called into question. NGOs have also been critical of the content of the modernizing or development process. Leaving aside the question of the role NGOs might play in political development, these bodies have much to contribute in the field of socioeconomic development. Clearly, the scope of the development *problematique* in the Asia/

Pacific region makes it a sine qua non for all sections of society to be mobilized and lend their skills and abilities if there is going to be a significant and lasting improvement in the conditions of life in the countries concerned.

The past several decades since independence have already seen the failure — massive in some countries — of many government-dominated programs to provide the masses of people with the basic minimum needs to lift them out of the poverty, hunger and squalor of their everyday life. The Brandt Report in 1981 estimated that more than 800 million people in the world lived in "absolute poverty," and from table 1 it can be seen that a considerable proportion, perhaps as much as three-quarters, are found in the Asia/Pacific region. Table 1 also shows the wide gap between Asia and the industrial market economies (IMEs) in some select economic and social indicators as of 1980 and 1981. In the worst-off Asian country, daily per capita calorie intake and life expectancy were only about half the levels found in the average IME. The infant mortality rate was about twenty times greater than in the IMEs, partly as a result of the Asian countries' having thirty times less doctors, while the number of children enrolled in secondary schools as a per cent of the relevant age group was nine times less. These grim statistics are by no means extraordinary. Although it may be conceded that some progress has been made in most countries when one compares nationwide social and economic indicators with those of twenty years ago, e.g., number of doctors, number of schools or the infant mortality rate, the nationally aggregated statistics almost certainly conceal considerable internal differences; and it would be difficult to dispute the charge that for the bottom fifty per cent of the population in the majority of countries in the Asia/Pacific region, the conditions of life have not improved much.

Meanwhile, the rapid growth of population has wiped out some of the gains made in economic and social development; and in the future, it threatens to be an even greater factor than today in exacerbating low incomes and unemployment. Of the nineteen countries listed in table 1, no less than twelve — Afghanistan, Bangladesh, Nepal, Pakistan, Burma, North Korea, Laos, Malaysia, Mongolia, Philippines, Vietnam and Papua New Guinea — will double their population within thirty years or less, based on existing estimates, while India, Sri Lanka, Indonesia and Thailand will double theirs within thirty-five years.

TABLE 1
Asian and Pacific Countries: Recent Socioeconomic Indicators

Country	Daily Per Capita Calories Supply (As % of Require-ment) 1980	Population per Physician 1980	No. Enrolled in Secondary Schools (As % of Age Group)	Infant Mortality Rate (Age 0-1) 1981	Life Expec-tancy at Birth (Years) 1981	Population Size (Millions) 1981
Industrial Market Economies	134	554	89	11	75	
Afghanistan	73	16,730	10	205	37	16.4
Bangladesh	84	10,940	15	135	48	92.8
India	87	3,640	28	121	52	688.6
Nepal	86	30,060	21	148	45	14.4
Pakistan	106	3,480	15	123	50	88.9
Sri Lanka	102	7,170	51	43	69	15.3
Burma	113	4,660	20	98	64	35.2
China	107	1,920	34	71	67	985.0
Indonesia	110	11,530	28	105	54	149.4
North Korea	126	440	n.a	33	66	18.3
South Korea	128	1,690	85	33	66	38.9
Laos	97	20,060	17	126	43	3.6
Malaysia	121	7,910	53	30	65	14.3
Mongolia	111	450	89	53	64	1.7
Philippines	111	7,970	63	53	63	48.9
Singapore	134	1,150	55	12	72	2.4
Thailand	104	7,180	29	53	63	48.3
Vietnam	90	4,190	48	97	63	54.9
Papua N.G.	90	13,590	12	102	51	3.3

SOURCES: World Bank, *World Development Report, 1983*, tables 23, 24 and 25, pp. 192-97; Far Eastern Economic Review, *Asia Yearbook 1982*, pp. 8-9.
NOTE: Table excludes countries of the Middle East and certain Far East and Oceania countries where data is not available.

A factor of special significance that threatens to cancel out gains even in the most equitable or dynamic development ideologies in the Third World is the process of rapid urbanization. It was long assumed that the majority of the Third World's people live in the countryside, and that the eradication of differential income levels and access to services between the urban and rural population formed an important priority in social development planning. However, recent figures indicate that the rate of urban growth has accelerated so quickly that by the year 2000, 44 per cent of the population in less-developed countries will be living in urban areas and that 50 per cent of these city dwellers will be struggling for survival in slums and shanty-towns.[9] In East Asia (excluding China),[10] the urban population will increase from 53 per cent in 1975 to 73 per cent by the year 2000, meaning that rural areas will see a continuous loss of population. Meanwhile, eastern South Asia will go from 21 to 35 per cent urban in the period 1975-2000.[11] For the period 1975-2000, the average annual urban growth rate is estimated to be almost nine times that of the rural (3.90 urban versus 0.45 rural). These figures, translated into development terms, imply very critical times ahead for the poor living in the cities and towns. Not only will most of them not benefit from the amenities, services and economic opportunities that urban areas have to offer, but they will be hard pressed to survive even at the most marginal levels of life.

Socioeconomic Prospects in ASEAN Countries

While the development outlook in the less well endowed Asian/Pacific countries looks very grim, it is only slightly less so in the majority of the ASEAN countries, which not so long ago were touted as Asia's second economic and social miracle after Japan and the East Asian countries of South Korea, Hong Kong and Taiwan. Enjoying exceptional growth rates (an average GNP per capita increase of over five per cent a year from 1970-80), the region and the individual countries it comprises seemed to have found the magical developmental recipe that would not only enable them to break away from the Third World countries in general, but also, in the minds of some future-oriented planners and scholars, to actually overtake Japan and the West in the future.

Today, the rhetoric about ASEAN and the Pacific Rim's boom has sobered considerably. Growth rates have dropped drastically, and the economies have begun to limp noticeably. In most of the countries, the inequalities between rich and poor and the social trauma caused by rapid (and, some would argue, superficial) development have worsened; and in at least one country, the Philippines, the unprecedented unrest and discontent must be seen as having its roots in the dominant laissez faire developmentalist strategy and its failure to generate authentic and sustained economic and social change. The gap between ASEAN and the industralized countries of the West in some basic social and economic indicators continues to be yawningly large (see table 2). For example, Indonesia's GNP per capita in 1978 was estimated to be about twenty-five times less than the average industrialized market economy's (IME), while the infant mortality rate in most of the region was between three to five times higher than in the IME countries. Only 22 per cent of the population in Thailand had access to safe water as of 1975, compared with 100 per cent in the IME countries.

TABLE 2
ASEAN: Some Social and Economic Indicators

	Indicator	Indonesia	Thailand	Philippines	Malaysia	Industralized Countries (Av.)
1.	Adult literacy rate (%) 1975	62	84	87	60	99
2.	Life expectancy at birth (years) 1978	47	61	60	67	74
3.	Energy consumption per capita (kg. of coal eq.) 1978	278	327	339	716	7,060
4.	GNP per capita ($) 1978	360	490	510	1,090	8,070
5.	Infant mortality (age 0-1) 1978	?	68	65	31	13
6.	Child death rate (1-4 years) 1978	20	6	7	3	1
7.	Population per physician 1977	14,540	8,170	2,760	4,350	630
8.	% of pop. with access to safe water 1975	12	22	39	62	100
9.	Daily calorie supply per capita 1977	2,272	1,929	2,189	2,610	3,377
10.	No. enrolled in secondary school as % of age group 1977	21	27	56	43	87

SOURCE: World Bank, *World Development Report, 1980,* annex tables, pp. 110-55.

What NGOs Contribute to Social Development

To begin with, it should be emphasized that the problems of development in the Asia/Pacific region are not new. To a certain extent, they are the outcome of processes that are complex, having their roots in the major historical developments in the economic and sociopolitical structures of the world for at least the past two hundred years. It is impossible, therefore, to talk about development (by which we mean economic and sociocultural well-being), under-development or overdevelopment without taking into account modern imperialism. Imperialism produced enormous profits for the imperial powers through economic exploitation of the colonies' natural resources and labor. Besides bringing in profits from the colonies, it enabled West Europeans to settle in large parts of the New World, kill off or subjugate the indigenous people and, through racially discriminatory immigration laws, prevent the movement of population from overcrowded lands to less crowded ones. The latter is still practiced today. The significant difference in the standard of living between European and non-European peoples in the world is not merely an outcome of the superior material technology or social organization of the Europeans; it is partially a result of the physical division of the world's lands in the eighteenth and nineteenth centuries, a division enforced by the West through the use of superior military technology and still perpetuated today.

There is, however, one important difference in the crisis of development in the Third World today compared with that of thirty or forty years ago: whereas in the past it was colonial systems and a small group of foreign interests that were primarily responsible for the lack of development, today the blame cannot be put on foreign exploiters or imperialist powers as unequivocally as before. More than most other participatory groups, NGOs seem to be cognizant of the need to focus on the internal forces and interests that stand in the way of the struggle for economic and social well-being.

Besides playing what is often a risky watchdog role, especially for the poor and unrepresented, through monitoring and criticism of corrupt politicians, exploitative businessmen and unscrupulous or inefficient bureaucrats, NGOs are often in the forefront of demys-tifying the conventional wisdom of development that might be promoted by vested interests. In its mildest form, this manifests itself in protests against specific cases of destruction of essential natural resources, impoverishment of groups of people, etc., which are seen as examples of government weakness that can be corrected through greater bureaucratic caution, better planning, etc. At a higher, more critical level, these grievances are linked to a more fundamental rejection of the conventional development strategy, which is regarded as not only inappropriate, but anchored to an unacceptable social and economic structure. The fiercest exponents of this line of criticism maintain that it is the social and economic substructure that must be changed before a transformation of the superstructure comes about.

In place of existing development strategies, NGOs have emphasized alternative approaches that offer different values and means. Among them are access to essential resources for the poor, self-reliance within communities, ecological management geared to protecting medium- and long-run access to resources, redistribution of resources where they have been denied, accountability of public or private power holders, etc. Stress also is laid on the ethical norms of development and the need to incorporate elements of freedom, justice, identity and a sense of meaning and proportion in material development.

The most visible impact of NGOs has occurred where they have campaigned on specific problems, e.g., squatter eviction (Tondo in the Philippines), environmental pollution or abuse (National Park and Papan in Malaysia), birth control education (Thailand). Here, NGOs with their expertise often act as catalysts or mediators by constantly publicizing the issue, organizing people to raise their voices, applying a strategy of pressure politics (mass campaign action, rallies, demonstrations) and soliciting support from other segments of society and the international community. This articulation of popular interests helps to encourage participation by those who cannot develop influence by themselves.

Also, many conservative and even liberal NGOs in the region devote important parts of their programs to providing services to various depressed communities. Here, their strength is in their innovative approach, usually stressing self-reliance, community organization, etc; but their effectiveness is often severely hampered by their lack of resources.

To offset the disadvantages of their lack of resources, many NGOs have carefully nurtured relations with the mass media so as to bring about a degree of neutrality, if not support, for their work. Solid research and data collection also enable them to present a powerful case for the issues they take up, while unconventional and creative tactics, including the identification of the human dimension in development problems, help prevent public apathy or boredom. An increasingly useful weapon in the armory of NGOs is to pressurize the existing legal system to bring about desirable change. In the past, the legal system was seen as the preserve of the rich and powerful. NGOs have helped ordinary people see the possibilities of change through legislation (both public and criminal law) that specifically addresses social problems, e.g., laws and regulations that concern pollution, safety and health of workers, allocation of land or water resources, etc.

Unlike the first two approaches, where the role and impact of NGOs is mainly educational, here NGOs have moved into more action-oriented positions by taking up cases on behalf of aggrieved groups, canvassing the public on the need for consumer or environmental laws, etc. This approach has considerably enhanced the impact and effectiveness of NGOs in many areas of life.

Review of NGOs in ASEAN

Malaysia

More than in the other ASEAN countries, NGOs in Malaysia are urban-based because of the domination of the rural areas by political parties. It also reflects to some extent the higher stage of economic (though not necessarily social) development and the large size of the Malaysian middle class. The leadership of NGOs here, as elsewhere in the region, is firmly in the hands of intellectuals and university graduates, mainly because of their higher levels of formal educational training and easier access to resources, contacts, the media, etc.

Support for NGOs in Malaysia from the middle and professional classes is often more tacit than active. Even where active support is forthcoming, it tends to be on an issue-specific basis, dissipating after some time. Although there is as yet little evidence of comprehensive and sustained mass support, there are encouraging signs of a slowly growing consciousness on issues such as consumerism, environmentalism, corruption, etc. and an increasing disillusionment with the party and communal politics that presently dominate Malaysian political and social life. This is mainly due to the untiring efforts of a small number of pioneering NGOs. Among them is the Consumers Association of Penang (CAP), which has campaigned against eyebrow pencil laden with lead, mosquito coils containing DDT, condensed milk loaded with sugar, and ginger cherry and other local junk food whose colors are derived from Red Dye No. 2 (banned in many parts of the world as carcinogenic). It has also called to attention the plight of poor fishermen displaced by mechanized trawler boats that deplete fish stocks by dredging shallow waters with small-mesh nets and of farmers who suffer from exploitation by middle men. Because consumers rarely notice the plight of small producers in their concern with the high price of goods in the marketplace, the educative work of the association in linking consumer problems to the conditions of production becomes vitally important. Prominent in the annual seminars on consumer problems organized by the association since 1978, which have become an important listening post for the country's academics, bureaucrats and professional class, is the theme of an unacceptable structural imbalance in the country's development process dividing center from periphery, city from country and modern from traditional.[12]

While CAP questions conventional development approaches by focusing on the plight of squatters, poor housewives, fishermen and other impoverished communities that have suffered from badly planned projects or the excesses of the market, Aliran, a multiracial, nonpartisan reform movement, has sought to encourage reflection and debate on the nation's future by putting forward for discussion what the movement sees as common values and principles and by articulating public issues and grievances. Aliran's stand on issues – a catalogue of which includes ethnic relations, communal politics, corruption, constitutional and administrative structure, education, culture, language, workers, trade unions and labor laws – is in many ways a holistic critique of the prevailing system found in the country. In its own words, Aliran represents a search for "a genuine understanding of development based on fundamental spiritual values upheld by all the community."[13]

More recent has been the establishment of environmental organizations such as the Environment Protection Society of Malaysia (EPSM) and Sahabat Alam Malaysia (Friends of the Earth Malaysia, or SAM). Until ten years ago, discussion of the ecological balance was conspicious by its absence from universities, public fora and the media, and development strategies were ecologically ignorant or blind. This followed the pattern in the West, where the social sciences, with the exception of social anthropology, where the man-environment relation and its ramifications have been more difficult to ignore, have dealt mainly with industrial civilization. Today, however, localized ecological disasters and a growing fear of further national environmental deterioration have given organizations such as EPSM and SAM a boost in their advocacy of ecodevelopment,[14] that is, a style of development that calls for specific solutions to the particular problems of each ecoregion in the light of cultural and ecological data and of long-term as well as immediate needs.[15]

Thailand

In Thailand, the active participation of NGOs in social development can be considered to have begun a decade ago, when the country enjoyed a brief period of relatively free political activity and parliamentary rule. However, this was followed by a spell of repressive conditions, and more recently, by a certain amount of liberalization which has enabled a large number of NGOs established earlier to work more actively and to appear more often in the public eye. Today, it is estimated that there are more than 200 NGOs in the country, run by a handful of unpaid volunteers and with only a small number of paid and full-time staff.

The early NGOs tended to be dominated by church, wealthy elite or government groups more concerned with proselytization, status acquisition or business ends. The newer NGOs have been the result of increased social awareness among Thai intellectuals (including university lecturers, doctors, lawyers, religious leaders and trade unionists) seeking an outlet.

Although some Thai NGOs are concerned with social development in the broad sense of the term, a large number are more oriented toward the provision of services than their counterparts in Malaysia or the Philippines. These Thai NGOs carry out a large number of development projects of a utilitarian nature (primary health, drug cooperatives, child care centers, rice banks, vocational training, etc.). Unlike similar government-run projects, NGO projects are seen as providing the necessary conditions for the development of social consciousness among the communities involved to a level in which they come to understand their situation and learn how to work together for more collective control over their lives. While the objective of consciousness-raising might have been attained, it has been admitted that these operations, sustained with much difficulty by the meager human and financial resources of NGO supporters, cover only a minute fraction of rural and urban needs and have yet to achieve any great impact or success in terms of concrete development results.

It is difficult to gauge the degree of public support for Thai NGOs, but generally, it has been assessed as limited, although selective NGOs have done well, e.g., those working on child labor or family planning. The problems Thai NGOs face are both internal and external. Internally, many of them are plagued by organizational defects stemming from a lack of professional and experienced workers. As one Thai activist within the movement put it:

> Most NGOs are organised and administered in a rather unsystematic and amateurish way, not conducive to the development of their workers and the organizations themselves. Information and experiences gained in the work often go unrecorded. Scientific methods are lacking in follow-up and evaluation of work, and in collection and analysis of data. Administrative structures and division of duties are often clumsy and inefficient.

An important outcome of these defects has been the slow accumulation of development knowledge and experience suitable for Thailand and reliance instead on imported theories and knowledge.

The political climate in Thailand has also tended to fluctuate considerably in terms of the openness of the system and official support provided to NGOs. There is probably a higher degree of security consciousness among local authorities (compared with Malaysia or the Philippines) in their reaction to NGO work, especially since the weakening of more radical social forces, such as the students, has brought more concern for the "adverse" impact of NGOs.

Notwithstanding these problems, which are inevitable to young social movements operating in a circumscribed political context, Thai NGOs have done well and are generally acknowledged to have contributed to more innovative approaches to development. Especially impressive have been the efforts of a number of NGOs in promoting health care reform. Several small groups, each with limited resources and programs, have realized the importance of coordination and joint compaigns. During the past few years, representatives of the various groups have met from time to time to exchange ideas, information and experience. They have also held joint campaigns to educate the public about drug abuse. One successful campaign held in January 1983 was the movement to abolish the utilization of APC (aspirin, phenacetin and caffeine) combination drugs, whose use was popularized among workers for many years. The campaign raised great public support and resulted in the authorities asking the drug manufacturers to stop producing APC combination drugs within one year. There is at the same time an ongoing campaign against *Yachud*, which is the local term for a combined set of tablets composed of different drug items, with 3-9 tablets placed in one bag. There are several sets of *Yachud* easily available in the market; the most common is used for colds, backaches, malaria, allergies, stomach pains, etc. It has been alleged by some NGOs that more than 75 per cent of people who buy drugs from shops receive ready-packaged *Yachud*, and since every set is composed of antibiotics, steroids and analgesics, this leads to dangerous side effects and the overconsumption of drugs.

In February 1983, a coordinating group of health reform groups in Thailand was established. Today, there are 16 members. Their activities include running an information center, production of a newsletter, organization of conferences and health projects, and generally, in the words of the organizers, "to campaign and educate the people to solve their health problems on the principle of self-reliance." Whether such coordination and networking amongs NGOs will further increase their impact remains to be seen.

Philippines

Of all the ASEAN NGOs, the Filipino ones are the most numerous, the most radical and the most innovative in terms of tactics and strategies. There are NGOs in almost every sphere of life, leading to a great complexity in the social and political process. They have also been most able to reach down to the grassroots, and on a number of occasions, to solicit and obtain the active support of the lower classes. Much of this success is due to painstaking grassroots organizational work by full-time organizers and a people-oriented approach to problem solving, although some Filipino activists will disclaim that NGOs have done enough mass work.

It is also in the Philippines that the ferment of alternative development strategies and alternative systems is most pronounced.

How much of this is due to the more radical Filipino popular political culture and how much to a reaction to the perceived excesses of authority is not clear. Obviously, too, the faltering economy, which has badly affected both the lower and middle classes and which has especially aroused the ire of the latter, has been an important factor in explaining the radicalization of Filipino NGOs. Finally, the church, with a segment of its clergy preaching the theology of liberation, has influenced the moral and ethical basis of many NGOs; but the links between the two are very complex, and it can be said that the church acts as a constraining factor as well as broadening the horizons and assisting the work of NGOs.

The evidence of the larger impact and longer outreach of Filipino NGOs over the past twenty years has been impressive. The urban-based, middle-class, limited-group ferment of the late 1960s has given way to a more broad-based ferment. Although Filipino NGOs have been fairly successful in developing a counterconsciousness to the status quo's own ideology, and to a lesser extent in organizing and mobilizing aggrieved communities to assert their rights, there is still much to be done in the area of formulating, presenting and realizing alternatives. The failure to present clear alternatives can be attributed to an overriding emphasis on problem analysis dealing with specific issues at the local, national or international level. Very little is done to link specific concrete issues with one another in order to have a more comprehensive macro view of sociopolitical and economic processes.

Indonesia

In Indonesia, NGOs have managed since 1965 to survive and consolidate under military rule in the absence of strong oppositional political parties. This in itself is a considerable success. Although their influence on the government has been marginal and at the pleasure of government leaders, government (or at least certain sections of it) has recently begun listening to various NGOs, because it is obvious that they reflect an important segment of the public view.

Among the most active and articulate NGOs are the Legal Aid Institute and various religious organizations, whose impact on government is proportional to the belief that they have public support. The Lembaga Bantuan Hakum in particular has been able, over a period of fifteen years, to arouse some public consciousness of legal, economic and human rights which the government finds difficult to ignore. Pesantren is not only an Islamic school, but also an active vehicle for conscientization, with branches all over Java. Elsewhere in the country, the small ideological changes in the past few years have marginally favored other NGOs, making them more legitimate, while the growth of a highly educated middle class has supplied them with some resources. But strong and continuing opposition from the more conservative elements of society has caused deep concern, as has a proposed law that seeks to limit and control NGOs even more.[16]

Besides the active NGOs, there are a large number that lack a critical and independent position and which see their role as supplementing and supporting national development programs, e.g., family planning, health, nutrition, etc. These NGOs are guided by the government and formal leaders, so their activities are in accordance with government programs. It is often impossible to make a distinction between their activities and those of the government.

Conclusion

In summary, it is important to see NGOs in the region not as a part of an international movement, with their stimulus coming from outside or their program direction influenced from abroad. Nor are the issues which NGOs raise direct transplants of grievances or problems that are foreign. Other clear indications that NGOs are indigenous forces are:

a) All the leadership positions in the most visible NGOs in the region are occupied by nationals.
b) The most prominent and successful NGOs are unique in their philosophy, objectives and modus operandi. They tend to have no precise equivalents in the West.
c) Most of the critical NGOs espouse a developmental strategy that is not biased towards any of the contending ideological systems in the world.

If planners and governments can grasp the notions above and acknowledge that NGOs, being closer to the ground and thus more sensitive to the problems of the community, have a legitimate role to play in social development, then the impact of NGOs in assisting with the resolution of social problems can be greater, and the path to social development can be smoothed. However, should there be greater insistence on a strategy of directed change, i.e., a pattern of centralized control and administration in which the objective and means of development are determined by government agencies working closely with small groups of elites, leaving little or no room for expression of the people's interests through alternative organizations, then both social and political development will be endangered.

Finally, it should be emphasized that despite great pressure, NGOs have persisted in working for social reform and change through peaceful means and open approaches that cut across traditional racial, religious and other social and class lines. They have also articulated the important view that if society is to survive, it must take a long-term and more holistic view of such issues as resource utilization, patterns of consumption and production, and lifestyle and place equity and justice considerations in the forefront of development. These views differ considerably from the short-term, fragmented views of development indulged in by politicians and other vested interest groups in society.

Notes

1. For example, in 1970 there was only one consumer organization in the ASEAN region; today, there are 11 in Malaysia alone and 9 in Thailand.

2. Aliran Kesedaran Negara, *Aliran Speaks* (Penang: Ganesh Printing Works, 1981), pp. 74-5.

3. See, for example, the Worldwatch Institute papers and books, many of which focus on citizen involvement in alternative development strategies, especially Bruce Stoke's "Local Responses to Global Problems: A Key to Meeting Basic Human Needs," Worldwatch Paper 17 (Washington, 1981). See also Ralph Nader and Donal Ross, *Action for Change: A Student's Guide to Public Interest Organizing* (New York: Grossman Publishers, 1973); George Lakey, *Strategy for a Living Revolution* (San Francisco: Freeman and Company, 1973); and Stuart Langton, *Citizen Participation in America* (Lexington, Mass.: D.C. Heath and Company, 1973).

4. See, e.g., "The Fight to Save Malaysia," *New Scientist* 87:1217 (4 September 1980); "Caveat Consumer," *Asian Wall Street Journal* (10 April 1980); and Ruth Norris, ed., *Pills, Pesticides and Profits* (New York: North River Press Inc., 1982).

5. An exception appears to be the Green Party in West Germany, which began its life as a citizens' movement in the field of environment but recently made the decision to participate in the political process directly by offering its own candidates for election. This decision spawned a wide-ranging debate among the movement's supporters, many of whom felt that the movement could contribute more to German society by remaining outside the electoral process.

6. James C.N. Paul and Clarence J. Dias, "Law and Legal Resources in the Mobilization of the Rural Poor for Self-Reliant Development" (unpublished paper, International Center for Law in Development, New York, July 1980), p. 4.

7. Hans Dieter Evers in his useful historical sketch of bureaucratization in three ASEAN countries argues that the "emergence of new strategic groups, i.e., a modern bureaucracy, a modern military, and a modern intelligentsia, might... be seen as taking over the functional roles of the *dewarajas* and *Sultans,* of the *priyayi* and *sakdina* lords, of the monk, priest and *mullah* of pre-colonial Southeast Asia." See his "Bureaucratization and the World Economy in Thailand, Malaysia and Indonesia, 1870-1980," (unpublished paper, Bielefeld, 1983), p. 26.

8. Paul and Dias, "Law and Legal Resources," p. 5.

9. John J. Donohue, "Some Facts and Figures on Urbanization in the Developing World," *Assignment Children* 57/58 (1982): 21-42. The figures following are taken from the article.

10. In the U.N. Population Division, this category contains Hong Kong, the Democratic People's Republic of Korea, the Republic of Korea, Macau and Mongolia.

11. In the U.N. Population Division, this category contains Brunei, Burma, Democratic Kampuchea, East Timor, Indonesia, Lao People's Democratic Republic, Malaysia, the Philippines, Singapore, Thailand and Vietnam.

12. The seminar papers of the earlier years have since published. See, e.g., Consumer Association of Penang, *Development and the Environmental Crisis — A Malaysian Case* (Penang: Sun Printers, 1981) and *Health, Food and Nutrition in Malaysia* (forthcoming).

13. Aliran, *Aliran Speaks*, preface.

14. A term made popular by Ignacy Sachs, a European environmentalist.

15. EPSM, SAM and a small number of other environmental and academic groups have succeeded, for example, in pressing the government to enact an Environment Quality Act, to stop logging in a proposed national park and to reverse a decision to construct a huge dam for a hydroelectric project that would have drowned thousands of acres and displaced traditional settlements. These were significant victories. For details of these campaigns, see Sahabat Alam Malaysia, *State of Malaysian Environment 1980/81* (Penang: Sun Printers, 1981) and *State of the Malaysian Environment 1981/82* (Penang: Sun Printers, 1982).

16. This law is similar to legislation in Malaysia which in 1981 aroused much concern when a bill was introduced in Parliament to amend the existing act and give to the Registrar of Societies, a government appointee, and the Minister of Home Affairs sweeping powers over the activities of societies and associations. The attempt met with strong opposition from over 100 societies. Describing the proposed changes as a serious curtailment of the freedom of association and expression, the societies argued that development "presupposed the critical and creative participation of people rather than the restriction of civil rights." They pointed out that "the numerous societies and associations... had contributed much to the development of healthy and constructive activity in the cultural, educational, religious and socio-economic spheres." (Press release by Coordinating Committee Against the Societies [Amendment] Act 1981, 4 April 1981). The determined resistence put up by the societies and strong public support for their position eventually forced the government to make major concessions in an amended act passed in 1983. Similar opposition has emerged among a wide range of public opinion in Indonesia to prevent the enactment of the new legislation controlling societies and nongovernmental organizations, but it is not yet known whether these efforts have been successful in making the government change its mind.

CHAPTER 32

Adjustment With a Human Face

Richard Jolly

There is no need to describe at length the tragic and deteriorating human situation in many parts of the world today — of rising malnutrition, increasing poverty and a general slowdown and often reversal in the human indicators of development. Already, it is clear that historians of the future will document the early 1980s as a period when nutrition levels in many parts of the world started to deteriorate sharply. The most obvious and the most extreme situation is that of Africa, where the disaster of drought follows a decade or more of misdirected development, national and international, and has pushed some 30 million persons to the extremes of hunger, starvation and often death.[1]

But this is only the visible tragedy. There is a much broader crisis of growing malnutrition which too often remains hidden through a lack of visual and statistical evidence. The World Bank estimates that the number of persons malnourished in Africa has risen from 80 million to 100 million since 1980.[2] UNICEF has been documenting the evidence of child malnutrition from a number of countries, the majority of which show rising levels of both moderate and severe degree malnutrition among the 0-5 age group, the most vulnerable of all.[3] In Ghana, for example, not a drought country, the rate of malnutrition among children age 6 months to 3-½ years doubled from 1980 to 1983.[4] Evidence from Botswana, Malawi and Kenya shows a similar picture. In Zambia, a comparison between surveys of the early 1970s and the early 1980s shows an increase in stunting and a decrease in height for age among all age groups and for both sexes of the under-15 group.[5]

This paper was originally presented as the Barbara Ward Lecture at the 18th World Conference of the Society for International Development in Rome in July 1985. It draws heavily on work, thinking and action in UNICEF over the past year. I am especially grateful for close partnership with Paul Altesman, Andrea Cornia, Denis Caillaux, Farid Rehman, Gerry Helleiner and Frances Stewart. Hans Singer has provided useful comments and endless inspiration. The paper is, however, a personal statement.

In Latin America, starting from levels of nutrition and welfare much higher than in Africa, there is evidence from a number of countries of rising levels of malnutrition, increases in morbidity and a slowdown in the long-term downward trend in infant mortality — and, as in the case of Costa Rica, even some increase in infant mortality. In Asia, where economic growth and dynamism have been better maintained, the picture appears to show continuing progress. But even in the industrialized countries, the tougher economic policies adopted are having a deleterious effect on the poor. In the United States, for example, the nationwide percentage of households below the poverty line has started rising again. In New York City, for example, the proportion of children in poverty is reported to have increased from 15 to 40 per cent.[6]

These reversals are the result of both national and international factors — and in no way should one pretend that the causes are solely, or even mainly, international. In most cases, international and national factors are inextricably linked in ways that are causing severe downward pressures on living standards and welfare services, particularly for the poor. Two years ago, UNICEF undertook a survey of the impact of world recession on children which analyzed the process in a dozen diverse countries — rich and poor, left-wing and right-wing — around the world.[7] This revealed that a multiplier mechanism was at work, transmitting the impact of recession in the industrial countries to the developing countries and within the developing countries, from urban to rural areas and to different income groups and classes. At each stage, the linkages mostly served to multiply the impact rather than diminish it as one moved further along the chain from rich to poor. We termed this "a reverse shock absorber effect" in which the impact on poverty and vulnerability was increased rather than absorbed.

But none of this was inevitable. The reverse shock absorber reflects the ways policies and institutional mechanisms, national and international, are allowed to work. It would be possible to arrange them to work in a different way, like a normal shock absorber.

Conventional adjustment policy serves as a good example. As it mostly operates at the moment, adjustment policy, national and international, transmits and usually multiplies the impact on the poor and the vulnerable. The result, as shown in many countries, is rising malnutrition in the short run — and in the long run, reinforce-

ment of a style of development which will primarily rely on accelerated growth and trickle down, if it works at all, to reduce malnutrition
in the future.

Yet this form of adjustment is no more than the form of adjustment conventionally adopted at present. There are alternatives. It
would be possible consciously to recognize that the human consequences of adjustment should not be left as an inevitable and unfortunate by-product, but treated as an essential concern. The protection of minimum levels of nutritional status and other basic human
needs could be monitored and made as much a part of the objectives
of adjustment as the balance of payments, inflation and economic
growth.

Such a broader approach to adjustment is not only a matter of
human welfare. To miss out the human dimension of adjustment is
not only a human tragedy; it is an economic error of the most
fundamental sort. Much evidence already exists of the economic
returns to investment in human resources.[8] To fail to protect young
children at the critical stages of their growth and development is to
wreak lasting damage on a whole generation, the results of which
may well have effects on economic development and welfare for
decades ahead. Moreover, in the short run, it is plainly absurd to
imagine that economic dynamism can be fully restored when an
important fraction of a country's workers remain malnourished — or
even lacks, as among small-holder peasants in many African countries
today, enough basic goods to buy to provide incentives for extra
effort. Consumption needs are a matter of proportion and degree.
Not every cutback on consumer expenditure is wrong or counterproductive. But there comes a point beyond — or rather, below —
which the cutbacks and reductions of an adjustment process become
absurdly counterproductive to the economic process, let alone to the
political and human viability of a country.

Let me also add here a particular word on giving specific attention
to women in the adjustment process. In part because many of the
important activities of women are not counted in conventional
economic statistics, their vital economic contribution is often underestimated. This is likely to be even more the case with adjustment,
where many forms of cutbacks impinge especially hard on women,
particularly those engaged in small-scale and informal sector activities.
Yet there is much evidence to show that in terms of economic
contribution, use of local resources in place of imports, returns to

investment and employment creation, many women engaged in household and informal sector activities make a disproportionately large contribution to the economic welfare of the poorer sections of the population.[9] Their contribution should therefore be especially encouraged in the adjustment process – not ignored, let alone cut back.

A More Human - Focused Approach to Adjustment

A broader approach to adjustment – "adjustment with a human face," as one might call it – would involve three things.

First, a clear acknowledgement in the goals of adjustment policy of *concern for basic human welfare* and a commitment to protect the minimum nutrition levels of children and other especially vulnerable groups of a country's population.

Second, the *implementation of a broader approach* to the adjustment process itself, comprising four components:

a) Actions to maintain a minimum floor for nutrition and other basic human needs, related to what the country can sustain in the long term.

b) Restructuring within the productive sectors – agriculture, services, industry – to rely more upon small-scale, informal sector producers and to ensure their greater access to credit, internal markets and other measures which will stimulate growth in their incomes.

c) Restructuring within health, education and other social sectors to restore momentum and ensure maximum coverage and benefits from constrained and usually reduced resources. Already there are important examples of what can be done to reach all of a country's population, but still at relatively low cost.

d) More international support for these aspects of adjustment, including the provision of more finance, flexibly provided and with longer-term commitments. The extremes of the present situation will often require a ceiling on outflows of interest and debt amoritization if the protection of human needs is to be feasible in the short run.

Third, *a system for monitoring nutrition levels* and the human situation is needed during the process of adjustment. We should be concerned not only with inflation, balance of payments and GNP growth, but also with nutrition, food balances and human growth. The proportion of a nation's households falling below some basic poverty line should be monitored and treated as one of the relevant statistics for assessing adjustment.

Let me note in passing that in respect of disasters, a number of countries (with the support of international and national agencies) have already made a start with early warning systems for famine, which focus in part on household food security and nutritional indicators. We now need to apply the same concerns not merely to natural disasters but to the man-made consequences of adjustment, and not merely to warn but also to avert the human consequences which often follow.

I have stressed the need for restructuring within the social sectors, in addition to the continued concern with restructuring the economic sectors. Here I must make another general point of fundamental importance. Adjustment policy with a human face will remain a sham — "an attempt to paint a smile on a face with tears" — if it is seen only as a matter of a change in the macroeconomic policy of government. Instead, it must involve a move to a more people-focused process of adjustment, a more fundamental restructuring — a shift to much greater self-reliance, to decentralization, small-scale production and community action, empowerment of people and households. These are the groups and approaches which in fact provide the goods and services and which generate income for the low-income sections of most populations. These are also the sectors which are often squeezed by adjustment approaches as conventionally implemented. Yet for sheer cost-effectiveness, as well as protection for the poor, these are the approaches that matter.

Let me give an example of the type of approach required. Over the last year or two, numerous examples have demonstrated how infant mortality can be reduced and child health and welfare can be improved at a fraction of the cost and a multiplier of conventional effectiveness if people's action and social mobilization are used to apply new technologies on a national scale, using the media and enlightened government leadership. As many will know, this is leading to a dramatic increase in immunization coverage and largely home treatment of diarrhea by ORT (oral rehydration therapy). It has already led in 1984 to an estimated reduction in child deaths by a million per year.[10] This is already making the 1990 goal of universal immunization seem a feasible reality and not just a utopian dream.

This example illustrates the potential and opportunities available but also makes some vital points about adjustment with a human face. It must get down to specifics, both to mobilize public interest and awareness and to make the case with ministers of finance and visiting missions – and to carry this through to planning and implementation when the case is accepted. Macroeconomics can provide a supporting frame, but only when community leaders, sector specialists and a host of others are involved will such an approach work. There are many other areas of alternative approaches to draw upon. They include many of those advocated by basic needs proponents, appropriate technology enthusiasts and community activists in health, housing, small-scale agriculture, water, local manufacture of clothing and transport. Relevant low-cost approaches exist across virtually the whole field of basic needs.

I would stress the need for these groups, including community leaders and sector specialists, to present their case in ways which show its importance for the goals of adjustment. At the moment, the tough, people-oppressing features of many adjustment policies are often supported because the policymakers involved see little alternative. If alternatives are made clear in specific terms, and with cost tags attached, they may often prove more acceptable, even desirable. There is, after all, a political payoff from action which visibly benefits the majority – and this can be an important force for change, especially at times of severe constraint.

To show the possibility for doing more is the first step toward winning political support. There is also a critical need to restructure expenditure in a more difficult and continual area – to reduce the resources flowing to the armaments and the military. Armaments and military expenditures are probably the greatest single area of neglect in adjustment policy, as in economic development analysis. In spite of the constraints of foreign exchange and the tough cutbacks forced by adjustment, in the majority of countries military expenditure has been rising, at least until 1984. In some cases, increases in military expenditure have been greater than financial cutbacks in health and education. Moreover, as Barbara Ward so eloquently and so frequently pointed out, military expenditure is the greatest inflationary factor in the modern world. Military expenditure adds to the difficulties of adjustment and often defeats its purpose. Its enormous use of national resources, especially foreign exchange, for producing a product which is neither bought nor sold makes it a prime force for increasing taxation, inflation or debt, and usually all of them. And the accumulation of armaments not only increases risk and insecurity, but also adds to domestic repression and violence.

There are some particular reasons at this time for reviewing the links between adjustment policy and rising military expenditures, most clearly shown in Latin America. Over the last few years, most Latin American countries have moved dramatically, and mostly democratically, to elections and elected governments. These changes still rest on a fragile base, with a new ne d fo those in power to maintain support from the electorate, ofte. ~ .ch the military still waiting in the wings. The cutbacks and constraints of adjustment on incomes and social expenditures on basic services for the majority hardly make this an easy task, as a number of recent examples make only too clear. Nevertheless, in this world of tight economic constraints, the choice between cutting military expenditure and cutting health, education and other basic services becomes an increasingly direct and evident tradeoff, attracting attention from many parts of the electorate. Combined with measures of collective action (regional or global) toward greater security, these conflicting interests might even be turned to encourage some measure of reduction in military spending.

An Example: Britain During World War II

British experience during World War II provides an example of incorporating nutritional concerns in an adjustment program and of the fact that this can be done even in extreme circumstances, concurrently with successful implementation of adjustment measures.

The adjustment problem faced by Britain during the war was to reduce imports very drastically and restructure industry and the economy for the war effort. All this had to be done very rapidly for a war originally predicted to last no more than 18 months. But in contrast to World War I, protection of the nutritional status of the whole of the British population was made an integral and conscious part of the adjustment process (as it was in a number of other countries). Nutritional needs were defined for each group of the population: babies, young children, older children and adults, pregnant and lactating mothers, and so forth. At Churchill's direction, no distinctions were made between different groups of the population except on the basis of physiological need. Churchill at times explained and defended the program in Parliament, summing it up on one occasion with the memorable phrase: "There is no finer investment than putting milk in babies" – an early and eloquent example of the human capital agrument. (If UNICEF had had a hand in the drafting, we would no doubt have pointed out that milk from mothers is always preferable to milk from bottles!)

Before leaving this example, let me make three points about this experience.

First, it shows there is nothing theoretically or operationally impossible in combining an adjustment program with the objectives and measures required to protect the nutritional status and basic consumption needs of a country's population. This is not to say that other countries can or should do it the same way, but there are sound reasons in all countries to ask how it might be done in their particular circumstances.

Second, the British experience was remarkably successful in nutritional terms. By the end of the World War II, in spite of all the hardships and constraints, the nutritional status of the British population was better than ever before in British history and probably as good as or possibly even better than today.

Third, and this is a point Barbara Ward herself would surely have stressed, it provides a superb example of what the vision and practical leadership of a few people can achieve.

One key figure in this case was Jack Drummond, a professor, scientist and expert in nutrition, who was appointed a month or two after the war had begun to be responsible for the decontamination of food from poisonous gas – a hark-back to the gas fears of World War I. Within three months, Drummond had redefined his job as protecting the nutritional status of the whole of the British population – a much bolder and more fundamental task. That was an example of real vision and scientific initiative.

Another key figure was Lord Woolton, the minister of food, who provided the political leadership and advocacy of the program in Parliament and outside. His inspiration and human concern had grown out of earlier experiences working in the Liverpool slums. The professionalism of the whole program was heavily influenced by Woolton's scientific background and the small circle of top professional scientists he had gathered around him.[11]

Indeed, the whole program was built on a framework of professionalism and science, turned to the protection of basic needs. Keynes, in the background, provided the macro framework for combining a policy for maintaining minimum consumption needs with the pressing claims on resources and government expenditure for the war effort, setting all within a pragmatic combination of government planning and the use of market forces. Those with an admiration for creative journalism might note that the essential elements of all these were originally set out in three articles by Keynes in the *London Times* and then published in early 1940 under the title, "How to pay for the war." Keynes also introduced two other ideas: the child allowance, initially of five shillings per week, designed to provide additional financial support to a family in relation to children's needs, and the idea of constructing what might today be called a "basic needs price index" to monitor the changes in the price of goods required to meet minimum consumption needs.

Before leaving the lessons of history, let me jump ten years forward to the early 1950s and the formative years of the United Nations. As during the war, in the early years of the U.N. one is struck by the creativity and professionalism of so much of the work undertaken. In the U.N. it was applied for peace, international economic relations and the early postwar efforts to tackle economic and social development problems. The names of those involved on the economic side conjure up some sense of the quality of their contributions — though of course at the time, the reputations of many of these persons had yet to be made.

It is not the names I emphasize, but the fact that from this group of international servants and others poured forth a stream of ideas, analyses and proposals which influenced both the international debate and led in a number of important cases to practical and specific action: the World Bank's IDA and the compensatory export finance facility of the IMF, both proposals made in the U.N. itself during the 1950s. This work ultimately led to the creation of UNCTAD.

New Roles for the International Community

This brings me back to today, and to the greater role which I believe the U.N. today could and should play in supporting a broader approach to adjustment. The U.N., in the sense of the core of agencies directly under the Secretary General, has some very natural comparative advantages in fulfilling such a role. The technical agencies of the U.N. are multidisciplinary and already concerned with a variety of the broader, but often neglected, areas of development: women's concerns, children's needs, urban problems, environment, etc. They include the regional commissions, with their special knowledge and focus on the main regions of the world. They also include four major agencies with the resources to support development: UNDP, WFP, UNICEF and UNFPA, which together provide some $2.5 billion of grant support to developing countries each year. Outside this circle are the specialized agencies of ILO, WHO, FAO and UNESCO.

The common element among this core of agencies and the four outside it is their human focus and concern — a human focus which is by no means absent from the programs of the World Bank, but which is certainly less marked in the World Bank and the IMF than in these other agencies. It would be a natural approach to bring the U.N. agencies together in support of some form of special and coherent commitment to the human dimension of adjustment, not merely as a short-term, stopgap arrangement, but as a means for strengthening long-term revival and development on a new basis.

There would need to be, of course, close links — closer links — with the World Bank, but not so close as to merge identities. There are great advantages in approaching the human dimensions of development with human concerns and human-centered objectives uppermost in one's mind, rather than approaching them from the perspective of an instrumental view of people primarily as human capital or of an input into some abstract process of development. Closer links between development agencies of the U.N. and the World Bank and a clearer definition of their respective roles would greatly help, but a merger would be unfortunate.

The IMF raises different issues. Although some of us passionately believe that the IMF needs to take more conscious account of malnutrition and other indicators of human welfare, there will be, I suspect, a strong consensus for keeping its operations limited to the economic and financial mechanisms of adjustment.

The IMF view, as I understand it, is that it has neither the staff, the mandate, nor the technical capacity to extend its analysis and actions much beyond the existing frame. This need not matter, provided the IMF consciously accepts the fact that the human impact of adjustment in the short run, as well as in the long run, is a matter of vital concern. It also needs to ensure that its own guidelines and approaches are broad enough to permit governments and others to take positive actions to protect the nutritional status of vulnerable groups wherever, and with whatever priority, a country chooses. Note that such concerns are already provided for in principle in the IMF's articles, which identify multiple objectives for the Fund's actions, including providing and maintaining high levels of employment, incomes and economic development as primary objectives.

Indeed, there already are precedents for the IMF to look at the nutritional effectiveness of food subsidies and food arrangements. The critical change will require not so much an alteration in the IMF terms of reference as in its willingness to be more positive about specific welfare measures when a government proposes them, and in the acceptance of a more flexible and pragmatic approach to the use of such policy instruments as targeted subsidies. Thus the macro frame for adjustment must be adapted to measures to protect nutrition and improve the incomes of the poorest in two senses. Micro rules must also permit sectoral efficiency in protecting human needs with the resources available and in ways in keeping with the economic, social and cultural context of each country. For instance, approaches to cost recovery of water, education, health services, etc. ought to be matters left to national strategy and political style, taking account of basic needs objectives.

The other requirement of macro adjustment policy relates to the total flow of financial resources available to support countries undertaking adjustment. Almost certainly, the protection of minimum human standards as part of the adjustment policy in a highly constrained economy will require some additional financial support from outside; and such support will have to be sustained over a longer period to permit adjustment to be more gradual. Already this is widely recognized in principle and provides the justification for the World Bank and other development institutions and donors to provide such support. There are two organizational problems which need to be tackled, however.

First, in most cases, the negotiations with the IMF on adjustment policy take place earlier and separately from the broader discussion of development policy. At best, this leads to economic inefficiency, in the sense that the adjustment parts of the program are not fully integrated with the long-term development parts and with the resources required and available to support them. But in the worst cases, demands for an adjustment process are set in motion in an ad hoc and haphazard way, with different donors and voluntary agencies left to deal later with the neglected human dimension. A more coherent and integrated approach is primarily a matter of institution-alizing a coherent discussion of the human and development issues at the time and as part of the original adjustment discussion. In practical terms, the consultative group meetings called by the World Bank and the Roundtable meetings organized by the UNDP would be appropri-ate fora, especially if these meetings formally adopted a commitment to the protection of minimum living standards as part of their agenda.

The second and major omission of macro adjustment at the moment is the inadequacy of the total flow of resources. In the case of Africa, the challenge is as much in decreasing the annual outflows of interest and amortization payments on debt as in increasing the gross inflows of development support. It is not my purpose to enter into a full discussion of these issues; much has been written, and many proposals have been put forward. But I wish to underline the link between the minimum floor for nutritional and basic needs support needed within countries and the minimum flow of finance required from outside.

There comes a point beyond which no variations in adjustment policy can succeed in both protecting the nutritional and welfare needs of the population and in maintaining the outflow of foreign exchange required for servicing very high levels of debt. At that point, a choice must be made. As President Nyerere has said, the choice becomes one of repaying one's debt or starving one's children.

Yet there are examples in history where the need for a ceiling on debt repayments has been recognized. In the case of reparations (the high levels of payment by Germany after World War I), Keynes argued eloquently, but without success, for a reduction. His failure to convince the authorities in time stimulated, as many have recog-nized, the rise of Nazism and the inexorable moves toward World War II.

In the 1930s, a number of Latin American countries called *force majeure* on debt servicing, and some repayments were never completed. An interesting African tradition, known at least in West Africa, is for victors in tribal warfare to take cattle and property from the vanquished, but never so much as to leave women and children with too little to eat. How civilized, compared with our present institutionalized international arrangements!

I do not propose how the issues of debt restructuring, retroactive terms of adjustment, increases in debt prices or increases in financial aid should best be tackled at the moment, especially for the poorest countries in Africa.[12] All I know is that while such issues have long been debated, very little has been done. Must the efforts of countries to protect the nutritional standards of their population be abandoned through lack of international support?

There are, as Barbara Ward eloquently reminded us, benefits to the industrial countries, in terms of economic returns as well as of political stability, of concerted international action to increase support for the poor countries. She proposed a twenty-year Marshall Plan for the Third World, which the Brandt report further elaborated. The fact that this idea is still not a serious item on the international agenda reflects not lack of need or inappropriateness, but the current economic ideology of the dominant and their lack of vision and international leadership. For this reason, much of the Third World languishes. Yet the inadequacy of current inaction will in time be recognized in the North, as it already is in the South, and serious debate on forward movement will return. We who are convinced of the need for change should not falter in our convictions, but should rather explore ways to turn vision into action.

I come finally to the last and most difficult question: what makes me imagine that any of those involved have the slightest interest in a change in approach? Let's not make it seem too easy; but neither should we make change seem impossible. History shows endless examples of the citadels of power and the wisdom of the day resting on sand — sometimes shifting sand, sometimes sinking sand, swallowing up all. The more uncertain the foundations, the stronger the protestations that the base is solid rock.

Keynes proposed that the power of vested interests was vastly exaggerated compared to the power of ideas. Barbara Ward said more poetically, "We learn from the visionaries, we do not learn from the practical men of **affairs**. They are marvellous, once the direction is set, but you will not find them in the forefront. They were not in the forefront in the nineteenth century, they are not in the forefront in the twentieth century."

Certainly there is today much questioning — sometimes rethinking — on adjustment policy among those directly involved, in the international agencies and among the bankers.

It is not difficult to think of Third World leaders struggling to protect or implement a more human-focused approach. Not every Third World leader is concerned, but why should we withhold support from those who are?

And there are also industrial country supporters for a more human-focused approach — governments in a number of cases, and probably a sizable proportion of the population in many others, especially if they knew the facts.

The outpouring of popular support for Africa followed after the ordinary television viewer saw what was happening. The dramatic change of government policies and support *followed that.* Would donor country governments remain so unmoved on debt and adjustment issues if their populations realized what was really happening?

So, stirrings are afoot in many quarters — but existing approaches, with only minor changes, remain in place. And the inefficiencies and absurdities continue, and the people suffer.

What holds us back? Inadequate evidence? Weak arguments? The adequacy of the present situation? The radical nature of alternatives? Every day I become more convinced it is none of these, but the factors systematically ignored by social scientists and too many others: vision, values and leadership.

Here I must quote Barbara Ward again, for she makes the point so much more eloquently than others:

> Virtually everything that works began with a vision and with a group of idealists prepared to work for it. Things which would have seemed inconceivable in early days of history, began with as unlikely a group as the small Quaker movement dedicating itself to the abolition of slavery. Everyone assumed that slavery was part of nature. Yet we have lived through a period in which slavery was abolished. Or take the great events which started with the American Revolution. Or who would have conceived in the 1880s that imperialism would be dissolved in another hundred years?... Our visionary perspective is the true realism and that is what we have got to pursue.[13]

Notes

1. The documents prepared by African ministers of planning and submitted to the OAU meeting provide a sober overview.

2. World Bank, *Towards Sustained Development in Sub-Saharan Africa: A Joint Programme of Action* (Washington, D.C., 1984).

3. UNICEF, *The Neglected Human Dimensions of African Development* (forthcoming).

4. UNICEF, "Situation Analysis of Children in Ghana," (mimeo, Accra, 1984).

5. UNICEF, "The Impact of Recession on Children," Part IV, *State of the World's Children Report* (Oxford University Press, 1984).

6. See, for example, *New Yorker* (April 1985) and also Arden Miller, "Infant Mortality in the U.S.," *Scientific American* (July 1985). The Congressional Budget Office study, *Reducing Poverty Among Children* (May 1985), shows that 22 per cent of all children in the U.S. were classified as poor in 1983 — the highest percentage since 1969, when it was 14 per cent.

7. UNICEF, "Impact of Recession" *SWCR* (1984).

8. See for instance, the World Bank's special issue on the human dimensions of development policy, *World Development Report* (Oxford University Press, 1980).

9. See for instance, *State of the World's Women*, prepared for the Nairobi Conference on the United Nations Decade for Women (1985).

10. See, for a summary, UNICEF's *State of the World's Children Report* (Oxford University Press, 1985).

11. As he explains in *Memoirs of the Rt. Hon. the Earl of Woolton* (London: Cassell, 1959).

12. The report of the SID's North South Roundtable provides some excellent analyses and specific proposals. See Khadija Haq, ed., *The Lingering Debt Crisis*, (Islamabad: North South Roundtable, 1985).

13. These final quotations are from the last public address Barbara Ward gave at the SID/North South Roundtable meeting on the Brandt report held in Sussex in July 1980. See "Beyond Brandt: Menace and Hope," summarized in *Development* 22:4 (1980).

CHAPTER 33

The Human Dimension in Development:
An IDB Perspective

Georges D. Landau

Descriptions of the situation in Latin America these days tends to resemble a long catalogue of woes.[1] Virtually every major economic indicator points to a critical downturn in the region's development infrastructure. After two decades of improvements in social welfare, Latin America has suffered the most from a convergence of factors, including a worldwide recession, depressed commodity prices, falling exports, abruptly rising international rates, the unprecedented appreciation of the U.S. dollar and a crushing burden of external debt.

These factors threaten to wipe out the achievements of these last twenty years, with nefarious consequences in the social context.

Today, Latin America's per capita income is below that of 1976; its output has fallen to pre-1979 levels; investments have sharply declined in every sector; marked contractions have occurred in net capital and credit flows to the region, including export credits; and, contrary to expectations, the recent recovery in the global economy has brought about not an increase or an improvement in the terms of trade of the region, but rather a further deterioration in these terms, higher real rates of interest, sharp declines in imports and significant net outflows of capital.

These grim data, however, conceal pronounced differences between countries, as well as some positive elements. With reference to debt management proper, the Latin American countries espoused a moderate and most responsible approach to the problem and, following some imperative reschedulings under the aegis of the IMF, have strived to honor their commitments by keeping their payments current, thus earning themselves the respect of the international financial community when it would have been easy, and indeed tempting, to go the other way. The rescheduling agreements already concluded have relieved much of the tension, and commercial bankers the world over have sighed with relief.

The structural adjustment programs exacted as part of the price for these reschedulings have proved to be a bitter medicine; but one cannot but admire countries which, albeit at a tremendous social cost (perhaps comparable to that of the industrial revolution in Europe), have adopted stringent austerity measures to cope with these requirements and by so doing are building a better future for their societies. In terms of sheer will power and a capacity for purposeful sacrifice, it has been an impressive performance, and much can be expected from peoples capable of an effort of such magnitude.

The Current Situation in Latin America

Latin America and the Caribbean account for approximately 8 per cent of the world's population, 11 per cent of the world's arable land, 5 per cent of the industrial production and more than 40 per cent of the developing countries' debt. The record shows that the countries of the region, taken as a group, showed notable achievements in economic and social development over the two decades beginning in 1960. Whether one looked at the modernization of their productive structure, their integration into the world economy, the expansion of coverage of social services or the growth of their economies, at the beginning of the 1980s many of the countries in the region could look forward to no longer being considered "less developed" by the end of the present decade.

Statistics alone cannot convey the full consequences of these indicators for society and for the still fragile texture of the democratic institutions in the developing countries of the western hemisphere. The sudden lowering of living standards and widespread economic insecurity engendered by drastic adjustment measures put into effect by Latin American and Caribbean governments in an attempt to bring their payments accounts into balance produced a dramatic rise in social tensions and violence. Rising unemployment, rampant inflation, deep cuts in fiscal expenditures and widespread contraction of business activity profoundly undermined the people's self-confidence and the belief, consolidated by two decades of remarkable progress, that an even brighter future was at hand.

The full significance of the recession that has buffeted the economies of the countries of Latin America and the Caribbean since 1981 and which continues to have severe repercussions despite some signs of an incipient recovery[2] can be appreciated from the fact that the region's total GDP in 1984 was about the same as in 1980, whereas in the intervening four years, the population had grown by more than 33 million.

And yet, since the region's GDP rose in 1984 by more than 2 per cent, even though living standards have not yet begun to improve, that recovery arrested the decline in the per capita product experienced in previous years. This contrasts sharply with per capita GDP declines of 3.3 per cent and 5.3 per cent in 1982 and 1983 respectively. Despite these extraordinary challenges, the Latin American and Caribbean region showed its resiliency by completing another year of difficult adjustment, thanks in no small measure to an additional large trade surplus, based partly on an improved export performance and not just on a curtailment of imports, as had taken place in 1983.

Role of the Inter-American Development Bank

One should consider in this context the role of the Inter-American Development Bank, which was created in 1960 and whose mandate is to foster the long-term economic and social development of the region. This is done primarily through lending directed both towards productive projects — which are not only self-liquidating, in that they produce returns that repay the investment, but which also make a net contribution to a country's economic health — and to others of a developmental nature, aimed at the improvement of the quality of life of peoples within the region.

In carrying out that mandate during the past quarter-century, the Bank has lent over $30 billion for projects whose total investment cost exceeds $100 billion. In December 1983, the member countries of the Bank ratified a general increase in its resources which will enable the institution to lend over $15 billion over the four-year period 1983-86, thus increasing the yearly lending at a nominal rate of 14 per cent per year, rising from approximately $3 billion in 1983 to over $4 billion in 1986. This program is being carried out. Approximately 70 per cent of the funds are expected to flow to the low-income smaller and medium-sized countries of the region, while the remainder will be devoted to projects in the four larger countries — Argentina, Brazil, Mexico and Venezuela — which of course also contain pockets of acute poverty and are in dire need of socially oriented projects.

From the start of the Bank's operations through 1984, about 22 per cent of lending went to help finance projects aimed at expanding agricultural production and improving standards of living in rural areas; about 27 per cent has been devoted to energy projects; another 18 per cent went for social development projects, including water supply and sewerage systems, education, health facilities and urban renewal; and some 16 per cent was used to extend credit to industry, mining and tourism. The remaining 13 per cent has been devoted to economic infrastructure (major roads, ports and communication facilities). Looking at the current (1983-86) four-year capital replenishment period, the IDB's lending activities are being concentrated in three broad investment areas: agricultural and rural development, urban development, and energy. Although the Bank provides funding only for specific development projects, it was nonetheless able to take a number of measures which eased some very difficult situations. Such measures included the provision of additional funds for projects which were in jeopardy because of a shortage of local counterpart resources; the shifting of resources to higher priority undertakings; and the provision of import financing to facilitate industrial recovery, not only for the purpose of generating revenue, but also as a means to absorb large contingents of unemployed or underemployed manpower.

As a development financing institution, the Bank has continued to provide resources on concessional terms for socially oriented programs considered to be of paramount importance by the concerned countries themselves in the context of balanced development.

Against the backdrop of Latin America's cogent needs for investments in the social aspects of development (education, health and human welfare), the creation of the IDB in 1960 responded to the region's long-standing aspiration for a financial institution capable of promoting both economic growth and a more equitable distribution of its benefits. Thus, a mandate to foster the human dimension in development has been embodied in the IDB's charter from its inception at a time when no other international financial institution envisaged the inclusion of the social sectors in its lending portfolio, as only projects involving the infrastructure of growth were then deemed eligible for financing. Only much later did development come to be equated with growth-cum-equity, and it can be said that the Bank, with its unblemished record of loan repayments by its Latin American borrowers (holding the majority of the institution's shares), played a major role in that regard.

Given the fact that due to per capita ceilings and other restrictions on concessional financing by other institutions, the Bank is still the principal purveyor of credit to Latin America, the importance of its operations in the social sectors of development in the region can easily be assessed. An impressive array of statistics can be marshaled to this effect. For instance, the Bank has been a major contributor to Latin America's social development in that during the period 1960 to 1980, the percentage of the region's urban dwellers provided with potable water systems rose from 40 to 75 per cent, i.e., from 41 to 168 million; life expectancy has been extended by six years, whereas infant mortality has dropped significantly, from 9.2 to 7.2 per thousand during the same two decades; and while the total population increase was during that period on the order of 70 per cent, Latin America being a region with one of the highest demographic dynamics in the world, primary education enrollment advanced by 186 per cent, secondary enrollment by 354 per cent and enrollment in higher education by 782 per cent. Altogether the Bank, during its first twenty-five years of existence, extended credits totaling some 30 billion dollars at the current rate of over $3.5 billion per annum, making it possible to finance development projects costing more than three times as much.

Nevertheless, the progress achieved by the region during two decades of unprecedented growth at the average rate of 6 per cent per annum is in real danger of being completely wiped out, with a vengeance, by the current economic and financial crisis, as the per capita product plummeted by nearly 10 per cent, imports fell by 40 per cent, the debt burden climbed to a virtually intolerable burden of $370 billion for the region as a whole, and Latin America became a net exporter of capital on a massive scale, due mainly to interest payments on the outstanding debt.

While operations have been launched to meet this radically changed situation — for instance, industrial rehabilitation loans designed to cope with the growing idle capacity in the region's manufacturing sector, or starting a special operating program geared to promoting the timely completion of priority ongoing projects threatened by acute shortages of counterpart funding, as well as initiating urgently needed new ones — the truth is that notwithstanding the availability of IDB concessional resources, by virtue of structural adjustment programs to which the critical debtor countries are subject, there is a much-reduced demand for lending for social development purposes, inasmuch as the domestically available counterpart financing tends to be used for export-oriented projects and others which can generate revenue linked to debt servicing and amortization.

This situation may, if allowed to persist, lead to pronounced social imbalances in the region which, coupled with widespread, growing unemployment and underemployment and a potentially explosive situation in large metropolitan centers already incapable of providing essential services to their burgeoning populations, could result in unbearable social and political tensions exceeding the resilience of Latin America's relatively fragile democratic systems.

Education

While it is today regarded as a self-evident truth that the human element in development is a fit subject for capital investment, with a high multiplier effect, this was not always so; and the IDB has pioneered in the field with its loans for education, science and technology. Over the years the Bank has helped, with loans in excess of US$ 1.3 billion, to modernize, expand or improve 3,176 learning centers throughout Latin America, including 142 universities and research centers, 109 vocational or technical schools and 2,925 primary or secondary schools. The Bank continues to invest heavily in the educational sector, particularly in the vocational field, including such far-reaching unconventional projects as the establishment of revolving funds for student loans benefiting some 750,000 students, a scheme for education by radio in Colombia, training for craftsmen under a small-projects financing scheme aimed at grassroots groups normally beyond the pale of creditworthiness, and other innovative initiatives, including the training of scientists and other researchers in priority areas of applied technology.

The Bank's initial lending in the education sector, complemented by technical cooperation and, in particular, preinvestment operations, was primarily oriented toward higher education, which was perceived as yielding the highest rate of economic return in terms of training of skilled instructors for all other types and levels of education. The areas emphasized were agricultural science, engineering, natural science, public health, economics, public administration and business management, with the object of contributing to the development in each borrowing country of a critical mass of highly qualified personnel capable of filling the need for human resources in the priority sectors required by economic growth and development. In these early years, when the Bank stood alone in providing external financing for the education sector, the accent was placed on institutional development of the concerned public agencies, the design of appropriate scientific and technical curricula, the gradual introduction of full-time teaching, the combination of teaching and research and the reorganization of universities.

In subsequent years, the Bank has been emphasizing loans to secondary and technical vocational education in order to augment and improve the supply of skilled personnel for both supervision and technical functions in industry, trade, and agriculture. Moreover, the Bank has been investing in rural elementary education within the framework of integrated rural development projects, which the IDB also helped to pioneer among international financial institutions. The same applies to credits for student loans, whereby the Bank has assisted in providing access to education for students of low-income families.

By the mid-1970s, it became apparent that the Bank should reexamine the functional scope of its operations for the financing of social development projects in the light of the pronounced changes which had taken place in Latin America since the institution's founding.[3] The need was felt, for instance, for a reconciliation of supply and demand for skilled manpower, with its corollary in an increase in capability for educational planning. Furthermore, it was found that the promotion of social development, as part of the Bank's mandate, would necessitate a comprehensive approach to both urban and rural areas. In the field of education, this reassessment could not but take account of the fact that, partly due to the Bank's own efforts, enrollment in higher education within the region had jumped from less than 600,000 in 1960 to more than 4 million by 1976, and that in view of the extremely high capital investment that would be required to defray the cost of new educational facilities at all levels needed just to accompany the pace of demographic expansion, far surpassing the region's financial resources, new financial resources and new financial formulas would have to be devised.

This led the Bank to sponsor three seminars on the financing of education in 1976, 1978 and 1980 with the participation of outstanding experts and, at the third one, of government representatives as well.[4] This led ultimately to a review of the Bank's policy guidelines for lending in the educational sector, reflecting the new directions already mentioned. It was found at these seminars, for instance, that the emphasis in credit for the sector at both the national and the external financing levels would have to be shifted from high unit-cost secondary and postsecondary levels to low unit-cost primary levels, with the attendant social and economic benefits accruing to lower-income groups, especially the marginal sectors of the population in both urban and rural areas. In that context, forms of vocational training and technical education were considered that might enable new kinds of nonbudgetary fiscal resources (e.g., social security) to be brought to bear on the problem.

A fairly typical example of the Bank's lending in the educational sector was an operation recently approved by the board for Haiti in the form of a loan of US$ 11.9 million, plus $ 1.5 million in grant technical cooperation, to expand primary and normal school education in that country — the least developed in the western hemisphere.

The quality of instruction in primary schools in Haiti, particularly in rural areas, is marked by serious deficiencies. Only an estimated 5 per cent of the rural population speaks French. Thus, one of the objectives of the educational reform program established in 1980 has been to introduce Creole as the basic language of instruction in the first four years of schooling. Accordingly, the Haitian government has awarded high priority to the upgrading of education under its 1982-86 development plan. The total cost of the project is estimated at US$ 14 million, of which the Bank loan will cover 85 per cent.

The loan will be used by the Haitian Education Ministry to carry out a program designed to improve the physical infrastructure of the public school system in the rural areas and to expand basic education coverage and enrollment in normal schools. This will involve the repair and construction of classrooms, the construction of teacher housing at schools in remote areas, and the expansion and outfitting of workshops at the normal schools, as well as providing furnishings and equipment for all these schools, printing and distributing textbooks for students' and teachers' manuals, training 3000 teachers for public and private primary schools in the implementation of new educational methods and programs, and developing a new curriculum for the normal school and new textbooks and manuals for teachers.

The loan was extended from the Bank's Fund for Special Operations for a term of forty years, at an interest rate of 1 per cent per annum for the first ten years and 2 per cent thereafter. It will be disbursed in dollars or other non-Haitian currencies which make up the fund and will be repaid in semiannual installments, the first of which will be due ten and a half years after the date of the loan contract. While other loans made by the Bank for the advancement of education in Latin America may not be quite as concessional as this one to Haiti, this particular operation may be regarded as representative for the sector.

The broad sector of education also includes training in the context of the Bank's loans, which often include a technical assistance component, frequently in the form of grants designed to provide the specific skills required by the operation of, e.g., new equipment financed by a Bank loan, or to strengthen the borrowing country's institutional development in the concerned sector. It can be estimated that the Bank has helped to train no less than 35,000 persons over the years in particular development-related skills.

Housing and Urban Development

In the area of housing and urban development, again, the IDB was active long before other international lending institutions, having started its activities in this field by supporting the financing of credit for housing low-income families. This was not easy to achieve, because the income levels of the intended beneficiaries were not high enough to keep up with the required amortization of the credits made available; and in practice, the criteria for eligibility in many of these programs had to be expanded to include groups with higher incomes able to pay the mortgages. In 1971, concerned with an insufficiently dynamic return on capital invested in this field in the face of competing social claims, the Bank revised its policy by reorienting its lending toward the support of urban planning and development, including participation in integrated urban development programs in which housing is only one of many components, and where coordinated investments may include the provision of services such as water, sewerage, transport, health, education and community development. Financing for sites and services programs has largely replaced direct support for housing (in which IDB funding nevertheless had made it possible to build or improve 407,900 units), and recognition of the informal (marginal) urban sector as a field for lending is another recent innovation by the Bank.

Social Sector

A general characteristic of the Bank's activities is the high priority given by the institution to the support of low-income groups, so much so that for its fifth capital replenishment exercise covering the period 1979-82, the board of governors of the Bank, reflecting its paramount concern for the distributive impact of the IDB's lending, directed that about half of the lending program for that period be directly oriented toward benefits to the lower-income groups, primarily through projects aiming at the creation of productive employment in both urban and rural areas. The same orientation was preserved in the Bank's current replenishment exercise (1983-86). Results for 1984 reveal that 40 per cent of the benefits of the loans from the Bank's own resources accrue to low-income groups, even though the loan programs in 1984 and 1983 were typical, since many of the Bank's loans in those two years went for supporting export-oriented industries and providing additional financing for projects already in execution.

Although Latin America experienced moderate recovery in 1984, the labor force continued a grow at a faster pace than new jobs. Open unemployment in urban areas is at the highest level recorded since 1970. The average unemployment rate in the region rose by more than 4 percentage points from 1970 to 1984, rising from 6.5 per cent to nearly 11 per cent.

Underutilization of labor, which characterized the region in the 1970s, expanded considerably during the recession. During the earlier period, open unemployment affected primarily the secondary labor force, consisting mostly of young people not generally heads of households, while persons with middle-level education tended to experience greater difficulties in locating jobs.

A new IDB report emphasizes that the new unemployment is more critical in that it exerts direct pressure on family income.[5] A significant portion of the increase in unemployment involves previously employed workers in the 25 to 44 age group. Adults working in industry and in the construction trades, who have lower levels of education, have been particularly hard hit. In many cases, employment in the public sector has also declined. This means that the public sector has not been able to play the countercyclical role expected of it during economic recessions.

Reduction in the length of the workday and a decline in minimum wages, as well as in industrial and construction wages, have also accompanied the crisis. Industrial and construction wages have reached lower levels in 1983 than those of 13 years ago in real terms. An increase in the informal urban sector, characterized by low productivity and meager incomes, has also been noted, contributing to the reduction in average incomes.

The intensity of the crisis and the consequences of adjustment policies have varied among the Latin American countries because of the different policies adopted by each of them and because of variations in the level of socioeconomic development. For the region as a whole, however, employment and wages have been very adversely affected. Faced with the economic and social consequences of falling incomes and deteriorating income distribution patterns, a number of Latin American governments have initiated special employment programs and provided subsidies for the hiring of labor, increased shifts in industry and promoted recovery in housing contruction.

The financing of social investments has faced particularly severe restrictions in the region. In an effort to ameliorate the situation, the Bank in 1984 approved a number of projects in education, expansion of the social infrastructure and health.

Public and Environmental Health

Yet another sphere of operations of the Inter-American Development Bank, and indeed, one in which it pioneered among international financial agencies, is that of environmental and public health. The Bank's very first loan was made in 1961 for upgrading the water supply system of the city of Arequipa in Peru at a time when the supply of water and sewerage systems was quite limited in Latin America, particularly among the urban and rural poor. Of around 200 million people inhabiting the region in 1960, of whom half resided in cities (the proportion is now 67 per cent and rising fast), only 40 per cent had access to potable water in their homes. The availability of sewerage systems was quite restricted in the urban areas and very limited in the countryside. For the Latin America and

Caribbean region as a whole, the provision of potable water and sewerage systems, of which IDB financing accounted for no less than 6,445 facilities, has represented an important contribution toward health improvement, noticeable in particular in the reduction of infant mortality and the raising of average longevity to the age of 65. In addition, the bank has helped to build or equip public health facilities ranging from rural clinics to full-fledged hospitals for some 13 million persons. For instance, a rural health program in Honduras, financed in part with resources from the Norwegian Trust Fund, led to substantial improvement in the country's health care services. Moreover, several technical cooperation projects were approved in the areas of human resource training, socioeconomic research and studies to improve social infrastructure services.

As an active member of the Committee of International Development Institutions on the Environment (CIDIE), launched in 1980, whose guiding principles are reflected in the IDB's internal policies for the sector, the Bank is consistently endeavoring to strengthen its credit and technical cooperation operations so that borrowing countries in Latin America and the Caribbean can preserve their natural resources by giving proper attention to the environmental impact of their own national development plans.

Agriculture and Rural Development

The Bank was the first international institution to venture into the financing of rural development on a large scale. During the early period (1961-67), the Bank's financing in this sector focused on agrarian reform, land settlement, potable water supplies and rural roads. During a later period (1968-74), these efforts were expanded to include support for productive activities of small-scale farmers through the financing of irrigation and farm credit, marketing programs, research and extension services. The Bank's loans for agriculture represent 22.8 per cent of its cumulative portfolio over a quarter-century, which reflects the countries' changing explicit or implicit priorities. Thus, Latin American agricultural production has generally been increased during the 1960s and mid-1970s by extending the land under cultivation through irrigation or land colonization. In this regard, the Bank has helped to improve some 15 million hectares of agricultural land. The agricultural credit programs were mainly complementary to the objective of area expansion. Simultaneously, the Bank has had a permanent interest in financing small-holders through irrigation, colonization and land reform, and integrated agricultural and rural development. While the nomenclature of these projects has changed over the years, their objectives and designs have not been greatly modified.

Lessons have been learned in organizing complex agricultural investment projects which require the integration of several subsectoral activities and normally involve the participation of different organizations in the preparation and execution of the program. This often leads to complex coordination among these organizations, requiring agreements on a comprehensive set of factors which include the definition of responsibilities, timing of execution, supervising roles and reporting mechanisms, to mention just a few. Different institutional styles and organizational structures with their respective policies and procedures create the need to devote a great deal of effort to coordinating work among the different project participants.

In recent years, in view of the changing emphasis from land expansion to greater agricultural productivity, the bank has responded by supporting technological development through the International Agricultural Research Centers in Latin America, CIMMYT in Mexico, CIAT in Colombia, and CIP in Peru, all three linked to the Consultative Group on International Agricultural Research (CGIAR) coordinated by the World Bank, of which the IDB has become an important supporter. The Bank has also extended loans and technical cooperation to national research and extension programs. Moreover, agricultural global loans and rehabilitation and irrigation loans, among others, now tend to stress complementary technological development within each subsector. Natural resource management has become a critical factor in promoting the conservation of renewable resources and increasing productivity on existing lands. The Bank has responded to government interest in these activities through the support of river basin and regional development programs.

The Bank's participation in agriculture has suffered from the chronic shortage of agricultural investment projects in the region, and it has been learned that traditional preinvestment lending is not well suited to agriculture, because project identification and preparation work in this sector are very complex, costly and time-consuming. As governments assign higher priority to agriculture, attention to project identification and preparation activities becomes a major concern.

Nevertheless, the agriculture sector in Latin America has in recent years (since 1975) failed to reach the growth rates that characterized it before that year, and the growth in output has barely kept up with the region's demographic increments. There is a long-term trend toward a decline in the relative share of agriculture for the region (17 per cent in the early 1960s, 11.8 per cent in 1983). However, the sector's dynamics must improve significantly if it is to play a major role in the economic recovery of the region in the years to come. There is no question but that the policy environment at the beginning of this decade, marked by a forced drive toward the improvement of the trade balance for the principal debtor countries and therefore by a dramatic reduction of investment, negatively affected the agricultural sector's performance. Despite the fact that the Latin American region has traditionally been a large net agricultural exporter, especially of foodstuffs, its imports for the sector have risen much more swiftly than its exports. In particular, food imports rose by 128 per cent between 1973 and 1983.

This situation points to the critical need for integrated food strategies, which the Bank has been promoting throughout the region, partly in cooperation with the World Food Council. The Bank has likewise conducted an in-depth review of its internal policy for the financing of nutritional projects so as to better adapt it to the requirements of the poorer segments of the population. Operations in certain subsectors, such as livestock production, fisheries and aquaculture, have also been intensified. In the latter subsectors, it is noteworthy that the Bank has made cumulative investments on the order of $300 million, which should enable per capita production of fish products (22 kilograms per annum, of which only 7 kilograms are food intake) to double over the next few years.

The Bank's institutional concern for the welfare of the lowest-income groups of the population in both rural and urban areas was reflected in the creation in 1978 of a Small Projects Financing Program designed to bring the benefits of credit to poor and largely uneducated persons beyond the pale of creditworthiness so as to bring them into the economic mainstream as useful producers of goods and services. Under this program, the Bank extends a loan — not a grant, although the terms are very soft indeed — for a maximum of $500,000 to a nonprofit intermediary organization such as a cooperative foundation or producers' association, which then on-lends the money to low-income people and guides them (sometimes with the help of additional Bank-financed technical assistance) in the production of crops, handicrafts and other goods. This program has been remarkably successful, and the $55 million or so lent since its inception have directly benefited some 50,000 low-income farmers, small-scale entrepreneurs and craftsmen. Along with the credit, beneficiaries receive assistance in planning and improving their production and in marketing their products.

One corollary of this particular program, as well as of the implementation of Bank policies in several sectors, is the direct benefits it has brought to women, heretofore largely bereft, as a group, of the social benefits of development. In Uruguay, for instance, the program has financed a women's handicrafts cooperative with such success that it is now an exporter, with sales skyrocketing tenfold within a very brief period, thus bringing about a marked improvement in the quality of life of its members. Indeed, the cooperative has now launched a five-year expansion scheme which will offer employment to 500 new craftswomen.

The Special Role of Women in Development

In 1976, females in Latin America comprised only 49 per cent of total primary and secondary school enrollment; but between 1960 and 1976, the percentage of women in universities went from 30 to 41 per cent of total student enrollment. The annual growth rate of women's participation in the labor force in Latin America is estimated for 1980-85 at 3.8 per cent, compared with 2.6 per cent for men. At this rate, the ranks of women workers will more than double by the year 2000. More women within the region than men are migrating to the cities — 58 per cent of the total female population lives in urban areas. Many of them are single parents. Around the world, one out of three households is headed by a woman. In parts of Latin America, the figure is as high as 50 per cent. Single or married, with or without children, women are becoming an ever more important earners of family income. Changes being brought about by development are pointing to major needs for training or retraining women in the labor force. While progress in the form of mass-produced goods and modern services has alleviated some of women's household chores, it has often deprived them of small income earned from activities they have traditionally performed; and frequently, when production methods are modernized, opportunities to learn new skills are made available first to men. In both instances, loss of income serves as an added incentive to women to migrate to the cities in search of jobs. The Bank, attentive to the problems derived from women's role in development, has been endeavoring through a variety of policies, notably in the educational sector, to further their chances of employment in both urban and rural areas as well as to provide extra services such as day-care centers which can help working mothers keep their jobs.

The Financial Equation

With a current population of some 370 million inhabitants (which amounts to a per capita external debt of US$ 1,000), predicted to increase through the year 2025 — when the expected population will be of 845 million, or 550 million by the end of this century, barely fifteen years hence — it is obvious that Latin America and the Caribbean and the development institutions serving them must vigrously pursue the twin goals of economic growth and social justice. These demographic indicators mean that in order not to surpass its present high unemployment rate, since reducing it appears infeasible, the region is faced with the well-nigh impossible task of creating an average of four million jobs annually over each of the next 30 to 40 years, nearly all of them in the cities[6] — most of which are already lagging behind deplorably in the provision of even the most essential social services.

From the foregoing, it will be seen that the Inter-American Development Bank has been active in the promotion of a number of human elements of the development process, consistent with its original mandate and, indeed, before any other multilateral financing institution found such elements eligible for the provision of international credit.

But it should be equally apparent that the magnitude of the resources involved exceed manifold the aggregate capability of all the external financing agencies operating in the area, the bulk of the investment having to come from the countries themselves — as has always been the case — and, to a much larger extent than before, from the private sector in the form of foreign direct investment and, as regards lending, complementary financing operations.

Direct investment should be bolstered by the recent creation of mechanisms such as the Multilateral Investment Guarantee Agency (MIGA) of the World Bank group and, in the case of Inter-American Investment Corporation, a new affiliate which should become operational early in 1986. As to complementary financing, which has enabled the IDB to channel resources (amounting by the end of 1984 to $642 million) from commercial banks and other financial institutions from nine OECD countries to development projects in Latin America, this is a means for capital mobilization that has yet to reach its full potential.

Consisting as it does in the sale of participations to the financial institutions submitting the most competitive bids for the full amount of loans made by the Bank (and without recourse to it) in given projects, the nature of the projects, whether for directly productive purposes or for social development goals, becomes immaterial. In such arrangements, the loan terms are frequently more favorable to the borrower than if the resources had been secured independently and, due to the Bank's intervention in the analysis, implementation and financial management of the project, often permit the borrower to raise capital which would not otherwise have become available. As an added feature, since the complementary financing loans are, technically speaking, also IDB loans, they have not been subject to either defaults or debt rescheduling, thus making them an attractive and secure investment in these troubled times.

Of all the Latin American and Caribbean countries suffering from the current financial crisis, the hardest hit are obviously the least developed in the region. The board of governors of the Bank accordingly decided at a special meeting held on September 24, 1985, to broaden the scope of the IDB's financing operations to provide increased support for these countries during the 1983-86 period, thus taking into account the difficulties being experienced by them, as well as by the other nations of the region, in raising local counterpart resources for their development projects.

Under the expanded criteria, the Bank will be able to provide foreign exchange credits for up to 90 per cent of the total cost of social infrastructure projects. Moreover, as of 1986, a portion of the foreign exchange resources of the Bank's concessional window, the Fund for Special Operations (FSO), will be eligible for allocation to investments in selected areas of agriculture, rural development and urban development, provided that they mainly benefit low-income population groups.

Under the Bank's sixth replenishment agreement, covering the 1983-86 period, the IDB's capital resources were increased by $15 billion and the FSO by $703 million. All the resources of the Fund are to be devoted to the Bank's least-developed countries, which include Bolivia, the Dominican Republic, Ecuador, El Salvador, Guatemala, Guyana, Haiti, Honduras, Nicaragua and Paraguay. FSO resources in those countries are being primarily targeted on social infrastructure projects in education, health and nutrition and water and sewerage systems benefiting mainly low-income groups, as well as on preinvestment studies.

Development financing institutions worldwide have begun to suffer the "aid fatigue" that has set on in some of the principal donor countries. This poses the challenge of devising new formulas for the mobilization of resources intended for development, as well as new delivery systems that will optimize the effectiveness of such aid. Just as structural adjustment is a harsh medicine that debtor countries have to take, with certain caveats, with a view to bringing their finances into order, so is the rationalization of aid-rendering a sometimes painful, but ultimately healthy, process of attuning often ponderous institutions to the new realities we are witnessing on the international economic scene. Among the institutional galaxy of multilateral development-oriented agencies, the UNDP and the regional development banks consistently stand out as institutions which have demonstrated their ability to respond swiftly to these new challenges. The growth of regional development banks in Africa, Asia, the Islamic countries and even at the subregional level illustrates a welcome trend towards the regionalization of aid and points up the need for linking it to strict investment banking criteria designed to optimize the effectiveness of the capital made available to the recipients. Furthermore, the ability of the regional development banks to tap private sector resources and associate them with their own credits under various cofinancing schemes augurs well for the mobilization of resources for long-term development programs and projects at a time when official development aid is all but drying up.

Conclusion

The challenge of financing social development projects in Latin America and the Caribbean is a significant one. The Bank is both aware of its responsibilities in this regard and willing to experiment with innovative formulas to assist its borrowing member countries in mobilizing the required resources. This is so despite — and indeed, with particular cogency, due to — their current severe financial crisis. It is essential that the human dimension in development be not only preserved during this crisis, but even further enhanced. The key word in this context is innovation. Clearly, the new challenge with which the international community is confronted, which in essence amounts to the maintenance of human dignity in the face of increasing economic dislocation, calls for new, untried approaches, ranging from high statesmanship to the grassroots level. The resources of Latin America and the Caribbean, human as well as natural, represent a vast and only partially tapped endowment which, with proper undertaking, can be of incalculable benefit to all mankind. The demographic time bomb can indeed be turned into an asset.

What it requires is an openness of spirit to new solutions and the political will to put them into effect. With reference to Latin America and the Caribbean, it is therefore of critical importance to bear three points in mind:

a) The problems faced by developing countries are long-term ones, and solutions need to be devised accordingly to resolve fundamental structural and financial issues. Deep-rooted recession cannot just disappear.

b) Any attempted approaches to the solution of the developing countries' economic and financial crisis must take account of their profound social and political effects in these countries, which could affect their stability. Economic instruments do not operate in a social vacuum.

c) Nothing that is attempted by way of a solution to the problems confronted by developing countries fails to have consequences for industrial nations as well. In today's world, interdependence is a fact, not a myth.

Overcoming these structural problems while enhancing the quality of life and the stature of man demands a synergism, an intertwining of wills for the common good and an innovative approach to development which from every perspective considers the human dimension, of which we so often lose sight.

Notes

1. For the sake of convenience, the expression "Latin America" shall be construed in this article as comprising the Latin nations of North, Central and South America, as well as those, whether or not of Latin stock, of the Caribbean.

2. IDB, *Annual Report for 1984* (Washington D.C., March 1985).

3. IDB, "The Role of the Bank in Latin America in the 1980s" (Washington, D.C., April 1981).

4. See, e.g., IDB, "The Financing of Education in Latin America" (Washington, 1978).

5. IDB, "Economic and Social Progress in Latin America" (Washington, D.C., 1985).

6. See Robert W. Fox, "Population Issues and the Pace of Change in Latin America" (IDB Reprint Series No. 119, 1982), p. 82.

CHAPTER 34

International Institutions and Human Development: A Critique

Uner Kirdar

All development must be seen as a process through which one lives, learns and participates, rather than as a static phenomenon. In global development, a concern of the international community for the past four decades, the praiseworthy efforts made at both the national and international levels, have doubtless brought about direct and manifold improvements in human conditions unprecedented in the annals of history. Yet for many developing countries in the mid-1980s, this process shows distinct signs of faltering. The development gains of four decades now appear at risk. Drawing on the rich experiences of those forty years, what are the lessons to be learned from the achievements and from the failures?

In the postwar era of the late 1940s, '50s and '60s, most development efforts were based on the neoclassical belief that successful growth could best be ensured through a massive transfer of capital resources from developed to developing countries, which would permit urban industrialization and modernization. This belief probably emanated from the achievements of Marshall Plan — the multi-billion-dollar grant form of aid from the U.S. to Europe in the late 1940s — which ensured the speedy, miraculous postwar recovery of the European countries.[1] However, the Marshall Plan was not an exercise in development, but rather an initiative to help restore economies which were ravaged by war — economies in which there was a strong human and institutional infrastructure, and where the only requirement was the transfer of capital.

Later, in the 1960s and 1970s, while recognizing the continuing need for sustained capital assistance, the importance of better terms of trade and increased trade flows from developing countries was highlighted. In the current decade, monetary aspects of the development process have gained prominence.

Each of these aspects, albeit highly relevant to the process of development, is a *means* to achieve development, but cannot be considered as the *objective* of development. It has frequently been overlooked that individual people are at the core of *all* development efforts, and that human skills and human capacity determine the success or failure of these efforts. It is now becoming more widely recognized that one of the underlying obstacles to the development process in many developing countries is the insufficient attention given to the development of human resources. In many cases the "capacity and management gap" between developed and developing countries has not been bridged by international financial assistance, which is used predominantly for physical capital formation.

In the early 1970s, a new interest was born at the international level in the issues of poverty alleviation, income redistribution and the satisfaction of basic needs. But the ways and means of how to fully and best utilize the human resources of the developing countries in pursuing these objectives were not adequately assessed, nor was the potential for exploring the complementarity between these objectives and growth realized. Moreover, this era of concern with equity and basic needs proved to be short-lived, as it was overtaken by the oil and international debt crises of the 1970s and 1980s. In the midst of an ongoing world financial and debt crisis, adjustment measures in most developing countries have been secured, unfortunately, at high human costs — high in terms of lost output, depressed employment and rising poverty levels. Austerity programs at the implementation level have resulted in a serious curtailment of investment in human resources.

In brief, the deficiencies and shortcomings of the policies and strategies of the past four decades, which relied too much on capital and natural resources and neglected the human element both as an input and as an objective of development, are becoming increasingly clear. Looking at the record of the past forty years, the international community is compelled to reconsider the very essence and objectives of development, as well as strategies for its achievement. Certainly, there is no one and only way to ensure development. Development is a complex process. Each country varies in size, political system, population, climate, resources, heritage, etc. The economies of the developing countries at present are diversified. Their needs may vary according to their stage of development. Therefore, one cannot claim to design a single, miraculous, universal strategy for development. However, one fact is clear: in the development process, solutions which do not take the human dimension properly into account will fail to provide an enduring answer; and until the human resources needed for sustained economic growth are developed, real development will remain a dream. Literate, educated, motivated people are the fundamental resource required for development.

During the past forty years, the organizations of the United Nations system have played an important and prominent role in promoting international policies, shaping global strategies for economic and social development and ensuring their implementation. The subject of this paper is to examine the role and evaluate the performance of these organizations in highlighting the importance of human development in the overall development process and, in so doing, to advocate the need for the elaboration of a multidisciplinary and multifaceted development policy in this respect.

Sectoral Organizations

Since their creation, the sectoral specialized agencies and organizations of the United Nations, such as the International Labor Organization, the World Health Organization, UNESCO and UNIDO, have performed commendable tasks and functions in developing operational programs and doing research work in human resource building related to their respective areas of competence. These activities, however, have been understandably confined to the sectors with which they are mainly concerned and have remained within the limited classical definition of human resource development, namely, education, training, skill formation, etc. As this paper aims to review the institutional aspects of human development in the broader sense, the sectoral agencies' and organizations' performances are not considered, and only those of the central institutions of the U.N. system are examined.

The United Nations

Taking into account the reasons for the failure of the League of Nations at San Francisco in 1945, it was clear to the signatories of the United Nations Charter that durable international peace and a security system could not be achieved unless effective measures were taken to solve major economic and social problems. Accordingly, a series of articles concerning economic and social cooperation were incorporated into the charter. Its preamble declared that "the peoples of the United Nations [were] determined to promote social progress and better standards of life... to employ international machinery for the promotion of the economic and social advancement of all peoples." Article I stated that "the purpose of the United Nations [is] to achieve international co-operation in solving international problems of an economic, social, cultural and humanitarian character." Articles 55 and 56 pointed out that "the United Nations shall promote... higher standards of living, full employment and conditions of economic and social progress and development" and "take joint and separate action" for the achievement of these purposes.

During the past four decades, the United Nations and its related organizations have had an undeniable impact on the world economic scene. The impact cannot be measured simply in terms of financial expenditures. For years, the research work and operational programs of the United Nations have provided indispensable and invaluable services to its member states and their citizens. Global conferences convened under U.N. auspices, such as those on environment, population, food, trade, industrialization, science and technology, and women, have influenced national policies by gathering scientific evidence, mobilizing public opinion, recommending lines of action and focusing the attention of political leaders on hitherto neglected national and international problems.

However, when it comes to the shaping of comprehensive and coherent global strategy and policies on human development, fuelling public opinion and attracting the attention of political leaders to this neglected area of the development process, the performance of the organization has, unfortunately, been much less remarkable. There are several causes for such a meager achievement in this area.

Intergovernmental Level

The following may be identified as main sources of poor performance at the intergovernmental level.

a) International policymakers, whether at the Second Committee of the General Assembly or the Economic and Social Council, have unfortunately been the prisoners of ill-conceived development policy perceptions of the *means* rather than the true *objective* of development. Since the preliminary days of the Second Committee and the Economic and Social Council, issues related to the promotion of the economic and social welfare of the developing countries were considered mainly under two distinct rubrics: (i) provision of technical assistance (later, "operational activities for development") and (ii) financing of economic development. Since the mid-1960s, consideration of issues related to the second heading has been transferred to UNCTAD.

b) A truly integrated approach to the consideration of problems affecting development and international cooperation has not yet been adopted. So far, economic development issues have been considered at the Second Committee of the General Assembly and so-called social problems at the Third Committee, by different governmental representatives, in total isolation.[2] Therefore, an artificial separation has been created in policy consideration of issues related to "human development." More inadvertently, never has an item on "human development" per se appeared on the agendas of the General Assembly or of ECOSOC.

c) Since human development and poverty-related issues are politically sensitive and primarily affect the policies of national governments, representatives of certain developing countries have been reluctant to give them predominance in the development dialogue in the United Nations. Instead, they have been more interested in discussing subjects related to ensuring economic growth, with special emphasis on the transfer of real resources and technology from developed to developing countries, trade liberalization and monetary issues. By contrast, in order to camouflage their poor performance on international development assistance, the representatives of some developed countries became the overwhelming advocates of the "basic needs approach."

Though true development comprises a twofold task, namely, to accelerate economic growth and to eradicate absolute poverty, many governments at the United Nations pursued one cause without paying adequate attention to the other. Thus they failed to understand that the pursuit of growth without reasonable concern for equity is socially destabilizing, and that the pursuit of equity without reasonable concern for growth merely tends to redistribute economic stagnation. Development is clearly not simply economic progress measured in terms of gross national product. It is something much more basic; as Robert McNamara once stated, "it is essentially *human development*; that is, the individual's realization of his or her own inherent potential."[3]

d) In the development strategies formulated by the General Assembly, whether in the case of the First, Second or Third Development Decade, too much attention was paid to statistical targets for overall performances, and not enough emphasis was given to fundamental policy choices, especially in the area of human development. Successive appraisals of the implementation of these strategies now give enough proof that quantitive targets, though perhaps useful in monitoring progress, do not by themselves guarantee the adoption of fundamental and appropriate policies.

Secretariat Level

Effective policymaking by governmental bodies largely depends upon the quality and timeliness of policy support and options which they receive from their secretariat. The need for strengthening the capacity of the U.N. Secretariat in the areas of intersectoral analysis and synthesis in order to formulate policy options for the consideration of relevant intergovernmental organs was recognized a decade ago.[4] Some measures have been taken through the restructuring exercise. Nevertheless, the question may be asked whether the U.N. Secretariat has adequately provided the required leadership, especially in the domain of "human development"; and, further, whether it has played the role of an "early warning system" in this area.

One of the main weaknesses of the central Secretariat as it has developed over the years may be attributed to the fragmentation of research activities resulting from many sectoral units. For instance, in the area of social development, one notices that several in-depth research activities are carried out concerning the development of women, youth, the elderly, crime prevention, etc., but none in a multidimensional manner which would assist in the development of a comprehensive strategy for human development.

High-quality research requires a high proportion of intellectual investment. For instance, the United Nations Secretariat has so far not succeeded in producing, in the domain of human development, research work of a quality equivalent to that of the World Bank's

World Development Report 1980 and 1981. Similarly, though there is a definite need for an annual report on "The State of the Human Condition" to provide for regular monitoring of world poverty levels, there is no sign that such an undertaking is on the way, either on the part of the United Nations or from the UNDP Secretariat.

Moreover, a decade ago, a recommendation was made to establish a joint research unit in the United Nations composed of high-level staff, seconded from various organizations of the system, for durations depending on requirements. This unit was to ensure effective multi-disciplinary support and in-depth intersectoral policy analysis for the United Nations system. Regrettably, this useful proposal has not yet seen the light of day.[5]

The United Nations Development Programme

Policies and Operations

The present United Nations Development Programme is the end-product of the merger in 1965 of the two earlier existing mechanisms for multilateral cooperation, namely, the Expanded Program of Technical Assistance (EPTA), created in 1949, and the United Nations Special Fund, established in 1959. At present, the UNDP is regarded as the major funding organization for human resource development.

Strangely, neither the constitutional documents of the UNDP nor those of EPTA or the Special Fund make any direct reference to human resource development as their specific and primary objective.[6] In practice, however, hundreds of millions of U.S. dollars were invested by EPTA, the Special Fund and later by the UNDP for the development of human resources in developing countries in different sectors through expert advice, manpower training, skill formation, etc.

Both the first Administrator and the present Administrator have been firm believers in and strong advocates of human development. As early as in the 1950s, Paul J. Hoffman, the first Administrator of the UNDP, said:

All countries tend to make better use of their physical resources than of their human. It is rather hard to conceive of a nation neglecting its diamond mines or overlooking its petroleum deposits. Yet human potentials of an immeasurably greater worth are wasted, and frequently for most unreasonable reasons. This is not only a great injustice, it is terribly costly as well. The real job is to reduce this waste of human resources by speeding up the education and training of people.

The present Administrator, Bradford Morse, fully shares the viewpoint of his predecessor. In fact, twenty years ago, when as a U.S. congressman he was invited to address a symposium at Stanford University, he said, "The trick is people." His thesis was a simple one:

Not only is the improvement of the conditions of life of human beings in developing countries the objective of development, but human beings in developing countries are and must be regarded as the principal instruments of development. In many developing countries, shortages of human skills and inadequacy and inexperience in administration and management are major constraints on growth and investment.

During the past ten years of his tenure in the post of Administrator, he has never missed an opportunity to stress the vital role of human resources in the development process and to warn that neglect of this factor in itself significantly retards long-term and self-sustaining development. Together with Robert S. McNamara, former President of the World Bank, Mr. Morse picked up the banner very vigorously over a decade ago and has been the main international campaigner for human development in recent years. Though this has been the case for the Administrator, this has not been translated into the research and policy activities of the UNDP. Unfortunately, during the same ten years in the UNDP, very little research resources have been devoted to supporting human development strategies and policies.

World Conference on Human Resource Development

The Administrator for some years gave thought to convening an international conference on the role of technical cooperation in the process of development. This idea was first discussed at a brainstorming session of the senior staff of the UNDP in 1982, but the proposal of convening a global conference on human resource development had only been made in 1984. The Administrator informed high level government officials in his letter of invitation to them for the thirty-first session of the UNDP Governing Council in June 1984 that it was his intention to propose the convening of such a conference.

Subsequently, in his annual policy address to the Council, he made a strong plea to the governments in that respect:

> The time has come to recognize that human resources development has been a neglected element in the development process which has not only inhibited economic and social progress in developing countries but has also meant that the maximum benefit has not been achieved from the funds that have been provided on the capital side... No investment can be sustained, maintained or maximized unless the developing country in which it is made has the indigenous human capacity to sustain, maintain and maximize it... Given the increasing recognition of the critical role of human resources in development by scholars and practitioners alike, why has the resource flow to accelerate the expansion of human capacities continued to be accorded relatively low priority in official development assistance? Is it because that process itself is not readily visible, or its results easily measurable? Is a more definitive analysis of the importance of human resources development needed? Or is it only that the international community must be further sensitized to its demonstrated value and productiveness?

He therefore proposed that a World Conference on Human Resource Development be convened in 1987 so that such questions could be addressed in a multidisciplinary way and definitive answers provided. He suggested that all elements of the U.N. system, particularly the ILO, UNESCO and the World Bank, should be involved at all levels of this undertaking in order to ensure the essential multi-disciplinary character of the conference.

Many delegations from both developed and developing countries expressed support for the proposal of the Administrator, and a draft decision endorsing it was presented to the Council. The representatives of some specialized agencies expressed concern about the proposal, since they considered that human resource development fell into their agencies' area of competence.

Due to an unresolved political question related to a country program, the Council was unable to take any action on this matter until the last hours of its session. When the draft decision finally came for adoption, considerable support had emerged both from the developed and developing countries in favour of the proposal, but the representative of one country declared that he was not in a position to join the consensus, as he had not received the necessary instructions from his government. In the light of this situation, the Administrator stated that it would not be inappropriate for him to pursue the objectives and the course of action outlined in the draft decision at the forthcoming session of the General Assembly of the United Nations. The Council approved the course of action outlined by the Administrator.[7]

Referring to this subject at the second regular session of ECOSOC for 1984, the Administrator stated that the Governing Council had authorized him to pursue his proposal for convening a world conference on human resource development at the General Assembly. He commended this authorization.

Later, however, in view of the lack of enthusiasm on the part of some countries for convening a global conference due to their skepticism about the effectiveness of such a conference and possibly heavy financial implications, the Administrator did not pursue his proposal at the thirty-ninth session of the General Assembly. Instead, he informed the General Assembly that he had decided first to initiate a process of consultations, in-depth study and research in order to launch a worldwide campaign of reflection and action to strengthen the role of the human factor in development. In pursuit of this objective, he established a Human Resource Task Force within the UNDP. The Task Force was mandated to consider various approaches, such as the possibility of convening regional workshops or seminars, and to cooperate with governments, United Nations system organizations, the scientific community, nongovernmental organizations and the private sector in mobilizing the necessary support for its activities. On the basis of these and other initiatives, "distilled ideas" were promised to be submitted to the Governing Council's thirty-second session in June 1985.

Nine months later, when the Council met, it was presented with a progress report that restated the Administrator's directives presented to the General Assembly and which informed Council members of the convening of "a small international workshop of eminent experts" in March 1986, as well as other plans for activities of this type at the regional level.[8]

Thus, another good idea which could have helped the promotion of human development has been shelved for an unknown period of time. Fortunately, at its last session in June 1985, the Governing Council decided to have a policy discussion at its next session in 1986 on the subject of "the unique role of UNDP in human resources development and development cooperation in the 1980s." This may be regarded as a valuable opportunity for the Administration to come forward with concrete, forward-looking operational policy options in the area of human development.

The Bretton Woods Institutions

The World Bank

According to the Articles of Agreement of the World Bank, one of the main purposes of the Bank is "to facilitate the investment of capital for productive purposes, including... the development of productive facilities and resources in the less-developed countries."

Though this may be the case, investment in the development of "human resources" was not considered a "productive purpose" by the World Bank for at least two decades. During this early period, according to the Bank's practices and policies, community projects such as housing, primary health care, education, etc., which are the essential needs of the developing countries and the fundamental requirements for economic and social development, were not bankable.[9]

Up to the early 1970s, the Bank acted like a private investment bank, and the bulk of its financing went to projects such as electrification, industry, etc., as they were regarded as revenue-producing in the short term. In selecting the projects, the Bank wanted to be certain that the money lent was so invested as to yield a quick, satisfactory return. The rationale of such conservative lending policies was that the Bank depended for its own financing on borrowing from the private capital markets, and therefore, it had to follow very strict and sound criteria.

In the 1970s, under the able leadership of Robert S. McNamara, there was a major qualitative change in the Bank's lending and development policies. That change arose out of the understanding that investment in human potential was very sound economics. Development was clearly not economic progress, to be measured simply in terms of gross national product, but essentially in terms of human development — namely, the individual's realization of his or her own inherent potential. Poverty severely impaired the individual's pursuit of that potential.[10]

The need to devise policies and investment programs to assist human development consequently acquired a special importance. Throughout the 1970s, the Bank made a determined effort to help its member countries to devise such policies and to finance and implement such projects. It devoted a high proportion of its intellectual resources and a growing share of its expanded lending to this objective. During the period 1964-68, such loans of the World Bank, in accordance with its own calculations, amounted on average to only $60 million per year and accounted for less than 5 per cent of the total lending. In 1980, they grew to $3.565 million and accounted for over 30 per cent of the total lending.[11] In that year, the Bank also issued one of its best *World Development Reports*, dealing specifically with poverty and human development issues.

With the departure of Robert McNamara from the Bank, these people-oriented human development strategies and investments, unfortunately, lost their popularity. Their international constituency, which had been built up with great difficulty, was also eroded. Thereafter, the *World Development Report*s no longer dealt properly with the state of human conditions, nor did they provide professional analyses, numbers and absolute figures on these issues, as they had done in the past.

It is for this reason that both the Istanbul and the Vienna Statements adopted at the end of meetings on World Monetary, Financial and Human Resource Development Issues organized jointly by the North South Roundtable and the UNDP Development Study Programme strongly recommended that concerned international institutions undertake the preparation of an annual comprehensive study on the state of the human condition and development as a counterpart to the *World Development Report* and the *World Economic Outlook*. It has been suggested that such a report should assemble the relevant statistical data to enable a regular stocktaking of the year's reverses and progress, review various countries' experiences, provide different paradigms of human development and demonstrate the results of the present adjustment programs and conditions in terms of human and social costs and long-term losses in terms of productivity. It was felt that this type of report could be a first step in a process to rebuild a world-scale constituency for supporting human development efforts and issues.

The International Monetary Fund

In its outward form, the International Monetary Fund was not designed to be a lending agency to finance the economic development of developing countries. However, from its early days, the Fund played an important role in the economic development of these countries. Since this aspect of the Fund's operations was not much publicized in the 1950s and 1960s, most of the authors who studied the problem of financing economic development were led into the mistake of not giving sufficient emphasis to this role.[12]

In the 1980s, as its lending operations increased substantially, the Fund has acquired a much greater importance and attracted considerable attention. The actual amount of the IMF's financing of developing countries' deficits is small when viewed in the context of overall international financing; yet the role of the IMF, its conditionality requirements, and the policies which govern its financing are decisively important.

Unfortunately, the results of the IMF's policies concerning human development have been most disturbing. To date, most of the Fund's stabilization programs demand major curtailments from concerned governments in their spending for welfare services, food, education, health, poverty programs, etc. According to its Managing Director, such policies "no doubt involve difficult social choices regarding education, housing, health and even public employment, but these choices have to be made."[13]

As the impact of the IMF's policies on human development was examined in detail in one of our other studies,[14] our comments here will be limited to emphasizing the existing similarities between IMF policies today and the ill-designed lending policies of the World Bank of the 1950s and 1960s, whose shortcomings and negative impact were recognized so frantically later.

The predictions of the former President of the World Bank in this respect are astonishing. In his farewell address to the Bank's board of governors in 1980, Mr. McNamara expressed his deep anxiety as he foresaw that the current adjustment process would in all likelihood be more difficult than the earlier ones of the 1974-1978 period. He stated :

> Most of the developing countries are facing a new, an unanticipated, and what is certain to be — for at least the next several years — a very difficult situation.
>
> Their rates of growth are going to be low. Their capital requirements are going to be high. And there are going to be severe pressures on their governments to adopt austere budget allocations for every activity that is not considered of immediate priority.
>
> In these circumstances the temptation will be strong to push aside and postpone anti-poverty programs. The argument will be that poverty is a long-term problem, and that the current deficits are a short-term emergency : that poverty can wait, but that deficit can't.[15]

The World Bank's *World Development Report 1984* in fact showed that as a percentage of total central government expenditure in low-income developing countries, expenditure on education declined from 16.4 per cent in 1972 to 5.9 per cent in 1981. The fall was just as dramatic in the health sector — from 6.2 per cent in 1972 to 2.9 per cent in 1981. Similar falling proportions of expenditures in all these sectors were also the case for all lower-middle-income developing countries, for oil-importing middle-income developing countries and even for high-income developing countries.[16]

Thus, these statistics dramatically prove the accuracy of Mr. McNamara's predictions and worries and emphasize the short-sightedness and negative impact of the Fund's policies.

Conclusions

Institutions are not ends in themselves; they are merely a means to achieve objectives. Therefore, the only yardstick to evaluate the success of the United Nations system in the area of human development is the extent to which the institutions have been effective in highlighting the required policies and ensuring their implementation. The present survey, unfortunately, gives us the impression that the system has not so far been as effective as it could be in promoting the importance of the human element in the development process. In 1975, we wrote the following:

In its thirtieth anniversary year, the United Nations has reached a turning point. In one direction lies the prospect of new capacity to cope with the central issues facing mankind in the decisive last quarter of the twentieth century. In the other direction lies the danger of a decline in the effectiveness and timeliness of the actions of the United Nations.[17]

Ten years have passed since then. In the view of the present writer, we still cannot conceive of a world without a strong United Nations system for the benefit of humankind. The human race presently faces major challenges, such as the human dimension of development, which can only be met through multilateral action. A logical place for this action is the United Nations system. Yet, paradoxically, there is widespread, growing doubt as to whether the United Nations system has the capacity to function as the main instrument in meeting these challenges. That doubt will be removed, and the United Nations will assert its pivotal importance in global development, only when human resources are accorded their decisive role in development.

Notes

1.   During the early years of the operations of the World Bank, the lion's share of its lending went to industrialized countries for financing their reconstruction projects. The first reaction against this allocation took place at the seventh session of ECOSOC, and subsequently, at the third session of the General Assembly. ECOSOC, by its Resolution 167 (VII)E, recommended that the Bank should contemplate paying more attention to the problems of development rather than reconstruction, as "other sources of financing" were available for reconstruction needs. "Other sources of financing" was an implied reference to the Marshall Plan. Developing countries in later years persistently requested a similar grant-aid form of financial assistance but never received it. For more details on this subject, see Uner Kirdar, *The Structure of United Nations Economic Aid to Underdeveloped Countries* (The Hague : Martinus Nijhoff, 1966), pp. 165-166, 197-201.

2.   The Group of Experts on Structure of the United Nations, in their 1975 report on "A New United Nations Structure for Global Economic Co-operation" (DOC E/AC. 62/9), took this need into account and recommended that the Second Committee be named the "Development Committee" and that those items on social development be transferred from the Third to the Second Committee after case-by-case examination. Neither of these recommendations, however, has yet been implemented.

3.   *Address to the Board of Governors* (Washington, D.C., September 30, 1980), p. 19.

4.   Kirdar, *Structure of U.N. Aid,* pp. 19-25.

5.   Ibid., p. 25.

6.   The purpose of EPTA, which was stated in paragraph 1 of the general principles laid down in Annex I of ECOSOC Resolution 222 (IX), reads as follows: "To help underdeveloped countries to strengthen their national economies through the development of their industries and agriculture with a view to promoting their economic and political independence in the spirit of the Charter, and to ensure the attainment of higher levels of economic and social welfare for their entire populations."

The objective of the Special Fund is stated in para. 1 of G.A. Resolution 124 (XIII): "To provide systematic and sustained assistance in fields essential to the integrated technical, economic and social development of the less developed countries and thus facilitate new capital investments either feasible or more effective."

7.   See "Report of UNDP Governing Council for 1984," Doc 3/1984/20, p. 12, para. 27.

8.   See document DP/1985/22.

9.   See *World Bank Policies and Operations* (Washington, D.C.: 1960), p. 40, and Kirdar, *Structure of U.N. Aid,* pp. 116-123.

10.   See *Address to the Board of Governors,* p. 22.

11.   Ibid., p. 30.

12.   On this point, see Kirdar, *Structure of U.N. Aid,* pp. 144-163.

13.   See J. de Larosier's lecture to the Africa Center for Monetary Studies, *IMF Survey* (January 1980), pp. 23-28.

14.   Uner Kirdar, "Impact of IMF Conditionality on Human Conditions," in *Adjustment with Growth: A Search for an Equitable Solution* (Washington., D.C.: North South Roundtable, 1984).

15.   Ibid., p. 18.

16.   *World Development Report 1984,* annex table 26, pp. 268-269.

17.   Group of Experts, "New Structure," p. 1.

APPENDICES

APPENDIX A

PARTICIPANTS AND CONTRIBUTORS

[All participants attended in their personal capacities. Participants' affiliations given here are those at the time of the meeting and not necessarily their present affiliations. An asterisk (*) before a name indicates a contributor to this volume. A double asterisk (**) indicates a contributor who could not attend the meeting.]

Yesufu Seyyid Abdulai, Director General, OPEC Fund for International Development, Vienna

* *Omar Akin*, Head, Department of Architecture and Computer Science, Carnegie Mellon University, Pittsburgh

* *David Beckmann*, Adviser on Poverty, International Relations Department, World Bank, Washington, D.C.

* *Francis Blanchard*, Director General, International Labor Organization (ILO), Geneva

* *Mercedes Pulido de Briceno*, Assistant Secretary General and Coordinator for the Improvement of the Status of Women, United Nations, New York

G. Arthur Brown, Associate Administrator, United Nations Development Programme (UNDP), New York

** *Headley Adolphus Brown*, Director General, Planning Institute of Jamaica, Kingston

** *Shahid J. Burki*, Director, International Relations Department, World Bank, Washington, D.C.

* *Choo Hakchung*, Director for Special Studies, Korean Development Institute, Seoul

* *Ihsan Dogramaci*, President, Council of Higher Education, Ankara

* *Louis Emmerij,* Rector, Institute of Social Studies, the Hague

Kaya Erdem, Deputy Prime Minister of Turkey

* *Henry Ergas,* Director, N.M. Rothschild Sons Limited, London

* *Just Faaland,* President, OECD Development Centre, Paris

Ivo Fabinc, Rector, Ljubljana University, Ljubljana

* *Goh Keng Swee,* Deputy Chairman, Monetary Authority of Singapore

Khadija Haq, Executive Director, North South Roundtable, Islamabad

H.R.H. Crown Prince Hassan Bin Talal of Jordan

* *Hakan Hellberg,* Director, Division of Health for All Strategy Coordination, World Health Organization (WHO), Geneva

* *Ryokichi Hirono,* Professor, Seikei University, Tokyo

* *Henri Hogbe-Nlend,* President, International Centre for Mathematics, Nice

Dean Jamison, Chief, Education Policy Department, World Bank, Washington, D.C.

* *Richard Jolly,* Deputy Executive Director for Programs, United Nations Children's Fund (UNICEF), New York

Frank Judd, Director, OXFAM, Oxford

* *Nemir Kirdar,* President and Chief Executive Officer, Arabian Investment Banking Corporation (INVESTCORP), Bahrain

* *Uner Kirdar,* Director, Division of External Relations, United Nations Development Programme (UNDP), New York

* *Ernst Knappe,* Senior Vice President, AB Volvo, Goteborg

* *Rahmi M. Koc,* Chairman, Board of Directors, Koc Holdings AS, Istanbul

* *Georges D. Landau,* Alternate Special Representative, Inter-American Development Bank, Paris

* *Lim Teck Ghee,* Professor, Center for Policy Research, University Sains Malaysia, Penang

* *A. M. A. Muhith,* Research Program in Development Studies, Woodrow Wilson School, Princeton University, Princeton

* *Sudipto Mundle,* Professor, National Institute of Public Finance and Policy, New Delhi

* *Raghu Nath,* Professor, Graduate School of Business, University of Pittsburgh, Pittsburgh

** *Oscar Nudler,* Senior Research and UNU Project Coordinator, Bariloche Foundation, Bariloche

* *Dominique Peccoud,* Director, Agricultural Program, World Centre for Informatics and Human Resources, Paris

* *J.C. Ramaer,* Adviser to the President on International Relations, Philips International BV, Brussels

* *Gustav Ranis,* Professor of International Economics, Yale University, New Haven

Howard A. Reed, Director, Undergraduate International Studies Program, University of Connecticut, Storrs

* *Dan Resnick,* Director General for Programs, World Centre for Informatics, Paris

* *Jean-Guy St-Martin,* Vice President for Policies, Canadian International Development Agency (CIDA), Hull

* *Abdus Salam*, Nobel Laureate and Director, International Center for Theoretical Physics, Trieste

** *Zul-Kifl Salami*, Minister of Planning, Development and Statistics, Benin

* *Mihaly Simai*, Member, Hungarian Academy of Science, Budapest

David R. Smock, Vice President, Program Development and Research, Institute of International Education, New York

Janez Stanovnik, former Executive Secretary, Economic Commission for Europe, Geneva

* *Frances Stewart*, Institute of Commonwealth Studies, Oxford University, Oxford

Mamoudou Toure, Minister for Finance and Economy, Senegal

* *Aurelie V. Wartensleben*, Chief, UNCTAD Advisory Service on Transfer of Technology, Geneva

Dafallah El Haq Yousif, Investment and Business Consultant, Khartoum

Conveners

Bradford Morse, Administrator, United Nations Development Programme (UNDP), New York

Maurice F. Strong, Chairman, North South Roundtable and Executive Coordinator, U.N. Office for Emergency Operations in Africa, New York

APPENDIX B

NORTH SOUTH ROUNDTABLE

The North South Roundtable, established under the Society for International Development, is an independent intellectual forum in which key national and international policymakers, academics and eminent leaders of thought from 60 developed and developing countries get together to identify and analyze major world issues, particularly those affecting North-South relations. It serves as:

- A forum for the clarification of global development issues.
- A sounding board for new policy proposals in the mutual interest of North and South.
- A force for the mobilization of national and international support for such proposals, backed by solid analysis.
- A contributor to and monitor of North-South negotiations underway in official bodies.
- A public educator on global development issues through direct briefings and through the dissemination of NSRT publications.

The activities of the NSRT take various forms, such as full Roundtable sessions involving over 160 members, smaller Roundtables on specific issues, and country and regional dialogue missions. Ideas evolved in the Roundtable process are disseminated to all relevant national, regional and international organizations and associations, and research and educational institutions.

NSRT activities are funded by governments, international organizations and foundations; its policies are determined by a Steering Committee. Maurice F. Strong is Chairman of NSRT, Enrique V. Iglesias and Saburo Okita are Vice-Chairmen and Khadija Haq is Executive Director. The Roundtable Secretariat is located at P. O. Box 2006, Islamabad, Pakistan.

UNDP DEVELOPMENT STUDY PROGRAMME

The Development Study Programme of the United Nations Development Programme (UNDP) was established by the Governing Council of the UNDP in 1981 in order to:

— Promote a greater understanding of the issues concerning development and technical cooperation.
— Strengthen public and governmental support for development and technical cooperation.
— Generate new ideas and innovative solutions to the problems of development and technical cooperation.
— Mobilize additional resources for development and technical cooperation.

The activities of the UNDP Development Study Programme take different forms, such as seminars, lectures and informal discussion groups. Participants at the various events held under the auspices of the Programme are drawn from among high-level national policy-makers, government representatives, senior officials of the United Nations development system, leaders of public and private enterprise, representatives of the media, academics and others.

The UNDP Development Study Programme is financed by voluntary contributions from governments, international public and private institutions and foundations. Contributions may include the provision of hosting facilities and collaboration in organizing joint seminars and meetings. The Administrator of the UNDP is Bradford Morse, and its Director is Uner Kirdar. UNDP Headquarters are located at One UN Plaza, New York, NY, 10017, USA.